# Classic Writings in Law and Society

# Law & Society Series

Contemporary Comments
and Criticisms

# Classic Writings in Law and Society

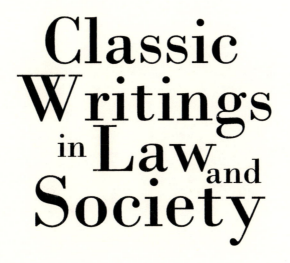

Edited by

# A. Javier Treviño

Transaction Publishers
New Brunswick (U.S.A.) and London (U.K.)

Library of Congress Catalog Number: 2006044460
ISBN: 978-1-4128-0611-4
Printed in the United States of America

Library of Congress Cataloging-in-Publication Data

Classic writings in law and society : contemporary comments and criticisms /
  A. Javier Treviño, editor.
      p. cm.
  ISBN 1-4128-0611-9 (pbk.)
    1. Sociological jurisprudence.  2. Law—Social aspects.  3. Rule of law.
  I. Treviño, A. Javier, 1958-

K370.C56  2007
340'.115—dc22                                                    2006044460

# Contents

# Acknowledgments

The editor gratefully acknowledges Transaction Publishers for permission to reproduce the following copyright material:

1. Dante J. Scala, "Introduction to the Transaction Edition." From Henry Sumner Maine, *Ancient Law*. Copyright © 2002 by Transaction Publishers, pp. vii-xxxix.
2. Piers Beirne, "Introduction to the Transaction Edition." From Gabriel Tarde, *Penal Philosophy*. Translated by Rapelje Howell. Copyright © 2001 Transaction Publishers, pp. xi-xix.
3. Dario Melossi, "Introduction to the Transaction Edition: The Simple 'Heuristic Maxim' of an 'Unusual Human Being'." From Georg Rusche and Otto Kirchheimer, *Punishment and Social Structure*. Copyright © 2003 by Transaction Publishers, pp. ix-xlv.
4. Tim Griffin, "Introduction to the Transaction Edition." From Oliver Wendell Holmes, Jr., *The Common Law*. Copyright © 2005 by Transaction Publishers, pp. xi-xxvi.
5. A. Javier Treviño, "Transaction Introduction." From Roscoe Pound, *Social Control through Law*. Copyright © 1994 by Transaction Publishers, pp. vii-xlix.
6. Klaus A. Ziegert, "Introduction to the Transaction Edition." From Eugen Ehrlich, *Fundamental Principles of the Sociology of Law*. Translated by Walter L. Moll. Copyright © 2002 by Transaction Publishers, pp. xix-l.
7. Alan Hunt, "Introduction to the Transaction Edition." From Georges Gurvitch, *Sociology of Law*. Copyright © 2001 by Transaction Publishers, pp. xi-liv.
8. A. Javier Treviño, "Introduction to the Transaction Edition." From Nicholas S. Timasheff, *An Introduction to the Sociology of Law*. Copyright © 2002 by Transaction Publishers, pp. ix-xxxix.
9. Marshall B. Clinard, "Transaction Introduction: Corporate Crime: Yesterday and Today—A Comparison." From Marshall B. Clinard

# Introduction: The Classic Tradition

Over against such reference volumes as encyclopedias, which are intended to provide an overview and summary of a subject, and dictionaries, which define a series of terms, "commentaries" consist of a collection of lectures or essays that discuss and explain in some detail particular topics and sources. In law, the best known and oldest of these is William Blackstone's *Commentaries on the Laws of England* (1765-1769). Others, which are equally prominent, include James Kent's *Commentaries on American Law* (1826) and Joseph Story's *Commentaries on the Constitution of the United States* (1833). This volume is presented in the spirit of the aforementioned treatises in that it consists of several essays of contemporary comments and criticisms (but in this case, prepared by various writers), intended generally to inform and educate.

In introducing the commentaries in this book it is necessary to begin by stating their dual collective purpose. First and foremost, they are intended to acquaint a new generation of students with thirteen classic books written by diverse sociolegal scholars of the first importance—ranging from Henry Sumner Maine, Oliver Wendell Holmes, Jr., and Hans Kelsen to Eugen Ehrlich, Nicholas S. Timasheff, and Richard Quinney. Second, they endeavor to demonstrate the contemporary theoretical relevance, the continuing legacy, of these classic writings. Accordingly, the commentaries discuss each of the scholars' work in general, how the particular book under consideration fits into that corpus, and how the book is assessed in a contemporary context. Singly and collectively these books have a clear relation to the "classic" tradition in thought—a tradition that, although not always acknowledged, is of great significance to current theorizing in law and society.[1]

## The Classic Tradition in Law and Society

It is important to recognize that the social scientific study of law as we know it today is directly and fundamentally premised on the classic tradition.[2] Moreover, as will be demonstrated below, in some of its more interesting, more "radical," present-day expressions, the study of law and society seems to be revisiting its conceptual "roots" in the classic tradition.

Simply put, the social scientific study of law involves an explanation, interpretation, and/or critique of the relationship between law and society, the social organization of law, the social interactions of all who come in contact with law (lawyers, judges, offenders, corporations, nation-states, legislators, etc.), and the meaning that people give to their legal reality. The keynote of this volume is the *classic tradition* in the study of law and society—an intellectual approach that implicitly contains a *modernist* interpretation of law's operations in modern social life.

It is not easy to say when the social scientific study of law began. Clearly, ideas from the ancient world, in, for example, Plato's *The Republic*; from the thirteenth century, in the writings of St. Thomas Aquinas; and especially from the eighteenth century, in the thought of the Enlightenment *philosophes*, Montesquieu, Voltaire, and Rousseau, contributed importantly to social scientific thinking in law. But it was only in the second half of the nineteenth century that scholars began to systematically consider the role of law in social context. In this respect we are on safe ground in saying that one of the earliest—"classic"—works of this kind was Sir Henry Maine's *Ancient Law*, first published in 1861, in which he traced the historical development of archaic legal ideas (particularly those of Roman jurisprudence), and explained their influence on modern social institutions. A little later, in *The Common Law*, Oliver Wendell Holmes, Jr., in writing that "law embodies the story of a nation's development," expressed what is now a commonplace notion: that there exists an inextricable, if not fully understood, association between law and society. These conceptualizations were succeeded, in 1882, by Herbert Spencer's analysis of legal evolution in *The Principles of Sociology* and by Émile Durkheim's six lectures titled "The Nature of Morals and of Rights" and delivered at the University of Bordeaux between 1890 and 1900, on ethics, civic morals, property, and contract.[3]

By the early decades of the twentieth century social scientific scholarship on law blossomed with the writings of Gabriel Tarde, Karl Renner, Max Weber, Leon Petrazycki, William Graham Sumner, Eugen Ehrlich, Roscoe Pound, and Karl N. Llewellyn. Not long thereafter came the ideas of Evgeny B. Pashukanis, Bronislaw Malinowski, Georges Gurvitch, Hans Kelsen, Georg Rusche and Otto Kirchheimer, and Nicholas S. Timasheff. During the third quarter of the twentieth century classic sociolegal analysis was explicit in the work of Richard Quinney, Donald Black, Alan Hunt, Marshall B. Clinard, and Peter C. Yeager. It was not until the last quarter of the twentieth century, however, that the classic tradition in sociolegal thinking began to be to seriously challenged by the "postmodern turn"—a *postclassic* social approach to law. Postmodernism's intellectual challenge, intended as a substantial preemptive critique of the classic tradition, continues until today.

Although the writings of the aforementioned sociolegal scholars are subsumed under the rubric "classic," it bears pointing out that the classic tradition does not form a unity; it does not mean the same thing to all its adherents. Indeed, the classic theorists did not even agree on how to understand society, or for that matter, on how to conceptualize law. Consider, for example, that Gurvitch examined law only in those social contexts—those "forms of sociality"—that he terms "mass" and "community," while Quinney specifically placed criminal law—derived from what he called "criminal definitions"— in "the politically organized society." And as concerns the notion of law itself, consider the subtle yet highly significant distinction of law's conceptualization between Holmes and Kelsen: For Holmes law consists of nothing more than "the prophecies of what the courts *will do* in fact," whereas for Kelsen, law consists of a combination of impersonal norms that state what the courts *ought to do* relative to a delict. Consider, moreover, that the classic theorists differed on what *aspect* of law should be the focus of analysis. Thus, while Ehrlich contended that sociolegal study should target the "living law," "the law which dominates life itself even though it has not been posited in legal propositions," Timasheff believed that law should be understood as "ethico-imperative coordination," which means locating it at the intersection of power and ethics.

## The Classics: Modernist Conceptual Methodologies and Questions

While it is doubtless profitable to discuss the intellectual conflicts, tensions, and dilemmas that have plagued the classic perspective throughout its history, in this introductory essay I will instead focus on a few of its commonalities as a way of getting a clearer sense of the classic tradition. So despite the classic theorists' many and varied positions relative to law and society we can nonetheless identify at least three fundamental conceptual methodologies endemic to their work in general: (1) the principle of social reciprocity; (2) the consideration of the variability of law; and (3) the strategy of critique, or the use of critical reflection on the dilemmas of sociolegal existence. All three conceptual features are played out in a theoretical understanding of law in social conditions that are particularly and uniquely *modern*. Thus, regardless of the several important differences between the thirteen classic authors featured in this volume, each is concerned with the reality of legal-social life during the modern period. Moreover, the three conceptual methodologies that the classic theorists employed are themselves defining social characteristics of the modern condition. In this sense, not only are the classic writers modern theorists, they are also theorists of modernity.[4]

## The Principle of Social Reciprocity

The study of society—sociology—as an analytic enterprise has long understood social interaction as a pattern of mutually contingent exchange of gratifications between actors. Indeed, this general notion forms the very core of George C. Homans's (1958) explanation of the elementary forms of social behavior, his analysis of "social exchange" that looks at the mutual reciprocity of rewards and costs between persons. Similarly, Talcott Parsons (1951: 38ff; Parsons and Shils 1951: 190ff) based his explanation of the viability of the social system partly on "the double contingency" and "the complementarity of role-expectations," or the idea that a social system is and will remain in equilibrium to the extent that ego and alter, as role players, conform with one another's expectations of each other.

In language that is more nearly "legalistic," Erving Goffman further developed this theoretical thread in positing that social interactions, or "face engagements" as he called them, have their basis in an exchange of rights and duties. Thus, when people come together they make an implicit communication contract with one another:

I have suggested some reasons why individuals, at least in our society, are obliged to keep themselves available for face engagements, and I have also suggested some of the dangers persons open themselves up to in so doing. These two opposing tendencies are reconciled in society, apparently, by a kind of *implicit contract* or *gentleman's agreement* that persons sustain: given the fact that the other will be under some obligation, often unpleasant, to respond to overtures, potential initiators are under obligation to stay their own desires. A person can thus make himself available to others in the expectation that they will restrain their calls on his availability and not make him pay too great a price for his being accessible. Their *right* to initiate contact is checked by their *duty* to take his point of view and initiate contact with him only under circumstances that he will easily see to be justified; in short, they must not "abuse" their privileges. (Goffman 1963: 106, emphasis added)

This statement from Goffman can be compared with the following explanation of what constitutes social order proposed by the Russian-Polish jurist, Leon Petrazycki: "According to Petrazycki the social order is based on an elaborated network of interrelations between official and intuitive law... [H]e maintained that...different networks of official laws—especially intuitive 'contracts,' 'gentlemanly agreements,' and accepted 'rules of the game'...constitute the very core of existing social order" (Podgórecki 1980-81: 192).

Similar, if not exactly identical, to sociology's conceptualization of social interaction, the study of law as a practical endeavor has long regarded the contract as a bilateral relationship in which each party involved has reciprocal duties. *Black's Law Dictionary* (8th edition) gives as a first definition of contract: "An agreement between two or more parties creating obligations [duties] that are enforceable or otherwise recognizable at law" (2004: 341). Thus, given this conceptual orientation in sociology as well as in the study of law, it is not surprising that the classic writings in law and society—with their focus on rights, obligations, expectations, and their concomitant sanctions—punishments—are frequently (albeit not always explicitly) organized around the principle of reciprocity. This is typically the case whether the relationship under consideration is between and among "juristic persons" (including social actors and corporations) or between and among societies (including those that are stateless as well as those that are nation-states).

As applied particularly in the social scientific study of law, the principle of social reciprocity had its early expression in the work of British anthropologist Bronislaw Malinowski (1926) who noted that primitive law is enforced, not by coercion, but by "a specific mechanism of reciprocity." Similarly, Polish sociologist Adam Podgórecki (1974) maintained that legal norms consist of a "tetrad," or a set of four rights and duties, and that, as such, each party in a bilateral relationship has a right and a duty in relation to the other party, or as Podgórecki put it, "the tetrad conception of the law is based on the principle of accepted reciprocity." Moreover, according to

Podgórecki, any social relationship involving the mutual reciprocity of rights and duties possesses a legal-normative character.

The preeminent Marxist legal theorist in Soviet Russia during the 1920s and early 1930s, Evgeny B. Pashukanis, argued that the most fundamental and abstract juridical concepts, such as "legal norm," "legal relation," and "legal subject," are ultimately expressions of economic relations of exchange. For Pashukanis, the reciprocal interaction and exchange relationship between commodity traders— buyers and sellers of property—is reflected in the legal-social relationship. So, too, did Hans Kelsen strongly hint at the idea of reciprocal relationships between nation-states when he proposed that the basic norm of the international legal order was based on the rule *pacta sunt servanda*, which obligates states to honor the agreements they have made. Indeed, *pacta sunt servanda* constitutes the legal basis of all international treaties. And, of course, reciprocal sociolegal relationships—bilateral exchanges consisting of a set of four corresponding rights (claims) and duties (obligations) between individuals—was a major theoretical theme in the sociology of law of Eugen Ehrlich, Georges Gurvitch, and Nicholas S. Timasheff (see Treviño 1998: 168-72).

*The Variability of Law*

At the heart and center of sociolegal reciprocal relationships reside the two crucial elements in the study of law and society—namely "law" and "society" themselves—which the classic tradition typically treats in one of two ways: (1) either as reciprocal elements in relation to each other, seeing a kind of mutual dependence, or functionality, between law and society; or (2) it considers law as a dependent variable relative to society. The implications of these two approaches in classic sociolegal theory are, first, that law does, in fact, exhibit variability as it behaves dynamically, and, second, that law is never considered *sui generis*, independent of social reality.

During the past thirty years legal sociologist Donald Black (1976, 1989, 1998) has formulated his unique approach to assessing the variation, or "behavior," of law by treating law, very deliberately, as a dependent variable and thus posing the question, How does the influence of social life reflect law's location and direction in social space? To date Black's is perhaps the most sophisticated analysis of law as a "quantitative" variable that varies in time and place, but the nineteenth-century theorists also understood law and society as variables that presumably could be "measured" in some way. The first such attempt was undertaken by Émile Durkheim (1984) as he endeavored to gauge a society's type and level of integration. According to Durkheim, there exists a concomitant variation between the type and amount of law and the type and amount of solidarity in a society. He thus analyzed both law and society as nominal variables (as being either repressive or restitutive law; as being either mechanical or organic solidarity) and also as ordinal variables (counting the number of repressive and of restitutive laws and subsequently assessing the degree of solidarity). For Durkheim the greater the amount of repressive law in a society, the greater the indication of mechanical solidarity; and the greater the amount of restitutive law, the greater the indication of organic solidarity.

Because for the classic theorists understanding law as existing prior to and separate from modern society misunderstands both, they therefore saw law as responsive to social conditions, and in sharp contrast to John Austin's largely asocial analytical jurisprudence that regarded law, simplistically, as the command of a sovereign. Thus, against Austin's top-down command theory of law that had dominated jurisprudential thinking throughout much of the second half of the nineteenth century, Holmes argued that the true source of law was not the "sovereign" (the King, the House of Lords, and all the electors of the House of Commons), but rather "the will of the de facto supreme power of the community," and Pound made it clear that the true purpose of law was to fulfill and safeguard the needs, wants, and interests of a developing society. Relying on the Marxist causal analysis of economic determinism Pashukanis saw law as no more than a mere "expression"—an epiphenomenon—of commodity exchange relations, and Rusche and Kirchheimer examined the extent to which the various methods of punishment—galley slavery, transportation, forced labor, incarceration, etc.—were determined by the interests of the labor market. The classic tradition thus involves understanding law not only as an element dependant on dynamic social conditions, but also as a fluctuating, behaving variable that possess its own dynamism. It means seeing law, as Roscoe Pound put it, "in action."

And as for viewing law in mutual dependence with the social, Holmes maintained that the social environment—the economic, moral, and political milieu—alters over time, and in order to remain responsive to this changing environment, law too must change. But since law is also part of this environment and impacts it, there exists a continual reciprocity between law and the social arrangements in which it is contextualized. So too did Pound's sociological jurisprudence, which focused on the social character of law, regard law, simultaneously, as reflecting the needs of a well-ordered society and as influencing that society.

Thus, whether they approached law as a *dependent* variable or as an element *interdependent* with society, one thing is certain: The classic theorists never considered law as an autonomous and static entity. It was perhaps Timasheff who best summed up the classic position in this regard as he insisted that contrary to traditional jurisprudence—which he regarded as an idiographic science concerned with the descriptive study of legal norms—the sociology of law was to be a nomographic science that, through causal-functional analysis, examined law's variability in relation to society.

## Critique

Used as a verb since the eighteenth century, most particularly in the work of Kant, the word "critique" initially meant a critical examination or investigation, and Kant's *Critique of Pure Reason* was a critical examination of the cognitive powers of human reason in order to determine these powers' conditions, range, and limits. Hans Kelsen came closest to realizing this Kantian conception of critique in at least one important respect: Against the prevailing legal doctrines of the time Kelsen endeavored to delineate, though critical examination, a "pure" theory of law informed by rational cognition.

By the nineteenth century, especially in the hands of Hegel, "critique" (*Kritik*) approached more closely the meaning held by the non-Marxian classic sociolegal thinkers—such as Tarde, Holmes, Pound, Kelsen, and Clinard and Yeager—as referring to social scientific assessment or judgment for the purpose of fault finding. Tarde's *Penal Philosophy*, for example, may be read as a polemic against Lombrosian criminal anthropology and against the scientism of the Franco-Belgian moral statisticians. Holmes and Pound launched a sustained critique of the received doctrine in law called legal formalism in order to demonstrate how it was largely unresponsive to the practical imperatives of society. Clinard and Yeager offer a criticism of the general corporate culture—one characterized by a variety of unethical practices—that sometimes facilitates illegal decisions by top executives.

After Hegel, and in the hands of Marx, and later of the theorists at the Frankfurt Institute of Social Research, the term "critique" was extended to refer to theorizing with the practical intent "to liberate human beings from the circumstances that enslave them" (Horkheimer 1982: 244).[5] In this more narrow, and more political, sense, critique, or "critical theory," was the strategy of the Marxist-inspired sociolegal scholars, with the objective of emancipation. Georg Rusche and Otto Kirchheimer, for example, whose work was informed by the conceptual framework of the Frankfurt School, pointed out that punishment was deeply implicated within the class struggle between rich and poor. As such, they argued that only by guaranteeing everyone "a reasonable standard of living" can the repressive penal practices that throughout history have been used as a means of controlling the supply, demand, and use of the poor's labor-power, come to an end. In *Critique of Legal Order*, Richard Quinney called for a critical understanding of crime and the legal system—an understanding that, with the making of a socialist society, would cease the exploitation and oppression of the underclass. As Quinney put it: "Liberation is the ultimate objective of a critical philosophy of legal order."

## The Character of the Questions Asked

Aside from the aforementioned conceptual considerations—reciprocity, the law's variability, and critique—that have acutely informed the classic tradition in sociolegal thinking, that tradition can also be described by the kinds of questions that have guided it. Even when the classic texts seem to be dated, they nonetheless pose questions that continue to puzzle theorists of law and society today: What is the nature of the relationship between law and society? How does law develop? What are the varieties of legal form? What, following Pound, are law's responses to the pragmatic needs of a society? How, following Kelsen, do we assess the efficacy of international law? The main quality of these questions can be summed up in one simple statement: *Law is an active social force*. Or, to continue with the physics analogy and to borrow Ehrlich's elegant phrase, "the center of gravity of legal development lies not in legislation, nor in juristic science, nor in judicial decision, but in society itself."

Although the classic questions are important in their own right, they are not asked, or at least not asked as explicitly, by a postclassic—a postmodern—study of law and society. This said, the classic writings are not intended, nor should they be read, as a counterpoint to the postclassic works.[6] They are, in fact, part of a continuing legacy that has come to influence postmodern sociolegal studies. But this is a legacy that calls for and indeed requires a reassessment—a reinterpretation—of the classic writings in contemporary context.

## Reinterpreting the Classics

Reading the classics is useful in gaining a better understanding and keener appreciation of the essential foundation for a postclassic approach in law and social inquiry—an approach that can be found in such conceptual orientations as critical legal studies, critical race theory, postmodern feminist jurisprudence, autopoiesis of law, chaos theory of law, and legal semiotics. Indeed, the legacy of the classic tradition can be of great utility in postclassic theorizing about law and society today.

There is, of course, no bright line of demarcation separating the classic and postclassic approaches in sociolegal scholarship. To be sure, some of the classic theorists anticipated certain aspects of postclassic analysis. Richard Quinney, for example, in *The Social Reality of Crime* anticipates postmodernism in adopting a "nominalistic position" and arguing that we cannot be certain of an objective social reality beyond our conception of it. And yet, at the same time, in his theory of criminal definitions Quinney quite deliberately accepted some fundamental assumptions about people and society—having to do with process, conflict, power, and social action—that as *epistemological foundations* are central characteristics of modernity.

There is no denying that since the 1980s the social scientific study of law and society has had to seriously contend with the postmodern alternative that fundamentally challenges the classic tradition's core presuppositions—its metanarratives—including its three conceptual methodologies. Thus, whereas the classic approach has been closely informed by the principle of social reciprocity, postclassic inquiry looks instead to a multitude of nonlinear legal discourses through which a decentered subject is in the process of becoming. While the classic tradition considers law's variability and (mutual) causality in social space (i.e., the social life of culture and organizations), postclassic jurisprudential thought considers law's iteration and indeterminacy in hyperreal space—dominated as it is by a plethora of simulacra and cyber images.

Critique, however, is the one conceptual strategy that is generally shared by the classic as well as the postclassic sociolegal approaches. But in the latter case critical analysis is intended as a way of uncovering and "trashing" the hegemony of the rule of law in order to establish different discourses where diverse voices—female, American-American, Latino/a, gay and lesbian—may be expressed in law. It therefore differs significantly from the classic emancipationist critique in one important respect: Postclassic inquiry typically eschews the modernist notion of historical progress toward the realization of an idealized goal.

Postclassic sociolegal analysis, with its focus on disorder, paradox, nonlinearity, and indeterminacy, can no longer justifiably be dismissed as mere nihilistic gobbledygook. Indeed, it is now imperative that the classic writings in law and society be reinterpreted in the context of the issues problematized in postmodernity: globalization, multiculturalism, epistemic skepticism, and hyperrealization. Such reinterpretation poses a major challenge to contemporary readers who must account for law's dynamism in a far different lifeworld than that which the classic theorists considered. And yet, that is as it should be, since it is in the nature of all ideas, be they mundane or momentous, to become transformed with the inevitability of social change.

As we have noted, the classic writers were concerned with sociolegal matters in modern societies—regardless of whether these societies were in socialist or capitalist settings, or in the common law world or outside it. The ideas of scholars like Maine and Tarde, Ehrlich and Pashukanis were influenced by the Enlightenment, the French Revolution, the Industrial Revolution, and the Russian Revolution, while those of Kelsen and Pound, Gurvitch and Quinney were impacted by the Progressive era, the Nuremburg Trials, the New Left Movement, and the Civil Rights Movement. All of these thinkers were[7] unique products of their time, as they responded to the great social transformations that transpired, as well as to the political, economic, and legal challenges that presented themselves, during the nineteenth and twentieth centuries. For these theorists world shaking and paradigm shattering events such as the implosion of organized communism; the terrorist acts of September 11, 2001; the expansion of globalization; the genocides in Rwanda and the former Yugoslavia; as well as the invasion of Iraq, still lay in the distant and largely unforeseeable future. All this notwithstanding

the classic writings in law and society continue to be highly relevant; for without them postclassic sociolegal analysis would not
have been born. There is no denying that critical legal studies has
part of its intellectual heritage in Holmes's and Pound's critique of
legal formalism; that autopoiesis of law can trace its legacy to Talcott
Parsons's ideas about the legal (cybernetic) system's recursive character; that chaos legal theory can best be appreciated in light of the
mind boggling complexity illustrated in Gurvitch's discussion of
the 162 kinds of law he identified. Indeed, the "roots" of postclassic
jurisprudence penetrate deeply into the rich soil of the classic tradition.

*Diversity*

Given the importance and influence of multiculturalism in today's
postmodern world, a word about "diversity" in the classics is in
order. It is altogether to the point that the classic writers considered
in this volume focused their analyses primarily, but by no means
exclusively, on Western law and Western culture: that of the United
States as well as of Western and Central Europe. For example, Tarde
examined, in particular, the criminality and the penal issues of late-
nineteenth-century European countries such as France, Italy, and
Spain. Rusche and Kirchheimer concentrated on how the various
modes of punishment were determined by the labor markets of capitalist countries in Europe. Pound considered the social interests that
have been asserted in "civilized society" (by which he meant the
European countries in general, and England and the United States in
particular). Ehrlich examined the Austrian Civil Code as well as the
legal rules of Austro-Hungary's nine distinct ethic groups: Armenians, Germans, Jews, Rumanians, Russians (Lipowanians),
Ruthenians, Slovaks, Hungarians, and Gypsies. Clinard and Yeager
concentrated on the extent and nature of illegal activities in 477 of
the largest publicly owned industrial and manufacturing corporations in the United States. And Pashukanis's theoretical analysis of
the legal form was a critique that makes sense only in reaction to the
Western bourgeois state.

Notwithstanding the thirteen classic writings' excessive focus on
Euro-American legal and cultural processes, we may nonetheless
admit two significant and interrelated points. First, the classic tradition in sociolegal thinking is a central part of the cultural tradition of
Western civilization. Indeed, as Weber has shown, the emergence of

formal rational law in Europe demonstrated an elective affinity with institutions regarded as pillars of Western society: the Protestant Ethic, bureaucratized democracy, budgetary management, and profit making—and we may also add, very deliberately, the liberal (and social) democratic state. Second, and again with Weber, the classic scholar's Western project constituted the crucial starting and continual reference points for the progression of legal modernity. These reference points are informed by rationalizing processes that with the influences of "globalization" have been disseminated throughout most of the world and include the secularization of the law, the laicization of the adjudication process, the bureaucratization of political administration, and the continued proliferation of market economies worldwide.[8]

Criticisms of the thirteen classic writings' failure to render sustained and focused consideration of legal phenomena in non-Western settings—viz., in Africa, Asia, the Middle East, and Latin America—are only partially on target. While it is quite true that information on various types of indigenous, traditional, religious, and precolonial legal cultures and structures was readily available (most certainly to the twentieth-century theorists), Pound, Ehrlich, Pashukanis, and the other theorists included in this collection believed that it was first necessary that they grapple with the legal systems of their own cultures before developing a true comparative sociological study of law.

### The Volume's Five Organizing Themes

The classic tradition represents those books that have come to be considered the foundational texts in the social scientific study of law. The commentaries collected here discuss thirteen of these books that are generally regarded to be excellent examples of the kind of thinking that sociolegal scholars, who partake of the classic tradition, ought to engage in. The commentaries were previously published as new introductions written, for the thirteen canonical texts, by some of today's leading scholars of law and society, from Piers Beirne, Dario Melossi, and Klaus A. Ziegert to Alan Hunt, Marshall B. Clinard, and Dragan Milovanovic.[9] The new introductions and the classic books have been reprinted by Transaction Publishers as part of its Law & Society Series, of which I am editor.

To be sure, the commentaries in this volume address only a small number of books in the canon that constitutes the classic writings in law and society. Thus, this selection, as a somewhat arbitrary collection of texts, makes no claim to the comprehensiveness of the numerous influential works that may be regarded as the "classic writings." Many readers will no doubt find missing commentaries on their favorite books, and the choice of books discussed here might well be challenged. It is my hope that commentaries on some of these "favorites" will appear in subsequent expanded editions of this volume. All this notwithstanding, the relatively small sampling of canonical texts discussed here is indeed representative of the classic tradition as described above.

As arranged in this collection, the commentaries do not adhere to any chronology of publication, either in terms of the original appearance of the classic books or of the appearance of the new introductions to Transaction Publishers' reprinting of those books. Only after consolidating the commentaries did I arrange them into five more-or-less coherent units based on several important intellectual themes that give the volume as a whole a topicality—the classic approach—that remains of considerable value to today's study of law and society. These themes make up the volume's five parts.

Part I consists of commentaries that consider three early classic writings that set the standard for the social scientific approach in examining the issues of law and of punishment. To begin with, Dante J. Scala posits that Maine, in his most famous work, *Ancient Law* ([1861] 2002),[10] proffered a sophisticated explanation of the legal progress of society—from status to contact—that is part and parcel of a larger conceptual tradition that has long dominated the social sciences. Next, Piers Beirne, in his commentary on *Penal Philosophy* ([1890] 2001), claims that Tarde endeavored to develop a criminology and penal philosophy that reconciled the doctrines of voluntarism and determinism by considering the processes of imitation—both at the individual and collective levels. Dario Melossi then regards Rusche and Kirchheimer's *Punishment and Social Structure* ([1939] 2003) as a pioneering work that formulated a paradigm in the study of the relationship between the history of crime and punishment and economic conditions. These early classic writings, then, initiated theoretical approaches in the social sciences that as conceptual elaborations and extensions continue to the present day—approaches informed by the issues of sociolegal progress, imitation and learning, and political economy.

In Part II Tim Griffin explains that Holmes's main point in *The Common Law* ([1881] 2005) was that the common law judge must be creative not only in determining the changing needs of society, but also in discerning how best to address those needs in a way that is continuous with past judicial decisions. Following this I discuss how in *Social Control through Law* ([1942] 1997) Pound regarded law as a mechanism of social control that functions to balance the many competing interests of society. Of particular significance in these two classic writings is that they both promoted the now commonplace notion that law is a social phenomenon.

Part III contains commentaries on the classic writings of three pioneers in the sociology of law. In the first of these Klaus A. Ziegert discusses how the sociology of law has followed in a direct line of succession from the sociolegal theory and methodology first presented by Ehrlich in *Fundamental Principles of the Sociology of Law* ([1936] 2002). Next, Alan Hunt sees Gurvitch's *Sociology of Law* ([1942] 2001) as being, at root, a continuation of the efforts, apparent in the work of Max Weber, to resolve or integrate the dualism between law as a positive institution resting upon a framework of social power, while at the same time being a system of values or norms having some compelling internal strength and validity. Finally, I contend that Timasheff's *An Introduction to the Sociology of Law* ([1939] 2002) is a sophisticated treatise that makes two fundamental points: Law can, indeed must, be studied by sociology, and law is a combination of socioethical and imperative coordination of human behavior. Together these three classic writings constitute some of the earliest statements in the development of the sociology of law.

Part IV focuses on two juristic entities—business firms and nation-states—in the study of law and society. Included here is Marshall B. Clinard's commentary on his, and Peter C. Yeager's, *Corporate Crime* ([1980] 2006) in which he discusses the development of a criminological interest in corporate crime, explains the nature of corporate crime, reviews a number of issues involved in its study, and concludes with a comparative view of corporate crime twenty-five years after the book's original publication. I then offer a summation of Kelsen's "pure" science of international law, which he set forth in full in his *General Theory of Law and State* ([1945] 2005), and propose that he anticipated the founding of today's United Nations and the International Criminal Court, as ways of guaranteeing a stable and universal peace among nation-states.

The volume concludes with Part V, which presents commentaries on three classic writings that offer critical perspectives on law, crime, and society. Beginning with Quinney's *The Social Reality of Crime* ([1970] 2001), I contend that it represents an eloquent and important statement on crime, law, and justice as it presents a unique critical-social constructionist approach that has been of tremendous significance in the development of theoretical work in the fields of criminology, social problems, and the sociology of law. This is followed by Dragan Milovanovic's comments on Pashukanis's *The General Theory of Law and Marxism* ([1924] 2002), where he argues that the "commodity-exchange theory" of law contributed to the historical development of Marxist law as Pashukanis deftly traced the form of law, not to class interests, but to the logic of capital. Continuing with a Marxist critique of law, Randall G. Shelden asserts that in *Critique of Legal Order* ([1974] 2002) Quinney called for a critical philosophy that not only transcends the current legal order but that also seeks an egalitarian socialism based on true democratic principles.

## Conclusion

At the outset I mentioned that the first goal of these commentaries is to introduce to the rising generation of students some of the classic writings in law and society. Clearly, reading the classics is a useful aspect of the intellectual education of today's students of law and of social science. The commentaries collected here, however, are in no way intended to be a substitute for engaging with the actual texts themselves. With all due respect for the splendid efforts of the commentators at presenting the classic writings in contemporary context, it bears pointing out that the further removed the reader is from the primary work, the more likely it is that the arguments and ideas of the original author will be misrepresented. Thus, the student is advised, not just to engage in a mere ritualistic veneration of the classic thinkers, but to actually *read* them.

Today, more than any other time in the evolution of sociolegal history—marked as it now is by the oppositional extremes of similarity and diversity, of stability and change—it is imperative that we earnestly engage with the classic writings in law and society. We may never recover the epistemological certainties of the classic theorists, but if we are to maintain a defensible and sustainable notion of the sociolegal we need to continue to pose some of the same questions they did about the relationship between law and society. In this very significant regard, the classic writings are well worth reading and re-reading.

*A. Javier Treviño*
January 2006
University of Sussex

## Notes

1.  A brief statement on my use of terms in this introduction is in order. To begin with, I utilize the word "classic" rather than "classical" to avoid connection with the historical period of "antiquity." Indeed, I will equate classic with "modern," and against the "traditional" (or preclassic) on the one hand, and the "postmodern"—or postclassic—on the other. Further, I refer to the most contemporary forms of social jurisprudential thought as "*post*classic," rather than by the quite serviceable "neo-classic," in order connote the former's relation to *post*modern theorizing. By traditional jurisprudence I mean the study of the black letter law, or *lex scripta*, in relation to philosophic ideas. By the modern social scientific study of law I refer to an examination of law in action, the legal system, and legal relationships. By postmodern legal studies I generally mean seeing law as discourse and engaging in the deconstruction of the legal text.
2.  I do not here distinguish between the so-called law and society movement, the law and economics movement, the sociology of law, sociolegal studies, the anthropology of law, sociological jurisprudence, and other ways of understanding law in social context. While these distinctions are important, I am here concerned more broadly with the social scientific study of law, or what I will alternatively refer to as law and society, or sociolegal, scholarship, which encompasses all of the above.
3.  It was also around this time, in 1892 to be precise, that the term "sociology of law" was first coined by the Italian legal philosopher Dionisio Anzilotti.
4.  Of the company of classic thinkers presented here only Henry Sumner Maine did not look at modernity specifically—indeed, his primary interest was in "ancient" society. However, in his analysis of ancient law, Maine explicitly and consistently relied on the three aforementioned modernist conceptual methodologies.
5.  At least two of Marx's works contain the word "critique" in their titles: *A Contribution to the Critique of Political Economy* and *Critique of the Gotha Program*. The subtitle of his most famous work, *Capital*, is *A Critique of Political Economy*.
6.  The same cannot be said about the postmodern works that explicitly challenge—that quite intentionally endeavor to destroy, or to use Jean-Francois Lyotard's (1992: 30) term, "liquidate"—the grand narratives of classic law and society scholarship.
7.  Three of the sociolegal theorists in this collection—namely Clinard, Yeager, and Quinney—are still very much alive and active today. However, since most of the others have long since died, I will refer to all of the scholars in the past tense.
8.  Exceptions to legal secularization and the other rationalizing tendencies are found in those Islamic countries where *Shari'a* law, which makes no distinction between religious and secular life, governs: Sudan, Iran, Saudi Arabia, and portions of Libya and Nigeria.
9.  Of this list of classic authors and contemporary commentators, Clinard is the only one to reassesses his own book, a quarter of a century after it first appeared.
10. This referencing format denotes the book's original date of publication in brackets followed by its republication by Transaction Publishers.

# References

Black, Donald. 1976. *The Behavior of Law*. San Diego, CA: Academic Press.
———. 1989. *Sociological Jurisprudence*. New York: Oxford University Press.
———. 1998. *The Social Structure of Right and Wrong*. San Diego, CA: Academic Press.
*Black's Law Dictionary*, 8th edition. 2004. St. Paul, MN: Thompson/West.
Clinard, Marshall B., and Peter C. Yeager. [1980] 2006. *Corporate Crime*. New Brunswick, NJ: Transaction Publishers.
Durkheim, Émile. 1984. *The Division of Labor in Society*. New York: The Free Press.
Ehrlich, Eugen. [1936] 2002. *Fundamental Principles of the Sociology of Law*. New Brunswick, NJ: Transaction Publishers.
Goffman, Erving. 1963. *Behavior in Public Places*. New York: The Free Press.
Gurvitch, Georges. [1942] 2001. *Sociology of Law*. New Brunswick, NJ: Transaction Publishers.
Holmes, Oliver Wendell, Jr. [1881] 2005. *The Common Law*. New Brunswick, NJ: Transaction Publishers.
Homans, George C. 1958. "Social Behavior as Exchange." *American Journal of Sociology* 63: 597-606.
Horkheimer, Max. 1982. *Critical Theory*. New York: Seabury Press.
Kelsen, Hans. [1945] 2005. *General Theory of Law and State*. New Brunswick, NJ: Transaction Publishers.
Lyotard, Jean-Francois. 1992. *The Post Modern Explained to Children*. London: Turnaround.
Maine, Henry Sumner. [1861] 2002. *Ancient Law*. New Brunswick, NJ: Transaction Publishers.
Malinowski, Bronislaw. 1926. *Crime and Custom in Savage Society*. London: Kegan Paul.
Parsons, Talcott. 1951. *The Social System*. New York: The Free Press.
———, and Edward A. Shils, eds. 1951. *Toward a General Theory of Action*. New York: Harper & Row.
Pashukanis, Evgeny B. [1924] 2002. *The General Theory of Law and Marxism*. New Brunswick, NJ: Transaction Publishers.
Podgórecki, Adam. 1974. *Law and Society*. London: Routledge & Kegan Paul.
———. 1980-81. "Unrecognized Father of Sociology of Law: Leon Petrazycki." *Law and Society Review* 15: 183-202.
Pound, Roscoe. *Social Control through Law*. [1942] 1997. New Brunswick, NJ: Transaction Publishers.
Quinney, Richard. [1970] 2001. *The Social Reality of Crime*. New Brunswick, NJ: Transaction Publishers.
———. [1974] 2002. *Critique of Legal Order*. New Brunswick, NJ: Transaction Publishers.
Rusche, Georg, and Otto Kirchheimer. [1939] 2003. *Punishment and Social Structure*. New Brunswick, NJ: Transaction Publishers.
Tarde, Gabriel. [1890] 2001. *Penal Philosophy*. New Brunswick, NJ: Transaction Publishers.
Timasheff, Nicholas S. [1939] 2002. *An Introduction to the Sociology of Law*. New Brunswick, NJ: Transaction Publishers.
Treviño, A. Javier. 1998. "Toward a General Theoretical-Methodological Framework for the Sociology of Law: Another Look at the Eastern European Pioneers," pp. 155-202 in *Sociology of Crime, Law, and Deviance* 1, edited by Jeffrey T. Ulmer. Greenwich, CT: JAI Press.

# Part 1

## Foundational Works in Law, Punishment, and Society

# 1

# On Henry Sumner Maine, *Ancient Law*

*Dante J. Scala*

*Ancient Law*, the most famous work of the nineteenth-century legal historian Henry Sumner Maine, is known as a history of progress, and its reputation as such is perhaps an obstacle to its appreciation by today's readers. The danger is that first-time readers of the book may think they already know how Maine's argument is going to end before they begin reading it.

For those with a background in the social sciences, but who never have read *Ancient Law*, Maine's famous phrase "from status to contract" may still sound a familiar note about the progress of society. Maine's narrative of change spans the ancient world, in which individuals were tightly bound to traditional groups such as the Roman patriarchal family, and the modern one, in which individuals are viewed as autonomous beings, free to make contracts and form associations with whomever they see fit. It is part and parcel of a larger tradition in the social sciences. The dichotomy Maine drew between status-based societies and contract-based societies is a variation on a theme that has dominated the social sciences for a century: the distinction between *Gemeinschaft* (community) and *Gesellschaft* (society), elaborated upon by such scholars as Tönnies, Durkheim, Weber, Simmel, and Parsons.[1] All of these great minds, and many lesser ones, have considered the question of what we gained and what we lost when we left behind a social world held together by communal, primordial bonds, and adopted one allegedly held together by impersonal, temporary agreements among individuals. The analytical dichotomy between *Gemeinschaft* and *Gesellschaft* as a description of historical evolution, the sociologist Edward Shils observed, was an example of what he aptly termed "the tyranny of

tradition."[2] What was in Maine's day a fresh and interesting idea—
that law was now no more than a "mere surface-stratum," thinly
covering the "ever-changing assemblage of contractual rules" that
actually governed social arrangements[3]—has become in our day a rather
hackneyed concept in the social sciences. Thus one of the problems
confronting Maine's readers, who today live with daily tales of the
all-encompassing power of markets and globalization, is resisting
the lull of a too-familiar analysis of Progress and Modern Society.

One of the dangers of knowing (or presuming) the ending of
Maine's history is bypassing the more interesting question of how
we got from there to here. If human progress was the end, was the
end inevitable? Or, was there an indispensable means toward this
end? What was the vehicle of progress?[4] For Maine, the means toward the end of Progress was Empire: an unsurprising conclusion,
perhaps, for a Victorian Englishman.

The empire Maine had in mind, however, was one not composed
of troops and commerce, garrisons and administrations, but rather
one of words and ideas, those compiled under the formidable array
of Roman law. The law of the Roman Empire was the winning con-
tender in what Maine variously described as "the empire of ideas"[5]
and "the empire of primitive notions;"[6] the achievement of Roman
law should not only be measured in words on paper, or laws enforced, but in its effects on the Western imagination. Such effects
could be measured as physical empires are sometimes measured, in
terms of time and space; consider, for example, Maine's assertion of
the "known social law" that "the larger the space over which a particular set of institutions is diffused, the greater is its tenacity and
vitality."[7] How did an empire of words and ideas gain "tenacity and
vitality?" What were the mechanics of innovation and diffusion that
led to the success of this empire of the Western mind? These are the
questions which should guide today's reader of Maine's *Ancient Law*
beyond the well-traveled roads of the distinction between status and
contract, into the open, unsettled country of how societies innovate
and how knowledge is diffused.

In Maine's own day (a quite fruitful period of legal historiography in Europe, from Savigny to Maitland), he warned that the study
of jurisprudence had failed to answer these questions about the nature of progress. He regarded *Ancient Law* as an attempt to supply
the defects of previous studies and to increase knowledge of the
internal mechanics of progressive societies. One of the major prob-

lems in this field of scholarship, Maine argued, was the lack of understanding of how law develops over time. This failure to understand temporal processes, in relation to legal development, had led
to the creation of false dichotomies. The most pre-eminent of these
is the alleged division between the ancient and the modern, which
Maine described as an "imaginary barrier" at which modern scholars felt they must stop and go no further in their study of the ancient
world.[8] Maine's desire to breach this barrier led him to present a
much more complicated and nuanced analysis of legal evolution
than is captured by the signature phrase, "from status to contract."

This barrier between ancients and moderns was created in part,
Maine argued, by his contemporaries' overreliance on functionalism: This scholarly error was "the mistake of supposing that every
wheel and bolt in the modern social machine had its counterpart in
more rudimentary societies."[9] Progress, according to Maine, did not
consist of some ongoing process of replacing old, worn-out parts of
social machinery with newer, more efficient cogs, while the design
of the machine itself remained basically the same. Such a vision of
social progress made the faulty assumption that all societies performed more or less equivalent functions, and thus could be judged
along a continuum according to how well they performed those functions. In actuality, Maine argued, some ancient institutions had performed functions that had no modern equivalents:

> ...the warning can never be too often repeated, that the grand source of mistake in
> questions of jurisprudence is the impression that those reasons which actuate us at the
> present moment, in the maintenance of an existing institution, have necessarily any-
> thing in common with the sentiment in which the institution originated.[10]

The achievement (and ascertainment) of progress in legal development is difficult to accomplish, Maine argued, in part because of
the complicated relationship in which the ancient and the modern,
the old and the new, both converge and diverge. A measuring stick
for progress is difficult to devise because the utility of law is not a
sufficient explanation for its formation and development: "Nothing
in law springs entirely from a sense of convenience."[11] A society's
sense of convenience, of what is more or less useful or beneficial, is
shaped by the ideas that came before it. Options and alternatives are
constructed out of the materials of the past, which were in turn created with far different intentions in mind. Only in this way, Maine
argued, can it be said that ancient ideas are part of our modern "every-day mental stock."[12]

For example, in opening a chapter on the early history of testamentary succession, Maine attested to the following difficulties in explaining the development of the will as a legal instrument. The scholar's dilemmas are manifold. At the beginning of this particular line of legal development, one finds oneself "surrounded by conceptions which it requires some effort of mind to realise in their ancient form." At the end of the line, one is stuck "in the midst of legal notions which are nothing more than those same conceptions disguised by the phraseology and by the habits of thought which belong to modern times." [13] For the historian, understanding how this development unfolded means divorcing oneself from the notion of progress. In other words, the historian must resist the urge to view the ancient world as mere prelude to the modern one, in order to understand the past on its own terms, rather than in the idiom of the current day. Maine was determined that legal history should not take the shape of a "search for origins," assimilating past events in order to explain the present in an arbitrary fashion.[14] How Maine fashioned a superior kind of historiography will be clarified by an overview of his historical narrative of the development of ancient Roman law.

## The Importance of Roman Law

If one associates the modern mind with progress and a society's self-consciousness of that progress, then according to Maine, the Romans were the first moderns. In *Ancient Law*, the Roman legal code emerges as the linchpin to the development of progressive societies in the West—an accomplishment of great significance, given the paucity of such societies in a world where inertia has tended to govern. Part and parcel of social progress, Maine argued, is the improvement of the law of society. Such improvement is similarly rare. One finds cases of sudden, violent change in which one set of laws is upended in favor of another, as well as instances in which a code of apparently divine origin grows "into the most surprising forms, by the perversity of sacerdotal commentators." Only a small part of the world, however, has been graced with gradualism, that is, with a legal system which underwent slow, steady improvement over time. "There has been material civilisation," Maine declared, "but, instead of the civilisation expanding the law, the law has limited the civilisation."[15]

The paradigm of a legal system beating such long odds, the exception to the rule of failure, is the Roman system of law, which displayed a long, continuous, recorded history of successful improvement:

> The Roman jurisprudence has the longest known history of any set of human institutions. The character of all the changes which it underwent is tolerably well ascertained. From its commencement to its close, it was progressively modified for the better, or for what the authors of the modification conceived to be the better, and the course of improvement was continued through periods at which all the rest of human thought and action materially slackened its pace, and repeatedly threatened to settle down into stagnation.[16]

The success of Roman law, however, had implications far beyond the institution of a legal code. For not only did the expansion of the Roman Empire expand the sphere governed by the Roman code; in turn, the Roman law expanded the sphere of the Western mind itself. For Maine, Roman law was the *lingua franca* of the West: "To the cultivated citizen of Africa, of Spain, of Gaul, and of Northern Italy, it was jurisprudence, and jurisprudence only, which stood in the place of poetry and history, of philosophy and science."[17] The Roman law became the language of the Western intellect, providing a common grammar for various courses of thought: "I know nothing more wonderful," Maine declared, "than the variety of sciences to which Roman law, Roman Contract-law more particularly, has contributed modes of thought, courses of reasoning, and a technical language."[18] Such tools were necessary before advanced thought could even begin on a particular subject, and so in this way Roman law provided the architectonics of the Western mind: "Politics, Moral Philosophy, and even Theology, found in Roman law not only a vehicle of expression, but a nidus in which some of their profoundest enquiries were nourished into maturity."[19]

As an example of the far-reaching effects of Roman law on the thought of the West, Maine offered the development of Western theology as a stream of thought separate from its older source in the East. To be sure, this separation was prompted by causes beyond the reach of the law, such as the founding of Constantinople and the division of the Roman Empire into two parts. The separation of East and West left the latter not only politically autonomous, but intellectually independent for the first time from the venerated Greeks.

> For at least three centuries, philosophy and science were without a home in the West; and though metaphysics and metaphysical theology were engrossing the mental energies of multitudes of Roman subjects, the phraseology employed in these ardent enquiries was exclusively Greek, and their theatre was the Eastern half of the Empire.[20]

The separation of East from West, however, did not leave a complete vacuum in the latter, more backward part of the Empire. While the Latin of the common folk was deteriorating into various vernacular dialects, a Latin worthy of use for the endeavors of the greatest minds in the West had been retained in the Roman law codes. The jurisprudence of Roman law filled the gap left behind by the departure of Eastern influences, remaining the "one department of enquiry, difficult enough for the most laborious, deep enough for the most subtle, delicate enough for the most refined, [which] had never lost its attractions for the educated classes of the Western provinces."[21]

As such, Roman law became both midwife and nurse to the new intellectuals of the West, and left an indelible mark on their birth and development, especially on the ultimate subject of theology.[22] (In Max Weber's terms, the Roman code provided a means toward the routinization of charisma: the institutionalization of the personal charism of a divine figure in the corporate body of a church.) As the Middle Ages began, Christian theologians in the East remained devoted to the study of the nature and substance of the divine: How many persons was God? How could God be simultaneously fully divine and fully human? Such studies were undertaken in the idiom of Greek metaphysics. In regard to these deliberations, the Western members of the Christian Church had remained respectful but quiet spectators. As the halves of the Roman Empire diverged, however, Western theologians began to emerge from the shadow of their more mystical Eastern brethren, making over problems of the divine in their own image: that is, the image of Roman law and its particular mode of jurisprudence. It was no accident, Maine noted, that intellectuals who were imbued with the theoretical categories of Roman law (such as the theory of obligations created under Contract, or of the acquisition and removal of debt, or the continued legal existence of the individual through the principle of Universal Succession) would turn to a whole new set of theological questions: How can humans acquire original sin by means of inheritance from their predecessors? What was the nature of the debt owed by human beings, that it required divine atonement? How can free will coexist with an omnipotent God? When the Romans "ceased to sit at the feet of the Greeks and began to ponder out a theology of their own," Maine argued, "the theology proved to be permeated with forensic ideas and couched in a forensic phraseology."[23]

The importance of Roman law as a vehicle of progress, according to Maine, thus extended beyond the transmission of Roman law from the great, old Empire to the young Germanic nations which replaced it in the Western world. Roman law also provided the catalyst for the Western intellect itself. In this broadest sense, then, the ancient law is our law, too, the law of the moderns. All the more reason, then, to pay close attention to Maine's analysis of these first moderns, the Romans, and to come to an understanding of the progress of their law, as well as their understanding of that process. What was the Roman method of legal development? What were the mechanisms of innovation and diffusion that propelled progress? What was their perception of their own progress? Specifically, how did the Romans view their progress vis-à-vis their own "ancients," the Greeks, and in relation to *sui generis* law, the law of nature?

## The Development of Roman Law

A legal code, in Maine's view, is the most striking emblem of the mind of a young nation at work. The study of laws is the first collective, reflective exercise of the intellect that a young nation undertakes.[24] Such an intellectual effort marks the turning of a corner for that collective body. No longer is law regarded as the result of divine fiat, a gift (*Themis*) of the gods given to a king, a series of "separate, isolated judgments" unconnected by comprehensive principle.[25] Even after aristocracy replaced monarchy as the governing body, the law remained the province of a few, a collection of customs reposited in the memory of "a caste, an aristocracy, a priestly tribe, or a sacerdotal college."[26] The creation of a code of law such as Rome's Twelve Tables, however, marked a legal and political breakthrough: written, published tablets replaced the recollections of the elite as the carrier of law.[27] This great step forward in legal development might be attributed by some observers to democratic movements in the West, and Maine did admit that aristocracies' tight control over legal knowledge may have posed a serious obstacle to democratization. Maine stressed, however, that in the case of ancient Rome, as in other cases, a wave of progress in legal development was the result of several crosscurrents acting simultaneously. In this case, the crosscurrent was a technological innovation, the creation of writing, and its application to the law:

> Inscribed tablets were seen to be a better depositary of law, and a better security for its accurate preservation, than the memory of a number of persons however strengthened

by habitual exercise... [The legal codes'] value did not consist in any approach to symmetrical classifications, or to terseness and clearness of expression, but in their publicity, and in the knowledge which they furnished to everybody, as to what he was to do, and what not to do.[28]

The widespread dissemination of the law was a catalyst to the development of the young Roman nation. Before this period, Maine argued, the law developed spontaneously—that is, with hardly an inkling of purpose or deliberation; after the legal codes were made available, development was linked to "the conscious desire of improvement," or at the least, a widening of the goals of that development.[29] Maine went to great lengths to make clear that the development of law was the result of considerable exertion in practice, not merely in theory,[30] even offering a rough formula for measuring progress in legal development: the amount of the intellectual force in the nation devoted to the project must be measured, as well as how much time that force was devoted to the particular task.[31]

The elaboration of a legal code was an intellectual task equal to the inquiry into the First Things of metaphysics, yet an eminently practical project: "As soon as the mind makes its first conscious efforts towards generalisation, the concerns of every-day life are the first to press for inclusion within general rules and comprehensive formulas."[32] In Maine's mind, the everyday things with which the law is concerned present as difficult a challenge as the First Things of metaphysics. This challenge springs from the age-old dilemma of governing and regulating the great variety of everyday human situations by means of "general rules and comprehensive formulas:" How may a society apply abstract ideals of justice to the specific idiosyncrasies and irregularities of everyday situations, without either failing to do justice in the specific, or betraying the ideals in the abstract? Furthermore, how may the law respond to factors such as "social necessities" and "social opinion," which Maine argued is necessary for a progressive society, while still retaining the stability that is a hallmark of the law? The capacity to work out these sorts of questions in practice, Maine argued, is the peculiar genius of the Romans:

One of the rarest qualities of national character is the capacity for applying and working out the law, as such, at the cost of constant miscarriages of abstract justice, without at the same time losing the hope or the wish that law may be conformed to a higher ideal.[33]

## Progress as Recovery

As the author of a book that celebrates the achievements of progressive societies, Maine nonetheless was sometimes rather ambivalent and circumspect about progress—more specifically, he was cautious about the promise, or prospect, of progress. For all of his insistence that progressive societies belong among the few, great elite in human history, elevated to a station far above the rest, he also insisted that the select elite faced their share of dangers from the temptations of progress. The paradox here is that a society which devotes itself to such an ideal in its laws loses the flexibility which a system of laws needs to act as a means toward the end of progress.

A fine example of the dangers of progress emerges in Maine's discussion of the influence of Equity, or "justice," on the development of a nation's laws. Equity is a set of rules which exerts influence on the development of a nation's laws by acting as their foil. In England, for example, Equity became a distinct body of law created to address the shortcomings of the precedent-laden common law courts in supplying remedies for any and all injuries. Equity, in short, is a parallel, or shadow, system of jurisprudence. Its authority does not come from within the nation, it cannot claim the prerogative of an executive or the law-making capability of a legislature as its source of power. Nor is Equity like a legal fiction, a judicial tool which smuggles in new legal principles under old legal conceptions and categories. Instead, Equity is a foreign (even otherworldly) body of law, "founded on distinct principles and claiming incidentally to supersede the civil law in virtue of a superior sanctity inherent in those principles."[34] Equity does not claim its authority on the basis of consent, but rather demands that its authority be respected (and implemented into a nation's law) on the basis of "the special nature of its principles, to which it is alleged that all law ought to conform."[35]

On the one hand, Equity provides a plethora of tools to the jurist for making wholesale innovations to the legal code of the nation. With the use of Equity, the jurist is well-stocked for all the steps in a project of renovating the laws of a nation: the means of elaborating on first principles, making generalizations, drawing interpretations of the law, and providing "that great mass of limiting rules which are rarely interfered with by the legislator, but which seriously control the application of every legislative act."[36] For example, under the employment of the Roman Praetor, who was both the chief equity judge and the great common law magistrate,[37] no part of Roman jurisprudence was left untouched by the influence of Equity. Thus Equity appears essential to a progressive society's development of law to aid its evolution.

At some point, however, Equity outlives its usefulness, and threatens to become a hindrance to legal development rather than a help:

> A time always comes at which the moral principles originally adopted have been carried out to all their legitimate consequences, and then the system founded on them becomes as rigid, as unexpansive, and as liable to fall behind moral progress as the sternest code of rules avowedly legal.[38]

Maine's warning on the dangers of Equity eventually hamstringing progressive societies is reminiscent of his discussion of the danger of adherence to customs in less advanced nations. A society in the earlier stages of development takes on particular usages and customs, which tend in practice to be positive means to the development of the fledgling community; these usages, though unconsciously followed by the masses of a particular society, are in fact reasonable and well-suited toward development. Inevitably, however, "usage which is reasonable generates usage which is unreasonable."[39] Popular belief converts a generally salutary and expedient adherence to custom into widespread superstition:

> Prohibitions and ordinances, originally confined, for good reasons, to a simple description of acts, are made to apply to all acts of the same class, because a man menaced with the anger of the gods for doing one thing, feels a natural terror in doing any other thing which is remotely like it. After one kind of food has been interdicted for sanitary reasons, the prohibition is extended to all food resembling it, though the resemblance occasionally depends on analogies the most fanciful.[40]

The use of analogy in legal reasoning, while a useful tool for sophisticated cultures, is an onerous trap for a young society which unwittingly uses it to impede progressive development. Other sorts of dangers, however, await maturing, progressive societies: just as primitive societies blindly adhere to custom and allow "irrational imitation" to attach to the law "an immense apparatus of cruel absurdities,"[41] so mature societies might irrationally follow the demands of Equity without considering how to integrate these higher principles with their own system of jurisprudence.

A main reason why progressive societies are vulnerable to the attractions of higher-law jurisprudence is their own ambivalence toward their progress as a society.

Human beings, whether individually or collectively, are modest, even somewhat ashamed, of the notion that they are somehow an improvement over what came before them: "Nothing is more distasteful to men, either as individuals or as masses, than the admission of their moral progress as a substantive reality."[42] Human beings' psychological resistance to the acceptance of their own progress is such that when progress does occur, they tend to describe it not as a step forward, but as a recovery of what once belonged to the society, a return to a lost state of grace: "the recovery of a lost perfection—the gradual return to a state from which the race has lapsed."[43] Thus, despite the dichotomy Maine drew between the few progressive societies and the many backward ones, he did note that "advanced" peoples persist in some of the same habits as "backwards" peoples, especially a proclivity to adhere to the ways of old. Maine elaborated on this odd persistence of progressive societies in his discussion of the Romans' treatment of one of the most prominent examples of Equity, the natural law.

## The Romans and the Natural Law

The gradual incorporation of natural-law jurisprudence into the framework of Roman law was another example of the eccentric steps which progress takes, and of the odd crosscurrents which propel progress within a nation's code of laws. Maine began his discussion of Roman natural-law jurisprudence with a quotation from the Institutional Treatise published under the Emperor Justinian:

> All nations who are ruled by laws and customs, are governed partly by their own particular laws, and partly by those laws which are common to all mankind. The law which a people enacts is called the Civil Law of that people, but that which natural reason appoints for all mankind is called the Law of Nations, because all nations use it.[44]

The first odd twist in the Roman chapter of the history of natural law is that the above description—"that which natural reason appoints for all mankind is called the Law of Nations, because all nations use it"—sounds as if the Romans placed this type of law above all others; but, in fact, the law of nations, or *jus gentium*, began as a mere bow to expediency. In short, according to Maine, the *jus gentium* did not begin as a matter of principle drawn from the dictates of natural reason. Rather, it began as a matter of expediency in coping with the difficulties of maintaining an increasingly diverse political society, by creating a set of laws that would serve as the least common denominator among the various nations that made up the expanding empire. Faced with the basic governmental problems of maintaining police and ensuring commerce, made all the more difficult by the threat of instability which plagued all ancient governments, the Roman state began to extend its jurisdiction beyond the domestic sphere, to situations in which one or both parties were foreigners. Using the already-established Civil Law was not an option, because foreigners had been excluded from such privileges from the early days of the Roman republic. Employing the law of the foreigner's nation on Roman soil was considered a disgraceful option. The solution which Roman jurists chose was to paste together a compendium of laws which these foreigners shared, "a system answering to the primitive and literal meaning of Jus Gentium, that is, Law common to all Nations...the sum of the common ingredients in the customs of the old Italian tribes."[45] Thus the *jus gentium* took its place alongside the civil law of the Romans as an "ignoble appendage."[46] The lowly, inferior nature of the *jus gentium* cannot be overstated to the modern ear, Maine warned. We moderns, with our taste for discovering universality beneath diversity, tend to view the Roman creation of the *jus gentium* as a great work of legal excavation, or a distillation of largely irrelevant ceremony and ritual which reveals the simple essence of the primitive law of the Italian nations. The Romans who created the *jus gentium* would have none of that:

> ...the results to which modern ideas conduct the observer are, as nearly as possible, the reverse of those which were instinctively brought home to the primitive Roman. What we respect or admire, he disliked or regarded with jealous dread. The parts of jurisprudence which he looked upon with affection were exactly those which a modern theorist leaves out of consideration as accidental and transitory; the solemn gestures of the mancipation; the nicely adjusted questions and answers of the verbal contract; the endless formalities of pleading and procedure.[47]

The desire for simplicity, for a return to basic principles, was actually the result of innovation; the old Roman law actually was quite complicated and ritualistic. It took the importation of another foreign element, Greek philosophy—a byproduct of Roman conquest—to effect in Roman jurisprudence the transformation of the *jus gentium* into the *jus naturale*, or law of nature. This "progress" in jurisprudence, however, was actually viewed by Romans as *regress*, as a return to first principles; this perception was a product of the influence of Greek philosophy. Nature, according to the earliest Greek philosophers, was wonderful in its simplicity, and reducible to one single principle, be it "movement, fire, moisture, or generation."[48] Later generations of Greek thinkers extended this conception of Nature to the moral realm:

...just as the oldest Greek theorists supposed that the sports of chance had changed the material universe from its simple primitive form into its present heterogeneous condition, so their intellectual descendants imagined that but for untoward accident the human race would have conformed itself to simpler rules of conduct and a less tempestuous life.[49]

Thus the epistemological efforts of early Greek philosophy acquired a moral component in its later manifestation (most prominently in the thinking of the Stoics), namely, to live according to nature: specifically, to cast aside bad habits and vulgar indulgences in favor of self-control and faithful observation of the "higher laws of action."[50] It was this philosophical injunction to simplicity, amidst the "unbounded profligacy" of imperial Rome, that caught the attention of part of the ruling class—most importantly, Maine argued, Stoicism captured the imagination of the Roman lawyers. These lawyers composed one of the two main factions of Rome's ruling class. On the one hand, the leaders of the military, immediately responsible for the development of Rome from a simple republic to the head of a vast empire, headed the "party of movement." On the other, lawyers took the lead of the "party of resistance"[51] in the Roman regime, though their mode of resistance in fact led to considerable innovation.

The Roman lawyers' subsequent, and substantial, innovations in their nation's jurisprudence, then, were the result of a fundamentally conservative movement. Of what did this resistance movement consist? Maine argued that the innovations of the Roman lawyers should not be measured by such a crude yardstick as the number of laws that may be directly connected to the dogmas of Stoicism. Rather, the influence of Stoicism on Roman jurisprudence had to be considered in terms of the effects of its "great though vague" animating principle, "resistance to passion."[52] In reaction to a Rome awash in the throes of empire, the Stoics preached a return to a golden era of simplicity, and it was that spirit of calm asceticism that informed the innovations of the Roman lawyers. Progress was measured in terms of the amount recovered from the past, and the *jus gentium* became the vessel which the Roman lawyers filled with their interpretation of the past. After Nature "had become a household word in the mouths of the Romans," Roman lawyers slowly but surely became convinced that the *jus gentium*, that unfortunately necessary appendix to the civil code, was actually "the lost code of Nature," and thus belonged at the core of all Roman jurisprudence.

It followed, then, that the Praetor should use his Edicts (annual proclamations) as means toward the end of this program of recovery, "to supersede the Civil Law as much as possible by the Edict, to revive as far as might be the institutions by which Nature had governed man in the primitive state."[53]

Again, however, Maine stressed that recovery of the lost code of Nature was as much a matter of style as of substance. Stoicism, according to Maine, refined the palate of the Roman lawyers. Just as the early Greek philosophers had stressed "simplification and generalisation" in their understanding of Nature, so Roman lawyers were motivated to scrape off all the excesses from their code, like barnacles off the side of a ship: "simplicity, symmetry, and intelligibility came therefore to be regarded as the characteristics of a good legal system, and the taste for involved language, multiplied ceremonials, and useless difficulties disappeared altogether."[54] Thus, while the emperor Justinian provided the ultimate force behind legal reform within the Roman Empire, the lawyers were the architects behind the plan he carried out during his reign.

While the attraction and influence of natural-law jurisprudence were undeniable, its ultimate effects were much less clear-cut, due to two factors. The first of these was philosophical confusion over the implications of the theoretical existence of a law of nature. Theories of natural law were what Maine described as a "mixed mode of thought," a constant problem which crops up in efforts at speculation, both ancient and modern. The main thing which natural-law theories confused or obfuscated, Maine argued, was the correct placement of natural law within history: Was natural law a thing of the past, the present, or the future? The very concept of a law of nature necessarily seemed to carry with it an idea of an original state of nature that had been governed by such law. Curiously, however, Roman jurists did not spend much time dwelling on the importance of the state of nature, and were unwilling to state much about its specifics. In terms of practical applications, natural law was a thing of the present, "something entwined with existing institutions, something which could be distinguished from them by a competent observer." Yet confusion persisted here as well. The criteria employed to separate what belonged to the law of nature from "the gross ingredients" mixed in with this original code over time were "simplicity" and "harmony," the qualities which attracted the Stoic-influenced jurists. Yet the ultimate reasons for the deference accorded to the natural law were not said to be these qualities, but rather its origins in "the aboriginal reign of Nature." These inconsistencies and difficulties in defending the sovereignty of the law of nature were serious, but Maine stressed that the confusion of the ancients over this matter actually was less severe than that of the moderns, who "betray much more indistinctness of perception and are vitiated by much more hopeless ambiguity of language" than the Roman jurists. Modern interpreters of the law of nature, for instance, sometimes tried to avoid the problem of time altogether by casting the placement of the law of nature far into the future, conceiving it as a goal which all human laws aim to reach in time. This attempt Maine dismissed as an unwitting turning of natural-law theory on its head, influenced by the Christian expectation of perfection in the future; the ancients held no such hope or expectation that things would improve in the fullness of time.[55]

In addition to this confusion over the correct placement of natural law in human history, the Roman mode of implementing natural-law jurisprudence possessed a subtlety easily lost on the modern mind, which in Maine's opinion had become enamored with the apparent possibilities of natural-law jurisprudence as a tool for social and political change. For the Romans, the function of natural law was "remedial, not revolutionary or anarchical."[56] Unlike the ancient Greeks, whose leading minds were always inclined to allow speculation over matters of "pure law" to trump adherence to legal rules, the Roman jurists refused to surrender the primacy of their home-grown civil law to the purity of the natural law. Instead, they sought to maintain a balance between the two. For example, existing civil law retained its authority, even in the presence of higher natural law, unless it was specifically repealed; the system of natural law would only gradually be combined with civil law, rather than suddenly replacing it. For the Roman jurists, the equity of the natural-law system became a standard to be aspired to, rather than a superstition to be blindly followed.

> The value and serviceableness of the conception [of Natural Law] arose from its keeping before the mental vision a type of perfect law, and from its inspiring the hope of an indefinite approximation to it, at the same time that it never tempted the practitioner or the citizen to deny the obligation of existing laws which had not yet been adjusted to the theory.[57]

Maine's admiration for the Roman jurists' ability to integrate civil law with higher law reflects the priorities that he held highest as a legal historian. In dealing with the question of progress, he recognized that progress over time could not be properly understood in the abstract, without an appreciation of the concrete details of practical legal activity. Maine might well have agreed with Michael Oakeshott's reflection that "Activities emerge naively, like games that children invent for themselves. Each appears, first, not in response to a premeditated achievement, but as a direction of attention pursued without premonition of what it will lead to."[58] Maine's description of the development of ancient legal understanding indicates that the activity of law-making preceded theoretical speculation about the law. Law-making, from its very beginnings, was part of the activity of politics, that is, the activity "of attending to the general arrangements of a set of people whom chance or choice have brought together."[59] The development of theoretical or philosophic speculation on the subject of law did not obviate the need to understand law-making as an activity which takes place within the context of a particular set of people attending to its general arrangements. Maine taught that understanding ancient law in terms of its contribution to the present, or understanding a society's legal development in terms of abstract standards such as "progress" or "higher law" was significantly flawed, because "to understand an activity is to know it as a concrete whole; it is to recognize the activity as having the source of its movement within itself."[60]

With this in mind, readers must beware the temptation to reduce the meaning of *Ancient Law* to its most famous tag line, "from status to contract," for this catch-phrase merely scratches the surface of what Maine understood to be a most complicated and fascinating matter: the development of legal codes, and the beguiling paradoxes and antinomies found within such histories.

## Notes

1.    Shils, Edward, "Henry Sumner Maine in the Tradition of the Analysis of Society," in *The Victorian Achievement of Sir Henry Maine*, ed., Alan Diamond (Cambridge: Cambridge University Press, 1991).
2.    Ibid., p. 176-177.
3.    Maine, Henry Sumner. *Ancient Law* (London: John Murray, 1866), p. 305-306. Third Edition.
4.    Krishan Kumar, in a provocative essay on Maine and the history of the idea of progress, raises this question as follows: "But what should a theory of progress contain? There has always been some ambiguity about this—or rather, practically every major theorist of progress seems to have found it difficult to deal adequately with what are analytically two quite separate things. Should an account of progress

principally explain how or why societies evolve from one state or another, or should it rather tell us about the substance or content of progress? Ideally both, of course, but it is surprising how rare this has been in the history of the idea of progress." K. Kumar, "Maine and the Theory of Progress," p. 81-82, in *The Victorian Achievement of Sir Henry Maine.*

5.    *Ancient Law*, p. 103.
6.    Ibid., p. 289.
7.    Ibid., p. 17.
8.    Ibid., p. 135.
9.    Ibid., p. 310-311.
10.   Ibid., p. 189.
11.   Ibid., p. 233.
12.   Ibid., p. 171.
13.   Ibid., p. 171.
14.   The political philosopher Michael Oakeshott argued that "the activity of 'the historian' may be said (in virtue of its emancipation from a practical interest in the past) to represent an interest in past events for their own sake, or in respect of their independence of subsequent or present events... 'The historian' is disposed to decline the search for 'origins,' not because the expression 'origin' is ambiguous (opening the door to a confusion between a 'cause' and a 'beginning'), or because 'origins' are beyond the reach of discovery, or because they are of insignificant interest, but because to inquire into 'origins' is to read the past backwards and thus assimilate it to subsequent or present events...and imposes upon past events an arbitrary teleological structure." Oakeshott, Michael. "The Activity of Being an Historian," p. 170, 175-176, in *Rationalism in Politics and Other Essays* (Indianapolis: LibertyPress, 1991).
15.   *Ancient Law*, p. 23.
16.   Ibid., p. 24.
17.   Ibid., p. 341-342.
18.   Ibid., p. 340.
19.   Ibid., p. 340.
20.   Ibid., p. 341.
21.   Ibid., p. 341.
22.   Ibid., p. 364.
23.   Ibid., p. 363-364.
24.   Ibid., p. 361.
25.   Ibid., p. 4-5.
26.   Ibid., p. 11-13.
27.   Ibid., p. 14-15.
28.   Ibid., p. 15.
29.   Ibid., p. 21-22.
30.   Ibid., p. 360-361.
31.   Ibid., p. 360-361.
32.   Ibid., p. 361.
33.   Ibid., p. 75.
34.   Ibid., p. 28.
35.   Ibid., p. 28.
36.   Ibid., p. 67-68.
37.   For more details on the role of the Praetor in Roman law, see p. 61-68.
38.   Ibid., p. 68-69.
39.   Ibid., p. 19.

40.     Ibid., p. 19.
41.     Ibid., p. 20.
42.     Ibid., p. 70-71.
43.     Ibid., p. 71.
44.     Ibid., p. 45-46.
45.     Ibid., p. 49.
46.     Ibid., p. 52.
47.     Ibid., p. 51-52.
48.     Ibid., p. 53.
49.     Ibid., p. 54.
50.     Ibid., p. 54.
51.     Ibid., p. 55.
52.     Ibid., p. 56.
53.     Ibid., p. 56-57.
54.     Ibid., p. 57.
55.     Ibid., p. 73-74.
56.     Ibid., p. 77. On this point, and on Maine's perceived need for a balance of continuity and innovation in order to achieve progress, see John W. Burrow, "Henry Maine and Mid-Victorian Ideas of Progress," p. 64-65, in *The Victorian Achievement of Sir Henry Maine*. Kumar defines Maine's definition of progress "in Darwinian terms as the achievement of order without the sacrifice of the potential for change," p. 86.
57.     Ibid., p. 77.
58.     Oakeshott, "The Activity of Being an Historian," p. 151, *Rationalism in Politics and Other Essays*.
59.     Oakeshott, "Political Education," p. 44, *Rationalism in Politics and Other Essays*.
60.     Oakeshott, "Political Education," p. 46; also see p. 67-68.

# 2

# On Gabriel Tarde, *Penal Philosophy*

*Piers Beirne*

During the last decade of the nineteenth century and the first two of the twentieth, the writings of the French magistrate and scholar Gabriel Tarde (1843-1904) exercised considerable influence in continental Europe, the United States, and in other parts of the Anglophone world. His influence extended to and was subsequently recognized in such diverse fields as social theory, political philosophy, and psychology. Yet, Tarde's intellectual accomplishments also rightly merit a secure and honorable status in the history of criminology, where the focus of his labors was the more or less successful attempt to forge a compromise between the voluntaristic subject of classical jurisprudence and the overdetermined object of the positivist revolution. Among Tarde's endeavors in pursuit of this focus were his creative application to crime and penality of a general system of social psychological theory, his leadership in the struggle against Lombrosian criminal anthropology and against the scientism of the Franco-Belgian moral statisticians, and his well-publicized and occasionally quite acrimonious debates with Émile Durkheim about the supposed normality of crime.

However, Tarde's interventions in criminology are among the most elusive in the discipline. One among several reasons for this is that he was an insular and often bitter antagonist who cultivated neither the allies nor the disciples required of a systematic intellectual legacy. Indeed, almost to the end of his life, Tarde was unique among French academics in that, despising the intellectual domination of the metropolis, he had no secure position within the all-powerful French university system. Tarde's self-imposed isolation has doubtless contributed to the unfortunate fact that his many intellectual, political, and organizational interventions in the formative years of criminology tend nowadays to be relegated to the status of little more than a footnote in intellectual history. Whatever the specific content of that footnote, moreover, it is often given a decidedly presentist thrust. Thus, Tarde's criminology tends to be wrenched from its historical context and, instead, to be repositioned either as an aspect in the development of the ecological concerns of the Chicago school in the 1920s and 1930s or for the modern-day relevance of his emphasis on the roles of innovation and imitation in the growth of crime. There is very little sustained treatment of Tarde's criminology in English and only a small part of his voluminous output on crime and penality is readily available to an English-language audience. The few useful English commentaries on his criminology are, in different ways, intentionally limited in their respective scopes.[1]

Who was Gabriel Tarde? What is the significance of his criminology? Jean-Gabriel Tarde was born in March 1843, in the small town of Sarlat in the Périgord region of the Dordogne in southern France.[2] He belonged to an old family of minor aristocrats who for eight hundred years had staffed the municipal bureaucracy of Sarlat. His father, an examining magistrate, died when he was seven, and he was raised by his mother, a remarkable woman who combined an erudite and sensitive disposition with a deeply religious Catholic background. His first studies were held at the local Jesuit college, at which he received a broad classical education that was instilled by the famed discipline of that order. At this school young Tarde displayed an excellence in rhetoric that was to serve him well in future years, and he was a popular student although one regarded as too independent by his superiors. He gained his baccalaureate in Toulouse, and then in 1869, having moved with his solicitous mother to Paris, he received his license for the magistrature. Tarde at once returned to the environs of Sarlat, where he remained until the early 1890s. Here he held a variety of legal posts, among them that of examining magistrate. However, this employment was not too onerous for the energetic young Tarde, and he was able not only to cultivate his talents as artist, poet, and playwright but also to read extensively in the areas of social philosophy, psychology, and criminology.

By 1890 some of Tarde's friends were displeased that the high position occupied in the scientific world by the examining magistrate from Sarlat was not recognized by his professional superiors.

In 1891 his friends procured employment for him—which he was persuaded to accept—at the Ministry of Justice in Paris. Here, from 1891 to 1896, he directed the statistical bureau that produced the annual *Compte Général de l'Administration de la Justice Criminelle en France*. Between 1896 and 1900 he taught several courses in an informal capacity at the *École Libre des Sciences Politiques* and at the *Collège Libre des Sciences Sociales*. It was only in 1900, just four years before he died, that Tarde accepted his first full-time academic position, the chair of modern philosophy at the *Collège de France*.

Tarde's criminology was in part contained within, and in some respects ran parallel to, two major intellectual projects that he began while practicing as a *juge d'instruction* in the provincial town of Sarlat. The object of both projects was the construction of a program that would encourage national unity in a France that he saw as engulfed in a rising tide of social and demographic problems. In the first project, lodged in his writings on philosophy and politics and also intermittently in his sociology, Tarde attempted to forge the socio-psychological dimensions of authority and obedience into a general theory of political obligation. Deeply troubled by the evident decay of Christian morality and strongly opposed to the rise of Marxism, anarchism, and nihilism, Tarde consistently applauded the growth of political democracy as a necessary condition of national reunification. But it must be said that for Tarde the great value of democracy did not lie in its cultivation of a liberal political ethos. Rather, Tarde valued the operation of democracy as an elitist mechanism whereby responsible members of the intelligentsia could safeguard the national interest.

Tarde's second project was the construction of a system of social theory which, he believed, would develop sociology by bringing it down from the spectacular heights of grand but vague causes to the precise, real, and socio-psychological level of individual agents. This system he published in several books, including *The Laws of Imitation, Social Logic, Social Laws,* and *Universal Opposition*. The elements of Tarde's social theory were based on the regular repetition, opposition, and adaptation that he perceived in all social action. Tarde understood social action to be the result of a complex interplay between the imitation of custom and the imitation of fashion, between tradition and invention, and between social morality and unbridled desire. The conceptual pivot of this project was the notion of imitation, which operated in his social theory as a counterpart to the notion of obedience in his philosophy and politics. In this second project, especially relevant to his criminology, Tarde attempted to mediate the sterile dichotomy into which the respective legal subjects of the doctrines of voluntarism and determinism had fallen in the second half of the nineteenth century.

It was elements in this project that chiefly earned Tarde the reputation as the foremost criminologist in the France of his day. This reputation he established not only with his book *Penal Philosophy*—which was originally published in France as *La Philosophie Pénale* in 1890—but also with the short and rather polemical collection *La Criminalité Comparée*. In addition, Tarde published numerous essays on crime and reviews of criminology in scholarly journals such as *Archives de l'Anthropologie Criminelle* (of which in 1893 he was appointed coeditor, responsible for the legal and sociological sections), the *Revue Philosophique,* and the *Revue d'Économie Politique.*

The ideas in Tarde's criminology are not approached without some difficulty. The reader of *Penal Philosophy*, in particular, should be prepared to discover in any of its nine chapters a diversity of objects that are attacked with different modes of reasoning and which are supported by contradictory discursive techniques. Tarde's literary style is frequently convoluted and, although sometimes quite elegant, it is often irritatingly polemical and even obscure. It habitually indulges in a mass of embroideries and prolix secondary ideas. Nevertheless, in the rather unkempt maze of *Penal Philosophy* one can discern that the several strands of Tarde's criminology are designed as so many complementary approaches to a common object, namely, the procurement of an acceptable "neo-classical" basis for criminal responsibility and for punishment.

One of these strands, for example, can be found in his several arguments opposing the widespread popular belief in the existence of habitual "born criminals," collectively comprising a *classe dangereuse,* a group of poor, semi-proletarian, professional thieves— Hugo's *Les Misérables*—who were committed to a way of life dependent on the proceeds of crime. This belief had been encouraged in France by well-publicized increases in the recorded rate of recidivism. These recorded increases in recidivism had fostered a most receptive atmosphere for the invention and propagation of the concept of the born criminal, which was formally initiated in 1876 in Cesare Lombroso's book *L'Uomo Delinquente* and then furthered in key supporting texts by Enrico Ferri and Raffaele Garofalo. The many adherents of Lombrosian criminal anthropology believed that it would rescue the study of crime from the mire of metaphysics and the bog of superstition. Its reputation quickly extended beyond Italian circles and, in the late 1870s and early 1880s, its findings were tested in France and were received favorably by a number of influential converts, including the eminent scholar Alexandre Lacassagne.

Tarde's offensive against Lombrosianism occurred on several fronts. He was an organizer, active participant in and skillful orator at several conferences that were otherwise dominated by Lombroso and his followers. In this regard, Tarde's main contributions occurred at meetings of the International Congress of Criminal Anthropology in Rome in 1885, in Paris in 1889, and in Brussels in 1892, and at the third Congress of Sociology held in Paris in 1894. Next, in a series of journal articles and reviews published from the early 1880s to the mid-1890s, Tarde criticized Lombrosianism largely for its empirical inadequacies. As readers of *Penal Philosophy* may see, among the key arguments of Tarde's onslaught against Lombrosianism are that it is impossible to establish agreement about the imputed characteristics of the born criminal; that it is impossible to determine whether the manifestations of born criminality—and of associated concepts such as moral atavism—are a cause of criminality or the gradual effect of a long criminal involvement; and that variations in crime rates among different French *départements* were caused not by different concentrations of alleged born or habitual criminals but by local variations in the incidence of such factors as poverty and alcoholism.

In his immediate confrontation with Lombrosianism, Tarde offered no conceptual or theoretical alternatives to the concept of born criminality. Tarde believed, like Durkheim, that individual criminals are sometimes abnormal, inferior, and degenerate beings; only rarely did he and his contemporaries draw between biological and sociological categories the rigid distinctions that we nowadays do. While accepting that some criminals had inherited their criminality, Tarde therefore initially needed to engage Lombrosianism only on a counterfactual empirical level to refute the claim that all criminals are born to their misdeeds. His efforts, in concert with those of his colleagues and admirers in the juristic and anthropological communities, resulted if not in the complete defeat of Lombrosianism in France then in a very serious decline in its intellectual and political influence.

But Tarde also realized that empirical criticisms of the concept of born criminality tended to leave a pressing vacuum in penal policy. If there is among criminals neither a pathological relation established through degeneracy or mental alienation nor a physiological relation transmitted through some savage ancestry, then perhaps it is impossible to ascertain some characteristics through which criminals can be classified. If criminals cannot systematically be classified, then is it at all possible to construct a coherent theory of punishment and responsibility?

In developing a social theory of crime that would achieve a conceptual advance on his empirical engagement with Lombrosianism, Tarde began with what he understood to be the chief error of a second movement in the positivist revolution, namely, the discourse of the Franco-Belgian moral statisticians. The presociological discourse of this latter group, prominent members of which included Quetelet, A.M. Guerry, d'Angeville, and d'Ivernois, had identified an astonishing regularity in social phenomena such as crime. The main problem with their claim that crime rates were thoroughly regular and predictable was that, though this might have seemed to be true for a few years after Quetelet and his colleagues originally made the claim in 1828 (the year that national crime statistics were first introduced in the *Compte Général*), the vicissitudes of empirical reality quickly showed it to be false. Indeed, toward the end of the nineteenth century, France appeared to be in the throes of a pathological crisis. For example, the overall number of recorded crimes in France trebled and the number of misdemeanors doubled in the half century after 1830. According to official records, the numerous dimensions of the crisis were visible in the rapidly accelerating rates of divorce, alcoholism, juvenile delinquency, assault, murder, suicide, and admissions to insane asylums—all this at a time when population growth was either stable or declining.

Though the moral statisticians were mistaken in their specific claim about the constancy of crime rates, they had at least confirmed for Tarde the need for theoretical analysis of the relationship between social organization and crime. If criminal behavior is generally not a product of atavism or inherited mental or moral defect, then what factors in social organization lead to crime? What is social organization? If crime is somehow caused by social organization, then how can individual criminals be held responsible for their misdeeds? It is with these questions that Tarde grapples in *Penal Philosophy*.

Tarde constructs his explanation of criminal behavior around the concept of imitation. For Tarde crime is a social phenomenon like any other, and is operated on by the process of imitation like any other. Imitation occurs at the cerebral level, applies to the different psychological states and beliefs of individual actors, and always operates in a social context. Tarde viewed the individual as locked in a process of unceasing struggle and always placed at a crossroads of apparent choice: between theft and honest labor, for example, and between vice and virtue. An actor travels one road rather than another for both logical reasons, such as those connected with utilitarianism, and extra-logical reasons, such as the imitation of a superior by an inferior. A particular road may be chosen consciously or unconsciously, voluntarily or through coercion. Imitation has its source in the metropolis, in the nobility, and in the rich (the masses are typically tied through imitative bondage to the conceptions and fancies of their superiors); it typically travels outward and downward, to rural areas, to the peasantry and to the poor. However, according to Tarde, the process of imitation does not operate exclusively at the level of the individual. It is also present, socially and historically, in urbanism and in the growth of cities, in national institutions and even in international warfare. It traverses all social, racial, and religious boundaries. It permeates all aspects of social life, from art to architecture and from music to militarism. It propagates both good and evil. It encourages crime.

As an additional cause of crime, that is itself both an example of the processes of imitation and also closely associated with the impersonal social relations of modern urban life, Tarde identified the violence fostered by mass collective behavior. Most of Tarde's analysis of collective behavior entailed an aversion to any body larger than a small and orderly gathering. Shrill-sounding concepts such as somnambulism, paroxysm, and mental contagion Tarde frequently invoked to explain the abnormality and dangerousness of crowds and mobs during the Third Republic. While it is inaccurate to suggest that he explicitly equated the violence of these groups with the organized activities of the French working class, this tendency is nevertheless implicit in many of his arguments about collective behavior. Appalled by events such as a strike by mill workers in his native region of Périgord and by anarchist violence in the 1871 Paris Commune, Tarde asserted that the emotional turbulence of crowd behavior was most vociferously expressed in the deluded actions of striking workers, rioters, and revolutionary political movements. Conservative though some aspects of his criminology and penal philosophy undoubtedly were, Tarde opposed such movements not only because they threatened an orderly recovery from social and political crisis but also and chiefly because their imitative effects destroyed individual responsibility. For Tarde, individual responsibility must lie at the very heart of penal philosophy, and at both the psychological and the sociological levels the state has a compelling duty to cultivate it.

In attempting to rescue the volitional subject of classical jurisprudence, in constructing a sociological explanation of crime in which the individual is ultimately the principal actor, and in suggesting forms of penality whose principles avoided the determinist implications of the positivist revolution—in these ways Tarde's *Penal Philosophy* helped to forge the dominant features of the neoclassical terrain.

My hope is that this new edition of Tarde's *Penal Philosophy* will help rescue his ideas from the rather uninfluential silence to which posterity has condemned them. The present version of *Penal Philosophy* reproduces the text of the fourth French edition of 1903 which, under the auspices of the American Institute of Criminal Law and Criminology, was very capably translated into English by Rapelje Howell, introduced by the psychologist Robert H. Gault, and published by Little, Brown and Company in Boston in 1912. This translation was reprinted in 1968 by Patterson Smith, though it is now no longer available. The reappearance of Tarde's *Penal Philosophy* here is therefore most welcome.

## Notes

1.    See, for example, Terry N. Clark (1968), "Gabriel Tarde," *International Encyclopedia of the Social Sciences*; Steven Lukes (1973), *Emile Durkheim: His Life and Work* (Harmondsworth: Penguin), especially pp. 302-314; and Steven Lukes and Andrew Scull (1983), "Introduction to Durkheim," pp. 1-32 in Lukes and Scull (eds.), *Durkheim and the Law* (New York: St. Martin's), at pp. 15-19. The present introduction to this edition of Tarde's *Penal Philosophy* relies on material in Piers Beirne, *Inventing Criminology* (Albany: State University of New York Press, 1993).

2.    Detailed accounts of Tarde's early career as poet and playwright, of the series of chronic illnesses that plagued him in his provincial habitat, including bronchitis, asthma, and severe difficulties with his eyes, and of the interesting—if unsubstantiated—links between his family history and his subsequent intellectual output can be found in Alexandre Lacassagne (1904), "Gabriel Tarde, 1843-1904," *Archives de l'anthropologie criminelle*, 1, pp. 501-534; M. Geisert (1935), "Le système

crimaliste de Tarde," *University of Paris*, pp. 1-22; and G. Tarde (1909), *Tarde. Introduction et pages choisies par ses fils*, pp. 7-70. An intellectual history of the formative years of Tarde's work can be found in René Worms (1905), "La philosophie sociale de G. Tarde," *Revue philosophique*, 60, pp. 121-156.

# 3

# On Georg Rusche and Otto Kirchheimer, *Punishment and Social Structure*

*Dario Melossi*

The time indeed has come for a new edition of Georg Rusche and Otto Kirchheimer's *Punishment and Social Structure*. Not only has the book in fact become very hard to find, even in libraries, and therefore impossible to adopt in university courses, in spite of the fact that a whole generation of teachers would have gladly done so. It is also that, while the "high" on "culture" that has deeply affected the social scientific academia in the last quarter of a century or so is slowly waning, we may be in the position to exercise a more "sober" evaluation of both the strengths and weaknesses of a book like *Punishment and Social Structure*. Then we will be able to avoid both the dubious "Marxist" enthusiasms of the mid-1970s, and the outright rejection of the following purportedly "Foucauldian" years when "Marxism" was symbolically burnt at the stake, while honoring the totem pole of "cultural insight." It was a time when, while decrying "gross" Marxist analyses and discovering, with deep "disenchantment," the relativity of everything, former "leftwing" intellectuals blinded themselves toward the unfolding, under their very eyes, of one of the most classic turn of events described in "Marxist" literature: the management, by the capitalist elite, of a very deep re-organizational "crisis," with all the consequences that this political clash traditionally has on the economy, but also on such pivotal "cultural/institutional"

This essay was written during a sojourn at the University of California, Berkeley, made possible by the Exchange Convention between the University of California and the University of Bologna. I would like to thank the two universities, as well as the Center for the Study of Law and Society in Berkeley that hosted me.

forms as crime and punishment. Now that all of this has happened between the mid-1970s and the beginning of the new century, and we are slowly starting to take our blindfolds off, the time has come again to read the book by Georg Rusche and Otto Kirchheimer.

Not that this book was ever completely shelved since the date of its original publication in 1939, as the reissue of the original Columbia University Press edition by Russell & Russell in 1968 was crucial in saving it from being forever forgotten. Furthermore, as the reader of these introductory notes will come to appreciate shortly, hardly has the process of the production and publication (and re-publication) of a book ever been more embedded within the political, social, and cultural events that the book itself, directly or obliquely, tried to address. And such is the case, starting with the very first idea, or concept, of the book, by a fellow named Georg Rusche, whose life path was completely unknown until 1980,[1] in contrast with the rather stronger limelight shed on his unenthusiastic co-author, Otto Kirchheimer.

## A Rather "Unusual Human Being"

Georg Rusche was born on November 17, 1900, in Hanover, the son of a doctor and a Jewish woman, something that, as he himself described his situation, would mark his life as of "mixed" origins. After an education that was typical of the middle class German youth of the time, he had a remarkable university curriculum, taking courses in Frankfurt, Göttingen, and Köln and working with such luminaries as Max Scheler, Erwin V. Beckerath, and Leonard Nelson. He became a doctor of philosophy in 1924 and then a doctor of economics and social sciences in 1926, both at Köln University. In the rather progressive environment of Saxony in the late 1920s he became involved in prison work, at Bautzen prison, and doubtlessly that experience turned him toward a special interest in matters of punishment that had not yet appeared in his studies, both of his dissertations being of a more theoretical nature. Probably also under the influence of Karl Pribram, who was to become a very distinguished expert of labor economics and to whom Rusche was an assistant in Frankfurt, he elaborated the idea of an essay on the relationship between punishment and the labor market. Hereinafter, between 1930 and 1931, he published an article in the famed German daily newspaper of the time, the *Frankfurter Zeitung,* on "Prison Revolts or Social Policy: Lessons from America" (Rusche 1930), and was commissioned by the Institute for Social Research of the Frankfurt University—of which Max Horkhheimer had just become the new director—to write a book-length study on the relationship between the history of punishment and the labor market. In an article that would appear two years later in the Institute's journal, the *Zeitschrift für Sozialforschung* (Rusche 1933), he laid out the main passages and developments of such a study. The study itself, however, was not to be published until six years later, under the title of *Punishment and Social Structure*, co-authored with Otto Kirchheimer. As we will see, those six years were to be very intense, for the Institute, for Rusche, and for the project of the book, within the context of the turmoil in which Europe and especially Germany were thrown, after the Nazi takeover in 1933.

In both his 1930 and 1933 pieces, Rusche started from a criticism of the prevailing literature on punishment, with its emphasis on legal and philosophical themes, and claimed that punishment should be understood on grounds of the historically changing nature of economic relationships, and especially of the relationships that constitute the labor market. Indeed, such grounds would constitute true "limits" to penal reform that could not be overcome by philosophical or ethical aspirations alone. He went on to connect the goal of deterrence with the centrality of the situation of the labor market. Given that punishment is usually reserved—but for a few historically solitary exceptions—to the lowest strata of the laboring classes, the end of deterrence is shaped after their position in the labor market. Such a position would signal, so to speak, the minimum value of a free human being under given circumstances. In order to preserve deterrence, conditions of life in prisons—or, more generally, the administration of punishment—would have to guarantee a level lower than that minimum, according to a logic that had been developed especially by eighteenth-century social writers and called the "principle of less eligibility."[2] Hence, the labor market regulates life in prisons: whereas in the situation of a "tight" labor market, when labor is scarce, wages tend to be high and the lot of convicted offenders tends to be better, in situations where instead the market is overflown with the offer of labor, wages tend to shrink and conditions of life in prison deteriorate rapidly. While in the 1933 article such a mechanism would be applied as spanning from the High Middle Ages to the late nineteenth-century,[3] in his 1930 article Rusche would compare the situations in the United States and Germany at the onset of the Great Depression—something particularly interesting because, as we will see, those sections of Rusche's original manuscript where he dealt with this very period would never see the light in the final version, being completely replaced and reworked by Otto Kirchheimer.

Two corollary remarks, so to speak, emerge from these two early pieces by Rusche. The first is that, in order to keep wages down in times of a labor market favorable to workers, punishment may assume the nature of forced labor, something that would be explored more deeply by Thorsten Sellin in a 1976 work in part inspired by Rusche and Kirchheimer. The second is that, in order to sustain workers' income under conditions of deep economic crises, in the twentieth century labor unions and welfare legislation have introduced forms of labor policies that somehow cushion the effects of the labor market and, in so doing, keep also the condition of life in prison above their "natural" level. That is how Rusche explains, in his 1930 article, the different effects of the economic crisis that had just then started, on prison life in the United States and in Germany. Whereas in the former, the lack of social policies had precipitated prison conditions toward the abyss of hopeless overcrowding and bloody riots, the presence of social policies in Germany had instead somehow preserved prison conditions from turning as horrible as they had in the United States.[4]

The date was, however, already 1933, and the quickly deteriorating conditions in Germany following Hitler's takeover suggested that everybody leave. The Frankfurt Institute began the migrating itinerary that would take it to Columbia University in New York. Its members also left Germany for France and the U.K. Rusche took off for London, a common end of many refugees. In this period, both the destiny of what would become *P&SS*, and of its main author, started shaping up. Already in 1934 the leadership of the Frankfurt Institute was sounding out American academic authorities to see whether they would welcome the Institute's relocation to the United States. Consequently, the need for publications in the English language became paramount and Rusche was asked to translate his manuscript to English, something that he did in London with the help of a friend. In November 1934, Rusche's English manuscript was sent to the two prominent American sociologist-criminologists of the time, Thorsten Sellin and Edwin Sutherland, who were asked to review the manuscript and give an opinion about its possible publication. At this point, matters became quite intricate. To make a long story short, two things in essence took place: on the one hand, both Sellin and Sutherland recommended publication (even if with many reservations), so much so that Sellin even went on to edit the book which, by the end of 1934, would almost be ready to be published, but, on the other hand, Rusche at the same time "was not available" for the very final revision of the manuscript—that would be entrusted to Otto Kirchheimer about two years later.

What happened? Though the possible answers we can give to such questions are still of a conjectural nature, we now have enough elements to make rather solid conjectures. First of all, what were Sellin's and Sutherland's comments on Rusche's manuscript? They both certainly recognized the scientific value of Rusche's basic idea. Indeed, we find traces of familiarity with Rusche's conceptualizations in later works of both Sellin, in a more direct form,[5] and Sutherland, less directly.[6] They had, however, also trenchant and interesting criticism, especially with reference to the situation they knew best, the prisons of the United States in the 1920s and 1930s, which occupied a number of pages at the end of the manuscript and which both Sellin and especially Sutherland found portrayed in a too negative light. They also strongly cautioned against a too rigid application of Rusche's "heuristic maxim," as he had called it (Rusche 1933:7). Other factors, of a historical, cultural, and political nature—they claimed—have effects on the conditions of punishment besides the socioeconomic situation. However, all this said, they separately concluded their reviews emphasizing the value of Rusche's manuscript and, in the case of Sellin, accepting to work on it as an editor. When Sellin finished his work, he sent the manuscript back to Julian Gumperz—who had kept up contact between the Institute and American academics—with the indication that a few weeks of work would make the manuscript publishable.

Why did the Institute leaders not follow up on that recommendation? There are two possible answers to such question, and they are not alternative to each other. The first is that the leadership of the Institute decided to be quite cautious with what would be their first American publication in a very delicate period, when they were trying to get the support of American academia during a time in which the "Marxist" characterization of the Institute was certainly not a good recommendation. Indeed Lévy and Zander give evidence of the fact that this was a preoccupation on the mind of the senior members of the Institute during the successive rewrite of the manuscript by Kirchheimer, and it is after all a rather well-known fact among the historians of the Frankfurt Institute.[7] Sellin's and Sutherland's criticism of Rusche's manuscript, centered on the sections that were most critical of the American prison system, might have been the straw that broke the camel's back.

However, all of this may have been overcome had the Institute been more appreciative, to use a euphemism, of Rusche's personality. We have no direct information about Rusche's character during his youth and his most productive years, the late 1920s and early 1930s, just before his emigration to the U.K. We know, though, from Philip Urbach who, a recently graduated student, was hired by Rusche in 1941 as his assistant, that when he met Rusche the latter seemed to be unable of, or uninterested in, any kind of intellectual discipline. Urbach describes Rusche as "unscrupulous," with "no concept of loyalty or honesty" but, at the same time, "of extraordinary intelligence," "entertaining" ("a great storyteller"), "prodigiously well read." He was very fat ("he was a gourmand, not a gourmet") but also very fit, as his postmortem will ascertain, and he quarreled with everybody. Homosexual, after the war he would teach in schools for children of refugees and in "special" schools, but he would move frequently because he was often suspected for his relationships with the children. Accustomed to the good life from his middle class background in Germany, he apparently borrowed a lot and became involved in shady dealings. But all of this applied especially to Rusche after his internment—as we will see—an event that may have broken anybody's spirits. Is there any indication of what his personality may have been during his early years in Germany? Obviously, the "lack of intellectual discipline" does not seem to apply to that period, and we have evidence that, understandably, the need to leave Germany for the United Kingdom and the overall situation of being a refugee had a "depressing" effect on him, as told in a letter by J.J. Mallon, director of Toynbee Hall, of which Rusche was a resident, and who warmly supported him (Lévy and Zander 1994:15-16). At the same time, when Kirchheimer was asked to rewrite Rusche's manuscript in 1937, he seemed to have hostility, or at least mistrust, toward Rusche that went back to their apparently common attendance of a seminar by Scheler in Köln in 1925 (Lévy and Zander 1994:21-22).

In London, in 1934 and 1935—before moving again, this time to Palestine—Rusche was desperately looking for sources of income, from the refugee help associations, from the Institute, from fellowships for which he applied, all to no avail. In March 1935 it appeared in a small press article[8] that Rusche had become involved in a fake wedding scam, by means of which he pocketed a sum paid by a German family "in anticipation of a marriage settlement," something a bit ironic given his homosexuality. About such an episode we have copy of a letter by which Harro Bernardelli, a close friend of Rusche, seemingly answered a request of information by Neumann on this incident (dated March 19th, 1935).[9] The bride-to-be had gone to Bernardelli in tears, "with a letter from R. in her hand that gloomily hints to his psychosexual difficulties and nervous breakdown, and an explanation that he was not able to marry her for these reasons." Bernardelli seems to have come to the conclusion that the bride-to-be and her family were victims of "a very vulgar marriage sham." However, "exposing R. to blackmail is to be excluded: [these] people will not sue for 'breach of promise' to force him to marry, they will not threaten him with disclosures about his homosexuality, which they of course have come to know of in the meantime, none of that." He adds, "I myself am not able to understand his [Rusche's] behavior despite all the knowledge I have of this unusual human being." After a detailed but somewhat confused description of the comings and goings of Rusche between Cambridge, Amsterdam, and Köln, Bernardelli explains that at the moment Rusche is nowhere to be found, he is probably in Germany, and in any case "the next [judicial] hearing will take place next Friday. All that was humanly possible was done to inform R. about it. If he does not appear the result will probably be 'contempt of court.'" The conclusion of the letter is particularly interesting in order to shed light on Rusche's personality:

> You can imagine what painful conflict this affair has brought to me. I have almost no hope that R. will come out of this matter unharmed. I cannot find any reason that could justify his behavior. I find the most plausible explanation to be that he was overwhelmed by feelings of fear, uncertainty, and persistent depression, which you have always noticed in him, and that these drove him into this sad adventure. You still know from our conversations during the last year how much I feared that something would go wrong with R. It is painful to see the form in which the breakdown takes place.

From this it would seem, in other words, that Rusche—whom Neumann must have known well enough to "have always noticed" his "depression"—suffered from depression since Germany but also, understandably, that his condition had much worsened after his migration to the U.K. It appears also that Neumann was particularly interested in the possibility that Rusche might have been "blackmailed" for having set up the "scam" and/or for his homosexuality—that, after all, was still a crime at the time in the U.K.—a preoccupation that may not have been completely disinterested since all of this was certainly not the right kind of publicity for the author of the first English publication of a Marxist Institute that was trying to relocate to New York.[10] It is impossible to determine, at this point, how much of the decision not to entrust Rusche with the revision of the manuscript was made because Rusche was "unavailable"—as Horkhheimer claimed in his Preface to *P&SS*—a lack of availability that could have derived from Rusche's depressed state or from his being in Palestine (where, according to Urbach, he went the following year, in 1936), or because the Institute, at this point, decided that they did not want to have anything to do with him.[11]

It was only after a hiatus of almost two years, in 1937, that Neumann contacted Otto Kirchheimer,[12] an émigré in Paris and also frantically looking for help, to see whether he was interested in picking up Rusche's manuscript and rewrite it. From Lévy and Zander's reconstruction, we gather that Kirchheimer was not very enthusiastic about the task, he mentioned a past acquaintance with Rusche in Scheler's seminar rather sarcastically, and in the end he was almost forced to do it by the promise of future help from the Institute in his hopes to relocate to New York. Paradoxically, this meant that Kirchheimer, who could not write in English, rewrote his own manuscript in German based on Rusche's English manuscript—i.e., the one that, almost two years before, Sellin had declared needing only "three weeks of final editorial work"[13]—and was then helped by a Moses Finkelstein, later to become famous as the expert of ancient history M.I. Finley, in bringing it to the final English version.

All of this happened on the background of extremely tense relationships between the Institute and Rusche, who was now in Palestine. The Institute considered the possibility of publishing the book without Rusche's name, and Rusche was trying to resist what in his view constituted essentially an illegitimate appropriation of his work by a colleague with whom obviously there were no good feelings.[14] He even managed to have eminent personalities write to Horkhheimer expressing their outrage. The situation was so delicate for the Institute that Neumann came to the point of hiring a New York lawyer to evaluate all the legal technicalities of the case. In the end, as we know, the more reasonable solution of a co-authorship was found. This too was resisted by Rusche at first, but he was brought to accept it in view of the fact that, after returning to London in 1939, he again had the problem of making ends meet and his only hope— maybe at this point not a very realistic one—was once more the Institute in New York.

The volume was finally published in 1939 by Columbia University Press as the first publication of the "International Institute of Social Research" (the name the Frankfurt Institute took at Columbia), and was the fourth incarnation, so to speak, of Rusche's original project, which had gone through four transmutations: a) a first manuscript by Rusche in German; b) a second manuscript by Rusche in English, prepared in London in 1933-34; c) a first manuscript by Kirchheimer in German, prepared on the ground of b); and finally, d) a second manuscript by Kirchheimer in English, prepared in New York with the help of M.I. Finley. With all these transitions, it is a fair question to ask how much of Rusche's original plan transpired in the final version.[15] In his Preface, Horkhheimer stated that chapters II to VIII "retained in essence the underlying concepts of Dr. Rusche's original draft," whereas the last five chapters would be attributable entirely to Kirchheimer. This seems to be reasonable because chapters II through VIII represent substantially an expansion of Rusche's 1933 piece, organized around the "heuristic" guidelines of the labor market and of the principle of less eligibility. More interesting is to note what is in the book that was not in Rusche's original plan and what was in Rusche's original English manuscript that is not in the book written by Kirchheimer. If chapter IX, "Modern Prison Reform and Its Limits," still reflects the substance of Rusche's analysis—linking the better conditions of imprisonment to improvements in the life condition of the working class around the turn of the century[16]—the others, about the use of pecuniary punishments and penal policies under Fascism, are much less connected to the logic of Rusche's original argument and reflect Kirchheimer's legal training and background.[17] Furthermore, the discussion of the Depression years in America and in Germany[18]—that, as we have seen, had been the target of Sellin's and Sutherland's critique—was now gone and so was any discussion of European Fascism from Rusche's specific point of view. This is quite interesting because, during his exile in the U.K., Rusche was apparently planning to write a work on "The Economics of German Rearmament" and a possibly related article for the New York Institute journal on "the most recent developments of the German penal policy" that was characterized, he wrote, by an "unbelievable scarcity of workers." According to Rusche's general hypothesis, such a situation would have called for an extensive use of forced labor and would have connected the general theme of *P&SS* also to twentieth-century totalitarian regimes (on this, more below).

After returning from Palestine, Rusche tried again to find sources of support in the U.K., but to no avail. Then sometime between the end of 1939 and the beginning of 1940, he was interned as an "enemy alien," in spite of his being Jewish and in spite of his anti-Fascist leanings. Apparently this was a rather common experience, especially for left-wing refugees, in the period after the Molotov-Ribbentrop pact between Germany and the Soviet Union (August 23, 1939). Furthermore, under the panic caused by German successes on the Continent, the rounding up of enemy aliens was greatly accelerated in May 1940. We do not know when Rusche was interned. However, according to a letter by him, he found himself on the "Arandora Star," a ship that was transporting 1,587 people (about 1,200 internees plus the crew and British army soldiers) to Canada. The internees were 734 "Italians" and 479 "Germans," by which it was meant a collection of Nazi prisoners of war, political (anti-Fascist) refugees, and Jewish refugees. In the early morning of July 2, 1940, the ship was torpedoed by a German submarine and went down in about thirty minutes. Almost half of the men on board drowned (66 percent of the Italians). Rusche survived. His presence aboard the "Arandora Star" seems to be now confirmed by the story told by another survivor of the torpedoing, Rainer Radok. Radok recounts of how, aboard the ship that had rescued him, he was helping other survivors to come on board, and at some point he helped a "Mr. Rusche, a large, fat man, without clothes, who was exhausted. My hands could not grab at his oil-covered body and other people helped me to rush him into the hospital of the ship."[19] This is the only proof, independent from Rusche himself, that we have until now found of Rusche's presence on the "Arandora Star," but it seems a rather conclusive one—given by somebody who did not know Rusche, and even if one were to hypothesize a case of homonymy (the first name of Mr. Rusche is not given), the description of the person really leaves few doubts.

Like many other internees, Rusche was brought back to other internment camps until, at the beginning of 1941, he was released.

After a last effort to enlist support by the New York Institute in a letter that is among the most interesting for his biography,[20] Rusche seems to have given up on any hope about his contacts in New York. He also abandoned any attempt at writing, even if he would once again occasionally lecture, something at which he was apparently still brilliant. During the rest of the war, and in the years just after, Rusche managed to get by through teaching at various schools for children of refugees or "difficult" children, jobs that he had to change often for the known reasons. Things did not at all become easier for him—but the contrary. In the late 1940s he became involved in some shady "property dealings" which threatened to land him in prison. He used to discuss suicide at length with his most intimate circle of friends in his last years. The prospect of imprisonment may have been the last straw, and on October 19, 1950, he carried out such action, taking his own life by poisoning himself with domestic coal gas in the small Uxbridge house in London where he lived alone.

### The "Fortune" of *Punishment and Social Structure*

When it first came out, *P&SS* had a success "of esteem," as Lévy and Zander note. Many among the prominent criminologists of the time acknowledged the book or even reviewed it. However, the war was starting and certainly gave everybody other matters to be concerned about. Almost thirty years later, a fortunate decision by Russell & Russell to republish the book was to meet with a very different destiny. In 1968 a wide audience of college students, scholars, and professionals in various branches of knowledge were going to welcome a book about "total institutions," as Erving Goffman had called them (1961), a topic which was "hot" at the time, and from a perspective that was also coming into great cultural vogue. *Punishment and Social Structure* was therefore to become—to friend and foe—the certified *bona fide* Marxist view on punishment, also ushering in, at the same time, a whole tradition of quantitative studies on the sociology of punishment—centering on the "explanation" of imprisonment rate "behavior"—where Marxists would cross swords with proponents of other competing views (such as Alfred Blumstein and the "Durkheimian" hypotheses, see below). Whereas we know that *P&SS* had been deemed "Marxist" enough by the high echelons of the Frankfurt School to be worried about the reaction of American academia to it,[21] we know, at the same time, from Rusche's "cur-

riculum" of studies and research that his inspiration could be defined as one of social-democratic economism, where the main explaining factor was labor economics much more than labor struggle.[22]
But let's not quibble: in the 1960s the prevailing traditions in criminology or the sociology of law were so intellectually moribund, so
mired in some form of Whig history of progress—especially concerning penology—that the appearance of *P&SS* was rightly hailed
as greatly innovative. At the same time, it should be pointed out that
Rusche and Kirchheimer's book was "discovered" within the very
few programmatically "neo-Marxist" efforts of those early years.
That is, in the work by Ivan Jankovic, whose interests may have
derived from the lively Marxist heterodoxy of Yugoslavian culture
at the time, but whose encounter with Rusche and Kirchheimer was
certainly favored by writing his Ph.D. dissertation at Santa Barbara
under the supervision of Donald R. Cressey, i.e., Edwin H.
Sutherland's student and later co-author.[23] Other authors of such
"neo-Marxist efforts" were David Greenberg in New York
(Greenberg 1977), and Dario Melossi, in Bologna and Berkeley
(Melossi 1976, 1977).[24]

It was mainly in the United States therefore that the book was
rediscovered. *P&SS*'s "American" fortune derived, in my view, basically from two elements. The first was the particular strain of American "critical criminology" that, in the early 1970s, had found its
stronghold in Berkeley, in the School of Criminology and in the
journals there published—first *Issues in Criminology* and then, since
1974, especially *Crime and Social Justice*. After the closing of the
School in 1974 and the academic diaspora to which its members
were obliged—with the single exception of its most senior member,
Paul Takagi, the only one who had already obtained tenure at Berkeley—*Crime and Social Justice* became the rallying point of critical criminologists in the United States and the natural American cor-
respondent of critical criminology worldwide.[25] Between 1976 and
1980 *Crime and Social Justice* published an early version of my
own work[26] (Melossi 1976), a translation of both Rusche's 1930
and 1933 pieces, an English version of my Introduction to the Italian translation of *P&SS* (Melossi 1978), my own piece of 1980 where
I reconstructed for the first time the sparse biographical information
about Georg Rusche, and two articles by Ivan Jankovic (1977 and
1978) where he "tested" Rusche's hypothesis or, what would later
become famous as the "Rusche and Kirchheimer's hypothesis."

## The "Rusche and Kirchheimer's Hypothesis"

In short, what came to be the "Rusche and Kirchheimer's Hypothesis" in such literature was the idea that there should be a direct positive relationship between changing imprisonment rates and changing unemployment rates. This was a type of hypothesis apparently easy to "operationalize" and it was, I believe, its coincidental overlapping with the growing interest for quantitative research within American sociology (and even more specifically the borrowing of econometric techniques, especially time series analysis, from economics) that constituted the other reason for *P&SS*'s relative success in the U.S. The two pioneers in this kind of analytical tradition were Jankovic (1977) and Greenberg (1977)—at first in an exchange with a different view by Alfred Blumstein and collaborators (1973 and 1977) who, instead of working on the assumption of "exogenous" causes of change in imprisonment rates moved from the idea of an "endogenous" mechanism or a "stability" or "homeostatic" hypothesis.

It is impossible here to reconstruct a detailed history of the tradition of study that developed *P&SS* towards this quantitative direction. A very useful piece by Chiricos and DeLone (1992) took stock of this literature, which was mainly from the U.S. but carried contributions also from the U.K. (especially the work by Steve Box and Chris Hale), France (Bernard Laffargue and Thierry Godefroy) and Italy (Dario Melossi). The debate did not stop there, however, and other interesting contributions appeared more recently (D'Alessio and Stolzenberg, [1995 and 2002]; Jacobs and Helms [1996]; Sutton [2000 and 2001]; Western and Beckett [1999]). Under pressure from an increasing dissatisfaction with the more orthodox variants of Marxism that defined this whole period, Rusche's hypothesis was reframed in an increasingly less instrumental fashion and was instead characterized more and more in social symbolic, cultural, and political terms, as in the work by Box and Hale, Melossi, Jacobs, Sutton, and Western and Beckett.

With all due respect for this by now quite considerable body of work that has acquired an autonomy and a raison d'être quite of its own,[27] it is time to ask whether working with measures such as the size of the unemployed population and the size of the imprisoned population—however refined and complex the models in which they are inserted—is a good way to "test" Rusche's original hypothesis.

As we have seen, in fact, Rusche had not come to any conclusion about the size of the prison population. And we have already briefly mentioned that the hypotheses that can be directly drawn from his theoretical and historical reconstruction are essentially two. The first is that, in periods when the labor market is flooded with the offer of labor, conditions of life within prisons go down accordingly, together with wages and the general standards of living of the working class. The second is the converse one, according to which, in periods when labor is rare and therefore valuable, conditions of life in prison tend to become increasingly better, work is introduced in prisons, and there is also going to be an increasing recourse—engineered for the first time at the time of mercantilist policies in the seventeenth century—to forced labor, in order to use punishment, and more specifically imprisonment, to break the resistance of the working class outside. "Outside," in fact, the favorable conditions of the labor market translate into wage increases and, together with them, in an increase of organization, demands, and general resistance to exploitation of the working class.

The latest research on the so-called "Rusche and Kirchheimer Hypothesis" has generally shown the difficulty of finding a straightforward relationship between the size of the unemployed and the size of the imprisoned—especially if one extends the analysis to a much needed comparative dimension (Sutton 2001; Melossi 2001). The developments in the United States in the last twenty years or so, for example, are usually mentioned in order to contradict Rusche and Kirchheimer's hypothesis, because in that instance a cyclically oscillating unemployment rate does not seem to have anything in common with a vertically increasing imprisonment rate (one which is exceptional at a global level). That is why, in my analysis of the emergence of the "great internment" during the crucial period of capitalist reorganization in the United States between the energy oil crisis in 1973 and the early 1990s—when the American economy again took off[28]—I proposed that we should speak not so much in terms of unemployment but in terms of "pressure to perform" placed on the working class (Melossi 1993). In those roughly twenty years, if the unemployment rate was on the average higher than in the previous period, what instead changed much more dramatically was the decline in hourly wages (Peterson 1994), the level of inequality—which increased spectacularly (Kovandzic, Vieraitis, and Yeisley 1998)—and participation in the work force and the total of worked hours, especially by women, which also increased very much (Schor 1991). It is, in other words, as if sometime in the mid-1970s the "social system" started squeezing the working class for the juice of production, not with only one hand, but with two hands at the same time. The increased level of performance demanded of the American working class would have as a consequence—according to Rusche's hypothesis—a lowering of the threshold of "less eligibility" and an increasing pressure to perform also at the general social behavioral level, with the consequence of producing many more infractions of the law, many more punished infractions, and more severe punishments—all of which happened in the U.S. after the early 1970s.

Why did this not happen—or, did not happen to the same degree—in Europe, where, after all, "post-Fordist" transformations also started unfolding? Recent discussions on the sociology of punishment have started moving in a comparative direction (Sutton 2000 and 2001; Melossi 2001; Savelsberg 1999). John Sutton's comparative analysis of a group of "advanced" countries, e.g., has come to conclusions that are not inconsistent with the position highlighted above. Sutton has in fact found that, if the relationship between labor surplus and prison growth is much overstated, especially in a comparative perspective, an element that is associated with what we could call a "structural restraint" on imprisonment seems to be the strength of the unions (Sutton 2001). This will not surprise those who are aware of the long-standing position of the unions *vis à vis* prison labor, especially in the United States, a type of labor seen as forced labor and therefore unfairly competitive with free labor. However, beyond that, Sutton's result seems to me to speak to the kernel of Rusche's thesis, contained in the "less eligibility" principle. The idea of less eligibility, as we have seen above, postulates that the living conditions of the working class are a "dependent variable" of the labor market. Among such conditions is also the management of crime issues through the use of penality—linked to the labor market by means of the concept of deterrence. Rusche's "model" is a strictly "liberal" model where market forces rule uncontrasted—in this reflecting the historical reality of the periods he mostly studied. In the course of the twentieth century, though, as Rusche himself pointed out in his 1930 and 1933 articles (through an argument that the lack of sociological sensibility by the legal theorist Otto Kirchheimer would fail to develop), such a view became progressively less realistic, exactly as in Rusche's comparison of the softening effects of social policy legislation on prison conditions in Germany during the years of the Depression, *vis à vis* what happened instead in the United States. The strength of the working class—measured as well through the power of the unions and the creation of a social legislation usually sponsored and backed by unions—tends therefore to have a moderating effect on the "free" cyclical unfolding of imprisonment in the same way that it has a moderating effect on the "free" cyclical unfolding of the market.

Consider also a connected aspect, which is the discourse of human rights. Often one hears, especially from legal theorists, an argument to the effect that prison conditions, having to do with human beings' basic human rights, cannot certainly be "reduced" to lowly "economistic" arguments, such as those by Rusche. This was of course Rusche's starting move, as we have seen, when he claimed that, because such "lowly economic arguments" constitute an unsurpassable limit to the possibility of penal reform,[29] one has to understand the mechanism by which the two are connected. And the basic mechanism is one indeed that has to do with the "value" of a human being in a market society, where, according to Rusche, such value is dependent on the value of labor. In fact, as Marx had famously written in the *1844 Manuscripts*,

> [P]olitical economy…does not recognize the unoccupied worker, the workingman, in so far as he happens to be outside this labor relationship. The cheat-thief, swindler, beggar, and unemployed; the starving, wretched and criminal workingman—these are *figures* who do not exist for *political economy* but only for other eyes, those of the doctor, the judge, the grave digger, and bumbailiff, etc.; such figures are specters outside its domain (Marx 1844:120-121).

What is instead "inside the domain" of political economy is the value of labor. The value of a human being is therefore the value of his labor.[30] The strength of working class organizing, however—which shows up, in Sutton's analysis, under the guise of union power—is directed exactly against such view. It has, as its objective, the independent determination of the value of human beings and the imposition, through class struggle, of an independent concept of such value over the one determined by the market. So much so that, at the beginning of working class organizing, the early forms of unions were seen by the legal system as (criminal) "conspiracies" against the functioning of the "natural law" of the market (Mensch 1982).

Such "class struggle," if it appears in forms that may seem similar everywhere there is a similar "mode of production," is embedded within a physical and a social world that is at least in part autonomous from that mode of production—a "lifeworld" that, indeed, the mode of production continuously attempts at "colonizing."[31] The conditions, therefore, also "cultural" conditions, under which the main mechanisms of modernity—such as capitalism, forms of industrial production, imprisonment—are set in motion, are profoundly different from society to society—even among "modern" societies themselves! This is indeed a dimension that is foreign to Rusche's analysis but that can hardly be overlooked. Perhaps, following a famous distinction by Durkheim (1900), one could distinguish between the "quality" and "quantity" of punishment. Bending Durkheim's terms a bit to a different usage, one could hypothesize that whereas the "quality" of punishment—i.e. the specific historical forms that punishment assumes—tends to move in similar ways through the development of the modern world, albeit through unavoidable "gaps" in time, the "quantity" of punishment can hardly be predicted in ways that are independent from rather idiosyncratic cultural traditions and political contingencies. Specific religious traditions, forms of government, the sense of one country's role in the world, will hardly be uninfluential on the unfolding of punishment (Melossi 2001; Savelsberg 2002).

### Le *"Grand Livre" de* Rusche et Kirchheimer[32]

It is worth *en passant* noticing the homage paid to "Rusche and Kirchheimer's" book in what probably came to be the major reference point of the cultural debate on punishment (and not only)—Michel Foucault's *Discipline and Punish* (1975a). I believe it goes to the credit of Lévy and Zander (1994:53-55) to have shown in a way that has been overlooked by all other commentators Foucault's indebtedness to "Rusche and Kirchheimer's great work" (Foucault 1975a:24). This work is "great"—according to Foucault, in one of the very few references to secondary literature in *Discipline and Punish*—because it "provides a number of essential reference points" (*ibidem*), and these points can be summed up in exactly what had been Rusche's starting move, i.e. the grounding of the study of punishment not in philosophical and legal theories and ideas, but in historically concrete practices of punishment. It is in fact significant that the final section of the first chapter of *Discipline and Punish*, which starts with the mentioned homage to Rusche and Kirchheimer, goes on to outline some of the most crucial (and later famous) concepts elaborated by Foucault therein, such as that of the "political economy of the body" and of the "microphysics of power."[33]

## The "Rusche and Kirchheimer's Hypothesis" and Totalitarianism

Besides the want of comparative analysis, another criticism that is often heard about Rusche's original hypothesis and the line of work somehow inspired by it, is the lack of reflection on ambits different from capitalist democracies and in particular the lack of "reflexivity" about the very heavy presence of imprisonment and especially of forced labor in countries once defined as "socialist"— something quite ironical, it may be added, for a position that is often portrayed as representative of a "Marxist" standpoint. Indeed, there are interesting hints in Rusche's work of the direction his analysis could have taken with regard to "socialist" countries. Rusche had shown an interest in the issue of "coercive labor" that, as we have seen, was not later developed by Kirchheimer. The starting move in Rusche's analysis, especially for what concerns imprisonment, is the period of Mercantilism when, faced with a lack or scarcity of labor power, all kinds of policies were devised in Europe to "put people to work"—one of these being the "invention" of that proto-prison, or *Ur-Prison*, the workhouse.

Policies of coercive labor have accompanied the development of capitalism ever since, even if they have not been the policies "of choice" of capitalism, the norm of which seems to be the much more malleable and flexible instrument of a free labor market. Slavery, and slave labor, has therefore been disappearing from the general picture of capitalist development except for particular times and periods. Thorsten Sellin's interesting reconstruction of the relationship between the institution of slavery and the penal system—according to the closely related idea, by Gustav Radbruch (1938), that slavery constitutes the historical seedling of punishment—was in fact one of the research efforts most clearly marked, from its very opening pages, by Rusche and Kirchheimer's work (Sellin 1976:vii). Furthermore, Rusche seemed to think that the (to him) contemporary situation of Soviet Russia and Nazi Germany could lend itself to being analyzed according to similar lines. In 1939, in a letter to Horkhheimer in New York, Rusche stated that he was ready to write an article for the journal of the institute on "the most recent development of the German penal policy." This was, in his opinion, "the unbelievable scarcity of workers" that had caused, in Germany, "truly interesting new phenomena," among which may have been—though it is not clear whether Rusche had this in mind—the emerging forced labor camps. Years before, in 1934, while he was revising the manuscript of his book in London, he apparently wanted to extend his discussion to the cases of Russia and India. In Russia Rusche saw as the determining factor the scarcity of a work force, having as a consequence an extensive utilization of coercive labor (Lévy and Zander 1994:16, 66).

Indeed, one could extend these remarks by Rusche, connecting them with the particular conditions of Soviet Russia in the 1920s and 1930s. The "first country in the world to be ruled by the working class" came out of the war, the famine, and the embargo without an industrial section and therefore without a working class to speak of. The very first objective of Soviet rulers, whether in the early "soft" NEP version of Lenin, or in the later "hard" Five-Year-Plan version of Stalin, was the reconstruction of both industry *and* the working class—also as instruments to build the kind of defense that seemed necessary for engaging in likely future wars. Especially Stalin's 1930s years, with the forced collectivization of the agriculture and the forced industrialization of the country, were the years of forced labor—until at least the Twentieth Congress of the Communist Party in 1956. I would like to submit that, consistently with Rusche's general overview, one could very well see those years as a sort of compressed and accelerated "primitive accumulation" that unfolded across decades instead of across centuries—as it had happened in Western Europe—and that used similar instruments, among which were coercive labor, and that particular form of coercive labor, penal servitude. It seems to me therefore, that, contrary to any impossibility of using Rusche's hypothesis to understand the events of "realized socialism," Rusche's "simple heuristic maxim" (1933:7) is particularly viable in order to understand the events of totalitarian societies between the two world wars.

### The "Rusche and Kirchheimer's Hypothesis" and the Imprisonment of Women

Another aspect of imprisonment that Rusche and Kirchheimer have often been charged with not considering, and this time more rightly so, is the imprisonment of women. This is in a sense a bit awkward given that, especially in the writing and blueprints of all the reformers, starting with the usual seventeenth-century mercantilist policies of the workhouse, the separation of men and women and the construction therefore of specific institutions for women, usually loomed large. The most obvious reasons for such lack of consideration is probably the "marginal" role that has always been attributed to such institutions within a kind of project-making patterned after male actors, given the actual relevance, also numerical, of men within penitentiary institutions.[34] In fact, one could probably argue that, when we discuss "social control," what is left unsaid about women concerns much more the "outside" than the "inside" of prisons, in the sense that the type of social control reserved for women, in reflecting the patriarchal structure of society, is much more a "domestic" type of social control rather than a penal type of social control. If one may want to take the chance of a slight generalization, one could venture to say that whereas for men criminalized—and penalized—behavior corresponds to what we may perhaps call an "exaggeration" of male characteristics, for women rather the opposite is true. It is a negation of "female characteristics" that brings women to deal with penalization, their becoming more "similar to men," which essentially means their practice of autonomy from the patriarchal and familial structure. In such a connection, the relationship of gender with class and ethnic markers is what comes to the fore, as shown for instance in the work by Nicole Rafter (1985) on the history of women's reformatories in the United States, where the correction of "the rebels" has, as its end, the instantiation of proper, middle class "womanhood" (Rafter 1985:157-175).

## "Long Cycles" of Punishment?

Finally, I would like to suggest that the research tradition initiated by the work of Georg Rusche might reveal itself to be most productively developed by probing deeply in the direction of what has been called the "long cycle" or "long wave" perspective: the perspective, that is, advanced both by liberal socioeconomic thinkers and Marxist ones, according to which what is most significant in international socioeconomic development, whether this is considered in terms of technological innovation and/or class conflicts, happens in long cycles of roughly fifty years, where the peak and the trough of the cycle are separated by periods of about twenty-five years (very close to the span of a generation). This would be a historical-economic concept more readily connected and employed in order to understand phenomena of an essentially cultural nature—

like, for instance, those of penality, which tend to be characterized by slow and viscous movement in comparison with the more straight-forward "economic" movement, a movement that is instead better captured by the usual concept of the "short" business cycle.[35]

Why should this view connect with the substance, if not the letter, of Rusche and Kirchheimer's analysis? Once again, the labor market would furnish the linkage. The long-cyclical view sees the movements of the cycle as induced by the efforts of the actors in the economic arena—essentially entrepreneurs and workers, with "the state," i.e., political actors, as a third party increasingly important in the adjudication of the results of conflict between the first two. Each one of these actors tries to overcome the limitations imposed on its development and "freedom," so to speak, by the adverse activities of the other. Innovation would therefore constitute a crucial tool by which entrepreneurs undercut the power of labor in situations during which a prolonged spell of prosperity has placed workers in a privileged position. The result of innovation—usually backed by political-legal power—is to destructure and disorganize the type of economy in which the former type of working class had achieved its dangerous (for the entrepreneurs) power. Likewise, adapting to the innovations implemented, the "new" type of working class recruited under the new conditions—often from "lowly" "immigrant" quarters—would slowly find the way to reorganize and bring ever more effective blows (at least as effective as the "old" type of working class was able to bring) to the new setting of social relationships and power. At this point, the cycle starts anew, similar to the preceding one in pattern, completely different instead phenomenologically.

Why would all of this have something to do with Rusche's main hypothesis? Rusche's concept of a connection between punishment—and especially imprisonment—and the labor market can be framed as one of the slowly moving aspects of that larger picture, where imprisonment rises and conditions within prisons become harsher in periods when the entrepreneurial elite is on the attack to respond to the "intolerable" levels of power reached by the working class. Later on, after the reestablishment of entrepreneurial hegemony, when the working class is slowly reconstructing its power and organization, imprisonment would again be on the decline and conditions of penality would tend to become more prone to "reform." All such connections should not be thought of as an "understructure" determining a "superstructure" but rather—as Max Weber did—as a network of relations of affinity, where the long-cyclical movements are caused by the autonomous but interactive contributions—economic, political, cultural—of all the actors involved.

In the one effort today to develop such a line of analysis, Charlotte Vanneste identifies, on the grounds of existing literature, the location of the "peaks" and "troughs" of such long cycles (Vanneste 2001:56).[36] The "peaks" are of paramount importance in order to understand the logic of the "long cycle" argument in relation to change in imprisonment. It is around the peak, in fact, that a long spell of prosperity ends and turns into an "economic crisis." Prosperity means, from the standpoint of the working class, increasing extension and power, stronger organization, and a robust capacity for wage demands. On the opposite side—that of entrepreneurs— the strength of the working class translates to fast reducing profit margins and the necessity for change and innovation. Through innovation (which is often the result of a common feeling that the boundaries of the "old" social system are too rigid and suffocating for the development that the long period of prosperity has made possible) the most enterprising sectors of the elite are able to side-step at the same time both the long-established competitors and the type of working class that grew together with prosperity—not to mention what is most important in terms of class conflict: to smash the given organizational forms of the "old" working class.

During the prosperity period leading to the "peak" years, the years when the "showdown" between labor and capital takes place, punishment has become less of a "necessity" for the social system as a whole. When most people who look for work can find it, the general social attitude, according to Rusche's hypothesis, is one of good disposition even toward the lowest members of the working class. There is the expectation that even if left to himself in a condition of freedom, the first-time offender will be able to reenter society and find some source of income. One who has already committed a crime can still be rehabilitated through a short prison stint or through some "alternatives to imprisonment" and only the most callous criminals will be thought of as deserving long spells of detention. Furthermore, prison conditions will be decent, and it will be possible to work within the prison system, both because this is deemed to be a good tool for rehabilitation and because the high wages outside make it worth it to produce at least certain goods at "controlled" prices (something that the unions outside often tend to object to). Furthermore, the basic stability of periods of prosperity makes it so that no "strangers" have to be called in to work, and anyway, even if they are, the general climate of tolerance and the good disposition of society extend also to them.

The opposite happens in the following period. The defeat of the "old" working class as well as of the least competitive economic sectors translates into a progressive devaluation of human beings. There is an increasing recourse, especially around the "peak," to a "new" kind of working class—youth, women, immigrants—that do not share in the values and general "ethos" of the old one, with strong resentments, conflicts, and, what is most important, divisions, being created within the working class.[37] The number of the unemployed increases, "crime" becomes more and more associated with the "newcomers," tolerance disappears, prison work and "alternative programs" are also shelved, and a general mean feeling of envy and revenge takes hold in a society increasingly structured around lines of hierarchy, authoritarianism, and exclusion.

If we accept "measuring" all of this by means of the indicator of imprisonment rates—a very unsatisfactory one, as mentioned above, but for the time being the only one we have available—it may be a useful exercise to compare, if only in a merely suggestive way, the "slope" prediction of Vanneste's "long cycle" model with the actual behavior of imprisonment rates in two countries, Italy and the United States (see Figure 1). According to Vanneste's reconstruction, the peaks would be located *grosso modo* around 1870, 1920, and 1970, and the troughs around 1850, 1895, and the period of World War II. Because, according to hypothesis, the imprisonment rate should "behave" in countercyclical fashion, we would derive the prediction of an increase in imprisonment rates in the three "downswings," 1870-1895, 1920-1945, and 1970-2000, and a decrease instead in the three "upswings," 1850-1870, 1895-1920, and 1945-1970. Today we would find ourselves on the brink of a new decrease.

The axes marked in Figure 1 correspond to the mentioned "peaks" and "troughs." The behavior of imprisonment rates seems to—*roughly!*—correspond to the predicted one only for the twentieth century, i.e., the last two "long cycles," but not for the previous one in the nineteenth century. Furthermore, as we mentioned above, when we were distinguishing between an argument based on "quality" and an argument based on "quantity," whereas we may be able to predict the general direction of the slope, the specificity of the size of incremental change year by year may vary greatly in different countries and under different circumstances. If we compare, for instance, the U.S. and Italian rates in the 1895-1920 period, we can observe a strong decline in the Italian case and a slight one in the U.S. one. The years of the ensuing Depression on the other hand see a moderate increase in the U.S. and simply an interruption of the previous downward trend in Italy. After World War II, we have again a definite declining trend in Italy and a substantially stable situation in the U.S. Finally, after 1970, Italian rates edge up a little, amidst oscillations, while in the U.S. we witness the well known "great internment" of the last quarter of the twentieth century. At the very least, one should note that the "long cycles" should here be negotiated with a "secular trend" (Schumpeter 1939:193-219) that is strongly declining in the case of Italy and strongly increasing in the case of the U.S.

I believe that this last exercise is a good indication of the value of Rusche's hypothesis—especially if applied over the dimension where it seems to me it makes most sense: long-term development. On the one hand, there is no doubt that—as Sellin and Sutherland stated when they first read Rusche's original manuscript—Rusche's hypothesis has to be negotiated with many other aspects of social real-

**Figure 1**
**Imprisonment Rates per 100,000 in the U.S. and Italy[38]**

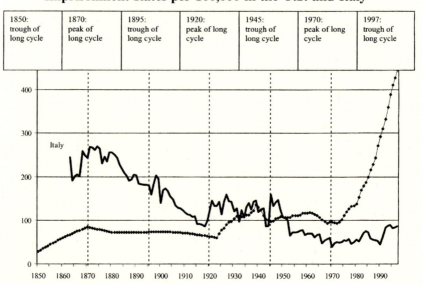

| 1850:<br>trough of<br>long cycle | 1870:<br>peak of<br>long cycle | 1895:<br>trough of<br>long cycle | 1920:<br>peak of long<br>cycle | 1945:<br>trough of<br>long cycle | 1970:<br>peak of long<br>cycle | 1997:<br>trough of<br>long cycle |
|---|---|---|---|---|---|---|

ity and especially with the historical specificity of each country's history. On the other hand, I think that the "heuristic maxim" laid out by an "unusual human being" at the end of the 1920s probably represents the most elegant and concise idea that the social sciences have produced today for helping to understand the social and economic context of developments in penality.

## Notes

1.  In 1980 I presented the most basic features of Georg Rusche's life (Melossi 1980). Such reconstruction was somewhat completed by the editors of the French translation in 1994 (Lévy and Zander 1994). The information that follows in the next section, about Rusche's life, is based on these two contributions. For all the details and sources please consult those. Here I will give information on the details and sources only of those few aspects of Rusche's life that emerged after the publication of Lévy and Zander's article.

2.  According to which, therefore, life in prison, or the meted punishment, would have to be less "eligible" than the "worst" type of "free" life. Even if Rusche does not, at times, literally state such a principle (Lévy and Zander 1994:63), it seems to me to be clearly at the center of both his 1930 (p. 42) and 1933 (p. 4) pieces and consequently also of his original plan for *P&SS*.

3.  Distinguishing six main periods with respect to the main analytical concepts used: High Middle Ages (favorable to labor), Lower Middle Ages (unfavorable), seventeenth-century mercantilism (favorable), the industrial revolution and the nineteenth century in Europe (unfavorable), the same period in America (favorable), and the turn of the new century and its beginning (favorable).

4.  As we will see, both Sellin and Sutherland, when they were asked to read Rusche's original manuscript of *P&SS*, were particularly critical of these passages.

5.  By Sellin, see especially his *Slavery and the Penal System* (Sellin 1976).

6.  Already starting with the 1939 Sutherland edition of *Principles of Criminology*, on to Sutherland and Cressey's 6th 1960 edition and then in the 10th and last Sutherland and Cressey's *Criminology* edition (Sutherland and Cressey 1978), Rusche and Kirchheimer are present in the second part of the volume, devoted to reaction to crime, in the chapters about variations in punitive policies, social-structural theories of punishment, and prison labor. I would also claim that the penal theory most original to Sutherland, the "consistency theory" of punishment, was influenced by Rusche's theory. See below about the relationship between Cressey and Jankovic.

7.  Generally, about the Frankfurt School, see Jay (1973:44, 105, 204). In particular, Franz Neumann—who, as a member of the Direction of the Institute, would be the one to approach his friend Kirchheimer for the rewrite of the manuscript—asked Kirchheimer "not to advertise on every page the superiority of Marxist theory" (Lévy and Zander 1994:22, see also p. 52). Also, one should keep in mind that the signing of the infamous Ribbentrop-Molotov pact between Germany and the Soviet Union bolstered the traditional anti-communism of the Western powers. As we will see, this was to become one more reason for treating "left-wing" refugees in the same way as "enemy aliens," even if staunchly anti-Fascist.

8.  We have a note, from Leo Lowenthal's file on Neumann, that reports news from the *Daily Herald* of March 14, 1935.

9.  Harro Bernardelli was a friend of Rusche from Germany who had written a thesis, under the direction of Horkhheimer, in mathematical economics, reviewed by Rusche

in the *Zeitschrift für Sozialforschung* (Bernardelli 1933; Rusche 1934). Later Bernardelli emigrated to New Zealand and became rather well known in academic circles until the early 1950s, contributing to economic theory and demography. The letter (in German) comes from Leo Lowenthal's file on Neumann. I would like to thank Martin Jay for having made the letter available to me.

10.     Later, Neumann followed for the Institute both the request to Kirchheimer to rewrite Rusche's manuscript and the rather stormy negotiations with Rusche in Palestine. The final greetings in Bernardelli's letter read, "Many greetings also on behalf of my wife to you." The picture that comes out of the letter, especially if we consider that Bernardelli had apparently been a student of Horkheimer (Lévy and Zander 1994:10), is that of a rather more intimate participation of the two friends, Bernardelli and Rusche, within the Frankfurt circle than until now suspected—certainly more intimate than one might think from the numerous denials of having ever known Rusche that I received more than twenty years ago when I addressed some of the most significant members of the School (Melossi 1980).

11.     That is literally what Neumann would write to Kirchheimer two years later (Lévy and Zander 1994:23 note 45).

12.     About the much better known biography of Otto Kirchheimer, see the usual two references.

13.     In a letter, alas!, dated March 1935 (see Melossi 1980:55).

14.     According to Lévy and Zander (1994:28), in a letter of June 1938 Rusche reported some malicious rumors about Kirchheimer and went on to label the "methods" of the Institute as similar to those of "gangsters."

15.     Both Melossi (1980) and Lévy and Zander (1994) entertain the issue.

16.     A similar argument had been made by Sutherland (1934) in an article that he had just published and that he mentions in his letter to Gumperz of January 3, 1936.

17.     Besides, they reflect the particular strain of analysis derived from Neumann's view inside the Institute (about this, see Lévy and Zander 1994, Melossi 1978, and especially Jay 1973:143-172).

18.     From Sellin's notes, pp. 413-26 of Rusche's manuscript dealt with the contemporary situation in America and pp. 427-75 with that in Germany.

19.     *Before and after the ReichKristallNacht. The history of a Königsberg family told by Rainer Radok* (see http://mpec.sc.mahidol.ac.th/Radok/).

20.     Once again, refer to my 1980 article.

21.     See note 7.

22.     In the end, we gather from people who knew him that he was an unabashed liberal. His educational curriculum, as we have seen, is not inconsistent with that. At the same time, a note of December 1, 1934 from the Society for the Protection of Learning and Science, which was trying to help the refugees, reported that Rusche had "prospects in the USSR." We may want to hypothesize that Rusche's political path was similar to that of many in his generations, ending in a deep disillusionment about socialism that was very common among refugees after the war—the kind of path most famously represented perhaps in the collection *The God that Failed* (Crossman 1950) (see especially Arthur Koestler's contribution).

23.     Jankovic's articles on *Crime and Social Justice* (Jankovic 1977 and 1978) originated from his dissertation work.

24.     Given that this is said at a time when to proclaim one's work—albeit past work—"Marxist" or "neo-Marxist" is no longer a sign of distinction but of eccentricity at best, I am not afraid of appearing immodest in stating this. At the time, I had derived the reference to *P&SS* not from any criminological text but from Maurice Dobb's *Studies in the Development of Capitalism* (1946) (Dobb had been among Rusche's supporters in the U.K). Lévy and Zander (1994:43 note 118) report a statement by

Heinz Steinert according to which, at the end of the 1960s, the British "new criminologists" (I assume Taylor, Walton, and Young) would have made *"circuler sous
le manteau dans les colloques"* the reference to Rusche and Kirchheimer's work. I
doubt it. I think that would happen only later (the turning point in this respect might
have been the *Autorenkolloquium* in Bielefeld [November 1-3, 1974], organized by
Alessandro Baratta and Karl Schuman about the just published *The New Criminology*, and where I presented a draft of the essay that would then be published in
*Crime and Social Justice* [Melossi 1976]). A reference to *P&SS* is in fact nowhere
to be found in *The New Criminology* (1973), which privileges a rather different
kind of "young Marx" Marxism, and if Taylor, Walton, and Young would have had
it *"sous le manteau"* they would have certainly drawn it out! Later on, Ian Taylor
especially, but also Jock Young, would be exceptionally and very kindly helpful in
the British side of my research about Georg Rusche's life that was then to appear in
Melossi (1980).

25.    A truly international phenomenon, from the "National Deviancy Conference" in the
       U.K., to the (still existing) "European Group for the Study of Deviance and Social
       Control" in Europe, to the many journals in German, French, Italian and Spanish in
       Europe and Latin America.
26.    Based on the research for my 1972 Bologna law degree thesis on "a Marxist theory
       of crime and punishment."
27.    I tried to summarize at least part of the debate in Melossi (1998).
28.    This is also the period many describe as a transition from a "Fordist" to a "post-
       Fordist" economy. For an attempt at connecting the particular version of "post-
       Fordist" argument developed by Hardt and Negri (2000) to the question of penal
       control, see De Giorgi (2002).
29.    Lévy and Zander, in their often mentioned Introduction, make this point very clearly.
30.    In the 1920s Soviet Union, E. B. Pashukanis (1924) made a rather similar point (see
       Melossi 1978).
31.    A story told both by the Marxist "imperialism" tradition (lastly Hardt and Negri
       2000) and Habermas (1981).
32.    From the original French edition of *Surveiller et punir* (Paris, Gallimard, 1975, p.
       29).
33.    Isn't this further proof, were there need for some, of the "family resemblance" of
       Foucauldian theory and a Marx-informed view on crime and punishment—if one,
       that is, goes to the very heart of Marxist theory, the connection between exploitation
       and work *discipline*? To the heart of it, even more explicitly than Rusche had
       done, given that Rusche's interest, closer to the tradition of market economics,
       had centered in the concept of the labor market rather than in what Marx used
       to call "the sphere of production." Instead, certain passages from Part Three of
       *Discipline and Punish,* the one in fact entitled "Discipline," sound at times like
       quotes from *Capital,* and the very central idea of a "productive" power sounds
       familiar to Marxist theory, almost as a kind of generalization of it. "Discipline"
       represents the linchpin that ties the place of production to the modern place of
       punishment in a way that is wholly derivable from Marx, and parallel to
       Foucault's (Melossi and Pavarini 1977). This is so, however, because Marx's
       teaching is part of Foucault's toolbox: as Foucault stated at the time in an interview,
       almost paraphrasing Bertrand Russell's famous quote about Christianity, the one
       who writes history today cannot help but call himself Marxist (Foucault 1975b).
       The relationship between the "Marxist tradition," Rusche and Kirchheimer, and
       Foucault is certainly much richer, more complex, and fertile and nuanced than it
       appears from Garland's treatment in *Punishment and Modern Society* (1990) (see
       Melossi 1998:xii-xiv).

34. See, however, Feeley and Little's interesting contribution showing otherwise for the period at the beginning of modernity (Feeley and Little 1991).
35. Schumpeter, Pareto, Sorokin, Kondratieff, and Kalecki are the names most commonly linked to some kind of cyclical theory of socioeconomic development (for a recent review, see Rennstich [2002]). Melossi (1985) and Vanneste (2001) have explored the possibility of applying such views to a Ruschean type of analysis.
36. Vanneste goes on to applying this theoretical framework to the case of Belgium.
37. History offers plenty of examples of such deviant representations of "strangers/workers." One has only to think of the "vagrants" that constituted the "original" proletariat in the process of so-called "primitive" accumulation (Marx 1867; Melossi and Pavarini 1977); of the "classes dangereuses" of the nineteenth century (Chevalier 1973); of the "hoboes" and the "wobblies" during the great transformation of North American working class in the early decades of this century (Anderson 1923); of the mass migration of former Southern and Eastern European peasants to the Americas around the turn of the century, and the panic about their "criminality" (Teti 1993; Salvatore and Aguirre 1996); of the mass migration of African-American rural workers from the South to the North of the United States between the 1920s and the 1950s, a mass migration whose later generations eventually went to feed what would come to be called the "American underclass" in more recent years (Wilson 1987); of the mass move of Southern Europeans, between the 1950s and early 1970s, toward Central and Northern Europe and, there too, the ensuing panic about crime (Ferracuti 1968); finally, the most recent example is probably the migration of Northern African and Eastern European workers towards the countries of the European Union, this time also Southern Europe, likewise marked by an outcry about the "criminal" invasion (Tonry 1997; Marshall 1997). In all these very different examples, we witness a bifurcation in the "moral economy" of the working class between a respectable "old" working class, expressing moral indignation at the mores of the newcomers, and a "new" working class, subject to extensive processes of criminalization. I have called this phenomenon the "cycle of production of *la canaille*," of the rabble, in my Introduction to De Giorgi (Melossi 2002).
38. Italian data are my elaboration of data assembled by the official governmental institute of statistics in Rome (ISTAT). They go from 1863 to 1997 and are equal to the sum of inmates in all adult prison institutions. U.S. data go from 1850 to 1997 and are equal to the sum of inmates in State and Federal prisons. They are based on an update of the data originally collected and elaborated by Margaret Cahalan (1979) (the line between 1850 and 1925 is a linear interpolation based on the years for which we have data, that is, 1850, 1860, 1870, 1880, 1890, 1904, 1910, and 1923). They do not include jail data.

## References*

Anderson, Nels. 1923. *The Hobo*. Chicago: The University of Chicago Press.
Bernardelli, Harro. 1933. *Die Grundlagen der ökonomischen Theorie: Eine Einführung*. Tübingen: Mohr.
Blumstein, Alfred, Jacqueline Cohen, and Daniel Nagin. 1977. "The Dynamics of a Homeostatic Punishment Process," *Journal of Criminal Law and Criminology* 67:317-334.
Blumstein, Alfred and Jacqueline Cohen. 1973. "A Theory of the Stability of Punishment," *Journal of Criminal Law and Criminology* 64:198.

* Please note: the dates after the name of the author (and in the text) refer to the date of the original edition of the work. The date at the end of the reference, if different, pertains to the edition used.

Cahalan, Margaret. 1979. "Trends in Incarceration in the United States since 1880," *Crime and Delinquency* 25:9-41.

Chevalier, Louis. 1973. *Labouring Classes and Dangerous Classes*. London: Routledge.

Chiricos, Theodore G. and Miriam A. DeLone. 1992. "Labor Surplus and Punishment: A Review and Assessment of Theory and Evidence," *Social Problems* 39:421-46.

Crossman, Richard. 1950. *The God that Failed*. New York: Harper & Row, 1963.

D'Alessio, Stewart J. and Lisa Stolzenberg. 2002. "A Multilevel Analysis of the Relationship between Labor Surplus and Pretrial Incarceration," *Social Problems* 49:178-193.

———. 1995. "Unemployment and the Incarceration of Pretrial Defendants," *American Sociological Review* 60:350–359.

De Giorgi, Alessandro. 2002. *Il governo dell'eccedenza*. Verona: Ombrecorte.

Dobb, M. Herbert. 1946. *Studies in the Development of Capitalism*. London: Routledge.

Durkheim, Emile. 1900. "Two Laws of Penal Evolution," *Cincinnati Law Review* 38:32-60, 1969.

Feeley, Malcolm M. and Deborah L. Little. 1991. "The Vanishing Female: The Decline of Women in the Criminal Process, 1687-1912," *Law and Society Review* 25:719-757.

Ferracuti, Franco. 1968. "European Migration and Crime," pp. 189-219 in M. E. Wolfgang (ed.), *Crime and Culture: Essays in Honour of Thorsten Sellin*. New York: Wiley.

Foucault, Michel. 1975a. *Discipline and Punish*. New York: Pantheon, 1977.

———. 1975b. "Prison Talk," pp. 37-54 in M. Foucault, *Power/Knowledge*. New York: Pantheon, 1980.

Garland, David. 1990. *Punishment and Modern Society*. Chicago: The University of Chicago Press.

Goffman, Erving. 1961. *Asylums*. New York: Anchor Books.

Greenberg, David F. 1977. "The Dynamics of Oscillatory Punishment Processes," *The Journal of Criminal Law and Criminology* 68:643-651.

Habermas, Jürgen. 1981. *The Theory of Communicative Action*, Volume Two. Boston: Beacon Press, 1989.

———. 1973. *Legitimation Crisis*. Boston: Beacon Press, 1975.

Hardt, Michael and Antonio Negri. 2000. *Empire*. Cambridge (Mass.): Harvard University Press.

Jacobs, David and Ronald E. Helms. 1996. "Toward a Political Model of Incarceration: A Time-Series Examination of Multiple Explanations for Prison Admission Rates," *American Journal of Sociology* 102:323-357.

Jankovic, Ivan. 1978. "Social Class and Criminal Sentencing," *Crime and Social Justice* 10:9-16.

———. 1977. "Labor Market and Imprisonment," *Crime and Social Justice* 8:17-31.

Jay, Martin. 1973. *The Dialectical Imagination*. Boston: Little Brown.

Kovandzic, Tomislav V., Lynne M. Vieraitis, and Mark R. Yeisley. 1998. "The Structural Covariates of Urban Homicide: Reassessing the impact of income inequality and poverty in the post-Reagan era," *Criminology* 36:569-600.

Levy, René and Hartwig Zander. 1994. "Introduction," pp. 9-82 in G. Rusche and O. Kirchheimer, *Peine et structure sociale*. Paris: Les Editions du Cerf.

Marshall, Ineke H. (ed.). 1997. *Minorities, Migrants, and Crime*. London: Sage.

Marx, Karl. 1867. *Capital—Volume One*. New York: International Publishers, 1970.

———. 1844. *Economic and Philosophic Manuscripts of 1844*. New York: International Publishers, 1964.

Melossi, Dario. 2002. "Discussione a mo' di prefazione: carcere, postfordismo e ciclo di produzione della 'canaglia,'" pp. 7-24 in De Giorgi (2002).

———. 2001. "The Cultural Embeddedness of Social Control: Reflections on the Comparison of Italian and North-American Cultures Concerning Punishment," *Theoretical Criminology* 5:403-424.

————. 1998. (Ed.) *The Sociology of Punishment*. In *The International Library of Criminology, Criminal Justice and Penology*. Aldershot, Hampshire: Dartmouth Publ. Co.

————. 1993. "Gazette of Morality and Social Whip: Punishment, Hegemony, and the Case of the USA, 1970-92," *Social and Legal Studies* 2:259-79.

————. 1985. "Punishment and Social Action: Changing Vocabularies of Punitive Motive within a Political Business Cycle," *Current Perspectives in Social Theory* 6:169-97.

————. 1980. "Georg Rusche: A Biographical Essay,"*Crime and Social Justice* 14:51-63.

————. 1978. "George Rusche and Otto Kirchheimer: Punishment and Social Structure," *Crime and Social Justice* 9:73-85.

————. 1977. "Prison and Labour in Europe and Italy during the Formation of the Capitalist Mode of Production," pp. 9-95 in Melossi and Pavarini (1977).

————. 1976. "The Penal Question in 'Capital,'" *Crime and Social Justice* 5:26-33.

Melossi, Dario and Massimo Pavarini. 1977. *The Prison and the Factory: Origins of the Penitentiary System*. London: Macmillan and Totowa (NJ): Barnes and Noble, 1981.

Mensch, Elizabeth. 1982. "The History of Mainstream Legal Thought," pp. 18-39 in D. Kairys (ed.), *The Politics of Law*. New York: Pantheon.

O'Connor, James. 1973. *The Fiscal Crisis of the State*. New York: St. Martin's Press.

Pashukanis, Evgeny B. 1924. "The General Theory of Law and Marxism," pp. 40-131, in E.B.Pashukanis, *Selected Writings on Marxism and Law*. London: Academic Press, 1980.

Peterson, Wallace G. 1994. *Silent Depression: The Fate of the American Dream*. New York: Norton.

Radbruch, Gustav. 1938. "Der Ursprung des Strafrechts auf dem Stande der Unfreien," pp.1-11, in G. Radbruch, *Elegantiae Juris Criminalis*. Basel: Verlag für Recht und Gesellschaft.

Rafter, Nicole H. 1985. *Partial Justice: Women in State Prisons 1800-1935*. Boston: Northeastern University Press.

Rennstich, Joachim K. 2002. "The new economy, the leadership long cycle and the nineteenth K-wave," *Review of International Political Economy* 9:150-182.

Rusche, Georg. 1934. Review of Bernardelli (1933) in *Zeitschrift für Sozialforschung* 3:147.

————. 1933. "Labor Market and Penal Sanction," *Crime and Social Justice* 10(1978):2-8.

————. 1930. "Prison Revolts or Social Policy: Lessons from America," *Crime and Social Justice* 13(1980):41-44

Rusche, Georg and Otto Kirchheimer. 1939. *Punishment and Social Structure*. New York: Russell & Russell, 1968.

Salvatore, Ricardo D. and Carlos Aguirre (eds.). 1996. *The Birth of the Penitentiary in Latin America: Essays on Criminology, PrisonReform, and Social Control, 1830-1940*. Austin: University of Texas Press.

Savelsberg, Joachim J. 2002. "Cultures of Criminal Punishment: Religion and Historical Contingencies," paper presented at the 2002 Annual Meetings of the American Sociological Association, Chicago.

————. 1999. "Cultures of Punishment: USA—Germany," paper presented at the Annual Meeting of the American Society of Criminology, Toronto.

Schor, Juliet B. 1991. *The Overworked American*. New York: Basic Books.

Schumpeter, Joseph A. 1939. *Business Cycles*. New York: McGraw-Hill.

Scull, Andrew T. 1977. *Decarceration: Community Treatment and the Deviant—A Radical View*. Englewood Cliffs (NJ): Prentice-Hall.

Sellin, J. Thorsten. 1976. *Slavery and the Penal System*. New York: Elsevier.

Sutherland, Edwin H. 1934. "The Decreasing Prison Population of England," pp. 200-26 in A. Cohen, A. Lindesmith and K. Schuessler (eds.), *The Sutherland Papers*. Bloomington: Indiana University Press, 1956.

Sutherland, Edwin H. and Donald R. Cressey. 1978. *Criminology.* Philadelphia: Lippincott.

Sutton, John. 2001. "The Political Economy of Imprisonment Among Affluent Western Democracies, 1955-1990," unpublished manuscript.

———. 2000. "Imprisonment and Social Classification in Five Common-Law Democracies 1955-1985," *American Journal of Sociology* 106:350-86.

Taylor, Ian, Paul Walton, and Jock Young. 1973. *The New Criminology: For a Social Theory of Deviance.* London: Routledge.

Teti, Vito. 1993. *La razza maledetta: origini del pregiudizio antimeridionale.* Roma: manifestolibri.

Tonry, Michael. 1997. (Ed.) *Ethnicity, Crime, and Immigration: Comparative and Cross-National Perspectives.* Chicago: The University of Chicago Press.

Vanneste, Charlotte. 2001. *Les Chiffres des Prisons.* Paris: L'Harmattan.

Western, Bruce and Katherine Beckett. 1999. "How Unregulated is the U.S. Labor Market? The Penal System as a Labor Market Institution," *American Journal of Sociology* 104:1030-1060.

Wilson, William J. 1987. *The Truly Disadvantaged: The Inner City, the Underclass and Public Policy.* Chicago: University of Chicago Press.

# Part II

## Law as a Social Phenomenon

# 4

# On Oliver Wendell Holmes, Jr., *The Common Law*

*Tim Griffin*

*The Common Law* is Oliver Wendell Holmes' most sustained jurisprudential work. In it the careful reader will discern traces of his later thought as found in both his judicial opinions and other writings, such as *The Path of Law*. However, the book can be difficult because Holmes' objective is not always clear. I hope that this introduction will shed new light on the work. Accordingly, I begin with a brief account of Holmes' life and the influences that played a role in shaping his thought. I then turn to a discussion of the larger concerns of *The Common Law* as well as certain of the significant particulars of his presentation that bear on it. Finally, I consider the relevance of Holmes' position for contemporary legal theory. Although *The Common Law* is difficult, students of law and jurisprudence will doubtless find their effort in working through it highly rewarding.

## I

Oliver Wendell Holmes, Jr. was born on May 8, 1841 into a prominent Boston family. His maternal grandfather, Charles Jackson, had served as a justice on the Supreme Judicial Court of Massachusetts. His father, Oliver Wendell Holmes, Sr., was a physician as well as a noted literary figure. In short, Holmes was born into a successful and well-established professional family.

As a young man Holmes was something of an idealist. He was, for example, passionately dedicated to the abolitionist cause and contemplated devoting himself to the study of philosophy. Neither of these positions was in accordance with his father's views or wishes for him. Nonetheless, in pursuit of the first of these ideals, abolitionism, Holmes enlisted in the Union army after his graduation from Harvard in 1861. He was commissioned a lieutenant in the Twentieth Massachusetts Volunteer Infantry and by the time he left the military in 1864, he had been involved in some of the worst fighting of the Civil War, had been wounded three times, and had been promoted to the rank of lieutenant colonel.

Holmes' military involvement may have taken much of the wind out of his idealist sails. This is hardly surprising given the divisive nature of the Civil War, and his firsthand witness of the cost, in this case in human suffering and life, of ideals, however worthy. This is not to suggest that the abolitionist cause was not just or that Holmes regretted his involvement in it. At least to my knowledge he never expressed any regrets. It has been noted, however, that the post-bellum Holmes was much more skeptical, if not cynical, about reform movements than the ante-bellum Holmes had been.

After his military service, Holmes considered various options before finally resolving to study law. In particular, he gave serious thought to pursuing a vocation in philosophy. In the end, he chose to enter Harvard Law School. He completed his legal studies and began to practice law in 1866. However, he remained interested in philosophy and in 1868 he began participating in the Metaphysical Club of Cambridge whose membership included such notable philosophical figures as Charles Sanders Peirce, Chauncey Wright, and William James. This association had a pronounced influence on the development of Holmes' theory of law.

Such were the events that shaped Holmes' outlook. From 1866 to the early 1880s his vocational focus was the law. In addition to his law practice, he was made a lecturer at Harvard Law School and coeditor of the *American Law Review*. In 1872 he married Fanny Bowditch Dixwell; that union would endure until her death in 1929. In 1873 Holmes published an edited version of *Kent's Commentaries on the Law*. Shortly thereafter, he began work on *The Common Law*, which appeared in 1881. The publication of this volume earned Holmes the rank of Professor of Law at Harvard Law School.

Holmes remained in this position for only one year. He resigned upon accepting an appointment as associate justice on the Supreme Judicial Court of Massachusetts, bringing to a close his brief stint as a practicing lawyer, academic, and scholar.

Holmes was sworn in as an associate justice of the Supreme Judicial Court of Massachusetts in 1883. In 1899 he was appointed the

Court's chief justice. In 1902, after serving nineteen years on Massachusetts' highest court, President Theodore Roosevelt appointed Holmes an associate justice of the Supreme Court of the United States. He remained in that position until his retirement from the Court in 1932. He died on March 6, 1935 and was buried beside his wife in Arlington National Cemetery.

During his lengthy tenure on the U.S. Supreme Court, Holmes displayed those characteristics that earned him the title "The Great Dissenter." It is important to note that Holmes did not receive this title because he dissented often, particularly by contemporary standards, but because he dissented effectively. In his dissenting opinions he often exhibited prescience for later developments by the Court—indeed, many of his important dissenting opinions were vindicated by subsequent Court opinions. Of course, it is difficult to say whether this success was owed to Holmes' aptitude for anticipating the direction in which the Court would move—an aptitude that Holmes would find among the most admirable for a legal thinker—or whether it was owed to the persuasiveness of his dissenting arguments. In all likelihood, his success was a matter of his powers of both prediction and persuasion.

It is noteworthy that the seeds of some of Holmes' most notable opinions are already present in *The Common Law*. For example, in his celebrated dissenting opinion in *Lochner v. New York* (1905), Holmes challenged the Court's position that the Due Process clause of the Fourteenth Amendment contained, by implication, substantive principles discoverable by means of reason. There is a clear relationship between this position and his rejection of the idea that the common law could be organized by means of philosophical principles or theories. To Holmes' way of thinking, judges must decide cases on the basis of facts—widely conceived so as to include considerations of social policy. Significantly, these attitudes already figure prominently in *The Common Law*, to which I now turn.

## II

Holmes greatly desired to make his mark as an author and scholar, and *The Common Law* was to be his vehicle for doing so. As noted above, prior to undertaking this project, he had edited *Kent's Commentaries on the Law*. Although the latter may have left him somewhat disillusioned with the state of the common law, it likely made him aware of the strengths of the common law system as well. In particular, he realized that the common law cannot be organized in accordance with one or another philosophical position. On the contrary, to attempt to impose order in this way would essentially compromise the common law's integrity. Thus, while it is possible to *discern* order in the actual workings of the common law, it would be a mistake to attempt to impose order on it from without so as to make it correspond to preconceived philosophical opinions. On this point, Holmes' position stood in stark contrast to that of many of his contemporaries.

At the time Holmes was writing *The Common Law*, there were movements afoot, in both America and England, to significantly reform the common law. The chief advocates of these movements, the utilitarians and the neo-Kantians/Hegelians, came from radically different camps. They agreed, however, that the common law was too disorderly and unsystematic to secure the larger aims for which a legal system exists. In particular, a crucial aim of the legal system is the imposition of order on society. However, the common law system itself seemed to lack order; the provisions of the law were therefore established on a case-by-case basis by judicial decisions.

Thus the difficulty, as the reformers saw it, was that the common law is a body of rules promulgated by judges in response to the particular facts of a given dispute. They recognized, of course, that a judge's decision is not entirely arbitrary. Common law judges must answer to precedent or *stare decisis*—the "rule of law" established in prior relevant judicial opinions. However, the determination of precedent is a tricky business in itself. There is, for example, the problem of determining exactly what the rule of law articulated in a prior case is—a task that is far more difficult than it might seem— and worse yet, there is always a question about whether a precedent case is relevant given the inevitable differences in fact situations between it and the case under consideration. Thus a common law judge must determine how closely the facts of the case under consideration match those of the precedent. If the facts in the prior decision are too remote, then the rule of the prior case may be disregarded or, in the language of the courts, "distinguished." Now obviously this is far more of an art than a science, and there is significant room for a judge's particular prejudices to enter into his interpretation and application of precedent. Thus, for those concerned with order and clarity, the common law appears sloppy and murky indeed.

Nor is the problem merely a matter of theoretical elegance and intellectual aesthetics. A more important concern is that individuals and the society as a whole rely on the law in ordering their affairs. But the fact that the common law allows so much room for judicial innovation makes its outcomes less predictable than they ought to be. This state of affairs is particularly scandalous in areas such as torts and criminal law, in which one who is held liable may suffer pecuniary losses or the loss of freedom. But the problem is not confined to these areas. Uncertainty in the law impacts the areas of property and contract as well; areas in which it is critical that one be able to rely on clearly defined rules to order one's affairs.

These are significant concerns, and Holmes' efforts to defend the common law system may seem surprising in light of them. However, he was convinced that the common law system possessed virtues that were overlooked or misunderstood by its critics. He held, moreover, that the concern for order of the sort envisioned by its critics was too simplistic. Thus, at the outset of *The Common Law* he observes that "[t]he object of this book is to present a general view of the Common Law. To accomplish this task, other tools are needed besides logic. It is something to show that the consistency of a system requires a particular result, but it is not all. The life of the law has not been logic: it has been experience" (p. 5). It is a mistake, Holmes thought, to attempt to impose an *a priori* order onto the common law simply for the sake of obtaining a rational legal order. There is more at stake than either logical consistency or certainty. The legal system must allow for the inevitable changes in society.

Of course, Holmes is not advocating the absence of order. His point is rather that there is order inherent in the common law that its critics have failed to notice. Furthermore, this order is more comprehensive, and therefore superior, to that which might be provided by a philosophical system such as utilitarianism or Kantianism. Thus, he continues, "[t]he felt necessities of the time, the prevalent moral and political theories, intuitions of public policy, avowed or unconscious, even the prejudices which judges share with their fellow-men, have had a good deal more to do than the syllogism in determining the rules by which men should be governed" (p. 5). In short, the aims of the law would not be met by a system in which the rule of law could be deduced as a conclusion from a syllogism, for such reasoning would not be responsive to the practical imperatives of society.

These remarks suggest that the law must be responsive primarily to pragmatic needs of the time, as disclosed in the thoughts, feelings, and even the prejudices that judges share with the general public. Indeed, a judge's ability to make decisions that are relevant to the community's current needs, by Holmes' reckoning, is one of the strengths of the common law. However, he is mindful of the threat that judicial innovation may pose to the stability of the legal system. As noted above, individuals need to rely on the law if they are to order their affairs in accordance with it. For Holmes, this reliability, or as he would prefer, predictability, is inherent in the common law's precedential structure. Thus, he completes his thought by indicating the important role of history in the eventual outcome of a judge's decision-making process: "The substance of the law at any given time pretty nearly corresponds, so far as it goes, with what is then understood to be convenient; but its form and machinery, and the degree to which it is able to work out desired results, depend very much upon its past" (p. 5).

Thus in the opening paragraph of *The Common Law*, Holmes provides a sketch of his general position. He is concerned to establish that the common law is able to meet the changing needs of society while preserving continuity with the past in order to enable individuals to rely upon it. A common law judge must be creative, then, both in determining the society's current needs, and in discerning how best to address these needs in a way that is continuous with past judicial decisions. In this way, the law evolves by moving out of its past, adapting to the needs of the present, and establishing a direction for the future. And to Holmes' way of thinking, this approach is superior to imposing order in accordance with a philosophical position or theory because the law would thereby lose the flexibility required of it in responding to the needs and demands of the disputing parties as well as the society as a whole.

### III

Many of Holmes' remarks in *The Common Law* seem to suggest that he is on a crusade to rid the law of philosophy. However, one must be careful not to make too much of his apparent distrust of philosophy. While it is true that he was opposed to the positions of those, such as the utilitarians and Kantians, who wished to reform the common law system in accordance with abstract principles, Holmes was by no means adverse to the application of philosophy to law. On the contrary, *The Common Law* owes a considerable debt to philosophy; a debt that one is apt to miss by taking Holmes' negative remarks too seriously.

As we have seen, Holmes was well grounded in philosophy and a member of the celebrated Cambridge Metaphysical Club, from which sprang the philosophical tradition known as "pragmatism." Whether Holmes' participation in the Metaphysical Club was the ultimate source of his philosophical conviction, his jurisprudence clearly bears the marks of pragmatism.

There are a number of pragmatist themes evident in *The Common Law*. First, pragmatism takes an empirical approach and emphasizes that experience is the ultimate source of knowledge. However, experience so conceived is not static, nor does it come piecemeal as many empiricists had maintained. Rather, experience is continuous. There is regularity in the experience of the environment that quite naturally leads to regularity in responses to it. And as responses to the environment become more patterned, predictions are possible. There is, then, a reciprocal relationship between the environment and the individual.

This point is closely related to a second important feature of pragmatism, namely, that the function of knowledge is successful adaptation to the environment. In this respect, knowledge is not a matter of grasping timeless truths or reporting the contents of immediate experience. Rather, it is a matter of moving forward to successfully encounter the environment. Consequently, knowledge is future-oriented, enabling the individual to anticipate future experience and accommodate to it. Yet while the *purpose* of knowledge is to enable one to anticipate changes in the environment and adjust to them, the *source* of knowledge is past experience.

Thus on both the frontside and the backside of knowledge one finds experience. Past experience shapes an individual in such a way that future experience may be anticipated. When one's expectations are borne out by subsequent experience, the tendency to reproduce the expectation becomes more pronounced. On the other hand, when the anticipated experience fails to materialize, the discomfort so occasioned results in an investigation to discover the source of the problem.

A third aspect of pragmatism is that it is primarily a philosophical method. As initially conceived by Charles Sanders Peirce, the acknowledged founder of the pragmatist movement, pragmatism is a thesis about the meaning of theoretical terms. In order to properly analyze a theoretical term, Peirce maintained, it is necessary to look at the experience to which it is connected. The outcome of experience is the test of the meaning of the term.

A further element of the pragmatist picture, and the final one that I shall mention in connection with this discussion, is the profound debt it owes to the theory of evolution. The influence of Darwin's theory on pragmatism is discernible in a number of places. First, as noted above, knowledge is conceived as part of an individual's "natural history," so to speak. It enables the individual to "adapt" to the environment and, on the basis of regularity in past experience, to anticipate the future. Second, an implication of the evolutionary position is that human beings are continuous with nature. Hence, a pragmatist rejects any conception that looks upon human beings as independent or outside of the natural order. Human beings may be more sophisticated than other creatures, but the fact remains that the principles by which human beings are acted upon by the world and in turn act upon it are continuous with those of other creatures. Third, it follows that those activities and institutions peculiar to human beings are also continuous with the natural order and explicable by similar principles. Finally, as with nature, human activities and institutions are always in the process of growth and change. Indeed, that which does not grow or change is dead. A human institution, particularly one like the law that guides human conduct, is useful only if it can adapt to meet the changing needs of the human community.

These features of pragmatism are all present in *The Common Law*. Indeed, it seems that pragmatism offers a near perfect explanatory framework for conceptualizing the common law. First, the common law is grounded in experience. The "law" in this system arises out of a particular controversy between (generally) two parties. The decision in the case is, accordingly, conditioned by the facts at issue and previous rules of law that are also owed to the facts of a specific case.

Second, it relies upon continuity in experience and in the similarity between situations giving rise to the controversy. It is this similarity that makes the doctrine of precedent effective. In a related way, continuity explains the manner in which the law grows and evolves. There is not a complete break between past and present, and yet the past is not perfectly replicated in the present. Accordingly, precedents are slowly extended and expanded to adapt to present circumstances. These features of experience explain, in turn, how it is that the common law is able to accommodate both the change that is necessary for adaptation and the regularity that is necessary for ordering one's affairs. Changes in the common law are typically slow, and its course of evolution is therefore predictable. And this is as one would expect, since the judge who decides a particular controversy is part of the environment and milieu that gave rise to it.

Third, the common law is fundamentally methodological. This does not mean, of course, that particular decisions are not based on abstract principles. However, the principles that inform particular decisions have arisen out of collective experience. They are not, then, read into the law antecedently but emerge from the experiences of the society, of which the judge is a member. This inductive aspect of the common law explains, in large part, Holmes' rejection of the idea that substantive philosophical or moral principles should be introduced as a means of ordering the common law system. The desire to do so displays, to his way of thinking, blindness to the proper role of principles in the law and, moreover, would curtail the law's natural evolution.

As we have seen throughout this discussion, the most pronounced feature of the common law, according to Holmes, is that it is ever changing and adapting to meet current societal needs. In this respect, not surprisingly, the common law mirrors the evolution of species. In the latter case, alterations in the environment produce innovations in biological species with the result that their subsequent generations are better acclimated to the natural habitat. There is, of course, no final fixed form, for the species so altered is also part of the environment. Consequently, one species' advance may serve as a catalyst for subsequent changes in the environment and so on. There are no sharp breaks in the process. Rather, the process of evolution is continuous in both space and time. That is, the modifications of evolution occur in an environment over time. There is no starting over—nature begins with what is present and adjusts accordingly. The result is that the innovations to a species may be such that progeny bear little resemblance to their ancestor.

According to Holmes, the law evolves in much the same way. The social environment—the economic, moral, and political milieu— that is, the background of legal intervention, alters over time. Therefore, in order to remain responsive to this social environment, the law must change as well. But, of course, the law is also part of this environment and impacts it. There is, then, a continual reciprocity between the law and the social arrangements in which it is contextualized. And, as with the evolution of species, there is no starting over. Rather, in most cases, a judge takes existing legal concepts and principles, as these are memorialized in precedent, and adapts them, often unconsciously, to fit the requirements of the case and present social conditions.

Holmes' commitment to pragmatism and evolutionary theory inform both the polemical and positive contents of *The Common Law*. As concerns the former, he was convinced that the utilitarian and Kantian/Hegelian theorists were mistaken about the common law system because they were insensitive to the actual processes that underlie it. Utilitarians were inattentive to the historical character of legal change. For this reason, although utilitarian virtues of utility and expediency are critical factors in a judge's decision, considerations of precedent and compatibility with previous cases are important as well. An uncritical and ahistorical application of the principle of utility to a particular controversy might produce unintended consequences that could significantly disrupt the social order.

Holmes is similarly critical of the tendency of Continental legal theorists who followed in the traditions of Kant and Hegel. These thinkers saw the law as a properly intellectual exercise that *ought* to be regulated by rationally deduced principles. Even the Hegelians, who placed such great emphasis on history, saw history as little more than a backdrop against which reason worked out its principles. In contrast, for Holmes history is important because change occurs only within a temporal framework, and while not random—change results from identifiable causes—it is not "rational" either. There is no preconceived end to which history is moving. History is rather an account of adjustments occasioned by the felt necessity of ever-changing circumstances.

Holmes' application of the theory of evolution is important for his positive contributions to legal theory as well. First, much of his discussion in *The Common Law* is devoted to the explication of legal expressions and concepts. He engages in this analysis in order to illustrate how the common law's application of these expressions and concepts has evolved. Thus the terms used in resolving earlier disputes may come to have different scope and meaning when employed in later opinions. Second, Holmes is concerned to show that the common law is an effective instrument for responding to and producing social change. When seen in this light, the application of the theory of evolution to the legal system is normative as well as descriptive. That is, it does not merely explain how the law grows and adapts in response to social change, but it establishes the law as a means of effecting such change in its own right. With this as background it may be useful to examine a particular example of this evolutionary approach from *The Common Law*.

## IV

While Holmes' theoretical commitments are not wholly absent from *The Common Law*, they are largely implicit. He does not develop his general position in a systematic way; rather he focuses instead on concepts, e.g., liability, in the respective areas of the law, e.g., torts, and traces the evolution of those concepts. He describes this evolutionary process in the following way:

> The customs, beliefs, or needs of a primitive time establish a rule or a formula. In the course of centuries the custom, belief, or necessity disappears, but the rule remains. The reason which gave rise to the rule has been forgotten, and ingenious minds set themselves to inquire how it is to be accounted for. Some ground of policy is thought of, which seems to explain it and to reconcile it with the present state of things; and then the rule adapts itself to the new reasons which have been found for it, and enters on a new career. (p. 8)

Holmes' intent is to expose the workings of this process. However, as noted, his aim is not merely descriptive. Rather, once the common law's process of evolution is properly understood, judges will be in a position to guide the process instead of being guided by it. Thus, while "hitherto the process has been largely unconscious," Holmes maintains that "[i]t is important, on that account, to bring to mind what the actual course of events has been. If it were only to insist on a more conscious recognition of the legislative function of the courts...it would be useful...." (p. 32). For Holmes, this means that judges will be in a position to consciously employ considerations of social policy in making their decisions. Of course, precedent will continue to play an important role in guiding the judicial decision-making process, but judges are not bound by precedents that no longer serve the public interest. Therefore, Holmes concludes, "[w]hen we find that in large and important branches of the law the various grounds of policy on which the various rules have been justified are later inventions to account for what are in fact survivals from more primitive times, we have a right to reconsider the proper reasons, and, taking a broader view of the field, to decide anew whether those reasons are satisfactory" (p. 33).

Such a position may sound surprising given Holmes' rejection of theoretical intrusions into the law. However, there is an important difference, for whereas the concern of a judge committed to a philosophical, political, or ideological position is the consistency of the outcome of a case with that position, the concern of a judge following Holmes' approach is to produce a beneficial social outcome to the extent that is possible. It is also worth noting that although a judge may have philosophical commitments that influence the final decision in a case, these commitments are part of the judge's milieu and not an external standard by which to measure the particular judicial outcome or the legal system itself. That is to say, philosophy and philosophical commitments are no more privileged in particular judicial decisions or the law in general than are other features of the environment in which a case is decided.

Holmes' treatment of the concept of liability—in both civil and criminal law—may serve to illustrate this point. His view, contrary to that prevailing at the time, is that the apparent moral elements of liability are vestiges of an early period of the law's development. Thus, in contrast to legal theorists who maintain that the focus on intention in the assignment of liability is an important and fairly late development in law, Holmes insists that the law's evolution has moved increasingly away from such "internal" considerations as concern with motives and intentions, and towards "external" considerations such as how the average person of reasonable intelligence would act; what level of care the average person would exercise in a given situation; whether the average person would have foreseen the harm produced by a particular course of action; and so on.

Holmes reasons as follows: Vengeance, or the desire for it, is among the most basic motives to justice and redress; it is a natural response when one is intentionally harmed by another. However, intention in this case is critical, and without it, vengeance is not justified. When liability is thus circumscribed many of the harms one receives are without remedy. After all, many, if not most, harms are caused by carelessness rather than intention. As the law evolved, it gradually made provision for rectifying these harms and it did so in a way that focuses on the harm itself and the way in which it results rather than on the mental state of the agent whose action produced the harm. Consequently, as noted above, the foreseeability that the harm would occur, that is to say, the likelihood that harm would result from a particular action, becomes more important than the offender's reasons for acting.

In the early chapters of *The Common Law* Holmes identifies the steps in the evolution of legal liability. First, vengeance involved physical violence in response to an intentional harm: the perpetrator, whether human or not, received corporeal punishment. However, this response was less than satisfactory because (1) it provided no remedy to the victim apart from the satisfaction of revenge, and (2) it often resulted in an inequitable loss of property. Consider, for example, a premodern agrarian society operating under such a rudimentary system of redress. In such a society, if my horse breaks free and tramples a neighbor's chickens, the remedy is to destroy the horse that caused the harm. And yet, in this case both my neighbor and I are losers. My neighbor loses insofar as the death of the horse does not replace the loss of the chickens, and I lose because the horse was valuable to me. Indeed, the horse's value to me is probably far greater than the value of the chickens my neighbor lost. Now, by tweaking this situation, by making me responsible (liable) for the horse's actions and allowing me to compensate my neighbor for the lost chickens, a better outcome is secured. This solution seems simple enough, but it does involve important innovations. In particular, it requires that liability is extended to one who has not acted and, therefore, does not have the necessary intention to justify vengeance. In fact, as the owner of the horse, I not only lack the necessary "internal" mental state to justify vengeance, my liability does not owe to any mental state at all. It owes rather to the absence of a mental state—presumably negligence or a lack of care on my part to ensure that my property does not harm another. Thus the assignment of liability to me in this case is a legal fiction. I am not, strictly speaking, liable because I do not have the requisite mental state for liability.

With this outcome, both my neighbor and I (not to mention the horse) are better off than with the doctrine that requires a mental state for the assignment of liability. In addition, the community as a whole benefits from this extension of the notion of liability. First, because it establishes a more desirable outcome for parties involved in future cases of this sort. Second, and more importantly, because in such a community a resource like my horse contributes to the commonweal. A judge is justified in considering this concern for social policy because the outcome and the reasoning of the case extend, by means of precedent, to the entire society, and because my neighbor and I (the parties) are members of that society.

One final comment is in order before moving to the concluding section of this introduction. It should be apparent from the foregoing that Holmes regards a common law judge's role as necessarily involving a legislative element. That is, in fact, the key feature distinguishing a common law tradition from the tradition of civil codes. Thus, although a judge does not enact legislation in the same way that a legislature does, a judge is no less concerned about the social implications of the decision in the case before her, and to ignore these implications is an injustice to the disputing parties (as members of the society) as well as the society as a whole. However, a common law judge must decide the case on the basis of the facts with which she is presented, as well as the relevant precedents and any relevant legislation. This feature of judicial decision-making often leads to the extension or modification of such concepts as "liability," and such extensions/modifications are one of the ways by which the common law evolves.

## V

Holmes' legacy and that of *The Common Law* are difficult to measure. He continues to be an important figure in the philosophy of law, though perhaps more on the strength of his judicial opinions and the small work *The Path of Law*. This is unfortunate because, as I mentioned at the beginning, *The Common Law* is Holmes' most systematic jurisprudential work, and therefore provides a more thorough basis for comprehending and evaluating his position than do his other writings or his judicial opinions.

In this connection, *The Common Law* may help to explain the divergence of opinions about Holmes and his jurisprudence. There are those, for example, who extol Holmes as a progressive and a forerunner of such innovative legal approaches as the Critical Legal Studies movement. There are others, however, who regard Holmes' legal theory as offensive in its aristocratic and totalitarian tendencies. There is some basis for these diverse attitudes but there is also much in them that is oversimplified and inaccurate.

First, it is true that Holmes was a central figure in the American movement known as Legal Realism, and it is true that that movement influenced the development of Critical Legal Studies (CLS). On the whole these movements, and particularly the latter, are associated with progressive agendas. According to most CLS scholars, law is a social institution subject to all the prejudices and limitations of the society of which it is a part. Thus, one of the central themes of the CLS approach is that the judges who decide cases are typically members of the dominant class. Not surprisingly, then, considerations of social standing, broadly conceived to include socioeconomic status, race, gender, etc., inform judicial decisions and thereby the law's form and substance. It is therefore wrong, the Critics maintain, to suppose that the rulings of the legal system are neutral or that they represent justice for everyone. In most cases, much to the discredit of the system and the disadvantage of those who are not members of the dominant class, the law serves to maintain the status quo. And this is not what one would expect or hope for in the legal system of a liberal democratic society.

Holmes would agree with much of the CLS position. Certainly on the level of description he would agree that judges are members of the dominant class and that their decisions reflect the prejudices and interests of that class. However, for Holmes this is an inevitable feature of the law and not necessarily an evil that needs to be corrected. Indeed, there is reason to believe that his commitment to Social Darwinism would lead him to assert that this situation is merely the outcome of evolutionary forces and ought not to be tampered with. In any case, Holmes' major concern was not to eradicate judicial prejudice or to level the playing field, so to speak. The larger concern for Holmes is that judges and legal theorists refrain from introducing external standards into the common law system by implementing global philosophical or ideological positions, whether progressive or conservative.

Second, there is some reason to suppose that Holmes' jurisprudence might lend itself to a kind of tyranny of the majority. He is not progressive about individual rights or the protection of the minority. Thus, in defending deterrence as a ground for punishment, he asserts that "the dogma of equality makes an equation between individuals only, not between an individual and the community" (p. 37). And, as part of the same discussion he responds to the Kantian objection that one should never treat another only as a means to an end by observing that "[i]f a man lives in society, he is liable to find himself so treated" (p. 38). Thus, while certain of Holmes' most notable dissenting opinions seem to advance progressive outcomes, the grounds for these outcomes were the benefits to the society and not the protection of individual rights.

This criticism is certainly valid, and one cannot read *The Common Law* without being struck by Holmes' pronounced preference for the societal good over individual interests. Still, his position in this regard is hardly simplistic. He recognizes that society benefits only when individuals are afforded certain legal rights. For example, freedom in the expression of alternative and unpopular opinions is necessary, according to Holmes, because such freedom advances the cause of society by introducing competition into the realm of attitudes and opinions. In short, it seems that Holmes avoids totalitarianism because, if for no other reason, he recognizes that the societal good (generally) requires individual rights.

Without question, the position presented in *The Common Law* is somewhat dated. In particular, the Social Darwinism to which Holmes subscribed has been discredited, and much of the common law system has now been codified. These facts notwithstanding, Holmes' position is important both because it is historically significant and because it continues to present a viable challenge to the omnipresent tendency to reconstitute the legal system to conform to one or another philosophical or ideological viewpoint. This tendency is currently manifest in the endorsement by many liberals of Rawlsian neo-Kantianism, as well as by many conservatives, who advocate a reading of the U.S. Constitution that is informed by the framers' "original intent." I think it is fair to say that Holmes would regard both of these partisan inclinations as mistaken. The liberal one because it seeks to impose an order that is foreign to the common law and that would curtail or artificially modify its growth and development; the conservative tendency because it assumes, wrongly, that the meaning of the terms and principles of the Constitution are static and fixed rather than living and therefore evolving. Regardless of how one feels about these issues, it is important to recognize the challenge that Holmes' thinking presents to such inclinations, and there is no better way of appreciating that challenge than by working through *The Common Law*.

# 5

# On Roscoe Pound, *Social Control through Law*

*A. Javier Treviño*

This republication of Roscoe Pound's *Social Control through Law* will no doubt be enthusiastically greeted by a new generation of jurists, legal theorists, and sociologists. Perhaps no other volume produced by Pound can, in one small package, better convey the whole of his thought. Many of the basic themes that Pound repeatedly expounds (albeit from different angles) in his numerous works are contained in this small book—the scope and subject matter of law, legal history and comparative law, the nature of law, law and morals, sociological jurisprudence, the jural postulates, the engineering theory, social control, and the survey of social interests. In *Social Control through Law* we find Pound as a jurist, philosopher, and scientist. To be sure, Pound possessed extended erudition in many kinds of scholarship besides legal scholarship. His breadth of reading and inexhaustible learning induced Oliver Wendell Holmes to proclaim that it made him tired just to try to remember the titles of what Pound "knows." Pound surveyed the law so widely and thoroughly that, at the time of his death, the bibliography of his publications consisted of close to a thousand titles, of which several hundred were books and major essays, many of which were intended for a general audience. My intention in this introduction is to briefly outline the principal aspects of Roscoe Pound's legal philosophy, as it was conveyed in several books, articles, and addresses, and show their relation to *Social Control through Law.*

## I

The broad details of Pound's academic career are relatively well known. He was born on October 27, 1870, in the frontier town of

Lincoln, Nebraska, the capital of the then newest state in the Union. His father, Stephen Bosworth Pound, was a successful lawyer and a district court judge. The young Roscoe was educated at home by his mother, Laura Biddlecomb Pound, until the time that he enrolled in Latin School. At the age of thirteen, Pound entered the University of Nebraska where he majored in botany, thus acquiring a thorough grounding in the method of the natural sciences. The importance that Pound gave to empirical investigation was to influence his approach to jurisprudence throughout his long and active career. Indeed, Pound had a penchant for collecting and systematically classifying and cataloging legal ideas much as a botanist would collect, classify, and catalogue various botanical species. This taxonomic approach is especially evident in Pound's *Outlines of Lectures on Ju-risprudence* (1903) where he engages in the scientific ordering, the "botanization" as it were, of minutely detailed judicial terms.

Pound graduated from the University of Nebraska in 1888 and the following year received his M.A. degree in botany. Although hardly surprising, it is nevertheless interesting that despite Pound's love of botany, his initial fascination with law was sparked by his father. During Pound's junior year in college his father gave him three books on jurisprudence which Pound repeatedly read: Holland's *Elements of Jurisprudence,* Amos's *Science of Law,* and Maine's *Ancient Law.* These three volumes may well have inspired Pound to pursue legal study in earnest. But since the University of Nebraska did not, at that time, offer professional training in law, Pound went East in the fall of 1889 to attend Harvard Law School. He spent only one year at Harvard, leaving the law school, as he put it, "a convinced utilitarian" and a follower of the nineteenth-century British legal philosopher John Austin. To be sure, Pound remained a social utilitarian throughout his life (even if his utilitarianism was continuously modified), but it was not long before he partially eschewed Austin's well-known proposal that the sanction of law is found in the threat of a sovereign. In contrast, for Pound the justification of law is found in the social ends that law, as an instrument of the community, must serve. Nevertheless, Pound seems to have retained Austin's idea that force is an essential element of law. As he states in *Social Control through Law,* "it is well to remember that if law as a mode of social control has all the strength of force, it has also all the weaknesses of dependence on force" (p. 20). Pound, however, makes it clear that force is only a means, not an end in itself.

Aside from his intensive year at Harvard Pound never again undertook any other formal study of the law or completed the prescribed requirements for a law degree. The scantiness of his legal education notwithstanding, he became one of the foremost legal scholars of all time. Some years after his Harvard experience Pound implored law teachers, or "legal monks" as he derisively called them, to supplement the traditional subject-matter of legal study to include a scientific understanding of the relations of law and society and of the needs and interests of modern industrial life.

Upon leaving Harvard Pound returned to Lincoln, qualified for the Nebraska bar, and began to apprentice at his father's law firm. Busy starting his practice in Lincoln, Pound initially wavered a bit between professions. In 1892 he founded and became director of the Botanical Survey of Nebraska, an organization with a university affiliation, which helped Pound launch his plan for the systematic botanical exploration of Nebraska. Five years later he completed his dissertation, *The Phytogeography of Nebraska,* a landmark scientific treatise on American plant ecology which earned him a Ph.D. in botany. The requirements for the degree included a minor as well as a major and Pound opted to minor in Roman Law. Shortly after graduating Pound resolved to embark on a legal career and started out by writing briefs with his father and by arguing appeals in state and federal courts. In 1899 he was appointed an assistant professor of jurisprudence and international law at the University of Nebraska College of Law.

Although Pound spent over sixty years involved chiefly in the administrative and teaching tasks of academe, he periodically enjoyed brief sojourns in the active practice of law. One such interval occurred in 1901 when, at the age of thirty, Pound was named as one of nine commissioners (auxiliary judges) of appeals of the Supreme Court of Nebraska in a move to expedite an overflow of judicial cases. The commissioner's "recommendations" were not superficial and cursory rhetoric on particular cases; rather they were taken, pro forma, as the judicial decisions of the court. While serving as commissioner Pound prepared recommendations in more than 200 cases.

In 1903 Pound relinquished his judicial duties and returned to academe, becoming dean of the College of Law at Nebraska. Around this time his formulation of sociological jurisprudence took its initial and foundational form. Apparently attracted to

Pound's "progressive" views, John H. Wigmore, dean of the North-western University School of Law appointed him professor of law in 1907. After only a short period at Northwestern, Pound accepted a professorship at the University of Chicago, and one year after that Dean Ezra Thayer brought him to Harvard as Story Professor of Law. In 1913 Pound was made Carter Professor of General Jurisprudence, a title that mote closely reflected his dominant interest. While at Harvard he served as dean for twenty years before being given one of the newly instituted University Professorships in 1936. Though he formally became emeritus in 1947 at the age of seventy-seven, Pound continued to publish prolifically until his death in 1964.

In addition to these regular teaching positions, Pound held a variety of distinguished visiting lectureships at several universities including Yale, Dartmouth, Cambridge, Tulane, and North Carolina. Many of his lectures were subsequently published as little books—*The Spirit of the Common Law* (1921), *An Introduction to the Philosophy of Law* (1922), *Law and Morals* (1923), *Interpretations of Legal History* (1923), *The Formative Era of American Law* (1938), *The Development of Constitutional Guarantees of Liberty* (1957), and several others. In point of fact, the four chapters comprising *Social Control through Law* constitute a series of lectures that Pound gave at Indiana University in 1941. He also delivered numerous addresses to bar associations and other public audiences in the United States, England, and on the Continent. Among the many accolades he acquired throughout his career, Pound received honorary doctorates from some sixteen universities at home and abroad. His accomplishments, however, were not limited to the halls of academe. Pound's nonacademic work included important practical aspects of law: international arbitrator to the American-British Claims Arbitration (1926-1927); consultant on administrative procedure and crime surveys, including the Cleveland Survey of Criminal Justice (1921-1922) and the Boston Crime Survey (1926); member of President Hoover's National Commission on Law Observance and Enforcement (the "Wickersham Commission"), which was concerned with the problems of national Prohibition (1929-1931); director of the National Conference of Judicial Councils (1938-1946); and advisor to the Chinese Nationalist government's Ministry of Justice, leaving for Nanking to undertake the task of setting up the courts (1946-1949).

## II

The intellectual influences that contributed, directly or indirectly, to Pound's juristic thought are too numerous to properly list here. However, particular mention should be made of two jurists, one philosopher, and three sociologists who had a indelible impact on Pound's thinking.

To begin with, two of Pound's major contributions to jurisprudence—the idea of historical relativity in law and the notion of jural postulates—were partly derived from the nineteenth-century neo-Hegelian jurist, Josef Kohler. The idea of historical relativity in law took form in Kohler as he looked at law not as a fixed and permanent entity suitable for all time, but as a dynamic phenomenon of human civilization. Kohler, in his *Philosophy of Law* (1914), maintained that since civilization is constantly developing and changing, so too must the law evolve and adapt to the changing needs and demands of culture. It follows, then, that for Kohler the law that is suitable for one period of civilization is not so for another.

For Pound as for Kohler, the task of the law is twofold: To maintain the existing values of civilization and to maintain, further, and transmit to their most complete possibilities the human powers of a given civilization. In *Social Control through Law,* however, Pound goes beyond Kohler in arguing that the ideal civilization must recognize competition and cooperation as two factors in achieving ulti-mate mastery over external and internal human nature. In Pound's view, human beings need the force of social control to keep their aggressive, self-assertive side in balance with their cooperative social tendency. He recognized that despite the law's three distinct meanings—namely, that of legal order, the body of precepts, and the judicial/administrative process—they could all be united by the idea of social control. Consequently, Pound approached law as a type of organized social control, which he describes in *Social Control through Law* as "the pressure upon each man brought to bear by his fellow men in order to constrain him to do his part in upholding civilized society and to deter him from antisocial conduct, that is, conduct at variance with the postulates of social order" (p. 18). Thus, for Pound, the subject-matter of law involves examining those manifestations of internal nature which, in asserting or seeking to realize individual expectations, require social control.

The law, in turn, is shaped by civilization's requirements for certain definite principles of law that Pound and Kohler term the "jural postulates" of civilized life. But whereas Kohler fails to specifically explain how the jural postulates are determined and derived, Pound, as will be discussed presently, conceives them to be presupposed by the de facto claims, demands, or interests made by human beings. Once Pound arrived at a method for determining the jural postulates of a given time and place he then proceeded to connect them to his idea of the scheme of interests.

From Rudolf von Jhering, Pound appropriated the notion of interests—the purposes of human existence—which, when given individual expression are characterized by *egoistical* self-assertion, and when given social expression involve collective cooperation through *ethical* self-assertion. In *Law as a Means to an End* (1913) Jhering views the law as an instrument for securing the social interests, that is, the general, objective, and organized purposes of a number of people. What is more, for Jhering a legally protected interest is a legal right. From these ideas Pound was able to formulate what became his highly popular "theory of social interests." Jhering's regard for the de facto interests that are asserted in a particular civilization, had a considerable impact on Pound. Additionally, Pound drew from Jhering's concept of *purpose* in the law; of law owing its origins to a practical motive, to an end. Pound was attracted to the fact that Jhering inquired into the more immediate social purposes and functions of law, rather than what had previously been considered important in nineteenth-century jurisprudence: the abstract nature of law.

From William James's philosophy of pragmatism, Pound acquired the ethical position, stated in James's essay "The Moral Philosopher and the Moral Life" (1891), that the end of ends is the goal for satisfying at all times as many demands as possible. Pound modified this utilitarian consideration in two significant ways. First, Pound states that the task of law should be to, at all times, satisfy as much of the total amount as it can for as many demands as it can. Or, as he puts it in *Social Control through Law,* the law as a mechanism of social control "makes it possible to do the most that can be done for the most people" (p. 64). However, since all desired resources—that is, the goods of existence, the scope for free activity, and the objects on which to exert free activity—are limited, people's appetite for goods and objects will inevitably conflict with or overlap those of their neighbors. In this case, Pound looks to the entire scheme of interests in dealing with a multiplicity of competing interests of a given situation. Second, and in contradistinction to James, Pound argues that implicit in the balancing of social interests and in the preservation of a pluralistic community's stability is the problem of values: the question of how to measure and appraise conflicting and overlapping social interests. Throughout his works, Pound repeatedly emphasizes that no legal philosophy can escape the problem of values. Indeed, Pound regards sociological jurisprudence as a prescriptive and valuative science. As such, his object is to give effect to the greatest total of interests or to the interests that weigh most in civilization, with the least sacrifice to the scheme of interests as a whole. However, in *Social Control through Law* Pound candidly admits that "[m]anifestly one cannot speak with assurance as to how we are in the end to value competing and overlapping interests in the present century" (p. 126).

Turning next to the sociological components of Pound's jurisprudence, it is widely recognized that they were derived largely from the writings of Lester F. Ward, Albion W. Small, and most especially E.A. Ross, who was a colleague of Pound's at the University of Nebraska during 1901-1906. Ward was an ardent advocate of government control and social planning who believed that legislation would contribute to the organization of human experience. Similarly, Small assumed that social reform could be carried out through legal means. Due to the influence of these two men Pound approached the law as a form of "social engineering." Indeed, the idea of law as an instrument of engineering and social control at all levels of government is an integral part of Pound's sociological jurisprudence. Toward the end of his life, Pound acknowledges his intellectual debts to Ross and Small in the preface to his magnum opus *Jurisprudence*. He writes: "Happily in the early years of the present century it was my good fortune to be associated with Edward A. Ross, then Professor at Nebraska, and thus to be set to reading Ward and to thinking about sociological jurisprudence. When I went to Chicago in 1907 I met Albion W. Small, and to Ross and Small,...I owe a decisive impetus at a critical point in my study."

In 1901 Ross published *Social Control,* a book that quickly became an early American classic, representing an elaborate inventory of the methods by which a society induces conformity into human behavior. Here Ross contends that of all the various instrumentalities of social control—public opinion, belief, social suggestion, religion, and so forth—law reigns supreme as "the most specialized and highly finished engine of control employed by society." Following Ross's lead, Pound thereafter focuses on the social character of law and sees the law, simultaneously, as reflecting the needs of a well-ordered society and as influencing that society. Accordingly, in *Social Control through Law,* Pound defines law as a "highly specialized form of social control, carried on in accordance with a body of authoritative precepts, applied in a judicial and an administrative process" (p. 41). The upshot of Ross's influence is that the notion of social control provided Pound's jurisprudence with a sociological starting point.

In light of Pound's efforts to purposefully forge intellectual ties and cultivate personal friendships with such early American sociologists as Ward, Small, and Ross (as well as with Harvard sociologists and Pound's colleagues, Georges Gurvitch, Nicholas S. Timasheff, Pitirim Sorokin, and Talcott Parsons), it is ironic that Pound's work is now scarcely considered in the sociological community. Clearly, Pound's sociological jurisprudence is an applied science in the tradition of empirical sociology. In "Philosophy of Law and Comparative Law" (1951), Pound underscores his preference for this tradition and acknowledges sociology's influence on him in stating that he, like other scholars trained during the early twentieth century, had been educated on the empiricism and sociology of Auguste Comte. The cumulative effect of these sociological influences is that Pound's philosophy of law significantly promoted the recognition of law as a social phenomenon. Little wonder that Pound felt justified in referring to his legal philosophy as *sociological* jurisprudence.

## III

The rise of Roscoe Pound's sociological jurisprudence is crucially interwoven with the vast institutional and ideological transformations taking place in the United States during the first quarter of the twentieth century. At this time the United States was shedding its frontier image and entering a period of modernity, an era characterized by increased urbanization (largely as a result of massive immigration) and industrialization. Rapid social change, triggered in part by enormous economic growth, helped the country achieve its status as a major world power. In the process, however, this rapid social change also generated immense social problems characterized by new and sharper levels of tension and conflict: poor working conditions in factories, political corruption, crowded city slums, the growth of the impoverished masses, the cartelization of the American economy, and the like.

Typically sluggish in keeping up with changing times, the American legal system entered the twentieth century in its traditional nineteenth-century guise, as formalist or analytical jurisprudence. Clearly the most pervasively influential school of jurisprudence, analytical jurisprudence was the most recent school at the time that Pound was writing. Austin—Pound's inspiration while a law student—was a key figure in nineteenth-century analytical jurisprudence as he suggested the development of a formal, logical closed system of law. The five schools of jurists and methods of jurisprudence that preceded the analytical school and that Pound details in *The Spirit of the Common Law* are the metaphysical school, the historical school, the utilitarians, the positivists, and the mechanical sociologists.

Analytical jurisprudence, being politically congruent with the liberal political theory of the post-Civil War period, had kept legal intervention and regulation in social and economic matters to a bare minimum. This laissez-faire policy did not signify the complete absence of legal oversight, it merely meant shifting the responsibility of control from artificial entities like the polity to "natural" ones like the marketplace. The self-regulating market was said to be guided by such universal economic principles as occupational specialization, the growth of wealth, and self-interest.

The notion of universal, or first, principles—that is, fixed axioms, eternal truths, predetermined conceptions—also affected the academic disciplines of biology, economics, and sociology. Indeed, during the nineteenth century there was an intense preoccupation with the idea that general absolutes governed the social and natural worlds; thus, it was only a matter of time before American legal doctrine was likewise attracted to the universal principle. However, not long into the new century the natural and social sciences—namely, biology, economics, sociology—made an abrupt about-face and abandoned the attempt to deduce know ledge from predetermined conceptions. In contrast, analytical jurisprudence tenaciously held on to the traditional notion of authoritative precepts and this made the law rigid and unyielding. Noting the law's inability to keep up with social progress, in his 1910 article, "Law in Books and Law in

Action," Pound wryly observed that the law had always been dominated by ideas of the past long after they had ceased being vital in
other knowledge-fields. Accordingly, legal doctrine ran into the problem of not being able to adapt to the changing social and economic
conditions of the time. Or, as Pound saw it, there existed a discrepancy between the law in books and the law in action. The traditional
legal doctrine revealed its inadequacy by failing to meet social, ends.
As Pound succinctly states in *Social Control through Law,* law "falls
short of what is expected of it, especially in dealing with the many
new questions and endeavors to secure newly pressing interests involved in a changing economic order" (p. 14).

Pound introduced sociological jurisprudence in a revolutionary
address that he delivered in St. Paul, Minnesota, on August 29, 1906,
before that most staid of legal bodies, the American Bar Association. He stated resolutely that the American court system was archaic and its legal procedures behind the times. Pound's speech was
a clarion call for the reform and modernization of what he saw as an
antiquated system of legal justice. Law, he remarked in characteris-
tically bold fashion, usually functions as a government of the living
by the dead. This speech was pivotal in American legal history because it marked the beginning of a new movement in law that shook,
challenged, and disturbed the existing system of legal orthodoxy.
As John Wigmore so eloquently put it, Pound's St. Paul speech was
the "spark that kindled the white flame" of legal progress.

In his 1908 article, "Mechanical Jurisprudence," Pound commented on the need for a scientific law. For Pound the word "scientific" had two distinct meanings: one refers to the art of abstract
systematization, the other to the technique of pragmatic application.
He states that analytical jurisprudence had transformed law into a
reasoned body of principles for the administration of justice. Analytical jurisprudence is scientific in the abstract sense because it is
marked by a conformity to reason, uniformity, and certainty. As such,
law is endowed with a certain degree of logic, precision, and predictability. Put another way, as a deductive system of law, analytical jurisprudence is scientific in that it reduces judges' biases,
ignorance, and possibility of corruption preventing their departure
from clearly articulated, predetermined rules. Pound, however, favored the notion of scientific law in its pragmatic sense. Thus, he
points out the shortcomings of a jurisprudence that is abstractly scientific as concerns the logical processes of its internal structure but

not concerning the practical results it achieves. According to Pound, since analytical jurisprudence regarded the law not as a means to a achieving an empirical end but as a means in itself, it had transformed lawmaking and judicial adjudication into a technical and artificial enterprise. Moreover, Pound notes that owing to the law's artificiality, lawyers tend to forget that the real function of scientific law is to adjust everyday relations so as to meet current ideas of fair play. Additionally, the rigid exposition of hard-and-fast rules in analytical jurisprudence prevents the law from adapting itself to the mutable culture of a modem, urban environment. As a result, the law had ceased having a utilitarian function in dealing with the realities of everyday life. It had turned into a hopelessly self-sustaining entity completely out of touch with the human condition and the new social needs that had arisen within the past half century.

Analytical jurisprudence, with its a priori concepts and deductive calculus, had become a mechanical jurisprudence. Pound urges jurists to reject the technical operations of mechanical legal doctrine, or what he sometimes referred to as "the jurisprudence of conceptions," and accept a more realistic and action-oriented "jurisprudence of ends." The central question to be considered, according to Pound, should be: How will a rule or decision operate in practice? His objective in asking it is to attain a pragmatic, sociological legal science that would make rules fit cases instead of making cases fit rules. In short, Pound's sociological jurisprudence—which regarded the actual operation of law rather than its abstract content—was a protest against the conceptualist jurisprudence prevalent among early twentieth-century judges.

In 1907, in his address to the American Bar Association's Section on Legal Education, Pound advanced the idea that the artificial and technical nature of mechanical jurisprudence had created a discrepancy between the conceptualism of the written law and the more sublunary sentiments of the American public. That is to say, that the law's rigidity prevents it from considering the practical needs, wants, and interests of the individuals the law is meant to serve. Accordingly, Pound maintained that American legal theory and doctrine had reached a degree of "fixity" prior to the emergence of the conditions that the law must address in a modem, urban, industrial society. However, in "The Need of a Sociological Jurisprudence" (1907), he notes optimistically that with the rise and growth of economics, political science, and sociology the time was ripe for a new tendency in legal scholarship that would consider the practical relations of law to society. A few years later, in "The Scope and Purpose of Sociological Jurisprudence," a lengthy three-part article that appeared in the 1911 and 1912 issues of the *Harvard Law Review,* Pound announced the emergence of sociological jurisprudence as a discrete and definable legal philosophy. Pound's sociological jurisprudence treats law not as a conceptual and logical system of formal rules, but as an institution operating within a larger societal context that functions to regulate social processes with the object of securing and protecting society's interests. With this notion of law Pound, through the theory of social interests, explains how the law accomplishes this objective. However, before the theory of social interests can be discussed, the jural postulates of time and place must be analyzed.

## IV

Inspired by Kohler, who in Hegelian fashion stressed the ideal rather than the non-rational elements of the civilization of a given period, Pound ultimately formulated a total of seven jural ideals or postulates that provided him with an organizing framework within which to locate his scheme of interests. In broad view, the jural postulates are a set of fundamental presuppositions that encompass the moral sentiments of reflective community and that are recognized and enforced by law concerning reasonable expectations of human conduct in a civilized society of the time and place. By "civilized society" Pound has in mind the English-speaking countries of Great Britain, the United States, Canada, Australia, and New Zealand. The deliberate exclusion of countries that did not develop their legal systems according to the conventions of English common law clearly reveals Pound's bias in favor of the Anglo-American legal tradition. Thus, at the present time when the ideas of cultural diversity and cultural equality have gained hegemony in the arts, humanities, and social sciences, Pound's remarks about the legal order of the civilized society of the time and place appear to be ethnocentric at best.

The jural postulates are expressed as expectations, claims, or "rights" and are procured from the great substantive branches of the positive law including criminal law, the law of torts (especially negligence and liability with-out fault), property law, contract law, and the law of restitution. The first five jural postulates for the domain of American law, at least, are articulated in Chapter IV of *Social Control through Law* as follows:

1.  In civilized society men must be able to assume that others will commit no intentional aggressions upon them.
2.  In civilized society men must be able to assume that they control for beneficial purposes what they have discovered and appropriated to their own use, what they have created by their own labor, and what they have acquired under the existing social and economic order.
3.  In civilized society men must be able to assume that those with whom they deal in the general intercourse of society will act in good faith and hence
    (a)  will make good reasonable expectations which their promises or other conduct reasonably create;
    (b)  will carry out their undertakings according to the expectations which the moral sentiment of the community attaches thereto;
    (c)  will restore specifically or by equivalent what comes to them by mistake or unanticipated situation whereby they receive, at another's expense, what they could not reasonably have expected to receive under the actual circumstances.
4.  In civilized society men must be able to assume that those who are engaged in some course of conduct will act with due care not to cast an unreasonable risk of injury upon others.
5.  In civilized society men must be able to assume that those who maintain things likely to get out of hand or to escape and do damage will restrain them or keep them within their proper bounds.

    In recognition of the two main directions that juristic thinking was taking—(1) concern for the concrete individual life rather than for the abstract individual will, and (2) concern for civilization as distinct from and contrasted with politically organized society—Pound, in 1959, proposed two new jural postulates in the first volume of his *Jurisprudence*:

6.  Everyone is entitled to assume that the burdens incident to life in society will be borne by society.
7.  Everyone is entitled to assume that at least a standard human life will be assured him; not merely equal opportunities of providing or attaining it, but immediate material satisfactions.

As social-ethical principles, the jural postulates for law have a practical three-fold purpose. First, they are meant to identify and explain the substantial totality of actual human claims, demands, or interests of a given social order. Second, they express what the majority of individuals in a given society want the law to do. Third, and relatedly, the jural postulates are meant to guide the courts in applying the law. Pound asserts that the jural postulates are neither eternal, immutable, or exhaustive. Indeed, he regards them as principles that overlap, conflict, and are in continuous dynamic transition. Pound's position toward the jural postulates is therefore one of relativity, for upon being recognized the postulates are legally protected only until the empirical facts of a changing society make them outmoded and obsolete. In the meantime, they are employed in the practical work of bringing a particular society's legal institutions into a condition of harmony with the jural postulates, and therefore into a condition of harmony with the de facto claims made by the majority of persons in a given society at a given time.

The link between the jural postulates and the scheme of interests is less than clear in Pound's work. In *Social Control through Law* he treats the jural postulates as simply a method for valuating social interests, one that was fast becoming less useful because society was undergoing the transition to a social order that had not yet formulated a generally accepted notion of the ideal. In *Jurisprudence,* by contrast, Pound refers to the jural postulates and the scheme of interests as two approaches that he finds useful in teaching law. In other contexts, Pound views the jural postulates as nothing more than general and universal expressions of the social interests. In any event, Pound does see a need for some connection, a mediating procedure, between the practical problems posed by the administration of justice and the jural postulates of the civilization of the time and place. This link consists of a set of interests which, like the jural postulates, also press for legal recognition and enforcement in that society. Pound rather ingeniously classifies certain claims of human beings to have things and do things by distinguishing between three ideal type interests: the individual, the public, and the social.

## V

In Chapter III of *Social Control through Law* Pound defines an interest as "a demand or desire which human beings, either individually or through groups or associations or in relations, seek to satisfy." Individual interests, he tells us, are "claims or demands or desires involved immediately in the individual life and asserted in title of that life." Individual interests divide into interests in personality, interests in domestic relations, and interests of substance. Public interests consist of "claims or demands or desires involved in life in a politically organized society and asserted in title of that organization." Finally, Pound defines social interests as "claims or demands or desires involved in social life in civilized society and asserted in title of that life" (quotations from pp. 66 and 69). Pound warns that these three types of interests are overlapping and interdependent and that most claims, demands, and desires can be placed in all three categories, depending upon one's purpose. However, as a practical matter, and in order to compare them on the same plane, he tended to treat claims, demands, and desires in their most general form, that is, as social interests.

It is no exaggeration to say that Pound's theory of social interests is crucial to his thinking about law and lies at the conceptual core of sociological jurisprudence. Pound first presented the theory in the keynote address which he delivered before the American Sociological Society in 1920. Considering that Pound's notion of social interests evolved through the years, a composite description derived from Chapter III of *Social Control through Law,* "A Survey of Social Interests" (1943), and the third volume of Pound's *Jurisprudence* (1959), yields the following definition: *Social interests are the prevalent and reasonable, de facto claims, demands, desires, or expectations that human beings collectively seek to satisfy and that civilized society must recognize and protect through law.* Because law protects social interests they are given the status of legal rights. Thus, a right is usually a legally protected social interest. In *Social Control through Law* Pound explains that the relation between interests and rights has to do with the fact that the latter conception is plagued with a multiplicity of meanings. At bottom, however, Pound rejects the idea of rights as being natural or inalienable—a quality inherent in humans as rational beings. Pound argues that what is natural are not "rights" but "interests."

In contrast to the abstract idea of right, social interests are strictly and precisely empirical entities because they are to be found solely in the law and legal processes of society. In other words, social interests are not abstruse propositions derived, through logical deduction, from such determinist sources as theological doctrine, philosophical ideas about human nature, or the psychological classification of instincts. Rather, social interests can be inferred only through the empirical investigation of such objective data as court decisions, legislative declarations, and what is written in a wide array of works (most of which, for Pound, are Western and especially English and American sources) referring to the law. In "A Survey of Social Interests," Pound explains that the first step in conducting such an investigation involves surveying the legal order (by which he means the regime maintained by a mature system of law in the latest stage of its development) and inventorying those social interests that have

pressed upon lawmakers, judges, and jurists for recognition and satisfaction. Through a painstaking and thorough analysis of hundreds of
legal documents, Pound inventories the social interests that have been
asserted and which must be acknowledged and secured by the courts
in order to maintain social order and attain civilized society. He proposes six broad categories of social interests and their subcategories:

I. *The social interest in general security* refers to society's claim
to be secure against those patterns of behavior that threaten its existence. This social interest takes five forms:

1. *Physical safety of the people.*
2. *General health of the population.*
3. *Peace and public order.*
4. *Security of acquisitions,* or the demands that titles are not vulnerable
   to indefinite attack.
5. *Security of transactions,* or the demands that previous commercial
   exchanges are not subject to indefinite inquiry, so as to unsettle credit
   and disturb business and trade.

II. *The social interest in security of social institutions* refers to
society's claim that its fundamental institutions be secure from patterns of behavior that threaten their existence or impair their efficient functioning. This social interest takes four forms:

1. *Security of domestic institutions.*
2. *Security of religious institutions.*
3. *Security of political institutions.*
4. *Security of economic institutions.*

III. *The social interest in general morals* refers to society's claim
to be secure against patterns of behavior deemed offensive to the
moral sentiments of the general population.

IV. *The social interest in conservation of social resources* refers
to society's claim that the goods of existence not be needlessly and
completely wasted. This social interest takes two forms:

1. *Use and conservation of natural resources.*
2. *Protection and training of dependents and defectives.*

V. *The social interest in general progress* refers to society's claim
that the development of human powers and of human control over

nature for the satisfaction of human wants go forward. This social interest takes three forms:

1.    *Economic progress.*
2.    *Political progress.*
3.    *Cultural progress.*

VI. *The social interest in individual life* refers to society's claim that each individual be able to live a human life in accordance with the standards of the society. This social interest takes three forms:

1.    *Individual self-assertion.* (This claim is expressed in those cases where self-help is allowed.)
2.    *Individual opportunity* refers to society's claim that all individuals have fair, reasonable, and equal opportunities.
3.    *Individual conditions of life* refers to the claim that each individual be assured at least the minimum living conditions which society can provide at that point in time.

Although Pound compiled this inventory of social interests between 1920 and 1959 with the intent of identifying the prevailing claims of his era, he was well aware of the fact that new values would emerge in the future. While he paid scant attention to predicting what interests *will* be recognized, he nonetheless seems to have foreshadowed claims that clamored for recognition and protection by American legislatures, courts, and administrative agencies during the 1960s and beyond. In *Social Control through Law,* Pound states with some foresight: "But some part of the path of the juristic thought of tomorrow is already apparent. It seems to be a path toward an ideal of cooperation rather than one of competitive self-assertion" (pp. 126-27). These claims of the 1960s, which developed out of the exigencies of particular political and moral struggles, were, to a measured degree, based on values of cooperation, stimulated in part by the principles of greater equality, tolerance, and social justice. In the zeitgeist of the 1960s, the claims, incited by a spirit of "cooperation"—expressed, for example, as "peace and love" by some leaders of the youth movement and by "understanding" by some leaders of the civil rights movement—were given voice by public opinion, public policies, and court decisions.

Numerous social interests, which many believed ought to be protected and promoted by procedures of law and government, were realized through the civil rights movement; the Warren Court's most

significant decisions including the school segregation cases; the
Johnson administration's war on poverty and war on crime; social
welfare policies and programs like aid to dependent children, Medicaid and Medicare; the Civil Rights Act of 1964; consumer protection legislation; questions of civil liberties; affirmative action; pro-
tections against self-incrimination; the environmental movement and
energy crisis. While Pound would probably have endorsed these
claims (though perhaps not the immediacy and urgency with which
they were made), it is highly unlikely that, despite his intensely activist drive, he would have approved of the political methods employed in publicizing the claims and reforming the laws suppressing them. Riots, boycotts, strikes, protests, and other types of "anti-
social conduct" are largely incompatible with Pound's efforts at social engineering which demanded the "weighing," "balancing," and
"ordering"—the reconciliation and harmonizing—of conflicting and
overlapping social interests for achieving stability of the social order.

## VI

Pound's juristic thinking has not aged well through the years.
One reason for this is that, like many persuasive intellectuals, Pound
became a victim of his own success. Indeed, at the height of his
long career from the middle of the first decade to the 1940s, his
focus on. the ends of law and his rejection of formalism. were readily
embraced by many jurists, including, and especially, the legal realists. This general acceptance of Pound's concepts within a generation or so after they were proposed made them outdated and "obvious." His ideas quickly became so commonplace and an integral
part of the legal culture that they soon ceased to be seen as pioneering or heretical. This is not to say that Pound's sociological jurisprudence is devoid of concepts with enduring value; it is to say that
there have been few attempts to extend or revise his ideas. For example, research on the role of interests in formulating and administering law has been virtually nonexistent.

Concerning this latter point, Pound was again a victim, a victim
of unpropitious timing. Toward the end of his life when he published his massive *Jurisprudence,* a five-volume work consolidating the sociological interpretations of law and legal ideas that had
occupied Pound throughout his career, a new model of society was
taking shape in sociology. The conflict model, initially inspired by

the works of by C. Wright Mills, Ralf Dahrendorf, Lewis Coser, and other social theorists writing during the late 1950s, began to supplant the consensus or pluralistic model that had been popular since World War II. The conflict theorists argued for a critical analysis of society and its institutions. They tended to view society, not as being characterized by consensus and stability, but by diversity, conflict, and coercion. They also regarded law, not as an instrument that functions outside of interests to resolve conflicts between interests, but as a *consequence* of the operation of interests. These two tenets directly challenged the political and moral assumptions of Pound's sociological jurisprudence and most especially his theory of social interests, both of which are premised on a pluralistic model of society that, rather benignly, and perhaps also naively, assumes that the legal order is created in society solely for the purpose of adjusting relations and ordering conduct. Jurists, legal sociologists, critical criminologists, and other scholars influenced by the conflict model-and several of its variants stemming from the New Left movement, social—conflict theory, the Frankfurt School, the various Marxisms, and, since the late 1970s, critical legal studies—have taken a radically different view of law and society. In general, these critical theorists maintain that law is not the product of the whole society nor does it serve those interests that are good for the whole society. Rather, for them, law incorporates the interests of a power elite— those specific persons and groups with the power to translate their interests into public policy. Thus, contrary to Pound's pluralistic conception of politics, law does not represent a compromise of diverse interests in society, but supports some interests at the expense of others. By the early 1960s Pound's theory of social interests was no longer given even passing consideration by sociologists and jurists. What the legal philosopher Julius Stone referred to as "the Golden Age of Pound" had, by that time, virtually faded into obscurity.

In addition, it must be said that while Pound's theory of interests provides fairly objective criteria for assessing the legal orders of the United States, Great Britain, and other English-speaking countries from which he drew his data, it offers far less for the comparative evaluation of countries uninfluenced by Anglo-American common law. Thus, in the age of the global village, Pound's theory seems to be seriously lacking in broad, multicultural explanatory power. Finally, and in fairness to Pound, it should be acknowledged that while he failed to produce a clear body of tenets, a rigorous set of methodologies or propositions about legal theory, there is one dominant intellectual theme that two of the most influential twentieth-century schools of jurisprudence—American legal realism and critical legal studies—trace directly to Pound: that the law had come to be out of touch with reality.

## VII

*Social Control through Law* is a remarkable book in manner and style. Here Pound adopts an admonishing tone from time to time, but his admonition is never overbearing as it is always tempered by polite regard for the positions of others. He gently (some may say, too gently) critiques the ideas of Hans Kelsen, Oliver Wendell Holmes, the legal realists, and others without mentioning them by name. Although he forcefully, and often persuasively, advances his ideas, Pound avoids crossing the line into callous dogmatism and polemics. Moreover, while he usually writes in generalities, and this is particularly the case with books like *Social Control through Law* which were originally delivered as lectures, Pound, nonetheless, exemplifies his remarks with instances of actual legal practice. One contemporary aspect of *Social Control through Law* is aptly demonstrated by our postmodern society and its skyrocketing rate of litigation. Now that the familial and religious institutions have lost much of their influence, the courts exert an unprecedented degree of control over the public and private lives of most Americans. To an extent perhaps unimagined by Pound, law remains the paramount agency of social control. In short, *Social Control through Law* is an insightful, concise summary of Pound's ideas that, after more than half a century, remains surprisingly fresh and relevant. It will doubtless continue to engage jurists, legal theorists, and sociologists for many years to come.

# Part III

## The Sociology of Law

# 6

# On Eugen Ehrlich, *Fundamental Principles of the Sociology of Law*

*Klaus A. Ziegert*

The question is in order as to whether there is a place for a reprint of a book based on research conducted at the beginning of the twentieth century and which was originally published in 1913. The following introductory remarks will come to the conclusion that the answer to such a question must be a resounding affirmative. The innovative and, in its quiet way, revolutionary scholarship of the eminent Austrian legal theorist and Professor in Roman Law, Eugen Ehrlich (1862-1922) is of such caliber that his work has not only held its place well in view of what legal theory, and especially sociological legal theory, has to offer as a major achievement. What is more, Ehrlich's concepts are still a powerful challenge to positions in legal theory that are no longer defensible.

It is another question as to why Ehrlich's work is not more widely known and used, apart from being just an item in the history of ideas in the sociology of law. After all, sociology of law, rather than sociological jurisprudence, followed in a direct line of succession from Ehrlich's observations and ideas as a new and special discipline linking jurisprudence with sociology. But many, if not most, sociologists of law today would be hard pressed if asked how their work was related to Ehrlich's foundation of the sociology of law. There are, of course, many reasons for the disappearance of references to Ehrlich's work, among them the unavailability of his texts in English, the fact that many of his ideas have become commonplace in sociolegal research and sociolegal theory and are no longer identified with his name, the very finding of Ehrlich's that the practice of law makes lawyers turn a blind eye to anything that is not deemed "legal reasoning," a number of misunderstandings and misconceptions about Ehrlich's approach, and, last but not least, a certain unfashionable simplicity—and today perhaps dated nature—of his theoretical concepts which are free of both legal and sociological jargon. We will address some of these reasons for the disappearance of references to Ehrlich's work by attempting to sketch the context in which Ehrlich worked and what his major tenets were (I). This will lead to a discussion of the argument that Ehrlich's work is still relevant today (II) and that he touched upon key issues in sociolegal theory and methodology which are still very much at the cutting edge of sociolegal research and a sociological theory of law (III).

The evidence is in Ehrlich's *Fundamental Principles of the Sociology of Law*, which is presented here as the reprint of the translation done in 1936. It is, without a doubt, the text that made Ehrlich famous. It does not represent all of his work and, with the benefit of hindsight, we can even say that it would in certain respects be misleading to judge Ehrlich's sociology of law by this text alone. But seen by Ehrlich's intention and the programmatic design of his work as a whole, it is the most fundamental introduction to his concepts and ideas. Most importantly, it is the only major work of his, which has to this day been translated into English.

Ehrlich presented this text, after more than twenty-five years of research and lively discussion with his fellow law professors, in 1913. It outlined, for the first time in the history of legal scholarship,[1] a consistent concept of the sociology of law. He summarized his findings inimitably in the famous foreword to his *Grundlegung der Soziologie des Rechts*:[2]

> At the present as well as at any other time, the center of gravity of legal development lies not in legislation, nor in juristic science, nor in judicial decision, but in society itself. This sentence, perhaps, contains the substance of every attempt to state the fundamental principles of the sociology of law.[3]

This radical assault on the traditional understanding of law and legal doctrine was followed five years later by an equally radical analysis of legal practice and legal reasoning in a second major contribution to sociolegal theory. Once again, he succinctly summarized his position in the foreword of the work *Die juristische Logik (The Juridical Logic)*:

For most lay people and for many lawyers it is evident today that the main task of judicial decision-making is to deduct the decisions in the individual case from what the law and statutes say. There is so much which is not evident from this evidence that it takes the combined forces of the theory of knowledge, legal history, logic, psychology and sociology to find out where this assumption which dominates all of the modern jurisprudence comes from, what it means, how far it reaches and where it leads to.[4]

Ehrlich's tragic death from tuberculosis in 1922, precipitated by the tumultuous postwar events in his home country, prevented him from completing the planned trilogy with a project on judicial decision-making,[5] but in the two books that he wrote Ehrlich presented a genuinely complete and innovative program for a sociological theory of law and for sociolegal research as a knowledge base for lawyers, judicial decision-making, and legal policy.[6] Ehrlich's distinctive observations had an impact on lawyers, especially the legal realists in the United States and Scandinavia in the thirties, legal anthropologists since the forties, and legal educators and sociologists of law in the seventies and eighties. However, each group received a different message from Ehrlich's work. The presentation of Ehrlich's work in its social and historical context makes it unmistakably clear that he was an academic lawyer who wrote for academic lawyers and received his most important inputs from academic lawyers. He saw in sociology a fruitful method, no more and no less, with which to confront the unavoidable question as to the scientific nature of jurisprudence. Ehrlich's radical, unconventional evaluation of what lawyers really knew about law provoked the criticisms of other legal academics, and even fellow-travellers[7] but did not produce, and was not intended to produce, general sociology. Ehrlich remained faithful to the juridical project of jurisprudence throughout. For him this project was about producing better lawyers and better legal doctrine to arrive at better decisions in finding the law. Better lawyers meant lawyers who were made more methodologically conscious of what they were doing and a better legal doctrine meant doctrine that was made more realistic and less self-deluding in its assumptions. However, while it is fair to dub Ehrlich's project "jurisprudence," his unconventional and uncompromising search for the *scientific reliability* of his findings (rather than their conformity with doctrinal orthodoxy) set his work clearly apart from conventional jurisprudence. It uncompromisingly pinpointed the errors and weaknesses of doctrinal legal reasoning and decision-making where it was held together by mythopoetical practice and tradition only. Ehrlich's committed empirical stance has produced remarkably useful and enduring arguments based on the distinctions between the different types of legal operations which have helped and still help to see law, its function and impact in a new light. These distinctions rather than a fully developed "sociology of law" have influenced and stimulated legal realists, legal anthropologists, and sociologists of law, and have provoked misunderstandings. Ehrlich was fully aware of the controversy and the dilemmas created by his suggestions. However, he saw the gulf between normative legal reasoning and scientific explanations of law as a practical difficulty only.[8] He did not contemplate, as one must today, that what he perceived as a methodological difference in approach is an *operative distinction by society*. It is this difference that gives law room "to maneuver" and it requires further (scientific) explanation. This lapse, no doubt influenced by his law reform agenda, in his otherwise so accurate observations, is a serious flaw in his sociological approach. What was required was more advanced theoretical thought and not simply "the hard work of generations of legal scholars to come."[9] Ehrlich, however, was undaunted, and set out—in this respect a lawyer through and through—to make a start on this work "for generations to come" and to at least lay the foundations for a sociological jurisprudence: "Also a beginning has once to be begun."[10]

# I

Eugen Ehrlich was born in 1862 in Czernowitz (today Cernovitsi in Ukraine), which was at the time the capital city of the Bukowina in southeastern Europe. He studied law in Czernowitz and Vienna, became Privatdozent (Associate Professor) in Vienna in 1894 and Professor of Roman Law in Czernowitz in 1897. Apart from travels to international conferences, he lived and worked in Czernowitz until his death in 1922. Behind the facade of this seemingly uneventful life in a remote province of the decaying Austrian empire, Ehrlich's life and work reflect dramatic cultural and political changes in Europe in the historical period leading up to the first World War.

The Bukowina was, like most of the Austrian Empire, a multicultural society. The slow economic development, predicated by the Austrian monarchy rule, kept this volatile socioeconomic and sociocultural mixture in the state of a pre-industrial, ethnic caste society. Ehrlich commented on the "tribal life" in the Bukowina,[11] in which the ethnic groups of Armenians, Germans, Gipsies, Jews,

Hungarians, Romanians, Russians, Ruthenians, and Slovaks lived side-by-side under the political umbrella of the Austrian imperial state at the brink of its collapse. When the collapse finally came, as a result of the First World War, most of the Bukowina was allocated to the new state of Romania. Thus, the Bukowina suffered the same fate as most regions of central Europe, southeastern Europe and the Balkans: Old states were retrenched and new "nation-states" were formed in shaky peace treaties with arbitrary allocations of national populations and contested territorial borders, giving rise to ever-present tensions which existed between dominating religious-ethnic groups and various large minority groups and were glossed over but intractable in the shadow of the permanent conflict between the European Great Powers for imperial dominance. Under these circumstances, notions of both a "common law" and a uniform "national" law are challenging propositions.

Ehrlich was a baptized Roman Catholic of Jewish descent. This fact is important to note in order to understand his keen awareness of the finer textures under the surface of the dominant culture of a nation state. As many other intellectuals of Jewish descent in Europe, Ehrlich was torn between a deep commitment to the perceived humanitarian values of the dominant German high culture and a rejection of the basic nationalist tendencies which that culture also embraced. A commitment to the professional rigor of uncompromising (positivist) scientific research seemed to provide a way out of the personal dilemmas for many of these intellectuals.[12]

The appointment to the Chair of Roman Law in Czernowitz and his teaching there since 1897 provided Ehrlich with a focal point for his critical mind: Roman Law, as taught in continental European faculties of law, integrates legal doctrine and historical research methodology. Ehrlich could easily develop his scientific approach as an extension of Roman law to legal-ethnographical research and noted it as historical method.[13] This approach enabled him to show that law in the Bukowina, like in ancient Rome, had none of the qualities which legal doctrine attributed to it but rather a host of qualities on which legal doctrine had nothing to say. It is this gap between the law as it operated and the law which legal doctrine explored that fascinated Ehrlich from his earliest works.[14] These early pieces are still dressed in doctrinal argument but they already foreshadow his critical probing of the soft underbelly of normatively wishful doctrinal thinking, using notions such as the "unity of the legal system" and the paradox of "tacit consent." He explored, with increasing methodological awareness, the contradictions in legal doctrine as a difference between legal myths and actual practice and he issued, ever more confidently, a call for a reform of legal practice.[15]

In 1910, he founded an Institute (Seminar) for Living Law. Its methodology was based on the empirical field work of contemporary South-Slavonic (Croatian) lawyers, especially V. Bogisic, who impressed Ehrlich with his formulation of a Civil Code for Croatia based on findings from interviews with the local population concerning their customary practices.[16] In his law reform proposals, he challenged the assumption of the traditional doctrine that all law is and must be found by a logical operation of deduction (subsumption) from existing legal propositions, be it in case law or formulated in acts, statutes and codes.[17]

Sociology was the cornerstone of Ehrlich's project to reform and revitalize jurisprudence. Through his intimate knowledge of Roman law and society he was no doubt aware of the claims of early Roman jurisprudence, for instance of Ulpian, to a place among the sciences (*jurisprudentia est divinarum atque humanarum rerum notitia, justi atque injusti scientia*). In this view, jurisprudence was, and always had been, the first social science, and it was a matter of retrieving that scientific position from under the layers of inward-looking legal doctrinal development which, especially with its turn to legal positivism, had allegedly lost sight of the objectives of jurisprudence. Sociology was the methodological vehicle for a modern version of legal science, extending the grasp of jurisprudence to areas and aspects of social life on which legal doctrine could no longer shed any light.[18] Although the objective of sociology was empirical and explanatory, and not normative and practical, it offered lawyers a methodology which was indispensable if they were to fulfil their obligations towards the community, namely legal work of the highest available standard of legal knowledge. Ehrlich was soon well known for his call to improve legal education by providing young lawyers with a portfolio of methodology and research techniques that comprised more than just doctrinal analysis. In 1912, he was asked to present the keynote address at the 31st Annual Meeting of the German Lawyers' Association (*Deutscher Juristentag*) on legal education. He delivered an address with an interdisciplinary vision of law as a subject of sociology, psychology, and economics.[19]

However, the idea of *Freirecht* (free finding of law) remained at loggerheads with the orthodox positivist legal doctrines in Austria and Germany,[20] and precluded any major impact of Ehrlich's sociology of law on legal education. He was more successful at influencing the contemporary discussion of legal theory in the United States and in Scandinavia. His concept of "living law" corresponded well with the anti-metaphysical and pragmatist (rather than sociological) propositions of the emerging schools of Legal Realism in North America and Scandinavia. In turn, Ehrlich assumed that English and American common law were less doctrinally hardened and freer on the level of judicial decision-making than the regime of the "adopted Roman and adjusted common law" on the European continent, which had become a straitjacket of state-law positivism turning lawyers into "virtuosi of obedience."[21]

There may have been a misunderstanding here on both sides. As will be shown below, the concept of "living law" is far more radically sociological than the notion of the Realists on both sides of the Atlantic.[22] And legal practice in England and the United States, which Ehrlich admired for what he believed was an approximation to his ideal of judge-made law, was known to him largely only through law books which said little about the traditional context. However, there is no doubt that, in particular, Roscoe Pound and the Harvard Law School under his deanship promoted Ehrlich's work as an important contribution to an, as it turned out, unrealistic program of social engineering through law and gave him a larger exposure than he would have had without that support. His publication in the *Harvard Law Review*[23] and the translation in 1936 of *Fundamental Principles of the Sociology of Law* (written in 1913) were available in the United States long before the works of either Emile Durkheim or Max Weber were translated. Without the support of legal theorists in the United States, the knowledge of European theoretical sociology of law there remained on the whole restricted to European refugee scholars—like Georges Gurvitch and Nicholas S. Timasheff— who had come to the U.S. in the wake of the atrocities of National Socialism and the Second World War. Perhaps the pinnacle of the legal realist project and the most accomplished legal realist analysis of society and its law anywhere is, unexpectedly, Gunnar Myrdal's epic, *An American Dilemma*. Following the tenet of legal realism, in a masterly interdisciplinary study Myrdal demystifies the American creed of a democratic constitution above and beyond the law with a wealth of empirical material taken from politics, economics, sociology and law.[24] However in this case, too, the realist message was not welcome in the political climate after the Second World War, and while Myrdal was safe in his home country, going on to win a Nobel prize, the American cooperators in the project ended up, ironically, being prosecuted for "anti-American activities" and found their academic careers subsequently in tatters.

Back in Europe Ehrlich's work suffered a similar fate. Apart from the controversy over Ehrlich's anti-formalist jurisprudence in the legal academic establishment, the disastrous end of the First World War and the increasingly vicious political climate in Europe further marginalized his legal reform ideas and humanist educational programs. Ehrlich died in Czernowitz in 1922, struggling with having to teach and write in Romanian[25] and being victimized for having been a representative of the German elite and their law.[26]

## II

On closer inspection, there are deeper, structural reasons why Ehrlich's break with the dominant doctrines of positive state law left him stranded in the no-man's-land between jurisprudence and other areas of knowledge, notably science and the social sciences. As pointed out above, this divergence was not always the case and developed over time. Ehrlich found conclusive explanations for this evolutionary development and they form an important part of his sociological jurisprudence. But the dominant perception was that these explanations applied to other legal systems and not to "law in its highest form," the positive state law of continental Europe, that is, law which could be changed rationally by state legislation and was accountable to the state only, or so it seemed. The proponents of this view, which was pretty much the collective establishment of European jurisprudence in all its different strands of contemporary legal theory, were hard to convince by "materialist" arguments. The dilemma, which caught up with Ehrlich most dramatically, but subsequently became the dilemma of all sociology of law—is the paradox that knowledge which helps to explain the operation of law is not necessary for its operation. Or simply: for law to operate it does not need to know what it is doing. Ehrlich came across this paradox of the "blind spot" of jurisprudence—and while legal positivism had pushed it to the extreme of an unassailable bastion of formalism and legalism, he and subsequently all sociologists of law tried their

utmost to make it disappear. Today, with hindsight and more sophisticated sociological theory to support us we can recognize that the
blind spot, which Ehrlich discovered, is not a fatal accident but part
and parcel of an evolved and differentiated structural design. It will
not go away unless law goes away, or in other words, law itself is a
paradox, which depends on this blind spot for its functioning and
development. Ehrlich's approach can also provide us with the requisite arguments for explaining this troubling finding. The point to
make about Ehrlich's sociological jurisprudence, then, is not that
his sociology of law is only a patchwork sociological theory of law
or that he got it "wrong" with his idea of a "living law." The point to
make is that he arrived through his research at arguments that proved
to be hardheaded. By hardheaded arguments we mean arguments
that survive severe empirical testing in the framework of scientific
methodology and philosophy of science theory, and which survive
the "test of time." This is more than can be said about practically all
legal theory and some sociological theory as well. In the following
we want to look at some of these arguments.

Ehrlich's major distinctions and those for which he became known
are concepts such as "living law," "the inner order of associations,"
"rules of conduct," and "rules of decision."[27] They are the result of
a systematic reevaluation and reconstruction of legal theory with a
view to drawing distinctions, not with regard to doctrinal (rhetorical) arguments but with regard to the observation of actual social
operations.[28] Such social operations can be found ("observed") in
socially related conduct and by both lawyers and laypeople at large.
Where could the legal methodology be found to direct such observations? There is none. What jurisprudence does is not only poor
scientific methodology, it is no scientific methodology at all. Jurisprudence promises something, which it cannot hold, and it does
something, which it cannot explain.

That law is a (skilled) trade and not a science is hardly a surprise
to common-law lawyers. Here practical skills and pragmatic results
have always dominated legal doctrine and legal education. However, the development of the Roman civil law as an academic discipline on the European continent led lawyers there to believe that
their law was the result of strictly rational "logical" reasoning, cul-
minating in the great systematizations of the codes and state legislation during the nineteenth century and at the beginning of the twentieth. These systematizations, in their turn, provided the legal deci-

sion maker with principles and supreme rules, from which strictly "logical" deductions would lead to finding the law in each individual case. "Forget logic!" Ehrlich argued[29]—there is no special logic in law or anything special in legal reasoning for that matter. Lawyers think, argue, and decide psycho*logically*, just like anybody else. What makes law special is not its logic—and even less any "higher" or magical normativity—but the lawyers' practice in producing enforceable decisions. Lawyers have, in the course of the development of modern law, "unlearned" to look at and understand social life as the major resource for producing enforceable decisions. Instead they have become transfixed by looking at and interpreting texts and they have become addicted to state power to enforce even the shoddiest and least meaningful legal decisions. There is no way back—but scientific methodology can help lawyers to learn (again) to use their observation and understanding of social life as a resource for producing better decisions and better law. This is the argument for why lawyers need to know sociological methodology. It follows from Ehrlich's crucial statement that every law is necessarily society's law and that making good law—be it in decisions, case by case, or be it by legislation and statutory interpretation—necessarily requires knowledge about society's ways of life.

Thus, it is important to note that sociology is seen here as a necessary and practical extension to legal reasoning. Sociology is supposed to recover the social link of law from the invisibility to which lawyers had relegated it by the development of positive law. And it must be sociology rather than psychology because the link between society and its law leads to social relations, that is, relations between people in contrast to any intrinsic "sense of justice" in individuals, which would be just another metaphysical assumption. Social relations hold the key to any understanding of the working of law, and working with law is a practical application of understanding how social relations work. This is Ehrlich's "practical concept of law,"[30] which he pits against the concept of law derived from doctrinally asserted legal propositions or texts only. It is a radical departure from traditional assumptions of legal theory[31] and it unveils legal theory as a normative rhetorical device unfit for scientific discovery. Nevertheless, Ehrlich's practical concept of law produces more questions than answers.

Ehrlich's fundamental distinction between what lawyers are actually doing and what legal doctrine tells them to think they are doing leads to observations which put forward hardheaded arguments related to the speciality of law among all social structures. This speciality is its practicality as a normative design. Law works because *norms* work. Norms are always social norms and they are always the result of social relations, working in the same way in all spheres of human practice; "legal" norms are no exception and do not constitute a "higher order" of social norms. There is no "sphere of ought" separate from a "sphere of 'is'."

> The legal norm is... merely one of the rules of conduct, of the same nature as all other rules of conduct (p. 39).

This observation states fundamentally that all legal operations are social operations, that is, operations that reproduce social structure, but that not all social operations are legal operations. It does not provide, as Pospisil later puts it, "a second path for legal thought,"[32] so as to constitute a dualism between "principles of actual behavior" = "living law" and "norms for decisions" = "official law."[33] Ehrlich's distinction holds simply that all law is made of the same material as social life at large. Norms as rules of conduct tie participants to a network of expectations, which are dependent on each other. Their normative force is given by the interdependence of the network or, as Niklas Luhmann puts it later, the fact that not all expectations of all people will ever change all at once.[34] The normativity of law and its certainty is all about this social (not individual!) "stubbornness" to learn.

The speciality of law as a social structure, then, has nothing to do with its normativity—which is society's domain—but is related to a differentiated practice by lawyers, or—in Ehrlich's distinction—the evolving differentiation between rules of conduct in general and rules for decisions developed by lawyers. Clearly, there is no room here for the suspicion that Ehrlich only shifts the mystique of legal normativity to a mystique of the normativity of social relations.[35] On the contrary, Ehrlich's finding of a historically differentiated *legal decision-making system within the legal system*—that is, everything that lawyers do in legal practice, jurisdiction and legislation—is the key to understanding the paradox of law and is empirically irrefutable. It is this differentiation of legal practice which closes the lawyer's unrestricted view of society and blocks an understanding of normativity—also law's normativity—as society's reflexive web of expectations. Instead, a differentiated legal practice refers lawyers

back to legal practice, for instance, to earlier decisions, statutes, and
other legal texts. Law begins to be decided by law only. The "blind
spot" comes into play. It helps to ignore any reference to the paradox
that law is decided by law and later in the development even rigorously
demands this be ignored, and drives the relentless development of an
ever more formalist (procedural) and legalist (positivist) law. This development, Ehrlich argues convincingly, has to be viewed critically
because the (specialized) legal decision-making system within the legal system has its own agenda, namely that of the "guild of lawyers"[36]
and, later in the form of positive state law, the agenda of state functionaries and politicians to tell, through legislation, lawyers and judges "how
to do their jobs."[37] Sociology can help to keep these agendas in
check, because positivist jurisprudence cannot.

Order is a factual outcome of the evolution of society. The power
and instrumentality of norms resides in society's reflexive web of
expectations that Ehrlich calls "the inner order of associations." Law,
as any normative idea, can—and indeed, as a normative design,
must—demand more than what is factually occurring.[38] However,
formalized by the legal-decision making system, law can never control the factual order but only itself:

> Man acts according to law first of all because social relations make him do so (p. 61).
> Criminal law is powerless when it comes to mobilizing forces which are not given in
> society itself; every criminal law can only achieve what it can achieve with the forces
> which exist in people (1966: 291).

The distinction of "(social) associations" and their "inner order"
leads to the concept of "living law." This concept, then, does not
claim—as Ehrlich's critics argue—a higher or "mystical" or different validity of law, for instance, as a "group will"[39] or a blind solidarity between the individual members of associations. It merely
spells out, in terms which can be empirically tested, where and how
the effects of law must be observed. It is an argument against the
"light switch" model of legal positivism, which assumes that law
has social effects because it exists and that legal propositions have a
social effect in their own right:

> The reason why the dominant school of jurisprudence so greatly prefers the legal
> proposition to all other legal phenomena as an object of investigation is that it tacitly
> assumes that the whole law is to be found in the legal propositions (p. 486).

In this way, the concept of living law was also devised to direct
attention at the requirement of empirical methodology which law-

yers must apply in order to understand law in a scientifically grounded fashion:

> We grope in the dark everywhere. We need but to open our eyes and ears in order to learn everything that is of significance for the law of our time (p. 489).

Society's reflexive web of expectations (the inner order of associations) makes law work. Everyday life is, on balance and for most, successful because living law is working. For Ehrlich, this is an order of "peace" and not of war or conflict. Debtors keep their promises to creditors, primarily because they are anxious to keep promises, not because they are afraid of credit law or sanctions:[40]

> If one reads a contract of usufructuary lease...one marvels how it is possible for the lessee to move at all within this barbed-wire fence of paragraphs. Nevertheless the lessee gets on very well.... One who is engaged in the practical affairs of life is anxious to deal peaceably with people (p. 497).

The concept of living law draws attention to the fact that the reflexivity of normative expectations precedes conflicts and that, in a few instances, conflicts can arise (only) because normative expectations exist. Living law, as an order of peace, is the condition which drives the legal decision-making system to develop ever more and ever finer norms for decision-making in dispute-treatment and conflict-resolution and, in that, gives rise to the jurisprudential view that the operation of law is restricted to conflict-resolution.

In spite of its clear foundation in empirical research methodology, Ehrlich's theoretical approach develops a remarkable constructionist reference to the historical dimension, which is evolutionary theory in its tendency, and free from crude functionalism:

> It is only a consequence of the deplorable limitation of the human mind that cause and effect are seen as separated in time; if our mind could be all-embracing it would easily identify all the effects timelessly interlaced with their cause (1966:180).

His concept of a differentiating special legal decision-making system leads to the discovery of a separate operative structure (the legal profession and the organization of courts and legislation), which is conditioned by the overall structure of living law but not identical with it. In fact, it is the closure of the decision-making system, which enables it to develop legal decision-making as a speciality regardless and independent of concrete information about its effects in society as the trademark of modern positive, that is, changeable law. Ehrlich does not deny the need for or the fact of legal specialization (differentiation). However, he can show the risks involved in this development, namely, that the closed operation of legal decision-making, conceptionalized by doctrinal jurisprudence, is fraught with self-aggrandizement and self-delusion:[41]

> The living law is the law which dominates life itself even though it has not been posited in legal propositions. The source of our knowledge of this law is, first the modern legal document, secondly, direct observation of life, of commerce, of customs and usages and of all associations, not only those that the law has recognised but also those that it has overlooked and passed by, indeed even those that it has disapproved (p. 493).

As far as the question as to the beginning of law is concerned, Ehrlich could show,[42] with his concept of the "inner order of associations," that the issue of the origin of law has never been a practical problem for legal decision-making and in legal practice. Normative decision-making in all societies can and always does refer to the preceding order of the living law because it can always be assumed and shown that the people who went before proceeded according to established norms of conduct.[43] The evolution of law driven by the differentiation of legal decision-making is an altogether practical affair:

> Jurisdiction was first of all the setting of a limit in order to avoid a feud in which the intervention of a court could be useful. Procedure was fishing for information in a complicated situation. Finding the law was a search for a decision which was so appropriate that even the belligerent party had to accept it (1966:13).

Accordingly, law does not "start" with legal propositions but it is an accepted practice, which gradually firms through closure and produces, among other things, legal propositions on its way. What makes legal propositions "legal" is not a "higher" normativity but the specialized (differentiated) performance of a subset of social operations (legal decision-making) by special people ("lawyers") who distil legal propositions:

> What initially provides interests with legal protection is not a legal proposition but above all the art of lawyers (jurists) and a free balancing of interests. The fact that the judicial decisional norm is recognized afterwards as a legal proposition only masks its internal contradictions but does not solve them (1966:27).

Legal decision-making or legal practice is society's response to the pressures of the uncertainty of an open future. This uncertainty can only be reined in by normative decision-making. Ehrlich calls this *Rechtsarbeit* (legal work). This work consists of finding normative decisions which resolve uncertainty and which are acceptable to all parties, including the stronger ones. Law has no higher or other power, and no other source, than the wisdom of the decisions derived from decision-making work. In other words, the authority of legal work simply rests on the conceptual creativity, inventiveness and—increasingly—consistency of the lawyers' work. To have "social effects," legal decision-making has to rely on the reflexivity of society's web of normative expectations (living law). "Ordinary jurisprudence," that is, one which is not assisted by sociology of law, ignores this fundamental interdependence between the self-referentially closed refinement of legal propositions by lawyers on the one hand and the reflexivity of (living) law on the other:

> The ordinary jurisprudence is always forced, in line with the purpose for which it exists, to pretend that all decisions—even and including the freely found ones—are based on legal propositions, and a number of exquisitely developed rules of the trade provide instructions on how this is done. These rules of the trade are the "juridical logic" of the ordinary jurisprudence: their result is the juridical construction. The juridical logic, understood in this sense, is essentially different from scientific logic in spite of all the strenuous efforts to refer the former to the latter. The task of juridical logic is not to verify a finding according to the rules of human thought but merely to make a finding appear as such (1966:74).

Ehrlich's model for legal decision-making, which strikes this delicate balance between factual norm-implementation—that is, normative decision-making which manages to interlace decisions with the reflexivity of living law—on the one hand, and the innovative creation of new legal propositions on the other hand, is that of the "wise judge." This model implies that if a legal (judicial) decision is to have social effects, the decision-maker needs to recognize not only the body of available legal propositions but also the social dynamics of the normative expectations of all the parties, including the community, who are involved, and must offer an attractive decision to all of them:

> The wise judge—a typical phenomenon of legal pre-history—is someone who has the best idea when it comes to decision-making. This requires a lot of experience, knowledge of human nature and intuitive insight into the given social relationships (1966:13).

The structural, systemic effect of legal work as a self-referential linking of decision-making operations to each other is given by their reference to the time-dimension: decision-making operations are operations in the present and at the same time, points of reference for future decision-making:

> Judicial decision-making...is already in legal pre-history exemplary for the future [and] saves the judge the hard labor of an inventor (1966:14).

Historically, the "hard labor of normative invention" eventually became the exception to the rule of a legal practice, which, like all human practice, derives certainty and communicative advantages from ritual, routine, and repetition as compared to *a novo* and *ad-hoc* decision-making. Legal propositions are an attractive alternative to other forms of authoritative decision-making, for instance, religious leaders or holders of political power. References to legal propositions give the appearance of an actual decision and supply this decision with the authority and reliability of past decisions. At the same time, the "art" or the trade of legal practice provides the practitioners with a frame of reference, which is exclusively controlled by the lawyers themselves and organized by the economic interests of the "guild of lawyers":

> The Roman and English reports relate the formalism of their legal actions (leges actiones) with the guild-interests of the lawyers....For the ever-increasing number of norms, which can only be learned from the master of the guild, effectively bars all those who have no access to this learning. It enables mediocrity, in the guilds like anywhere else, to rule by fearful obedience to the rules and to oppress dangerous, independent initiative. Foreign to the uninitiated, the guilds mask the practice of the guild in the glow of utmost importance and accumulate the economic success (1966:17).

The concept of the specialization of legal work in all its forms as the structural element in the formative historical process of the differentiation of law leads Ehrlich to conceptualize what constitutes the unity of law. Also here Ehrlich departs radically from both positivist and natural law jurisprudence. Supported by his findings, he can show that law is indeed a "system" but it is not a system of texts, or, in modern reading, of "discourses." Law is a system, which dynamically produces and reproduces its unity through social operations, which structure themselves and, in the process, reconstitute the "inner order" of society as legal order:

> Law can be seen as a real unity but it is not a unity made up by legal propositions. Legal propositions form a unity only in connection with the society in which they operate. If one wants to understand the unity of law one has to include in that not only the legal propositions but also the order, which exists in the legal relations. However, this order is not an achieved one but one which is constantly in the process of being achieved by dissolving the conflicts of interests in the social relations ultimately in legal regimes (1966:146).

Ehrlich's concept of "living law" is not designed as a dichotomy of "law and society" and the subsequent fashionable renaming of sociology of law as a discipline for "law and society" has not made it easier to understand the finer points of Ehrlich's fundamental distinction of living law. It states unequivocally that all law is *society's law* and that the differentiation of a special legal decision-making system drives the evolution of modern law over time.

The mystifying activities of the "guild of lawyers" in their doctrinal recursivity conceal this unity of law and invisibilize the (social) reflexivity of law. Positivist jurisprudence does not operate any references to society other than as legal propositions. In order to bring references to society back into the picture, a scientific approach is required. Sociological jurisprudence has the goal of emancipating legal practice from a "pure" doctrinal refinement of legal propositions *to a scientific observation of law in its social context*. Brought back into legal decision-making sociological jurisprudence can enrich the knowledge of the decision-maker and make decisions more attractive, that is, enforceable:

> Jurisprudence has no scientific concept of law...the jurist does not mean by law that which lives and is operative in human society as law but...exclusively that which is [important] as law in the judicial administration of justice (pp. 9-10).

> Practically all modern juristic writing and teaching...pretends to be nothing but a setting forth, as clear, as faithful, as complete as is possible, of the content of statute law44 and its finest ramifications and its remotest applications. Such a literature and such teaching cannot, however, be termed scientific; in fact, they are merely a more emphatic form of publication of statutes (p. 19).

> The logic of the practical jurisprudence as the doctrine of the trade (in contrast to a theoretical science of law) is in essence the same as other trade doctrines, for instance in engineering, and could hardly achieve the result that applying the law is the only task of jurisdiction. Since logic is independent of positive law, the logic of jurisprudence in each legal system should be the same (1966:2).

Ehrlich's notion of sociological jurisprudence as legal science demonstrates that he is fully aware of the highly invasive nature of modern law, especially of state law (legislation) and that he recognizes this as the result of a historical process of the differentiation of legal practice. However, he does not accept all the wrong reasons for the invasiveness of modern law. In Ehrlich's view, legal science offers a way out of the dilemma of modern law, that is, positive law which reconstructs the social order as an ever more closed legal order. By providing lawyers with scientific methodology additional to their doctrinal instructions on how to ply the trade, the cycle can be broken:

> It will be the matter of the logic of the jurisprudence of coming generations to show how the results of social science research can be utilized in legislation, in the legal literature and in the administration of justice. All of these are only the beginnings of a scientific foundation of jurisprudence. It will take several centuries for legislators, lawyers and judges to stand on firmly established scientific ground (1966:313).

## III

This brief introduction to some of the concepts that Ehrlich developed and used is not comprehensive and is necessarily selective. It leaves out large areas of further explications of his ideas and fascinating descriptive accounts of legal history, which was his domain. Nevertheless, the summary can give an insight into the approach that Ehrlich took and point out the advances of sociological jurisprudence that have survived the test of time as hardheaded arguments which have guided other legal and sociolegal scholars in this century, and can still do so today.

Ehrlich may have been ahead of his time and this adds an almost prophetic quality to his work, which can only be appreciated fully today. Obviously, the uncompromising radicality of his arguments made it difficult for them to be accepted in their full meaning during his time. Even the favorable reception of his ideas by the American and Scandinavian Realists proved to be a mixed blessing. The concept of "living law" seemed to offer support for the concept of the oppositional pair of "law in the books" and "law in action" used by Roscoe Pound.[45] However, there is a considerable difference between Ehrlich and Pound in their respective approaches to sociological jurisprudence and legal theory.[46] Ehrlich appraised European legal theory, whereas Pound, committed to American pragmatism, assembled tools for his vision of social engineering through law. In this attempt, only a few of Ehrlich's finer points of distinguishing "living law" as the methodological focal point for legal knowledge survived.[47] In spite of this, it appears that Pound's juxtaposition of "norms of decision" on the one hand and social operations on the other—law and society indeed—influenced later legal scholars very significantly, and more so than did Ehrlich's original approach.[48] A more subtle blending of Ehrlich's "European" sociological theory of law and Pound's legacy of American Legal Realism can be found in the writing of Julius Stone[49] who recognized in Ehrlich the inception of a non-doctrinal, scientific understanding and description of law as the foundation of a special discipline of "sociological jurisprudence."[50]

Another distinct group of scholars who carried the ideas of Ehrlich further was a group of legal anthropologists who were able to reference both European legal theory and American anthropological research methodology.[51] This interpretation of Ehrlich's work also appears to promote its own agenda, that is, positivist, behaviorist research, and to miss the point that Ehrlich's legal theory is not about individual behavior but about norms, normative structure, and the genuine function of normativity in society. Undoubtedly the concept of "living law" and the finding of an "inner order of associations" provided a forceful argument for legal anthropology in stateless and "law-less" societies, not least because Ehrlich had derived these distinctions from his own ethnographic research. However, the strong behaviorist bent of these writers goes too far in interpreting Ehrlich's distinction of "rules of conduct" as a feature of *individual behavior*.[52] They criticize Ehrlich for having fallen victim to the ideas of a (socialist?) "mystical 'group-will' that was distinct from the individual wills of the members of such a group,"[53] and for making "a group of people almost a living beast (thus giving rise to the "unfortunate Durkheimian trend in sociology and anthropology)."[54] No wonder, then, that Pospisil cannot find in Ehrlich's approach the "transmission of normativity" through (individual) leaders of groups,[55] which is so important for the understanding of social control and political order by anthropologists. This is reminiscent of Pound's criticism of Ehrlich for his "phobia of the State and of Sovereignty."[56] It is supported by the established positivist jurisprudence of European legal theorists, which is committed to the idea that the validity of law is given by the conjunction of law with state power and sanctions, ultimately using physical force. However, all these criticisms overlook what Ehrlich had established so clearly: the existence of a genuine "social" level apart from and in addition to the individual "psychological" level as the relevant fact in the operations of norms. This is, indeed, where sociological inquiry must start, that is, the level on which individuals relate meaningfully to each other and where relations between individuals and their actions are stabilized effectively as normative expectations. And only with this level as a precondition, individuals can relate to themselves and other as persons. This is the normative structure, the "inner order of associations," that individuals need as a reference point in order to construct themselves as "behaving individuals" and to expect from others what they can reasonably expect from themselves. This reflexive web of normative expectations, and only this, is the domain of law and it has nothing to do with "state," governance or sovereignty.

These arguments are supported by sociological research, which can follow Ehrlich's legal theory as an approach to understanding law "from the bottom up." This research confirms that the distinctions of "living law" and the "inner order of associations" identify authentic areas of sociological (field) research which lie outside the traditional areas of legal research. These approaches start from the assumption of the overlap and interdependence of a more or less differentiated law *and* a more or less undifferentiated law, and they move towards concepts of a "legal pluralism"[57] which challenge the assumption of the state-law equation. This has clear implications for a better understanding of the operation and effects of normative structures and—as Ehrlich intended—consequences for legal and social policies.[58] And there is room for further empirical research[59] and a refinement of the theoretical positions contained in Ehrlich's holistic approach.[60]

As far as positivist jurisprudence is concerned, doubts have been raised whether Ehrlich was able to capture all aspects of modern law with his approach.[61] And there were questions as to the position of what Ehrlich calls "sociological method."[62] Not surprisingly, Ehrlich has also been accused of a perverted "panjurism" in relation to how he defines "social norms." In this view, Ehrlich—by declaring all social norms legally relevant—is seen to water down an alleged accurate concept of modern law, or is deemed, at least, to be "excessively liberalist" by stating that the coercive power of the state is not an intrinsic part of law or may even be counter-productive to the proper functioning of law.

Do these criticisms hold? As Ehrlich has shown, positivist legal theory and practice are wedded to the idea of the coercive characteristics (*Zwangscharakter*) of law. For Ehrlich, this idea is neither reasonable nor scientific but is an evolutionary outcome. Not surprisingly, lawyers and the legal policy audience find the concept of a law without sanctions difficult to understand. Sociolegal research has persistently shown, however, that the effects of the coercive potential of law are vastly overestimated. Law and law enforcement are ineffective if not aimed at supporting the personal integrity of individuals.[63] The development of equal rights of modern law can be seen as a paradigm for the development of supportive human rights.[64] State regulation is more successful if collaborative styles are used[65] and "wise" discretion is exercised.[66] Conversely, law and order campaigns applying prohibitive and punitive legal policies have typically failed to achieve stated goals.[67] Recent social-psychological research on procedural justice[68] and a behavioral model of judicial decision-making[69] bear out Ehrlich's finding that a fair treatment of the parties and a just decision are the crucial agents in effective decision-making and produce the desired social effects—as hypothesised by Ehrlich—through the contextual and ecological awareness of the decision-maker.[70] It seems, then, that Ehrlich's finding that the effectiveness of law is not related—or is only insignificantly related—to coercion is not a flaw but is another hardheaded argument, which challenges the positivist conception of law, which sees legal violence as inevitable.

Hence Ehrlich's critical view of the state and state law is a direct consequence of his sociological observations of the evolutionary development of modern law. In this process, state law is only a historical stage among many and not necessarily the last one, let alone the "highest" one. Later sociological theory will apply the concept of adequate internal complexity as the key issue in this evolutionary development of law as a process of systemic differentiation.[71] However, the lack of a sociological concept of differentiation does not prevent Ehrlich from observing how the evolution of legal decision-making through legal practice conditions the social order for further evolution and specializes the court-based decision-making system as the effective hub of the living law.[72] In this analysis, there is no legal role for the state other than that of a powerful party, for instance, in the historical position of a "sovereign." While Ehrlich is well aware of the complexity of modern state operations, he insists that law through legal practice is—due to its historical conditioning—simply not able to achieve anything more than what the reflexive web of normative expectations in society at large (the "inner order of associations") is able to achieve factually. The historical conditioning of legal "work," on the other hand, must also be seen as a resource for society in achieving and stabilizing the requisite critical distance and independence of judicial decision-making from all forms of interference, political interventions and oppressive social interactions, including state operations and legislation. Ehrlich never tired of pointing out that only where state operations support the inner order of the associations, that is, are ruled by living law, can they be effective on a long-term basis.

His skepticism as to the social engineering capacity of *state law* is supported by modern sociological theory of law[73] and sociolegal research.[74] Where the specialized legal decision-making system (within the legal system) on its evolutionary path of amplifying deviance loses sight of an integrative concern for the interests of a collective public at large, societies lose their hold on large sections of society,[75] reflected, for example, in the dramatically growing prison populations.[76] Or they turn into "hour-glass" societies with a large majority of lawless citizens juxtaposed by powerful nomenklatura like the contemporary Russia in transition[77] and possibly soon China. On the other hand, where state law is concerned with such a contextual and ecological perspective on a supportive performance of law, as, for instance, in the Netherlands[78] and in the Nordic societies, fairly successful legislative programs can be designed on a "human scale" and with solidarity as an outcome.[79]

These introductory remarks should serve to whet an appetite for a study of Ehrlich's work and his *Fundamental Principles of the Sociology of Law* in all its captivating detail. The translation of 1936 may have suffered more from the passing of time than the original, as is the fate of translations. This introduction has tried to overcome some of those contextual shortcomings to which translators are exposed and to present Ehrlich's work in context and in view of the hundred years of sociological jurisprudence which followed. In this view, there is no doubt that Eugen Ehrlich has opened the way to new departures for the analysis of the social phenomenon "law." His approach of a scientific, empirically based observation of the observers of law, that is, the lawyers, in the framework of historically sensitive evolutionary theory has proved successful and will prevail as the main scientific paradigm, not only in sociology of law but in all social sciences, as we move on to the next millennium. Ehrlich's beginning of the sociology-of-law project was not only the necessary first step of a journey of a thousand steps but also a step in the right direction.

## Notes

1.    Issues of originality and first discovery are always difficult to determine with final certainty, especially in regard to the history of ideas in legal thought and jurisprudence which, not accidentally, is more densely and eclectically cross-fertilized than any other area of human thought. We shall see below that Ehrlich's work is no exception to such cross-fertilization, originating in a cultural and historical milieu which was teeming with anti-doctrinal, anti-formalist, and scientific legal thought. However, among contemporary legal scholars such as Leon Petrazycki, Anton Menger, Georges Gurvitch, Nicholas S. Timasheff, Karl Georg Wurzel, and leaving aside the sociologists Emile Durkheim and Max Weber who do not have a jurisprudential agenda, Eugen Ehrlich presented the most con sistent sociological approach to law for the first time.

2.    The translation of the term *Grundlegung* is actually "laying the foundation (of sociology of law)." The term thus indicates a more radical turn away from tradi-

tional legal doctrinal writing than is conveyed in the title and in the translation of the concept in Ehrlich's foreword as chosen by the translator of the Harvard University Press edition. After all, Ehrlich is suggesting here a different approach and a new methodology and not just a further addition of doctrinal principles to the vast armory of eclectic, and as Ehrlich shows, unprincipled and unscientific arguments of legal theory.

3.  See below, E. Ehrlich, *Fundamental Principles of the Sociology of Law.*

4.  E. Ehrlich (1918), my translation from the reprint version of *Die juristische Logik* (Ehrlich, 1966), preface.

5.  See as an outline, E. Ehrlich (1917), "Die richterliche Rechtsfindung auf Grund des Rechtssatzes" ("Judicial Decision-Making Based on Legal Propositions"), 67, *Jherings Jahrbücher für die Dogmatik des Bürgerlichen Rechts,* 203-252, and the announcement in Ehrlich (1918), op. cit, at 313.

6.  We shall see below that Ehrlich focused quite deliberately on core-elements of the operation of legal systems (reflexivity of normative expectations, legal communication and courts) in order to support his sociological jurisprudence with research evidence. This speaks against assumptions that Ehrlich was concerned with an early concept of "legal pluralism" and confirms, instead, that his objective was a non-doctrinal, scientific explanation for the function of law.

7.  See K. G. Wurzel (1991) at 199. Wurzel (1875-1931) is particularly interesting because he shared many characteristics of Ehrlich's biography. Like Ehrlich he was born in the ethnically, highly mixed region north of the Carpathian ridge, came from Jewish background, began his academic career at the Faculty of Law of Vienna University, pioneered sociological jurisprudence on a work on legal reasoning (1904) which predates Ehrlich's work on the same topic, and was promoted in the United States by legal realists, like Roscoe Pound and Jerome Frank in his Modern Legal Philosophy Series (Boston). Ehrlich refers to Wurzel in his *Fundamental Principles* (see below). In a later work (1924), Wurzel is nevertheless critical of Ehrlich's approach for being too sociological and too little concerned with a doctrinal (normative) "system" of legal reasoning (*Juristische Logik*). This rift foreshadows the reasons why Ehrlich's arguments still hold and Wurzel's became lost in obscurity.

8.  See his reformist suggestions for a "free finding of law" in Ehrlich's text below which contain the optimistic vision of such a harmonious marriage between normative decision-making and sociological jurisprudence.

9.  Ehrlich (1966), op. cit. at 313.

10.  Ibid.

11.  Ehrlich (1912), "Das lebende Recht der Völker in der Bukowina" ("The Living Law of the Peoples in the Bukowina"), 1 *Recht und Wirtschaft,* 273-279, 322-324 at 273.

12.  Immediate parallels can be drawn with his contemporaries, the lawyer Karl Georg Wurzel (1875-1931, see note 7 above) and the sociologist Emile Durkheim (1858-1917) both of whom were fundamentally influenced by the new discipline of clinical and experimental psychology and its behaviorist-positivist empirical approach pioneered by Wilhelm Wundt (1832-1920) at the University of Leipzig (Germany) from 1875-1917. This approach appeared to open the way for a "value-free" social science research. While Ehrlich acknowledged the new discipline, he kept largely to his own sociological observations and a historical-evolutionary methodology. The influence of the impressive experimental psychology of Wundt can also be found in the sociological jurisprudence of the Russian law professors (and later sociologists) Leon Petrazycki (1867-1931) and Georges Gurvitch (1894-1965).

13.    Ehrlich draws an important distinction between "legal history" used as another doctrinal subject and a *sociological method* of observing history as a field for research. For the English common law, see especially the work of John H. Langbein who draws a similar distinction.

14.    Ehrlich (1888), *Über Lücken im Recht (About Gaps in the Law)* Vienna; id. (1893) *Die stillschweigende Willenserklärung (Tacit Consent)* Berlin.

15.    Ehrlich (1903), *Freie Rechtsfindung und freie Rechtswissenschaft*, Leipzig, reprint Aalen 1973, partly translated as: "Judicial Freedom of Decision: Its Principles and Objects," pp. 47-84, in *Science of Legal Method*, The Modern Legal Philosophy Series, Vol. 9, Boston 1917; id. (1911) "Die Erforschung des lebenden Rechts," pp. 129-147, in 35 *Schmollers Jahrbuch für Gesetzgebung, Verwaltung und Volkswirtschaft im Deutschen Reich.*

16.    V. Bogisic (1874), *Zbornik sadasnih pravnih obicja juznih Slovena* (Collection of the principles in customary law of South Slavia), Zagreb; Ehrlich (1912), "Das lebende Recht der Völker in der Bukowina" ("The Living Law of the Peoples in the Bukowina"), 1 *Recht und Wirtschaft*, 273-279, 322-324; id. (1936) op. cit., p. 486 ff.

17.    Ehrlich (1903), op. cit.; M. Rehbinder, ed. (1967) *Eugen Ehrlich. Recht und Leben. Gesammelte Schriften zur Rechtstatsachenforschung und zur Freirechtslehre*, Berlin: Duncker & Humblodt. See also Wurzel (1991 [1904]) op. cit. at 37 with suggestions for reform based on the same finding but psychological explanations.

18.    Ehrlich (1913); id. (1917) op. cit.; id. (1918) op. cit.

19.    The full title of the address is: *Was kann geschehen, um bei der Ausbildung das Verständnis des Juristen für psychologische, wirtschaftliche und soziologische Fragen in erhöhtem Maße zu fördern?* ("What Can be Done to Enhance the Insight of Lawyers in Psychological, Economic and Sociological Issues"), Transactions of the 31st Annual Meeting of the German Lawyers' Association, 1912.

20.    Even Max Weber (1864-1922), another lawyer turned sociologist and contemporary of Ehrlich, suspected that Ehrlich's reform efforts were just another attempt to subvert the formal rationality of modern law by suggestions to revert to "rematerialized law." Weber's own sociology of law remained largely in the shadow of his theoretically far more ambitious project to explain the driving forces of the development of modern society more adequately than Marx; see Weber (1922), *Wirtschaft und Gesellschaft (Economy and Society)*, Tübingen: Mohr & Siebeck at 511. Arguably, the demands from his complex theory led Weber to gloss over important observations on law and lawyers and misrepresent others.

21.    For a more detailed account of the position of Ehrlich in the larger context of the history of ideas of sociology of law and sociological theory of law, see Ziegert (1975) *Zur Effektivität der Rechtssoziologie: die Rekonstruktion der Gesellschaft durch Recht (Towards the Effectiveness of Sociology of Law: The Reconstruction of Society Through Law)* Stuttgart: Enke, pp. 62-86 and id., (1979) "The Sociology behind Eugen Ehrlich's Sociology of Law," 7 *International Journal of Sociology of Law*, 225-273.

22.    See also Nelken (1984), "Law in Action or Living Law? Back to the Beginning in Sociology of Law," 4 *Legal Studies*, 157-174.

23.    Ehrlich (1922), "The Sociology of Law," 36 *Harvard Law Review*, 130-145: id. (1936) op. cit.

24.    See Gunnar Myrdal, *An American Dilemma, The Negro Problem and Modern Democracy*. Original edition published in 1944 by Harper & Row, latest edition in 1996 by Transaction Publishers, New Brunswick, NJ. Myrdal graduated and worked briefly as a lawyer in Sweden in the scholarly climate of legal realism and had close contacts with Axel Hägerström and Alf Ross, the major proponents of Scandina-

vian Legal Realism. However, since Myrdal's subsequent academic career was in political economy, the influence of Max Weber on his scientific approach to law and economics may have been somewhat greater than that of legal realism.

25. See Raiser (1987), *Rechtssoziologie. Ein Lehrbuch* (*Sociology of Law. A Textbook*), Frankfurt: Metzner Verlag, at 59.

26. For more detailed accounts of Ehrlich's life see Rehbinder (1967) *Die Begründung der Rechtssoziologiie durch Eugen Ehrlich* (*The Foundation of Sociology of Law by E. Ehrlich*) Berlin: Duncker & Humblodt; id. (1978) 403-418; Ziegert (1979) op. cit. pp. 228-230.

27. It is difficult to insist that Ehrlich "invented" these concepts because a look into the contemporary literature by legal academics in Vienna at the time can show that there was an ongoing discussion about them mainly following the earlier work of the Historical School of Carl-Friedrich von Savigny and the doctrine of interests developed by Rudolf von Jhering in Germany.

28. Social operations have to be distinguished from individual behavior as, for instance, in a behaviorist interpretation of Ehrlich by legal anthropologists E. A. Hoebel (1954), *The Law of Primitive Man*, Cambridge, MA: Harvard University Press; 1968:13, and L. Pospisil (1971), *Anthropology of Law: A Comparative Theory*, New York: Harper & Row (reprint 1974, New Haven: HRAF Press): 28,103, but also in a later approach of social engineering through law, for instance, P. Stjernquist (1973), *Law in the Forests*, Lund: Gleerup.

29. See Ehrlich (1966), op. cit. at 156.

30. See Ehrlich (1966), op. cit: at 1. It is important to note that "practical" refers, throughout Ehrlich's work, to (observable) actual social operations ("practice") and through that to an empirical grounding of legal theory which provides jurisprudence with a scientific (rather than doctrinal) foundation.

31. See also Pospisil (1971), op. cit. at 104.

32. See Pospisil at 28.

33. Pospisil, ibid.

34. See Niklas Luhmann, *Das Recht der Gesellschaft* (*Society's Law*), Frankfurt: Suhrkamp, 1993, at 80.

35. See especially Pospisil at 107 who contrasts here Max Weber's "sober approach" to legal pluralism favorably with Ehrlich's distinction, and Pound's criticism (1948) quoted by Nelken (1984) at 159.

36. Ehrlich (1966), op. cit. at 74.

37. Id. at 92.

38. This is a crucial concept for a modern sociological understanding of law as pointed out by Luhmann (1993) op. cit. at 219.

39. This is the main criticism of L. Pospisil (1971) at 103 who overlooks that Ehrlich is not concerned with individual behavior but with the (social) structure to which individuals can refer for adjusting their (individual) behavior.

40. Again, Ehrlich's argument is supported by all current research. Only very few customers in relation to the overall volume of credit transactions run up bad debts, and this overall success cannot be credited to law; see, for instance, K. A. Ziegert (1987), "Gerichte auf der Flucht in die Zukunft. Die Bedeutungslosigkeit der gerichtlichen Entscheidung bei der Durchsetzung von Geldforderungen" ("Courts on the Escape to the Future. The Insignificance of Judicial Decisions in Relation to the Collection of Debts), in E. Blankenburg and R. Voigt, eds., *Implementation von Gerichtsentscheidungen*, Opladen: Westdeutscher Verlag, 110-120.

41. See approvingly from the perspective of legal anthropology L. Pospisil (1971), op. cit. at 107, but curiously inconsistent Hoebel (1954), op. cit. at 27 in view of his earlier research together with Llewellyn; see K. Llewellyn and E. A. Hoebel (1941),

*The Cheyenne Way: Conflict and Case Law in Primitive Jurisprudence*, Norman: University of Oklahoma Press.

42.   See misleading D. Nelken (1984), op. cit at 173, who suggests that Ehrlich did not ask the question: "How do the norms of 'living law' arise?"

43.   This position is confirmed by Luhmann (1993), op. cit. at 57, who elaborates on Ehrlich's concept of law as a structure of social operations (communication) in the framework of the theory of operatively closed systems (without mentioning Ehrlich).

44.   Here one should read *"all written and declared (statute) law,"* i.e., all positive law. The American translation is misleading in this point by using a technical term, which only exists in English common law in order to distinguish case law from statute law. This distinction does not make sense in legal systems with codified law ("Civil law").

45.   See R. Pound (1910), "Law in Books and Law in Action," 44 *American Law Review* 12, and further on this point Ziegert (1979), op. cit. at 225.

46.   See Nelken (1984), op. cit at 159.

47.   Ibid. at 166.

48.   Ibid. at 160.

49.   See J. Stone (1966), *Social Dimensions of Law and Justice*, Sydney: Maitland Publications, 7, 44, 46-47, 645-46.

50.   Stone had, in contrast to Pound earlier, direct access to Ehrlich's original publications and background material through intensive cooperation with European legal scholars but appears to not have read Ehrlich's work in the original.

51.   See K. Llewellyn and E. A. Hoebel (1941), *The Cheyenne Way: Conflict and Case Law in Primitive Jurisprudence*, Norman: University of Oklahoma Press, E. A. Hoebel (1954), op. cit.; L. Pospisil (1971), op. cit.

52.   E. A. Hoebel (1968) at 13; L. Pospisil (1971) at 28, 103.

53.   L. Pospisil at 102.

54.   Ibid. at 102-103.

55.   Ibid. at 104.

56.   See R. Pound (1948), "Introduction" to S.P. Simpson and J. Stone, eds., *Cases and Readings on Law and Society*, quoted Nelken (1984), op. cit. at. 159.

57.   See, for instance, Nelken (1984), op.cit.; J. Griffiths (1986), "What is Legal Pluralism?", 24 *Journal of Legal Pluralism and Unofficial Law*, 1-55; G. Teubner (1996), "Globale Bukowina. Zur Emergenz eines transnationalen Rechtspluralismus" ("Global Bukowina. On the Emergence of a Transnational Legal Pluralism"), *Rechtshistorisches Journal*, 15, 255-290.

58.   See Nelken (1984) at 173.

59.   Ibid.

60.   Contenders for such further development are, as far as can be seen, a sociological theory of norms and systems theory. For the former, see for instance, D. Nelken (1984), op. cit; J. Griffiths (1986), op. cit., and for the latter N. Luhmann (1993), op. cit; K. A. Ziegert (1975), op. cit.; id. (1979) op. cit.; id. (1995) "The Political Fitness of a Legal System: English Law, Australian Courts and the Republic," 17 *Sydney Law Review,* 390-410.

61.   See M. Weber (1922), *Wirtschaft und Gesellschaft*, Tübingen, at 511, J. Carbonnier (1972), *Sociologie juridique*, Paris, at 86; K. A. Ziegert (1979), op. cit. at 236; R. Cotterrell (1992), *The Sociology of Law*, London: Butterworths, at 35; K. F. Röhl (1987), op. cit at 33; T. Raiser (1987), op. cit at 69.

62.   See R. Cotterrell (1992) at 35; T. Raiser (1987) at 69; H. Rottleuthner (1987) *Einführung in die Rechtssoziologie*, Darmstadt: Wissenschaftliche Buchgesellschaft, at 26.

63. See in the area of criminological research S. Cohen (1985), *Visions of Social Control: Crime, Punishment and Classifications*, Oxford: Polity Press, and with support from systems theory N. Luhmann (1993) at 156-157.
64. See Luhmann (1993), op. cit. at 115.
65. See for many studies in the area of "social steering through law," P. Stjernquist (1973), op.cit. and K. Hawkins (1984) *Environment and Enforcement: Regulation and the Social Definition of Pollution*, Oxford: Clarendon Press.
66. See R. Lempert (1992), "Discretion in a Behavioral Perspective: The Case of a Public Housing Eviction Board," in Keith Hawkins, ed., *The Uses of Discretion*, Oxford: Clarendon Press.
67. See, for instance, the wealth of empirical research detailed in S. Cohen (1985), op. cit.
68. See A. E. Lind (1994), "Procedural Justice and Culture: Evidence for Ubiquitous Process Concerns," 15 *Zeitschrift für Rechtssoziologie*, 24-36.
69. See Lempert (1992).
70. See Nelken (1984) at 172.
71. See Luhmann (1993) at 293.
72. See empirical support in Jeffrey T. Ulmer, "Trial Judges in a Rural Community. Contexts, Organisational Relations, and Interaction Strategies," *Journal of Contemporary Ethnography,* 23-1 (1994) 79-108.
73. See with further arguments Luhmann (1993) at 154.
74. See K.A. Ziegert, "Das Ende der sozialen Fahnenstange? Überlegungen zum sozialen Rechtsstaat und der Evolution des modernen Rechts" ("The End of Social Welfare? Observations on the Social Welfare State of Law and the Evolution of Modern Law), in R. Voigt, ed., *Evolution des Rechts*, Baden-Baden (1998) pp. 215-252.
75. See M. Gallanter (1974), "Why the Haves Come out Ahead: Speculations on the Limits of Legal Change," 9 *Law and Society Review*, 95-160.
76. See, for instance, R. P. Weiss and Nigel South, eds. (1997), *Comparing Prison System: Towards a Comparative and International Penology*, Gordon and Breach: Amsterdam.
77. See R. Rose (1995), "Russia as an Hour-Glass Society: A Constitution Without Citizens," 4 *East European Constitutional Review,* 34-42.
78. See, for instance, E. Blankenburg and F. Bruisma (1994), *Dutch Legal Culture*, Deventer/Boston: Kluwer.
79. See, for instance, A. Hetzler (1984), *Rättens roll i socialpolitiken* (Swed.: "The Role of Law in Social Policy"), Stockholm: Liber; B. Carlsson (1995), "Communicative Rationality and Open-ended Law in Sweden," in *Journal of Law and Society,* 22-4,475-505; K. A. Ziegert, "Debatt med Lund om moral, politik och rätt: The Double Modality of Law and Swedish Sociology of Law," in H. Hydén, red., *Rättssociologi—då och nu* (1997), Lund: Sociologiska Institutionen, pp. 95-104.

## Ehrlich's Major Publications

(1888)  *Über Lücken im Recht (About Gaps in Law)*, Wien.
(1893)  *Die stillschweigende Willenserklärung (Tacit Consent)*, Berlin.
(1903)  *Freie Rechtsfindung und freie Rechtswissenschaft (Free Finding of the Law and Free Legal Science)*, Leipzig, reprint Aalen 1973, partly translated as "Judicial Freedom of Decision: Its Principles and Objects," pp. 47-84, in *Science of Legal Method*, The Modern Legal Philosophy Series, Vol. 9, Boston 1917.

(1911)    "Die Erforschung des lebenden Rechts" (Research on Living Law), pp. 129-147, in 35 *Schmollers Jahrbuch für Gesetzgebung, Verwaltung und Volkswirtschaft im Deutschen Reich.*

(1912)    "Das lebende Recht der Völker in der Bukowina" (The Living Law of the Peoples in the Bukowina), 1 *Recht und Wirtschaft,* 273-279,322-324.

(1913)    *Grundlegung der Soziologie des Rechts,* München/Leipzig, reprint 1929,1967; Engl.: *Fundamental Principles of the Sociology of Law* (introduction by Roscoe Pound), Cambridge, MA, 1936.

(1917)    "Die richterliche Rechtsfindung auf Grund des Rechtssatzes" (Judicial Decision-Making Based on Legal Propositions), in 67 *Jherings Jahrbücher für die Dogmatik des Bürgerlichen Rechts,* 203-252.

(1918)    *Die juristische Logik (The Juridical Logic),* Vienna, Tübingen 1922, reprint Aalen 1966.

(1922)    "The Sociology of Law," 36 *Harvard Law Review,* 130-145.

(1967)    *Eugen Ehrlich. Recht und Leben. Gesammelte Schriften zur Rechtstatsachenforschung und zur Freirechtslehre (Law and Life. Collected Works on Socio-legal Research and the Doctrine of the Free Finding of Law),* Berlin: Duncker & Humblodt, ed. M. Rehbinder.

(1992)    "Die Gesellschaft, der Staat und ihre Ordnung" (Society and State and their Order), 13 *Zeitschrift für Rechtssoziologie,* 3-15.

# 7

# On Georges Gurvitch, *Sociology of Law*

*Alan Hunt*

## I. Introduction

Inquiries focused on the place of law within societies wax and wane in their interest in locating themselves within some explicit and elaborated general theory. In some periods this is seen as a matter of pressing importance while in others such projects are regarded as unnecessary indulgences that impede the pursuit of empirical and policy concerns. In general, in the process by which subdisciplinary specializations undergo institutionalization there are two stages. In the first, some general theoretical framework is pursued as a means of defining and asserting a new specialization. In the second phase, attention becomes focused on expanding the funding base for the new specialization and the pursuit of research and institutional funding imposes the logic of "practicality" and "relevance" and leads to the rise of an empiricist preoccupation.

The history of the intellectual engagement of the social sciences with law has often been written in terms of a division between two linked components: a theoretically oriented sociology of law existing alongside empirically oriented socio-legal or law-and-society studies. This distinction, descriptively useful though it is, implies the coexistence of two alternative intellectual styles. A more accurate chronology involves periods of alternation between shifting dominant styles of inquiry within the field.[1]

The institutionalization of social scientific engagement with the legal realm has followed an uneven path of development. In the early part of the twentieth century concern with law and legal phenomena was strongly evident within the mainstream development of sociology itself; this was particularly the case in the classic texts of Weber and Durkheim. This integration within mainstream sociological theory was also present at mid-century in the corpus of Talcott Parsons' systematization of social theory. In the interwar period there were important attempts to articulate a systematic sociology of law. The most significant of these was pioneered by Georges Gurvitch of which the present work was its most systematic expression. Another similar project was undertaken by the exiled Russian sociologist N.S. Timasheff (1936). These early attempts at systematic sociology of law gave rise to a partial institutionalization. In 1942 with Gurvitch now based like so many European scholars at the New School for Social Research, he launched the *Journal of Legal and Political Sociology*; the editorial board contained influential figures from both the legal and sociological fields such as Karl Llewellyn, Roscoe Pound, and Robert MacIver. This was not a propitious time for such a venture and by 1947 the journal had ceased to appear.

It was not until the 1960s that a renewed theoretical sociology of law emerged in the United States; this development was very strongly influenced by the dominant functionalist tradition, particularly the Parsonian version. Thereafter a protracted process of institutionalization occurred in which a suitable institutional location proved difficult to find. While law schools often had the resources they generally proved to offer an ill-equipped attic that reinforced the sense of isolation of social scientists who entered therein. In sociology departments rival claimants operating variously under the labels of "criminology" or "deviance" policed the entrance of sociological studies of law. These difficulties were gradually resolved and an expanding number of practitioners of the new subdiscipline came to make something of a virtue of the very mixed academic accommodation they found themselves occupying, whether it was in law schools, sociology departments or various self-standing institutes. By now they had created the appropriate apparatus of journals and professional associations.

Yet institutionalized sociological approaches to law lacked any sustained theoretical productivity. Much work took place within some variant of the still pervasive functionalism. The more formalized theoretical work took on an arid abstraction exemplified by Donald Black's (1976) behavioralist theory which, while attracting a few followers, failed to have any impact on the mainstream.

The major response to the pervasive functionalism expressed it-self in the form of conflict theory approaches to law; politically committed, but theoretically weak, it did little more than register an objection to the complacent vision of law's role in securing social integration. The emergence of a theoretically sophisticated "critical legal studies" in the mid-1970s was to have significant impact in stimulating debate, or at least controversy, within legal scholarship. It had surprisingly limited reverberations for sociological studies of law, primarily because of its overtly doctrinal frame of reference. Significantly there have been occasional sorties into the field of law by prominent social theorists such as Bourdieu (1987), Derrida (1990), and Habermas (1987; 1996). Most theoretical inspiration has come from the margins. It is not the intention to provide a comprehensive survey of the current state of the sociology of law. It is sufficient to mention that significant shifts of focus have arisen from a renewed ethnographic engagement with law, from the iconoclasm of the postmodernist controversies and from the penetration of the legacy of Foucault. Suffice it to say that the paucity of self-generated theoretical initiatives within the sociology of law makes it timely to revisit the legacy of Georges Gurvitch.

## II. A Brief Biography

Georgii Davidovich Gurvitch was born in Russia in 1894; he grew up in the political turbulence and intellectual excitement of Russia during the period between the revolutions of 1905 and 1917. His education had immersed him in classical, philosophical, and legal studies. He greeted the events of February/March 1917 with enthusiasm, being particularly impressed by the creation of Soviets and Factory Councils, which he saw as models of the pluralistic and decentralized political system which he had come to espouse. He was at the University in St. Petersburg in 1917; his intellectual and political interests brought him into contact with the margins of both Menshevism and Bolshevism. Theoretically, he was ambiguous about Marxism. Intellectually, he rejected Marxism because of what he perceived as the tension between its economic determinism and its political voluntarism. Yet the radical participatory democracy of the Workers' Councils and the Soviets left an indelible impression and was to form the basis of his distinctive lifelong socialist commitment. The path of political development after October 1917 disillusioned him as he saw the prospect of a pluralistic social order recede. Gurvitch left the Soviet Union in 1920. He obtained a university post in Prague (1921-1924), but then moved to France, where he became a naturalized citizen and spent the remainder of his life, except for a period in the United States during the Second World War.

Gurvitch was later to comment on the experience of the Bolshevik Revolution; he noted that he had "witnessed the almost total explosion of the old global social structure" which confirmed his "complete break with Marxism and Hegelianism" (1969:ii). His intellectual orientation took him through a series of engagements with neo-Kantianism in a quest to espouse both anti-individualist and anti-statist positions; during this period he was much influenced by Fichte. A concern with the tension between equality and liberty led to an interest in Rousseau. When he settled in France from 1925 he deepened his engagement with Proudhon and the tradition of French syndicalism that was to become a decisive influence on his thought.

In the first period of his life outside Russia, he focused on his studies of "social law" and was much influenced by French syndicalism and in particular by the writings of Proudhon. He wrote widely on developments in social philosophy, writing on the work of von Gierke and of Fichte, and upon the general growth of German social philosophy. In 1941 he managed to leave France and, along with many other prominent European intellectuals, took up a position at the New School for Social Research in New York. In 1942 he published his first English language text, *Sociology of Law*. He published another set of articles on legal issues (Gurvitch 1940; 1941; 1942a; 1942b) and a collaborative work with Wilbert Moore on the recent history of sociological theory (Gurvitch and Moore, 1945).

With the defeat of German fascism Gurvitch returned to France in 1945. Back in France he held posts, first at Strasbourg and then the prestigious professorship in sociology at the Sorbonne that had once been held by Durkheim. He became a major figure in French sociology. Over the next two decades his work was focused on the elaboration of his contribution to systematic sociological theory (Gurvitch 1950; 1955; 1962).[2] He died in 1965; prestigious though his wide-ranging contributions to French sociology had been, his reputation faded as a new wave of politically committed intellectuals had little time for his sociological formalism and reformist politics.

lée du Droit Social (1932a). This elaborated a critique of
traditions of analytical jurisprudence whose deficiencies
ied as stemming from their exclusive emphasis upon state
remedy he offered was to focus attention upon the social
is generated by each form of social collectivity. It is only
 foundation that state law develops.

 again the syndicalist influence that had the greatest signifi-
t only for his political thought, but also for his sociology of
 thrust of Gurvitch's ideas can be grasped as a response to
sical debate over "juridical socialism" that had long been
a of contention in socialist thought. The central issue re-
around the possibility of the transition to socialism being
 by legal-constitutional means. Engels, in his dispute with
y, set out the clearest articulation of the critique of juridi-
ialism (Engels, 1977).[3] Engels argued that for the bour-
 law represented what religion had provided for feudal-
amely a world view. For this reason socialists should not,
 any circumstances, replace the objective of the revolu-
y displacement of the bourgeoisie by a reliance upon an
nary philosophy of law offering the prospect of a socialism
ed by legal transformations, however "progressive" such
ts might appear.

rvitch exemplified just such a commitment to juridical social-
It was embodied in his lifelong commitment to the project of
 law. He elaborated his ideas on social law in a series of texts
ced in the 1930s, L'Idée du Droit Social (1932a), Le Temps
ent et l'Idée du Droit Social (1932b), and L'Expérience Juridique
 Philosophe Pluraliste du Droit (1935). He developed an ac-
t of the historical emergence of social law and was optimistic
t "its victorious march" in overcoming the individualism inher-
in the bourgeois forms of law. He counterposed social law to the
ived tradition of Roman law grounded in the state-centered view
 only sovereign states can create law and that law involved rela-
s between state and individual. Such individual law fulfills only
egative function, that of preventing harm to individuals. Histori-
ly, anti-individualism has tended to take anti-legal form as with
rx and Saint-Simon. In contrast:

Social law is for us the autonomous law of communion by which each active, concrete
totality is integrated in an objective fashion. This social law incarnates a positive value.
It is the law of integration. (Gurvitch, 1932b:11)

## III. Social

There are two dimensions of Gurv
to those concerned with the relation b
ences. The first is his politically comm
and the second is his theoretical mode
law. In the early phases of his writin
closely linked; it was his espousal of s
elaborate his model of the forms of la
ments became increasingly separated an
the time Gurvitch spent the war years in
sult, as we will see below, was that his soc
formalized theoretical form.

Gurvitch's lifelong commitment to soci
sive part played by his reflections on the
Revolution. Like many other members of
he embraced the successive eruptions of
enthused over the novelty of the transforma
the urban workers that produced the diver
and Workers' Councils that soon spread to
countryside. It was here that he identified the
order, one which was expressed in the new
zation which he identified as the formative
this he conceived as an expression of the self-d
of cooperation and solidarity.

Gurvitch became increasingly disquieted wit
subjugation of this spontaneous self-organizati
project of welding these inchoate forms into pa
in Lenin's "dictatorship of the proletariat." He
to identify the project of social law as a pol
potential alternative to Bolshevism. His most
commitment was to the syndicalist project of
organization of workers at the point of produc
provided a commitment to radical social and eco
der the generic label of socialism, while at the san
a critique of the state-focused politics of Marxism.
he deepened his acquaintance with the deep traditio
dicalism.

It was in this context that Gurvitch continued
with the concept of social law which took its most

in his *L'i*
the main
he identif
law. The
law that
upon thi
It was
cance n
law. The
the clas
an aren
volved
secured
Kautsk
cal so
geoisi
ism, n
under
tiona
illusi
secur
proje
Gu
ism.
socia
prod
*Prés*
*et l*
cou
abo
ent
rec
tha
tio
a
ca
M

Social law develops spontaneously and independently of the state, creating a juridical order from within the primary social associations.

Gurvitch counterposed social law to individual law manifesting a shift from "I" to "We." His key proposition was that social law was the law of cooperation, communion or solidarity. In positing these two types of law, individual and social, he found it necessary to add a third form, the law of subordination, a perversion of social law when individual law turned into an oppressive law as, for example, in the case of the law of the capitalist factory where the social law of cooperation is perverted by the law of property. His conception of social law provided the basis for his ideal of a socialist society grounded in Workers' Councils.

Gurvitch's general intellectual position became less and less overtly political. A trend that accelerated during his years in the United States, such an outlook was not characteristic of American intellectual life, but seemed to fit his sense of his stay in the U.S. as being a temporary sojourn. Gurvitch was attracted to the dominant motif of American sociology, the quest for a route of social development between capitalism and socialism. The undertaking was concerned to secure social integration, epitomized in the concept "social control"; this was enthusiastically taken up by Gurvitch as a means of mediation between individual and group interests. This shift in Gurvitch's sociological stance was articulated in his presentation of the history of sociology as a quest for social integration in his collaborative volume with Wilbert E. Moore (Gurvitch and Moore, 1945).

However, with the liberation of France in 1944, Gurvitch's interest in social law reasserted itself. In *La Déclaration des Droits Sociaux* (1944) and the very similar English-language version, *The Bill of Social Rights* (1946), he expounded a project for a legal transition to socialism in France via producers' and consumers' associations. The radical nature of Gurvitch's proposals is evident in the text he proposed. The preamble read: "Convinced that the absence of guarantees of the rights of producer and consumer may compromise the effectiveness of the rights of man and citizen, [the French people] has resolved solemnly to proclaim a Declaration of Social Rights, to complement and strengthen the Declaration of Political and Human Rights, the validity of which is hereby reaffirmed" (1944:91). Article IV set out the rights of producers:

The social rights of producers consist in: the right to work, guaranteed to every healthy man and woman in accordance with their ability and training, and providing remuneration to assure them of the dignity of that condition; the right of labor to participate on an equal footing in the control and administration and in the profits of the firm, the occupation, the industry and the entire economy, in functional, regional, national and international aspects; the right to leisure and to retirement; the right of trade union freedom and the right to strike.

In similar vein Article V specified the rights of consumers:

The social rights of consumers consist in: the right to subsistence in conditions worthy of man, freeing them from oppression through poverty; the right to share in the distribution of the products of the national economy; the right to economic security guaranteed by an independent insurance scheme, freeing them from threats and fear; the right of user associations to participate on an equal footing with producers in running services, firms and industries, and in the direction of the regional, national and international economy; the right of consumer cooperatives to participate on an equal footing with user associations in such direction, the right to freedom of cooperatives, user associations and their federations. (1944:91-3)

Somewhat more ambiguous is the stipulation in Article VI that "ownership confers obligations" and that "any ownership privilege contrary to the rights of labor and the dignity of man as such, as producer and as consumer or user, is abolished" (1944:94).

Despite much initial enthusiasm for Gurvitch's proposals, the hardening of divisions on the French Left and the onset of the Cold War removed them from the realm of practical politics. Yet traces of their impact persist. More recently François Ewald has promulgated a social law solution to the problems inherent in contemporary social pluralism. He argues that social law requires the socialization of the law, the conscious efforts of the legislators to organize the protection of "those interests judged by society as useful to protect," that is to protect "socially legitimate interests" (Ewald, 1986:51).

## IV. The Context of Gurvitch's Sociology of Law

A major shift in Gurvitch's intellectual orientation had occurred during the 1930s; a widening gulf opened between his commitment to the project of social law and his concern to elaborate a theoretically rigorous sociology of law. It is probable that as he watched the storm clouds gather over Europe with the rise of German fascism, he became less optimistic about the possibility of realizing the program of social law. The result was a shift from the promotion of social law to an increasingly rigid adherence to a separation between normative commitments and the pursuit of the quest for scientificity in social thought. He had little attraction to the Anglo-

Saxon empiricist version of the fact-value distinction; rather he pursued the project of an exhaustive elaboration of a theoretical model of the forms of law.

It is significant that it was his *L'Expérience Juridique et la Philosophe Pluraliste du Droit* (1935) that formed the basis of the English language work, *Sociology of Law*.[4] This work not only presented a much reduced political commitment to the project of social law, it also exemplified the value-neutralism or scientism that had come to characterize Gurvitch's other sociological writings.

Gurvitch occupies an interesting place in the development of the sociology of law. In the period immediately preceding its quantitative expansion, he produced an explicitly conceived systematic theoretical intervention. What is significant about Gurvitch's *Sociology of Law* appears in the first instance as a contradiction. His work has had very little lasting impact on developments within the field of the sociology of law; at best, his existence is occasionally footnoted, but engendered no great controversy or debate, nor does he have any active contemporary "disciples." However, despite the lack of attention, his work provides a concentrated expression of the theoretical problems that beset the field.

Gurvitch sought to articulate a theoretical framework as a precondition for any successful sociological treatment of legal phenomena. He was to move progressively away from, though never to abandon, his interest in the sociology of law as he moved towards general sociological theory. His self-conception was that of a major innovator initially in the sociology of law and later in sociological theory generally.

The core of Gurvitch's sociology of law is at root a continuation of the efforts, apparent in the work of Weber, to find a resolution or integration of the dualism which is conceived as so markedly affecting law. It is the apparent dualism between law as a positive institution resting upon the framework of social power, while at the same time being a system of values or norms having some compelling internal strength and validity. This concern with the dualism of law placed Gurvitch, as it did Weber, under the influence of the neo-Kantian tradition. In his effort to deal with law as a manifestation of these two dimensions, he was greatly influenced by the Russian jurist Petrazhitsky. Gurvitch took over and applied Petrazhitsky's definition of law as an "imperative-attributive" system, with its explicit assertion of the polarity of legal phenomena. Hence, Gurvitch refused to define law solely in terms of external constraint, but rather—and here again there are similarities with Weber—to recognize the possibility of constraint.

At the heart of this project lay a commitment to an integrationist social control perspective and an interest in the problematic of social integration—a problematic that has had such a pervasive influence on sociological theory, particularly through the legacy of Durkheim. The integrationist perspective is linked to an evolutionary and functionalist perception of the social division of labor, as a consequence of which social integration is located in normative processes of which human subjects are the bearers, but whose location lies within society itself. This view of social control finds its clearest presentation in the early writing of Durkheim, in particular in *The Division of Labor in Society*. In its general form, with its central focus on normative social control processes operating on the individual primarily through socialization or internalization, this perspective is seen as having some natural "fit" or congruence with the social phenomenon of law, and as a consequence has provided the underlying theoretical foundation for the subsequent development of the sociology of law and socio-legal studies. Gurvitch provides us with a systematic and coherent expression of this general position.

In order to engage fruitfully with Gurvitch's legal sociology it is necessary to touch briefly on some other features of its wider intellectual context. The elements which formed his intellectual orientation are complex and diverse. His thought rests quite explicitly on a philosophical basis; his sociology stems more immediately from philosophy than from sociology itself. The most direct source of influence is the phenomenological philosophy of Scheler and Husserl. Gurvitch went as far as to insist that a phenomenological perspective was a necessary precondition for the elaboration of sociological theory. Phenomenology arose from the attempt to resolve the Kantian epistemological dualism and sought to discover a position that could reconcile idealism and materialism. The phenomenologists insisted that phenomena are the objects of immediate experience and provide the raw material for cognition, which, by a process of direct inspection and intuition, may reveal the "essence" or "spirit" of phenomena. Phenomenology seeks to unite the object and the consciousness thereof.

The result is what may be described as a "subjective realism" which stresses the role of intuition. Gurvitch saw significant connections between his own epistemology and Weber's method of *Verstehen*, as well as with the pragmatism of James, which in turn finds an echo in the relativism and pluralism of Gurvitch's own thought. His theoretical strategy combined a radical empiricism with intuitionism. This epistemological position underpinned his major writings on the sociology of law. However, by the 1950s he had formally broken with phenomenology (Gurvitch, 1950). This change was directly associated with his increasing concern with general theoretical sociology. From this point on, he described his method as "dialectical hyperempiricism," but it should be stressed that his empiricism took a highly abstract form. He also emphasized the need for the separation of sociology and philosophy. His position became an even more extreme relativism, but he still retained his emphasis upon "experience" and his demand for sociology "in depth" and can thus be regarded as having retained the distinctive imprint of phenomenology.

Gurvitch's concern with the immediacy of experience places him in an intimate relationship with the predominant trends in the sociology of his adopted country, where the influence of Durkheim remained active. Hence, he found it necessary to react to the positivistic strand in sociology. The interaction with Durkheim's sociology is complex, being in part a reaction against, yet at the same time manifesting a continuation of a number of Durkheim's most important themes. On the one hand, they were united in seeking a scientific and sociological method of studying ethics. This is particularly evident in the central position in which Gurvitch placed the concept "justice" in his conception of law. Close parallels exist insofar as both asserted the distinct reality of social groups independent of the individuals who formed them, although Gurvitch accused Durkheim of allowing his notion of the collective to pass over into an unwarranted transcendence. In addition, there is a close correspondence between Durkheim's concern with the "forms of social solidarity" and Gurvitch's concern with the "forms of sociality." His classification of the three primary types of sociality as mass, community, and communion has a strongly Durkheimian flavor in that the basis of classification is the intensity of the reaction to the violation of norms.

In contrast, Gurvitch was anxious to repudiate many facets and implications of Durkheim's sociology. In essence, he regarded Durkheim's sociology as being over-mechanical and verging on the adoption of monocausal explanation. Thus Gurvitch argues that

Durkheim's two forms of social solidarity (mechanical and organic) obscure the complexity and plurality of social relations. In their place, he posits a bewildering complexity of forms of sociality, which he added to over time, and whose very plurality impedes their usefulness. One significant result is that he viewed Durkheim's binary distinction between repressive and restitutive law as concealing the diversity of legal relations and forms that are to be found within societies. Gurvitch attributed many of Durkheim's deficiencies to his insistence upon the homogeneity and unity of primitive society; in contrast he insisted that primitive societies were characterized by social pluralism. Gurvitch is perhaps the ultimate pluralist.

He was also strongly influenced by certain analytical and classificatory tendencies in sociology. It may be suggested that this influence was so potent that it had fatal consequences for Gurvitch's sociological thought. From von Weise he acquired a preoccupation with classification, and from Weber the associated fascination with the construction of typologies. In exploiting these techniques, he laid himself open to the charge of "sociologism," of providing such a rarefied conceptual schema that it is incapable of making contact with the social reality which it purports to analyze. Goldmann (1969), for example, accuses him of "concept fetishism" and of "highly intellectualized word play." It is hard to avoid the judgment that his proliferation of classifications and typologies obscured his capacity to offer a comprehensible vision of legal reality. It is undoubtedly true that his works do not make easy reading, but there is a more substantial criticism that may be leveled: namely, that his sociology is formalistic. It consists of posited relationships between a proliferation of conceptual variables with no means being disclosed as to how these are to be applied to the analysis or understanding of empirical data. This is made more confusing by his repeated insistence that his method is "realistic" and "empirical." The cautious observer is probably wise not to place too much reliance upon the self-designation of others. There are few sociologists whose work is less empirical than Gurvitch's, yet he remained insistent about its empirical character. Unlike Weber, he rarely interrupts his theoretical discourse to illustrate or demonstrate the applicability of a particular concept or classification by reference to historical or social data. For Gurvitch, "empiricism" is a declaration of faith rather than a description of his method.[5] His systematic sociology of law is abstract, formal, and remote from concrete empirical realities.

Much of the complexity and formalism of Gurvitch's writings arise from the fact that his work is explicitly ahistorical. He is insistent that unlike, for example, Weber and Durkheim, his typologies are not developmental. His overriding concern is with social phenomena at their most general level. As a consequence his work is beset by an inevitable abstraction as he strives to lift his concepts above any specific historical form. Thus the dialectical relationships between social phenomena which he seeks to study tend to be treated as if they existed in a cultural and historical void.

It is with these serious limitations that Gurvitch's sociology should be approached. He is guilty of treating social phenomena in a formalistic and theoreticist manner, without disclosing the mediation between his theoretical constructs and empirical reality. Yet, as Everett Wilson (1962:252) remarks, "one is impressed with the deft taxonomic legerdemain, and struck with the cavalier sweep across data-free centuries."

## V. Central Features of Gurvitch's Sociology

Gurvitch's sociology seeks to embrace a subjectivist frame of reference within an empiricist methodology that asserts the necessity of value-freedom. He is concerned with the meaning of social phenomena, conceived in terms of the values through which they are experienced. The role of values in human society is such that they form an irreducible basis for all social reality. His concern is with what he called the "sociology of the human spirit" or with the "sociology of spiritual values." He seeks to grasp the "total social phenomenon," the term "total" carrying connotations of the essence or underlying reality which constitutes the elemental and powerful forces coursing through social life.

An important dimension of Gurvitch's pluralistic perspective is to be found in his conception that social phenomena do not exist on a single plane of reality, but rather that they can only be fully understood as existing at a number of different "depths" or "levels." He describes his method as "an immanent downward reduction through successive stages towards whatever is most directly experienced in social reality" (p. 33). Such an approach carries with it the implication that the essence of social reality lies at the deepest level and is not to be found in its surface manifestations. His classification of the depths of social reality undergoes amendment during the course of his writing, but the main levels may be indicated:

(i)    the morphological level of the physical characteristics of objects and institutions;
(ii)   organized superstructures;
(iii)  standardized collective conduct;
(iv)   spontaneous social conduct;
(v)    "social symbols," "values," and "collective ideas";
(vi)   the deepest essence of reality is variously described as that of "collective mentality," "noetic mind," or "human spirit."

While Gurvitch denies that there are any value judgments associated with the ranking of these levels, it is difficult to avoid the conclusion that the greatest significance is to be found at the deepest level, conceived as the essence of social reality. Thus, for example, when he talks of "intuitive spontaneous law" which constitutes the deepest level of jural reality, he insists that "here is the most profound and dynamic level of jural reality" (1940:210). One is led to the conclusion that his quest for "sociology in depth" requires an acceptance not only of a group mind theory, but one which places the group mind at the very core of social reality.

One major strand in Gurvitch's sociology links him very directly with Durkheim. His sociological theory might, without too much distortion, be reduced to the proposition that the characteristics of specific social phenomena, be it law, morality, or any other institution, are manifestations of the different forms of "sociality." They are, for Gurvitch, the ways in which individuals are inescapably linked to the whole. He is explicitly concerned with the classification of these forms of sociality. In so doing, he rejects the oversimplification of Durkheim's dichotomous distinction between mechanical and organic solidarity; in its place, he develops a typology composed of a multiplicity of forms. He identifies twenty-seven different forms of sociality. The dimensions of the typology are based on the distinction between "spontaneous" and "organized" sociality. Within the former, he distinguishes between "sociality by partial fusion" ("we") and "sociality by interdependence" ("you," "him," "them"). These categories are subject to further subdivision on the basis of variation in intensity and function.

Gurvitch demarcates three levels or types of sociology. The first, "micro-sociology" is concerned with the analysis of the forms of sociality. The intermediate stage, "differential sociology," is concerned with the study of social groups and inclusive societies, while "macro-" or "genetic sociology" concerns itself with the change and development of total social systems. In relation to his sociology of law, these different levels of sociology manifest themselves in the delineation between "kinds of law," "types of law," and "systems of law," each of which he treats in sequence.

Gurvitch's delineation of the multiplicity of forms of sociality, of the different depth-levels of reality, added to the different levels of sociality, ensures that the classifications he generates are extremely complex. I will do no more than indicate in broad terms the frame-work of the constitutive variables of his classification while refrain-ing from any attempt to discuss in detail the constituents of any particular typology or classification. Rather, an unavoidably selec-tive approach will have to be employed by highlighting particular elements within his wider scheme. These elements will be selected on the basis of the light they throw upon the general character of his sociology of law.

## VI. Gurvitch's Sociology of Law

*The Status of the Sociology of Law*

Gurvitch gives extended attention to a discussion of the character and status of the sociology of law. In particular, this is to be found in the first part of *Sociology of Law* where, after discussion of the gen-eral relationship between sociology, philosophy, and jurisprudence, he devotes a considerable proportion of the book to a chapter en-titled "The Forerunners and Founders of the Sociology of Law," which occupies over 100 pages. The treatment spans the develop-ment of socio-legal thought from Aristotle to Durkheim, Weber, and in the English version includes Roscoe Pound and the American legal realists.

Gurvitch attributes the late and somewhat limited development of a sociology of law to the fact that it has had to "fight on two fronts" for its existence; it has encountered powerful opposition both from jurists and sociologists. The twin evils in his view are analytical jurisprudence and sociological positivism. He insists that a distinct and independent sociology of law is indispensable for those con-cerned with law both in their practical tasks and for their theoretical concerns.

Gurvitch sets out a demarcation of the respective intellectual projects. Jurisprudence or "legal science," as he prefers to call it, is defined in terms of the practical tasks of jurists and of courts; it is preoccupied, to use Pound's term, with social engineering. Hence, he argues that "sociological jurisprudence" is itself only a different and more modern technique of practical utility.

On the other hand, both sociology of law and the philosophy of law are theoretical disciplines and, as such, are primary. These two theoretical sciences constitute the twin bases for legal science. The sociology of law is concerned with the "objective description of the social reality of law valid in a given social milieu" (p. 9). Gurvitch therefore adopts a somewhat ambivalent attitude towards sociological jurisprudence. He welcomes it insofar as it represents a significant shift away from analytical jurisprudence, yet he is insistent that it does not constitute a sociology of law. Instead, he suggests that "the so-called sociological theory of law is merely the positivistic interpretation of the philosophy of law" (p. 52). All that it seeks to do is to substitute "sociology" for "philosophy" while remaining positivistic in seeking to derive values and norms from facts.

The sociology of law and philosophy of law as theoretical disciplines are both concerned with problems at a higher level of abstraction. Gurvitch views sociology of law as having a special relevance in the twentieth century. He argues that during the seventeenth and eighteenth centuries, natural law had a special and revolutionary role in overcoming the contemporary deficiencies of legal thought. Moreover, he claims that in the twentieth century, a comparable period of major social and legal change occurs and consequently needs liberating from the predominant intellectual framework of the previous period. Hence, he concludes that, "Under present circumstances the sociology of law alone is able to give jurists themselves a satisfactory solution to the problems of jurisprudence" (p. 11).

Despite this apparent primacy of the sociology of law, Gurvitch can be interpreted as subordinating the sociology of law to the philosophy of law, and to philosophy in general. He is emphatic that the philosophy of law has an independent existence, and therefore resists the attempts of some sociologists of law who seek to supplant legal philosophy. This position, taken in conjunction with his view that any sociological project requires the adoption of a specific philosophical orientation, comes close to asserting that the sociology of law is merely an adjunct to the abstract, purely theoretical philosophy of law which, while he leaves its content undefined, stands at the apex of legal science.

Gurvitch defines the sociology of law in the following terms:

The sociology of law is that part of the sociology of the human spirit which studies the full social reality of law, beginning with its tangible and externally observable expression, in effective collective behavior.... Sociology of law interprets these behaviors and material manifestations of law according to the internal meanings which, while inspiring and penetrating them, are at the same time in part transformed by them. (p. 48; emphasis omitted)

While this definition incorporates Gurvitch's aspiration to a sociology in depth, it does not tell us a great deal about the substantive content of the discipline.

## Gurvitch's Definition of Law

The starting point of Gurvitch's sociology of law is a definition of law which on first encounter appears to be quite distinctive. He defines law as, "an attempt to realize in a given social environment the idea of justice...through multilateral imperative-attributive regulation...[which] derives its validity from the normative facts which give a social guarantee of its effectiveness" (p. 47; emphasis omitted). This definition is constructed explicitly with reference to the differentiation of law from other modes of social control.

What is significant about this definition is the notion of "law as an attempt to realize justice."[6] The essence of legal reality is seen as manifesting collective spiritual values of which not only law, but the whole realm of social life is but the symbolic or superstructural reflection. Thus law is conceived as the collective realization of spiritual values. It is "the incarnation of realization of values in fact" (pp. 41-42). It is this last formulation which grounds his description of his theory as empirical.

Gurvitch's definition of law is notable for its breadth. It encompasses an arena of social reality wider than that embraced in the ordinary meaning of the term. Breadth in a definition is, in itself, unexceptionable; yet Gurvitch runs into the same problem as others who have sought to import a pluralistic conception of law. He used the term "law," rather as had Ehrlich, in an all-embracing sense, as the inner order of social groups and relations that embraces all forms of social coordination. Thus, despite his attempt to define law in terms of its differentiation from other forms of social control, his definition is so broad that it runs the danger of redundancy through excessive indeterminacy. In his usage, "law" often appears interchangeable with the word "social."

In constructing his definition of law, Gurvitch attempts to separate himself from what he regarded as the erroneous implications inherent in imperative theories of law. He contends that while law makes use of coercion or constraint, it must not be defined solely or predominantly in these terms. He goes even further when he argues that coercion is not a sufficient condition for the existence of law. Such a view posits a transcendental source of the legitimacy of the legal order. The transcendental source does not lie for him, as is the case in Hegelian influenced juristic thought, in some reified conception of the state. Consistent with his desire to define law as a natural social phenomenon, Gurvitch is anxious to reject the equation of "law" and "state."

The definition of law quoted above makes use of the concept "normative facts." This concept plays an important role in his thought. Its utilization is a reflection of his desire to avoid the identification of law and force. Law finds its obligatory force in the objective facts which give effect to intrinsic juridical and moral values. He seeks a middle ground between the idealist and the realist views of law by following what he terms an "ideal-real method." Hence, the source of both the legitimacy and the effectiveness of law is to be found in the active life of communities which create law by their activity, and which law in turn provides the basis for their very existence. In other words, "One cannot say either that the law pre-exists the community or the community the law, but that they are born and affirm each other together" (Gurvitch, 1932a:119).

The normative facts are the social relations and the values enshrined in communities, and as such the core elements of juridical life. While, as previously noted, such a view commits Gurvitch to a "broad" definition of law, he succeeds in evading some of the anti-statism of Ehrlich's view which places the "living law" as a preexisting condition for all other law (Ehrlich, [1936] 1962).

Throughout his writing, Gurvitch devotes considerable attention to the topic of natural law (1953b). His usage diverges from the traditional jurisprudential concept inasmuch as it is intimately connected with his concept of normative facts. He defines natural law as "that law which, grounded in the innermost nature of man and society, is independent of convention, legislation or other institutional devices" (1953b:284). At a more general level, he enshrines social law with such a special status that it becomes difficult to distinguish it from natural law. Its true existence, Gurvitch urges, is as an articulation of the normative facts of communities, that is, the values of the group mind.

Thus, law is, for Gurvitch, a central and basic feature of social existence; the "juridical experience" being central to the experience of social life itself. This juridical experience he locates, reflecting his hierarchical view of social reality, as being the "midpoint between the sense experience and the experience of the spiritual" (1935:77). Hence law is conceived as mediating between the ideal and the real. Law as the search for justice is thus not simply a disguised variant of natural law, but rather it is a much more complex, yet no less problematic, attempt to grasp law as a total social phenomenon.

Gurvitch's definition of law entails certain implications with respect to the social function of law. He attacks those who define law in terms of its functions. In contrast, his relativism requires him to insist that law has a variable historical function. Yet at the same time, his writings on law exude a very distinctive functional perspective. It is one that is consistent with his pluralistic political philosophy, namely that of providing social regulation or maintaining the social equilibrium in such a way that the fundamental spiritual values of the collectivity are thereby protected.

## The Typologies of Law

Gurvitch's predilection for complex typologies has been noted. In constructing his typology of the "kinds of law" (that is, the legal reflection of the forms of sociality), he succeeds as will be seen in isolating no less than 162 different kinds. This prodigious total stems from the complex of axes that he utilizes. Like Durkheim, he posited a direct reflection of the forms of sociality by forms of law, "to every form of active sociality there is a corresponding kind of law" (Gurvitch, 1941:22).

The primary axis is constituted by his distinction between the horizontal and vertical social differentiation. On the horizontal axis, he distinguishes between "spontaneous sociality" and "organized sociality." The former is the immediate realization of states of collective mind and collective behavior: it is this form to which he devotes the greatest attention, and thus by implication attaches the greatest importance. Organized sociality reflects the conscious superstructural forms that rely upon sanctions; these are not dealt with in any detail. Typically, it is the spontaneous forms that most interest him; they are more "fundamental" in that they "underlie" the forms of organized sociality.

Spontaneous sociality manifests itself in two distinct general forms, firstly, "sociality by interpenetration" or "partial fusion," and secondly, "sociality by interdependence." This distinction may most readily be grasped in terms of the participant attitude to the social bond created. Sociality by interpenetration, or by partial fusion, is characterized by the predominance of "We," while that of interdependence by "I-you-him-they." It will be observed that there is a very close parallel between this delineation and that drawn by Durkheim between mechanical and organic solidarity. They differ insofar as Durkheim presented an explicitly developmental classification, while Gurvitch's ahistorical approach suffers from the disadvantage of providing no criteria for the determination of the social conditions under which specific forms emerge. It is a formal classification, and consists of little more than the assertion that they are logically possible forms of social bonds.

The two forms of spontaneous sociality are further subdivided by reference to two further variables, namely the "intensity of fusion" and the nature of the "functions" that the particular form of sociality performs. In this context, Gurvitch devotes most attention to the way in which this further delineation affects sociality by interpenetration. He distinguishes three degrees of intensity (weak, medium, and intense) which give rise to three distinct forms of social interaction which he refers to as the "sociality of the masses," "community," and "communion" in ascending order of intensity. The greater the intensity of the fusion, the less reliance there is upon the "force of pressure" (sanctions and coercion) to sustain the relations.

Gurvitch next differentiates by reference to the function of the forms of sociality between "uni-functional," "multi-functional," and "super-functional" form. Logically, therefore, there are nine possible forms of sociality by interpenetration, but he argues that social life exhibits a distinct pattern in that "masses" are uni-functional relations, "community" has multi-functional relations, and "communion" involves super-functional relations. In other words, he contends that of the nine possible forms, only three are of empirical importance. He suggests a similar method of classification for the forms of "sociality by interdependence," but does not develop their classification in any detail.[7]

Along with the classification of the forms of sociality, Gurvitch considers the forms of law that correspond to them. With respect to his primary distinction between sociality by partial fusion and by interdependence, he posits the existence of two kinds of law: "social law" and "inter-individual law." In addition, however, he asserts the existence of a third kind of law, namely "subordinative law" or "the law of domination," which he regards as a perversion of social law. However, the law of domination is treated by Gurvitch as a residual category to which he devotes minimal attention other than to indicate that it is founded upon coercion.

The distinction between social law and inter-individual law suggests some similarity with Durkheim's distinction between repressive and restitutive law (Durkheim, [1893] 1964). This similarity has some basis in the parallels between inter-individual law and restitutive law in that both envisage atomized individuals coming into contact and being subject to rules designed to mitigate the potential conflict arising from their pursuit of individual ends. Durkheim, however, focuses his main attention on the forms of sanction involved, while Gurvitch, although mentioning contract as the prime example, fails to give any other indication of how this category is to be identified.

A much sharper distinction is apparent when repressive and social law are contrasted. They both refer to forms of social relations characterized by the predominance of collective sentiments. Yet they are sharply differentiated in that for Gurvitch, social law rests upon the intensity of the fusion in the collective, by the sentiment of being bound; hence the stronger the fusion the less reliance there is upon pressure or coercion. It is clear that the concept of social law is an uncompromising negation of Durkheim's conception of repressive law in primitive societies where the intensity of social solidarity elicits punitive responses to infractions.

Gurvitch distinguishes between social and inter-individual law in the following manner: "social law is based on confidence while inter-individual and inter-group law is based on distrust. The one is the law of peace...the other the law of war" (1940:204). While such a formulation has a certain polemical quality, it does not take us analytically beyond the distinction between integration and coordination.

Corresponding to his major subtypes of sociality, (masses, community, communion) Gurvitch identifies a "social law of masses,"

"community social law," and "communion social law." He advances
the proposition that there is an inverse relationship between the degree of fusion and the extent to which there is reliance upon pressure. Thus the "social law of masses" reflects the least intense degree of fusion and hence places maximum reliance upon pressure;
such law is characterized by retribution and repression. At the other
extreme, social law of communion rests on the most intense fusion
and thus is marked by minimum pressure, and as such is the least
stable form.[8] The most stable form of law is "community social law"
which manifests a mixed dependence on fusion and pressure. This
principle of an inverse ratio of fusion and pressure is an underlying
feature in all integrationist theories.[9] However, we again encounter
the problem of relating Gurvitch's conceptual framework to empirical data. The problem is simply that he gives us little or no indication as to how we are to recognize his three types of social law when
we encounter them.

Gurvitch's discussion of the subtypes of law that reflect sociality
by "interdependence" is even more schematic than his treatment of
social law. He advances three subtypes of individual law, namely,
"individual law of rapprochement," "individual law of separation,"
and "individual mixed structure law." The second type he regards
as legally sterile, and he sees the most pervasive form reflecting the
combination of rapprochement and separation. Gurvitch utilizes this
in a discussion of contract to integrate both a consensual and an
interest theory of contract, whereby contractual activity is characterized at one and the same time by the convergence and conflict of
rights between the parties. While this presentation is not fully developed, it may be suggested that his recognition of, and attempt to
synthesize, the integrative and agonistic elements of law provides
one of the most interesting features of Gurvitch's sociology of law;
but insofar as he fails to develop this analysis either systematically
or concretely, the potentiality remains latent.

Having considered the first dimension of his typology of the kinds
of law, we can more briefly indicate the vertical axis which sepa-
rates the different levels of jural reality. This section of his paradigm
is based upon three depth levels, firstly, "law which is fixed in advance," secondly "flexible law which is developed ad hoc," and
finally, "intuitive law." These levels are correlated with the distinction that has already been encountered between "organized" and
"disorganized" law. This part of his typology may therefore be re-

duced, not without some degree of simplification, to the model presented in Figure 1.

The polar types upon which Gurvitch lays the greatest emphasis in this typology are "organized fixed law" and "intuitive spontaneous law." In his treatment of these we encounter an instance which bears out the criticism made previously that, despite his disavowal of value judgment, he does imply an evaluative rank ordering of the types and levels of jural reality. Organized fixed law, which corresponds to the widely held positivist conception of law as a fixed body of rules applied through authoritative procedures (lawyer's law), is characterized as "the most rigid and superficial level of jural reality" (pp. 178-79). His category of intuitive spontaneous law, which exists at a deeper level consists in the direct perception of normative facts by individuals such that they are absorbed into their conduct without the need for pressure, is described as "the most profound and dynamic level of jural reality" (p. 179). Thus, his conception of intuitive law is nothing more than the actually held values that are collectively accepted as standards of right conduct. Such a conception results in the equation of "law" with "values," but at the price of law ceasing to exist as a distinct social phenomenon.

Gurvitch fell into the trap which confronts any attempt to advance a sociological framework for the study of legal phenomena.

**Figure 1**

|  |  | TYPE OF LAW | |
|---|---|---|---|
|  |  | ORGANIZED LAW | DISORGANIZED LAW |
| D E P T H  L E V E L | **LAW FIXED IN ADVANCE** | **ORGANIZED FIXED LAW** lawyers law, made law (statutes, etc.) | **FIXED SPONTANEOUS LAW** customary law |
|  | **FLEXIBLE LAW** | **FLEXIBLE ORGANIZED LAW** —discretionary law | **FLEXIBLE SPONTANEOUS LAW** negotiated settlement of disputes |
|  | **INTUITIVE LAW** | **ORGANIZED INTUITIVE** judicial activism, filling 'gaps' | **INTUITIVE SPONTANEOUS LAW** "most profound" self-goverance |

This trap consists of the need, often achieved polemically, to overcome the barriers raised by a legalism which posits law as a self-contained phenomenon. The insistence upon a general sociological perspective has given rise to the temptation to submerge the sociological significance of the most highly visible elements of legal systems (statutes, litigation, procedures, courts, judges and sanctions).

Gurvitch goes further and elevates as the most profoundly "legal" that which by any other criteria has no necessary legal substance. The task of the sociology of law is not to cast the appellation "law" on all aspects of regularity in social governance, rather it is to seek to identify the specific effectivity of law and to determine the forms of mediation between law and other forms of social governance. The unity of the social process cannot be "proved" by appending a common label to such a wide variety of social phenomena such that the term "law" ceases to have any distinctive meaning. All that he achieves is to embrace the totality of social regulation within the framework of law. Gurvitch is not alone in falling into this trap; nor indeed are its consequences totally negative. This limitation may be understood as a necessary stage in the development of the sociology of law. For such an approach to legal phenomena to emerge, it has had to fight a protracted battle to overcome the narrowness of legal positivism. Hence, much of what has been claimed as sociology of law has not progressed beyond the polemical level of asserting the desirability of asking a different set of questions, and in so doing it has often lapsed into the habit of denigrating the perspectives and problems with which the jurists have sought to grapple.

Gurvitch arrives at the position where his exposition of the two dimensions of "fusion" and "pressure" allows him to complete his typology of kinds of law. With respect to the horizontal axis, he has twenty-seven logically possible categories, and in the vertical axis he has six types. Combining the two axes, there are, he concludes, 162 different kinds of law. The limited heuristic value of this typology is revealed in the fact that he undertakes no substantive discussion of any of this multiplicity of kinds of law. There is a very real temptation to dismiss the whole framework of Gurvitch's method and results. To do so would, however, fail to give recognition to the extent to which he succeeds in taking forward aspects of the necessary debate on the nature and classification of law.

## Differential Sociology of Law

Gurvitch designates the second level of sociological enquiry as "differential sociology." He is concerned with the jural consequences of the existence of social groups which have produced different kinds of laws. Social groups are constituted around a combination of a number of different types of sociality. He advances a classification of social groups with reference to the social functions they fulfil; his six types of groups are: kinship, locality, economic, non-lucrative, mystic-ecstatic, and friendship groups. Each social group engenders its own jural regulation, and therefore each group produces its corresponding "framework of law." His consideration of these frameworks is somewhat sketchy. What stands out most sharply is his anti-statist attitude. As against the conventional primacy attached to state law, he stresses the importance of "economic law," the jural regulation arising from economic activity, which competes effectively with "the political legal order."[10] Gurvitch employs this thesis to provide a sociological foundation for the contention that international law has primacy over national law. It is within international law, as opposed to state law, that he sees the true repository of social law. He does not deny the pervasiveness of state law, but rather he sets up international law as the model for social law that is condensed within democratic state law; and in so doing lays the groundwork for contemporary human rights theory. The democratic pluralistic society which is his ideal is conceived as being constituted by the fusion of state law and social law within a democratic institutional framework.

## The Legal Typology of Inclusive Societies

The second area of the differential sociology of law identified by Gurvitch is the study of the legal systems of inclusive societies. His analysis is built around a number of variables: firstly, the extent to which a particular type of social group plays a predominant role, and secondly with respect to a "mysticism-rationalism" dimension.[11] The third factor is the form of the segmentation of the inclusive society.

Gurvitch is insistent that his typology is constituted from ideal types and that "none of these types is to be found in a pure expression in history" (p. 205). However, he does appear to suggest that his final type of legal system, namely the "transitional system of law" of contemporary society, is not such an ideal type, but rather has an empirical existence.

Despite his ahistorical and anti-evolutionary methodology, he mirrors fairly closely a conventional socioeconomic stages of development model. Further, his typology is, in its main constituents, very similar to the transition from irrational to rational forms of law posited by Weber. Gurvitch's first stage is that of "polysegmentary societies having a magical-religious base" in which collective responsibility is emphasized in a manner reminiscent of Durkheim's mechanical solidarity; but he rejects the latter's emphasis upon repressive law, developing instead a view that approaches Malinowski's focus on reciprocity (Malinowski, [1928] 1961).

The second type of legal system is very explicitly Weberian, "legal systems of societies given homogeneity by the theocratic-charismatic principle." Such a system is characterized by the emergence of the priest-king and of patriarchal social structures. This type merges without any clear demarcation into a stage where the domestic political group has achieved preeminence, forming the root of the developing institution of a state form in which magical and religious factors play a declining role. This is followed by a stage that is more explicitly a sociohistorical designation: the "law of feudal society" characterized by a hierarchized federation of patriarchal groups resting upon semi-rational and semi-mystical bases. Whereas more conventional views emphasize processes of standardization and centralization of law at this stage, Gurvitch stresses the pluralism of law in feudal society, with its overlapping and competing jurisdictions in which, for example, the central courts of the feudal state compete with ecclesiastical courts on the one hand and the municipal or guild courts on the other.

The stage which Gurvitch sees as fully reflecting the centralizing tendencies in law is that of systems of unified law associated with the predominance of either the city or the empire. Such legal systems are more rational and more secularized and reach their logical expression in the sixth type of legal system. This is one based on the predominance of the nation state. Such systems manifest rationality and secularization and "correspond to the classic capitalist regime from the sixteenth century to the end of the nineteenth century" (p. 221). At this stage, state or public law and the law of contract reach a high level of development, and inter-individual law comes to predominate over social law.

Gurvitch's seventh and final type is the most problematic. Under the label "transitional system of law of contemporary society," he discusses the characteristics of legal systems that exist within the framework of "organized capitalism," in which a central role is played by giant industrial enterprises, "vast organizations of domination," and as a reflex, trade unions and other forms of collective organizations are formed. He sees, very much under the influence of contemporaneous political events, two alternative paths of development: one towards fascism, characterized by the desperate efforts of the state to integrate both big business and labor within itself. The other possibility is towards a pluralistic society, a form of democratic syndicalism, expressing his commitment to social law, that seeks to realize the "development of the autonomous collaborative groups of economic activity which will one day be called on to limit the state itself" (p. 225).

It is undeniable that much of his discussion of the "transitional stage" is speculative, consisting of an imposition of political value judgments upon an apparently analytical model of types of legal systems. Yet he finds it immediately necessary to deny this and, in the same breath, to assert the self-evident truth of his value judgments. The passage is sufficiently revealing to quote at length:

> The sociology of law, like all sociology is concerned neither with predicting nor with evaluating the future.... The only thing which appears to us beyond question is the fact that the tendency towards pluralistic democracy is the most favorable to jural culture, to the safeguarding of the autonomy of social control through law contrasted with other spheres of control and regulation. (p. 225)

Closely associated with his observations on the types of legal systems is a brief chapter on "genetic sociology of law." This is concerned with the regularities and tendencies of change within legal systems; it is what might be labeled general theory. Gurvitch reviews some of the major developmental theories of law, rejecting Maine's status-to-contract theory, and also Durkheim's repressive-restitutive thesis, as well as Weber's irrational-rational model. In the place of these universalistic models, he maintains that each stage has it own tendencies. The features that Gurvitch indicates appear so particularistic that they are unable to take us beyond a purely descriptive sociology. Yet this feature of his discussion stands out as having a merit not contained within evolutionary models of legal development. He is at pains to stress the contradictory facets of the process of legal development, a manifestation of his dialectical sociology. Such an approach, although only sketched, deserves greater elaboration as a necessary corrective to the overwhelmingly unilinear models that have dominated the sociology of law.

Gurvitch views the major dynamics of legal systems as residing in the tensions and conflicts between various kinds of law and levels of depth. In addition, in a classically pluralist manner, he stresses the role of extra-legal factors in legal development paying special attention to ecology, economics, religion, and collective psychology. While, true to the pluralist tradition, he formally denies causal priority to any one factor, in practice he appears to concede it to collective psychology:

> [T]he most profound layer of social reality, penetrating all its manifestations and aspects, the collective mentality is virtually present underneath all the factors just enumerated. Collective psychology indirectly influences law through religion, morality, knowledge and even through economics and the morphological basis of society. (p. 238)

In the final analysis, Gurvitch seeks the determinants of the interrelation between law and society in a theoretical position fraught with all the conceptual and methodological problems inherent in a view that approximates a "group mind" or "collective conscience" concept. Gurvitch stumbles on the Achilles' heel of sociology: the problem of avoiding the inherently anti-social and atomistic pitfalls of methodological individualism, without, in reaction, lapsing into the over-organic view of society as existing above and beyond its participants. Insofar as it concerns his treatment of legal phenomena, Gurvitch's framework and his addiction to complex typologies results in a certain loss of contact with the empirical world, such that his work becomes arid and far removed from its purported empiricism. As a consequence, in his search for explanation and analysis of law, he gropes backwards through the depth of social reality attempting to grasp at some ultimate essence of reality. In the course of what must ultimately be regarded as a frustrating journey, he succeeds nevertheless in turning over some fruitful stones. It has been suggested that the most fruitful of these is a more dynamic approach which recognizes, without exploring, the role of conflict and contradiction, with respect to both the development and functioning of legal systems.

## VII. Conclusion

It would be wrong to dismiss Gurvitch on the grounds of his lack of subsequent impact upon the development of the sociology of law. No school applauds his contributions; few commemorative plaques in the form of footnotes in scholarly works record his achievements. Yet the very causes which underlay the rapidity of his passage into obscurity are the same that currently mark the theoretical frailty of modern sociology of law. Their weaknesses and deficiencies are the enduring weaknesses of mainstream sociology of law.

It is to be hoped that the foregoing discussion establishes that Gurvitch was no mere cipher for a self-evidently defective sociology of law; he certainly cannot be dismissed as mere purveyor of consensus theory to be dispatched with a few swift conflict blows. He offers to readers today a systematic theorization capable of providing some grounding for the again influential quest for a pluralist theory of law. Gurvitch's pronounced commitment to the syndicalist project of social law which was at its lowest ebb in the present text is still sufficiently present for it to serve as a beacon of the ongoing quest for a transformative vision of law.

## Notes

1. I have offered a detailed account of this trajectory that I called the "sociological movement of law" (Hunt, 1978).
2. For general accounts of Gurvitch's general sociology, see Balandier, 1975; Bosserman, 1968; Lemert, 1981; Swedberg, 1982. Since it largely post-dates Gurvitch's contributions to the sociology of law, I make no attempt to discuss this body of work in detail.
3. Engels' argument draws on Marx's discussion of the distinction between "political emancipation" within bourgeois civil society and its encapsulation in legal rights, and "human emancipation" which requires the transcendence of civil society and bourgeois right (Marx, [1843] 1975).
4. This volume combined a translation of much of *L'Expérience Juridique*, along with added elements involving a discussion of English-language sociology of law not present in the earlier text.
5. A similar criticism may be made of his "dialectical method." In practice, it does not amount to a detailed methodological prescription, but is rather an assertion of his multidimensional and pluralistic framework.
6. The concept "justice" plays an important role in Gurvitch's thought (1953a). Much influenced by Proudhon, he saw it as a means of effecting an equilibrium between "individualism" and "universalism." It is thus conceived not as a metaphysical standard with respect to which positive law may be evaluated, but rather as one of the elements of law itself. It is viewed as an intermediary between morals and law.
7. Corresponding to the mass, community, communion typology, he advances distinct forms of sociality, namely "rapprochement," "separation," and "combination of rapprochement and separation." Although not developed, this classification is one of the few points at which Gurvitch draws attention to conflict as well as integration in the forms of social relations.

8.    The tone of Gurvitch's discussion of "communion social law" suggests a close parallel with Weber's concept of charisma, associated as it is with the intensity of personal involvement and an inherent instability resulting from the difficulty of institutionalizing charismatic authority.
9.    A similar configuration of fusion and pressure is found in Timasheff's juxtapositioning of ethical and imperative elements in law (Timasheff, 1936).
10.   In this respect there is an interesting convergence with the Soviet jurist Evgeny B. Pashukanis (1980) who similarly stressed the primary link between economic and legal relations and with whom Gurvitch shared a commitment to the "withering away of law."
11.   Gurvitch acknowledges a close proximity to Weber's rational-irrational dichotomy.

# References

Balandier, Georges. 1975. *Gurvitch*. Oxford: Basil Blackwell.
Black, Donald J. 1976. *The Behavior of Law*. New York: Academic Press.
Bosserman, Phillip. 1968. *Dialectical Sociology: An Analysis of the Sociology of Georges Gurvitch*. Boston: Sargent.
Bourdieu, Pierre. 1987. "The Force of Law: Toward a Sociology of the Juridical Field." *Hastings Law Journal* 38: 805-53.
Derrida, Jacques. 1990. "Force of Law: The 'Mystical Foundation of Authority.'" *Cardozo Law Review* 11: 919-1045.
Durkheim, Émile. [1893] 1964. *The Division of Labor in Society*. New York: Free Press of Glencoe.
Ehrlich, Eugen. [1936] 1962. *Fundamental Principles of the Sociology of Law*. New York: Russell and Russell.
Engels, Frederick. 1977. "Juridical Socialism." *Politics and Society* 7: 203-220.
Ewald, François. 1986. "A Concept of Social Law," pp. 40-75. In Gunther Teubner (ed.) *Dilemmas of Law in the Welfare State*. Berlin: de Gruyter.
Goldmann, Lucien. 1969. *The Human Sciences and Philosophy*. London: Jonathan Cape.
Gurvitch, Georges. 1932a. *L'Idée du Droit Social: Nation et Système du Droit Social: Histoire Doctrinale Depuis le XVIIe Siècle Jusqu'à la Fin du XIXe Siècle*. Paris: Libraire du Recueil Sirey.
_____. 1932b. *Le Temps Présent et l'Idée du Droit Social*. Paris: Vrin.
_____. 1935. *L'Expérience Juridique et la Philosophe Pluraliste du Droit*. Paris: Editions A. Pedone.
_____. 1940. "Major Problems of the Sociology of Law." *Journal of Social Philosophy* 6: 197-215.
_____. 1941. "The Problem of Social Law." *International Journal of Ethics* 52: 17-40.
_____. 1942a. "Magic and Law." *Social Research* 9: 104-22.
_____. 1942b. "Democracy as a Sociological Problem." *Journal of Legal and Political Sociology* 1: 46-71.
_____. 1944. *La Déclaration des Droits Sociaux*. New York: Editions de la Maison Française.
_____. 1946. *The Bill of Social Rights*. New York: International Universities Press.
_____. 1950. *La Vocation Actuelle de la Sociologie: Vers une Sociologie Différentialle*. Paris: Presses Universitaires de France.
_____. 1953a. "Justice," pp. 504-514. In Edwin R.A. Seligman and Alvin Johnson (eds.) *Encyclopedia of the Social Sciences*, Vol. VIII. New York: Macmillan.
_____. 1953b. "Natural Law," pp. 284-290. In Edwin R.A. Seligman and Alvin Johnson (eds.) *Encyclopedia of the Social Sciences*, Vol. XI. New York: Macmillan.

_____. 1955. *Détermismes Sociaux et Liberté Humaine: Vers l'Etude Sociologique des Cheminements de la Liberté*. Paris: Presses Universitaires de France, Paris.

_____. 1962. *Dialectique et sociologie*. Paris: Flammarion.

_____. 1969. "My Intellectual Itinerary or 'Excluded From the Horde.'" *Sociological Abstracts* 17:i-xiii.

Gurvitch, Georges, and Wilbert E. Moore (eds.). 1945. *Twentieth Century Sociology*. New York: Philosophical Library.

Habermas, Jürgen. 1987. *The Theory of Communicative Action: Vol.II, Lifeworld and System*. Boston: Beacon Press.

_____. 1996. *Between Facts and Norms: Contributions to a Discourse Theory of Law and Democracy*. Cambridge, MA: MIT Press.

Hunt, Alan. 1978. *The Sociological Movement in Law*. London: Macmillan.

Lemert, Charles C. (ed.). 1981. *French Sociology*. New York: Columbia University Press.

Malinowski, Bronislaw. [1928] 1961. *Crime and Custom in Savage Society*. London: Routledge & Kegan Paul.

Marx, Karl. [1843] 1975. "On the Jewish Question," pp. 146-174. In *Karl Marx, Frederick Engels Collected Works*, Vol. III. London: Lawrence & Wishart.

Pashukanis, Evgeny B. 1980. *Pashukanis: Selected Writings on Marxism and Law,* edited by Piers Beirne and Robert Sharlet. London: Academic Press.

Swedberg, Richard. 1982. *Sociology as Disenchantment: The Evolution of the Work of Georges Gurvitch*. Atlantic Heights: Humanities Press.

Timasheff, N.S. 1936. *An Introduction to the Sociology of Law*. Cambridge, MA: Harvard University Press.

Wilson, Everett. 1962. "Review of Gurvitch *Traite de Sociologie*." *American Journal of Sociology* 68: 251-255.

# 8

# On Nicholas S. Timasheff, *An Introduction to the Sociology of Law*

*A. Javier Treviño*

## I. The Place of N. S. Timasheff in the Sociology of Law

Although the term "sociology of law" was coined by the Italian legal philosopher Dionisio Anzilotti in 1892, and Eugen Ehrlich's *Grundlegung einer Soziologie des Rechts* appeared as early as 1913, to date the sociology of law has not formally recognized its founders.[1] Several scholars, however, have made a case for bestowing that honor on, among others, the exiled Russian sociologist and legal scholar Nicholas S. Timasheff. Scheuer, for example, states that, "Timasheff, if not the founding father himself, can accordingly be placed among those who are the founding fathers of modern sociology of law" (1965: 435). Bierstedt (1970) identifies Timasheff, along with Roscoe Pound, Eugen Ehrlich, and Leon Petrazycki, as a "founder" of the sociology of law. Sheskin describes Timasheff as being "among the first to attempt the delimitation of the sociology of law" (1978: 116). Hunt considers him to be "one of the earlier pioneers of theoretical sociology of law" (1993: 62). More recently, I have included Timasheff, in company with Ehrlich, Petrazycki, and Georges Gurvitch, as one the "Eastern-European pioneers" of legal sociology (Treviño, 1998).

To be sure, Timasheff's place in the forefront of the sociology of law was established with the publication, in 1939, of his *An Introduction to the Sociology of Law*. However, despite the appearance of this important treatise—one of the earliest in the field—Timasheff's influence has not endured for several reasons. First, even though

Timasheff, up until the end of his career, hoped to release *Introduction* as a new edition in which he expected to make revisions, many of the key ideas contained in the book became passé almost immediately upon publication. This was primarily due to two factors.

Perhaps out of deference to his Russian compatriot, Ivan Pavlov, Timasheff's simplistic application of the behavioristic viewpoint to his sociolegal theory never progressed beyond an outdated Pavlovian reflexology. Thus, while Timasheff's application of Pavlov's theory of conditioned reflexes can adequately explain the fixation and automatism of legal behavior, it cannot explain the emotional character of the ethical motivation that contributes to that behavior.

In addition, Timasheff wrote *Introduction* during a very inauspicious period in history: just prior to Allied-Axis involvement in World War II and at a time when legal issues (e.g., genocide) and legal organizations (e.g., international legal tribunals) were on the cusp of undergoing developments and transformations of seismic proportion. In short, many of Timasheff's views on the social reality of law were quickly outrun by changes in behavioral psychology, the legal field, and world history.

A second reason for Timasheff's relative lack of recognition in the sociology of law is that following in the classical European tradition which was his heritage, he wrote on a wide variety of issues, most notably and most frequently about current events in Soviet Russia. This diversity of interests detracted both attention and time from his contributions to legal sociology. Third, Timasheff's writings on sociolegal matters—the majority of which where published during the 1930s and 1940s—did not always appear in mainstream sociological journals where they would be easily accessible to legal sociologists; rather they were published in law reviews and marginal periodicals that all but guaranteed their obscurity. Finally, there is the issue of religious prejudice. During most of his American career Timasheff was associated with Fordham, a Catholic university. Shortly after accepting the appointment at Fordham, Timasheff's life-long friend, Pitirim Sorokin, warned him that the stigma of being associated with a Catholic institution would prevent Timasheff from obtaining the distinction he deserved. Toward the end of his life, Timasheff admitted that Sorokin had been partially correct in this regard.

These, then, are some of the reasons why Timasheff has remained only a footnote in the annals of the sociology of law. This situation is regrettable because, as will be seen in section VI, Timasheff's work has the potential to be of great significance to contemporary sociology of law.

## II. Timasheff: The Man and His Work

Born in St. Petersburg on November 9, 1886, Nikolai Sergeyevitch Timasheff came from an old family of Russian nobility. His father served as the Minister of Trade and Industry under the Czar. On the basis of family tradition and personal inclination the young Timasheff was expected to follow in his father's footsteps and pursue a career in public administration. Circumstances and opportunities, however, eventually put him on a very different trajectory, one that culminated in Timasheff being recognized for his scholarly contributions to a variety of topics relevant to many scholarly fields including jurisprudence and sociology.

For all intents and purposes Timasheff's career path was set when he matriculated at the University of St. Petersburg and became a student, friend, and later, colleague, of the Russo-Polish jurist Petrazycki. This intellectual and personal relationship with Petrazycki was to have a significant impact on Timasheff's sociolegal thinking throughout his life work. Indeed, in 1947 Timasheff wrote a thoughtful and sensitive piece explaining his mentor's legal philosophy, and in 1955 he prepared the lengthy introduction to the English translation of Petrazycki's *Law and Morality*.

For his *magister* (master's) degree, which he received from the University of St. Petersburg in 1910, Timasheff wrote his thesis on the history of probation. It is noteworthy that his interest in this topic continued for some decades and eventually led to the publication of two monographs, *One Hundred Years of Probation* (1943) and *Probation in Light of Criminal Statistics* (1949). In 1914 Timasheff completed his dissertation on an analysis of criminal propaganda and was awarded the LL.D. Two years later he began teaching sociological jurisprudence at the University of St. Petersburg.

There is no doubt that owing to Petrazycki's influence Timasheff developed an interest in the sociology of law. Following, the Dean of the School of Law at the University asked him to offer a course on the subject. Outside of the outstanding exception of Eugen Ehrlich in Vienna, Timasheff was quite likely only the second scholar to ever teach the sociology of law.

But Timasheff's involvement with the law was not limited to academe. In 1915 the Minister of Justice appointed a committee—of which Timasheff was a member—to draft a law on enacting the Russian penal code of 1903. Their efforts did not bear fruit because the March revolution of 1917 broke out before the draft could be completed. Timasheff then worked for the Provisional Government drafting a law introducing necessary changes into the Russian criminal code. He was specifically entrusted with the preparation of a clause, concerning subversive propaganda, that made punishable public incitement of the violent overthrow of the democratic government. In an ironic twist of fate the Provisional Government declined Timasheff's draft on the grounds that it was undemocratic—a few months later the Bolsheviks overthrew the Provisional Government. Not surprisingly, from that point on Timasheff appears to have strengthened his conviction that a powerful central authority is essential to the law's efficacy.

Following the October revolution which had given power to the communists, Timasheff was appointed Professor of Sociology and Dean of the Law School at the Polytechnical Institute of St. Petersburg where he lectured on sociological jurisprudence. However, in 1921 he was implicated in an anti-Soviet conspiracy (the Tagantsev affair) and the following year had to flee his natal country under the threat of arrest and execution, and was never again to return. He subsequently emigrated to Germany where he wrote for French, Swiss, and Russian newspapers and, in 1923, was appointed Professor of Criminal Law at the University of Prague.

From 1928 to 1936 Timasheff lived in Paris and lectured at the Slavic Institute of the Sorbonne and at the Franco-Russian Institute of Political and Social Science. In 1932 he began his collaboration with fellow Russian émigré and sociologist, Pitirim A. Sorokin, on the monumental four-volume treatise, *Social and Cultural Dymanics*, for which Timasheff provided much of the material on war and revolution and the fluctuations in law. The two had known each other since their student days in St. Petersburg. At Sorokin's invitation Timasheff moved to the United States in 1936 and lectured for several years at Harvard (where Sorokin was chair of the Sociology Department) on the sociology of law and on modern social movements. In 1940 Timasheff joined the faculty of arts and sciences at Fordham University where he taught courses in the sociology of law, criminology, and Russian constitutions. Three years later he was naturalized as a U.S. citizen. During 1955-56 Timasheff lived in the Netherlands as a visiting (Fulbright) Professor at the University of Gröningen, during which time he conducted research on the Dutch penal system. Timasheff retired from Fordham in 1957 and after a long illness, died in Mt. Vernon, New York, on March 9, 1970.

It is estimated that during his long and distinguished career, Timasheff published hundreds of newspaper articles, about three hundred book reviews, approximately two hundred scholarly articles, and eighteen books (in several languages) on a wide-range of topics including law, jurisprudence, the sociology of law, probation, penology, the sociology of war and revolution, religion, ideology, sociological theory, social methodology, and post-revolutionary Russia. His most well-known works include *Religion in Soviet Russia, 1917-1942* (1942), *The Great Retreat: The Growth and Decline of Communism in Russia* (1946), and *Sociological Theory: Its Nature and Growth* (1955).

Timasheff's sociolegal ideas, including his running commentary on the sociolegal ideas of other scholars (in particular those of his early colleagues at the University of St. Petersburg, Gurvitch and Petrazycki) are to be found scattered in several articles (1922 [1964]; 1937a; 1937b; 1938a; 1938b; 1939a; 1939b; 1940; 1941; 1942; 1944; 1946; 1947; 1955; 1957) written over a period of about twenty years. However, the magnum opus in which he endeavored to articulate a systematic legal sociology is *An Introduction to the Sociology of Law*.

### III. *An Introduction to the Sociology of Law*

Between 1916-1920, while lecturing in sociological jurisprudence at the Polytechnical Institute of St. Petersburg, Timasheff sketched the first draft of *Introduction*. The manuscript, however, was lost when he fled Russia in 1921. The following year he published (in Russian) an essay, "Law as a Social Psychological Phenomenon," in which he attempted to orient the sociology of law to social psychology rather than to individual psychology. This essay comprised the book's fundamental ideas. Nearly fifteen years later, while lecturing on the sociology of law at Harvard, Timasheff resumed work on the project. The effort resulted, with Sorokin's help in arranging publication, in the appearance, in 1939, of *An Introduction to the Sociology of Law*.

The book's primer-like title is misleading as it gives the false impression that the volume is merely a textbook intended for classroom use. *An Introduction to the Sociology of Law*, however, is much more than this. It is, in fact, a sophisticated treatise that does nothing less than explain, precisely and methodically, the law's efficacy as a social force. More specifically, and more significant for the sociology of law, the volume makes two general points: (1) that law can, indeed must, be studied by sociology, and (2) that law is a combination of socio-ethical coordination and imperative coordination of behavior.

It may be asserted with confidence that one continuing thread that runs throughout *Introduction* is Timasheff's interest in the dialectical interplay between the positive law and the living law: the understanding and appreciation of the law's verbal formulas in conjunction with and opposition to its normative facts. To be sure, Hunt (1979) maintains that Timasheff's and Gurvitch's work share an interest in this dualism that affects the law—which I refer to as the dialectical interplay between positive law and living law—and explains it as follows:

> The common strand in [Timasheff's and Gurvitch's] respective sociologies of law is at root a continuation of the efforts, very apparent in the work of Weber, to find a resolution or integration of the dualism which is conceived as so markedly affecting law. It is the apparent dualism between law as a *positive* institution resting upon the framework of social power, while at the same time being a system of values or *norms* having some compelling internal strength and validity. (Hunt, 1979: 170, emphasis added)

Generally and simply, positive law (*jus positivum*) consists of statutes enacted or recognized by an external authority—a political superior or a sovereign. As Austin states, "Every positive law...is set, directly or circuitously, by a sovereign person or body, to a member or members of the independent political society wherein that person or body is sovereign or supreme" (1961: 405). Positive law is enforced in the courts and other tribunals. Furthermore, it is created by legislative, judicial, and administrative acts or by legal transactions (Kelsen, 1945: 115). According to Kelsen, the key to law's positivity "lies in the fact that it is created and annulled by acts of human beings" (1945: 114). Consequently, the greater the amount of formal and authoritative interference in law, the greater its degree of positivity.

By contrast, the living law is not dependent on an external authority but rather on the expression of ethical group conviction. The term "living law" (*lebendes Recht*) is widely used by Ehrlich who defines it as the law which dominates life itself even though it has not been posited in legal propositions. The source of our knowledge of this law is, first, the modern legal document; secondly, direct observation of life, of commerce, of customs and usages, and of all associations, not only of those that the law has recognized but also of those that it has overlooked and passed by, indeed even of those that it has disapproved. (1936: 493)

Timasheff's characterization of law as "ethico-imperative coordination" brings together the spheres of power and ethics. Accordingly, he considers the law's positive *and* living qualities.[2]

On the one hand, Timasheff contends that law is supported by power or authority. Power, or the imperative coordination of behavior, has a positivistic stamp to it as it entails an "external excitation" such as the act of the dominator through imperative words or gestures or through physical force. Social power, moreover, requires organized active power centers as well as a complex of interrelated individuals as a necessary condition for the law's externalization and "objectivity." This objectivity results from the fact that individuals have a tendency to reify transpersonal hierarchical power structures.

On the other hand, according to Timasheff, law possesses an ethical-normative element. An ethical system involves custom and morals: two forces that have their origins in the living law exhibited as the group conviction concerning duty of behavior. The nucleus of the ethical substructure of law, Timasheff makes clear, is that "no legal system has ever existed in which at least a large part of the fundamental rules would not have been directly recognized by large numbers of citizens as conducive to the common good" (1941: 246).

For Timasheff, positive law consists of legal propositions that are decreed by an external, organized authority that has achieved objectification—namely, the state. The law's positivity has to do with the extent to which it has been formally and logically manipulated by such an authority. Conversely, the living law (the ethical aspect of Timasheff's ethico-imperative coordination), that is, the law as it actually lives in society, may generally be characterized as customary, unwritten, and de facto. The law's deductive derivation from custom and morals (two categories of ethics), reflects these living qualities. Timasheff's ideas about the law in life and how it sometimes supplements but usually contradicts the law in the books is expressed in four theoretical themes that underlie *An Introduction to the Sociology of Law*.

## IV. Four Theoretical Themes

I maintain that Timasheff's focus on the dialectic between positive ("state law") and living law ("social law") is based on the four themes that inform his legal sociology in *Introduction*: antiformalism, normative study, functional control, and psychogenics. Although these theoretical themes are interrelated, for analytical purposes they may be considered as being distinct and will be discussed in turn.[3]

### Antiformalism

Timasheff's legal sociology emerged in direct opposition to the formalist jurisprudence prevalent, at least in the United States, from shortly after the Civil War until about the 1940s. Legal formalism—a view epitomized by John Austin who defined law, very simply and without regard to social factors, as the command of a sovereign—refers to the process whereby judges derive legal rules from abstract principles and then mechanically apply those rules, through logical and deductive reasoning, in deciding the outcome of a case. By the turn of the twentieth century legal formalism had created a system of law that was highly rational, autonomous, and conceptualist.

It is noteworthy that Timasheff wrote *An Introduction to the Sociology of Law* while at Harvard during the late 1930s, for this was the milieu in which the sociological jurisprudence of Roscoe Pound (who served as Dean of Harvard Law School until 1936) dominated legal scholarship. In Pound's view, legal formalism's overly scientific bent had transformed lawmaking and judicial decision-making into an abstract and artificial enterprise. He maintained that legal formalism's conceptual and technical nature had created a discrepancy between the positive law (law in books) and the more down-to-earth sentiments of the American people (law in fact). Pound's impact on Timasheff is apparent in that he cites no less than nineteen of Pound's works.

What is more, *Introduction* also bears the indelible imprint of legal realism. (Legal realist Hessel E. Yntema read the entire manuscript and made suggestions for improvement.) Perhaps the central characteristic of legal realism is its pragmatic approach which underscores the law's social and psychological realities. One of these realities is that judges are not confined to following abstract principles in deciding a case but rather frequently employ their discretionary powers. Timasheff firmly believed that completely eliminating the personal element from legal power structures—such as the discretionary power of judges and officials—posed a "danger for democracy" because in such a society persons with a strong tendency to dominate others "would be inclined to create a type of domination more suited to their preferences" (p. 212). Timasheff's approbation of the personal element made possible by antiformalism no doubt stemmed from his personal legislative experiences with the Provisional Government, and its subsequent demise:

> The Provisional Government consisted of persons inclined toward ultrademocratic theories. To show personal domination and to make use of force seemed to them to violate the principles of democracy. This might have been harmless in a country where everybody held the same views; but this was not the case. There were people there with clearly articulated inclinations toward becoming rulers of the personal type, namely the Communist leaders. And almost without struggle they became dominators of the country and proceeded to rule it in an absolutely undemocratic way. (p. 212)

Thus, having been influenced by Pound's emphasis on the law in fact, by American legal realism's pragmatic legal realties, and by his own personal experience in Russia, Timasheff's legal sociology is decidedly antiformalist in that it does not focus only on rational, or "scientifically grounded," legislation, rather, he examines seriously the law's free, intuitive, and discretionary aspects. That is to say, Tiamsheff considers the living law.[4]

In *Introduction* Timasheff locates the law's antiformalism in the realm of the collective ethical *ought*. This "oughtness" (that which binds individual consciousness into collective consciousness) that Timasheff attributes to law pervades his legal sociology, but it is perhaps nowhere more evident than in his concept of the self-limitation of power. According to Timasheff, a true legal order is possible to the extent that the political state rules by restraint. Only in such a situation is there found the real union of ethics and power (ethicized power, as it were) that constitutes the law.

The point that Timasheff continuously drives home is that law exists only as long as it is recognized by an active power center (the exercise of authority), which in modern society is typically the state, its administration and tribunals. This important premise, however, appears to be the exception in the case of international law, given that it lacks the support of a similar centralized power. Even in today's climate of the global village, neither the United Nations nor the international conference comes anywhere close to wielding the same

law-making authority as does the political state of a liberal democracy. It is, to be sure, questionable whether international legal rules
do in fact constitute the highest form of law. Even the "supernorms"
currently popular among international legal scholars, have not been
specified much less put into practice. The real problem, however, is
that there is no universal, supreme authority to justify or enforce
these supernorms or any other type of international law. And, since
Timasheff believes that a legal order must be engendered by power,
by coercive sanctions, "the question arises as to how it can be
maintained that [international laws] are of a truly legal nature"
(Olivecrona, 1948: 190). Timasheff's answer is that there are
sanctions (aside from socio-ethical pressure and official force)
that stem from the self-limitation of power and consequently
numerous informal, extra-legal motives restrict the tendency of
active power centers to violate the rules of international law.
Among these motives, which are grounded not in formal procedures but in the group's ethical conviction, is the resistance of
the people. Timasheff is convinced that the people (in the case of
constitutional law) or the international community (in the case of
international law) would simply not tolerate a situation of gross social injustice perpetrated by dominators through a failure to circum-
scribe their own authority.

Unfortunately, Timasheff's position on the self-limitation of power
takes him beyond the ethical practicalities and procedural formali-
ties of both the living and the positive law and, if not exactly into the
world of idealism, at least into the realm of the improbable. Self-
limitation by dominators has seldom been realized, at least not in
most of the cases of mass proportion. Despite the deterrent intentions of the Nuremberg Trials, the United Nations Genocide Treaty,
and the International War Crimes Tribunal, the post-Holocaust world
has nevertheless witnessed large-scale human rights abuses perpetrated on thousands of people by the governments of the Soviet
Union, China, Argentina, and Chile—to say nothing of Guatemala,
El Salvador, Cambodia, Rwanda, and Bosnia. Excepting those who
based their rule on "the One" (for example, Marcos in the Philip-
pines, Ceausescu in Romania, and Noriega in Panama, who were
deposed, at least in part, by the "mass" of citizens in those countries), in most cases neither the people nor the international community can or do take the necessary measures to stop the atrocities of
despotic government. However, Timasheff's point, even if it diverges

from the facts more often than not, is that the living law's free, intuitive, and customary—that is, antiformalist—aspects are evoked, not by impersonal rules, but when "the people" or "the international community" are compelled, by a moral belief based on what should or should not be, to rectify a perceived injustice.

## Normative Study

The "oughtness" exhibited in Timasheff's antiformalism is also manifested in the fact that, much like Weber, who considered *values* in reference to social action, he sees the study of *values* and *norms* as crucial to understanding law. Two points, however, need to be made in this regard. First, much to his credit, Timasheff avoids the common error—made by Ehrlich, Gurvitch, and Sorokin—of ascribing legal character to all socially recognized norms, or models of right conduct. This inclination to define the legal so broadly that it overtakes the study of custom serves only to muddy the theoretical waters as it unduly conflates jurisprudence with sociology. Despite his struggle in dealing with the interrelation between unoffical (living) law and official (positive) law, Timasheff, by contrast, does not lose sight of the crucial fact that while all legal norms are social, not all social norms are legal in character.

Second, although Timasheff persistently analyzes law as embodying the normative character of oughtness, he does not believe that the sociology of law should be a normative endeavor. For Timasheff, the sociology of law is not a normative science but a nomographic one that attempts to discover and explain recurring patterns—uniformities—in social phenomena. Contrary to the philosophy of law, the sociology of law cannot be involved with evaluating the ultimate ends to be attained by law:

> The sociology of law can formulate propositions in which the ends of positive legal regulations would be stated. But whether one or another of these ends should be pursued by law, whether within the competition of ultimate end systems (for instance, those of conservatism, liberalism, socialism, or fascism) this or that system should be preferred, can never be decided by scientific methods, such questions being beyond the scope of science. (p. 30)

This rejection of legal sociology's normative application notwithstanding, Timasheff makes it clear that the sociology of law should not ignore the fact that "law is related to the world of values" (p. 367) and "that values are recognized by men who accept for guidance norms oriented towards the realization of these values" (1941:

234). In other words, while the sociology of law does not prescribe norms and values, it does study them.

Timasheff's indication of the study of norms and values is salient in his analysis of ethical norms, or those rules that show the correct ways of actually behaving. No doubt inspired by Sorokin's notion that law and morals are the two subsystems of the system of ethics, Timasheff contends that behavior defined under categories of ethics is referred to as morals and custom. Law, moreover, is also a branch of ethics and is defined deductively from morals and custom.

In the case of custom, the individual complies with the system of rules only because of the socio-ethical pressure that he or she receives from others. Here, there is no power center (authority) exerting sanctions on the individual's behavior nor is the individual possessed of an inner conviction of duty. Custom, Timasheff contends, has to do with those rules of decency and politeness that inform people's everyday behavior and interactions. An example of a customary rule is the expectation that we will greet acquaintances when meeting them. Alternatively, morals are connected to the great religious or philosophical movements such as Christianity, ancient Greek philosophy, and Communism. Unlike custom, moral norms demand an "internal conviction"—an internalized (psychological) agreement—on the part of the individual. Consequently, in addition to socio-ethical pressure, another, more internal sanction is found in morals: remorse. Because remorse afflicts the conscience of the wayward individual, the first step which that individual must take toward reconciliation with the group is confession. Finally, law relies on the involvement of both custom and morals; and this is precisely why it derives its operative nature from "oughtness." This reliance on custom and morals gives law its special ethico-normative character.

*Functional Control*

Even the casual reader of *An Introduction to the Sociology of Law* is certain to note that Timasheff's legal theory repeatedly utilizes the notion of functional control; in other words, he relies heavily on the concept of social control in combination with a functionalist analysis of law and society. In accordance with his views, social control may be seen as a power that imposes its authority on persons or groups for the express purpose of coordinating, regulating, and constraining their behavior. Moreover, this power may be—but is not necessarily—coercive (in the form of physical force or psychological pressure) in that it enforces social rules and punishes those who violate them.[5]

Additionally, Timasheff's functionalist orientation allows him to view social control as having positive consequences for the total social system. Thus, for him, social control leads to conformity and uniformity of behavior and helps, therefore, to develop and maintain order, integration, and equilibrium in society. Indeed, Timasheff describes society in functionalist terms: "as a system in socio-ethical equilibrium" (p. 112). The most general function of law, as ethico-imperative coordination of human behavior, is to create social "order," expressed vicariously as "peace," "security," and "organization." As Hunt remarks, "[Timasheff] advances an 'equilibrium' or 'social order' model of society as a concrete system with an inherent tendency towards social equilibrium. He conceived society as responding with a Pavlovian reflex to anything that disturbs that equilibrium" (1979: 191). In addition to a Pavlovian influence, Timasheff's notion of social equilibrium is decidedly Paretian:

> The role of law securing equilibrium is obvious. Criminal law inhibits drives to violate it and, if the inhibition is insufficient, reinforces the totality of basic sentiments [behavior tendencies]. Civil law secures and, eventually, restores that distribution of goods and of services in which the social equilibrium is expressed. Constitutional law secures the distribution of dominance and submission within the social system. By many parts of modern "social law" the degree of co-operation attained in a given society is secured, etc. (Timasheff, 1940: 149)

Timasheff sees law as a "social force" that, with the support of an organized power structure, imposes on people certain norms of conduct for the purpose of producing uniformity and conformity in their behavior. To be sure, *without* law individual activities "would interfere with each other," but *with* law they "are transformed according to patterns which make them mutually compatible" (p. 334). Thus, only through law can social order be realized. Timasheff describes order as "a set of rules of conduct which the members [of a society] are supposed to follow and the violations of which are disapproved and reacted upon by the other members" (1946: 822).

He further maintains that legal relations between people are possible in large measure because these relations entail a "situation of having to act under actual or potential coercion" (p. 331). Simply put, people sometimes fulfill their legal duties (contractual obligations) toward each other because they fear sanctions. Although

Durkheim did not regard the contract as primarily coercive, he did point out, in similar fashion to Timasheff, that contractual law serves to maintain social equilibrium by regulating and determining the contract's legal outcome. It does this by constraining the bargaining parties to respect each others' rights and duties. For both Durkheim and Timasheff, the uniformity of behavior—brought about through the social force of law—is crucial to maintaining the equilibrium of society.

Given that Timasheff regards the sociology of law as a nomographic science that analyzes the uniformity of phenomena, in his consideration of functional control he distinguishes between three main types of behavioral uniformities. First, "natural uniformities" occur when similar causes produce similar effects, without efforts to create and enforce a uniformity. They have to do with those sets of similar acts (e.g., crimes, suicides, divorces) caused by factors external to the individual (e.g., poverty, rapid social change, unemployment). Natural uniformities are not acts to which individuals must conform in order to prevent disruption of society's equilibrium. Second, "imitative uniformities" are based on simultaneous choices made by large numbers of people of identical behavior patterns. They have to do with certain patterns of behavior that any number of individuals may freely choose to copy as, for example, with the introduction of a new fashion of clothing that is eventually adopted by some people. Finally, "imposed uniformities" are compulsive, they occur when "a certain behavior is 'imposed' on group-members as an obligatory pattern for their behavior" (p. 8). An obligatory pattern of behavior may manifest itself in one of two ways: (1) as a concrete act or a series of similar acts, or (2) as an ideal structure, that is, as an "abstract description of behavior to which individuals should adjust their conduct" (p. 117). An example of the first variety is seen when the courts of a given country follow the decisions of their supreme court concerning a particular legal matter. An example of the second variety occurs when a new ritual is established by a church council and the priests and believers perform it. For Timasheff, the uniformity of behavior created by law is always of the "imposed" types.

The imposing of behavior patterns is accomplished by the activities of functionaries whom Timasheff calls "supporters of patterns" and which include magistrates, judges, administrative officials, and legislators. Behavior conforming to the obligatory pattern in force is regarded as normal and said to be "coordinated." On the other hand, behavior deviating from the obligatory pattern is considered "abnormal." The process of imposing preestablished behavior patterns is termed "social coordination" and its purpose is to maintain social equilibrium. Put another way, the goal of coordination is the creation and preservation of social order.

Social coordination occurs in several forms. First, it may be classified as ethical or nonethical. Ethical coordination takes place when the imposition of patterns of conduct on individual wills is accepted by the ethical conviction of the group as a matter of conscience. A conviction is said to be an ethical one "insofar as its content is the evaluation of human behavior from a specific viewpoint, permitting the application of the term 'duty' to the behavior which is in conformity with a certain pattern, and of the term 'violation of duty' to the behavior nonconformable with it" (p. 13). On the other hand, nonethical coordination is not based on people's evaluation of behavior as being good or bad, right or wrong, just or unjust; rather, it relies on coercive sanctions alone to ensure desirable conduct. In this case, people obey the rules because they fear reprisal.

Second, the forms of social coordination may also be classified as centralized or decentralized. In centralized coordination, we find within a larger social group, a smaller group that Timasheff calls the "active center of power-structures." The dominant power center in society—i.e., the political state—exercises authority over the members of the passive periphery (viz., the citizenry) as it imposes patterns of behavior on them in order to determine their conduct. Thus, owing to this power imbalance, the social interaction between the active power center and periphery is an unequal one. Timasheff refers to this process as "imperative coordination."

In a situation of decentralized coordination there is no active power center—that is to say, no government—and, thus, the imposition of behavior patterns takes place as individuals of equal standing influence each other's conduct. Because the display of organized power is absent in this situation, Timasheff describes it as one of "nonimperative coordination." In this case, "every group-member influences all the others and every group-member is influenced by all others" (p. 106). Hence, it is not coercion or the display of power in the form of official commands and sanctions that accounts for the imposition, but socio-ethical pressure. Socio-ethical pressure (which is the sole sanction in premodern societies and which is not yet legal regulation) arises from the group conviction that a person "ought" to act in a certain way in given circumstances. Those individuals who transgress the ethical rules will provoke a hostile attitude or punitive reaction from the group.

Timasheff derives four types of social coordination from its two pairs of forms discussed above. These are: (1) nonethical and nonimperative, (2) ethical but nonimperative, (3) imperative but nonethical, and (4) ethical and imperative. The nonethical and nonimperative type does not exist in reality because without group conviction and centralized power, there is no effort at securing uniform patterns of conduct, and without some patterns of conduct, society is not possible. Ethical but nonimperative (purely ethical) coordination relies on group conviction but not on centralized power. In this case, custom and morals alone determine individual behavior. Imperative but nonethical (purely imperative) coordination depends on an organized central power but not on group conviction. The despotic rule of a totalitarian government unconcerned with the moral sentiments of its people serves as an apt illustration. Finally, the ethical and imperative type of social coordination requires both group conviction and an organized social power to authoritatively impose patterns of behavior on group members. The ethical and imperative type of coordination, Timasheff contends, is created by law.

Based on the foregoing remarks Timasheff concludes that ethical conviction and organized social power (i.e., political power) are the two major elements of social coordination. He distinguishes between the two elements: "The interaction resulting in giving force to ethical rules is an equal one: in this process everyone plays the same part, imposing the common will on others and feeling this will imposed upon him. Within power-structures, the social interaction is an unequal one—the waves of influence run only in one direction" (p. 171). Despite their differences, ethics and power combine to form a higher synthesis: law.

> Rules of behavior are created which are simultaneously ethical rules and general commands of an established power structure. They form a system of human behavior in society presenting simultaneously the features of efficient ethics and efficient power, of *law*.... Ethics and power are not two coordinated or subordinated phenomena. They may be thought of as two circles which cross one another. Their overlapping section is law (p. 248).

In other words, law is ethical—thereby revealing its living dimension—because "every legal pattern of conduct can be expressed in a proposition with the predicate 'ought to be'"(p. 15). At the same time, law is also imperative—and therefore possesses elements of positivity—because its "ought to be" is enforced by a centralized power-structure, a government. The law, therefore, is an ethico-imperative coordination. As Timasheff puts it, "legal order is constituted by patterns of conduct enforced by agents of centralized power (tribunals and administration) and simultaneously supported by a group-conviction that the corresponding conduct 'ought to be'" (p. 17). The law's functional control brings about "the realization of a perfect coordination of human behavior" (p. 321).

## Psychogenics

Although Timasheff takes a decidedly sociological perspective—in that he describes law as "one of the orders observable in human relations and social processes, an order imposed and enforced by politically organized men" (1946: 818)—as well as a social-psychological approach—in that he regards law as a type of "collective mentality" in which the "socio-psychological spheres of ethics and power synthesized are [its] basis" (1964: 207)—some of his key concepts tend to be psychogenic. In this respect Timasheff was influenced by the psychological ideas of Pareto, Pavlov, Piaget, J.B. Watson, Wilhelm Wundt, and especially those of his friend and teacher at the University of St. Petersburg, Leon Petrazycki, who understood law as a psychological phenomenon given that legal concepts such as "obligation," "right," and "contract" exist only in the human psyche (*psikhika*). Thus, for Petrazycki, the law's origins lie in people's "psychical experiences" for it is only in the mind that "legal impulsions" can be isolated. Although Timasheff emphatically disagrees with Petrazycki's individualistic theory of law (contending instead that law is socially determined), he nonetheless considers such "psychological"—and one could say, "living"—factors as psychic dispositions, behavior tendencies, and basic sentiments. Greatly influenced by the behavioral psychology of his time (Pavlov was conducting his experiments on the conditioned reflex in St. Petersburg at the same time that Timasheff lived, studied, and taught in that city) Timasheff premises at least part of his sociolegal theory on the notions of conditioning and reinforcement, stimulus and response.[6]

Timasheff's idea that power and punishment are ultimately based on people's biopsychic instincts (basic sentiments) begins with his view of ethics. Ethics, he maintains, serve to sustain society's equilibrium by reacting against anti-social or unlawful behavior. This reaction is a consequence of the instinctive emotional response—the "retributive tendency"—to punish behavior violating the group's ethical convictions. Thus, similar to G.H. Mead (1918), Timasheff pays special attention to the affectual reactions of the law-abiding members of society against the lawbreaker. It should be noted that, like Mead, Timasheff, at bottom, treats the notion of biopsychic experiences sociologically in that he considers these experiences to be part of a "collective mentality": a concept analogous to Durkheim's "collective consciousness." Following Durkheim, Timasheff does not reduce the social fact to the fact of the individual; contrary to Durkheim, he does not ascribe primacy to society. Instead, Timasheff steers a middle course when he considers such individualistic-collectivistic processes as biopsychic experiences.

Timasheff's reliance on many of the major concepts popularized by behavioral psychology is particularly evident in his explanation that "domination is conditioned by polarizing a social group, by separating it into an active center and a passive periphery" (p. 208). According to him, this process of polarization is based on a natural division between people that is manifested in social groups as some individuals, possessing an active personality ("psychic constitution"), exert their will to dominate, while the majority of individuals, possessing a passive personality, exhibit a tendency to obey. In this way, a relation of dominance-submission is created between dominators and subjects. The result is the emergence of a power structure, or "a complex of behavior tendencies and corresponding psychic dispositions in many interrelated individuals" (pp. 184-185) that involves dominance-submission patterns. The commands of the dominators emanate from the power structure's active center and are received by the subjects of the passive periphery. This unequal social relationship creates an imperative duty in which the subjects evince a disposition to carry out commands, for no other reason than that they come from the dominators. In time, the subject's submission to the dominator's directives becomes habitual and automatic, forming "reaction tendencies" and a "readiness to behave" on the part of those subordinate to the power center. The act of submission is therefore a conditioned response, a learned behavior. Timasheff explains concretely how the dominance-submission relationship molds the desired action:

Why does the soldier behave "correctly?" Because during a certain length of time certain sounds accompanied the display of an already existing tendency of submission (inborn or acquired). In the beginning, our soldier was impressed by the meaning of the words he heard and by the sounds as such; these meanings, through the complex mechanisms of voluntary action, resulted in the corresponding bodily movements, which were, of course, carried out quite inaccurately; later on, the nervous current engendered in the sense organ by sound was directed immediately toward the centers ruling the commanded movements, and these movements were performed automatically and, therefore, with more accuracy. (p. 181)

Timasheff's account of people's inborn instincts toward dominance or submission has prompted Hunt to declare that "a distinctive feature of [Timasheff's] sociology of law is that he approaches the role of psychological factors in the study of legal phenomena" (1979: 192). These psychological factors, or biopsychic experiences, illustrate the law's living character.

## V. Timasheff's Methodology

Possessing an exceptionally heightened methodological consciousness not given to the mass of social scientists, Timasheff expounds at length on what he regards as the essential methods to be employed in the social sciences, as systems of thought and action. He states, very clearly, that sociology is a nomographic science whose goal is to study the role of similar, related, or sets of related social phenomena through the principle of causality. Accordingly, the various methodological directives that Timasheff advocates in *An Introduction to the Sociology of Law* focus principally on the law's causal reality. Given that law is a secondary social phenomenon derived from the unity of power and ethics, Timasheff maintains that the sociology of law must begin by studying these phenomena from the causal-functional point of view and conclude by analyzing their joint action.

According to Timasheff, the object of every empiric science, including sociology, is to "access," that is to say, to establish and make sense of "facts." Timasheff identifies two types of facts as being important in the social sciences—physical facts and psychic facts. Whereas physical facts require the researcher to observe, through a variety of modalities, empirical culture and social action, psychic facts, consisting as they do of concrete states of mental processes through which meanings are ascribed to physical facts, require the use of historical evidence, interviews, and questionnaires.

Timasheff posits that the methods of individual observation (participant observation), introspection (self-observation), and mass observation (statistical analysis) be employed to show that law is, simply and concretely, "a fact of social life"—one that imposes uniform patterns of behavior on group members. Individual observation and introspection (as forms of immediate experience that help establish facts) are methods ideally suited for analyzing the intuitive and spontaneous nature of the living law. Indeed, "all of the basic propositions of the theoretical social sciences...are based on self-observation and interpretation, intuitive, emphatic, or inferential, of observations concerning mental processes of other persons" (1948: 263). By contrast, mass observation in the form of quantitative data is intended to help in empirical investigations of positive law. "By necessity," writes Timasheff, "the statistician abstracts from the majority of traits observable in the concrete phenomena and concentrates his attention on a few; his object of study is a 'population,' or a cluster of concrete phenomena looked upon from a particular point of view" (1945: 174).

Through individual observation, the researcher directly studies how overt human behavior is related to law. Thus, for instance, human behavior may be seen as a set of conditioned reflexes (e.g., the reflexes of freedom and submission mentioned by Pavlov) that determine which kind of social control the law will exert. The technique of individual or direct observation also allows the legal sociologist to examine the fact that rigid legal formulas are transformed in actual life.

Contrary to the behaviorism emphasized by individual observation, introspection involves reflexivity and employs the techniques of depth psychology. Timasheff's method of introspection is similar but not identical to that of his teacher Petrazycki who utilized the method to arrive at an understanding of people's psychic world and of their specific experiences in the context of legal relationships. Petrazycki's introspection is reflexive given that it involves "observation of one's own mental processes and body movement resulting from them; and inferring contents of the mental processes of others, by analogy, from their body movements" (Górecki, 1975: 4). Conversely, Timasheff describes introspection as the "accurate subsequent analysis of one's state of consciousness insofar as it is related to law (acting according to law; acting against the law; acting with intent to transform the law; reactions produced by another's acting in accordance with or against the law)" (p. 38). For example, introspection requires that the researcher—qua participating member of society—look within himself/herself in order to recognize those patterns of behavior (ethical rules) that he/she supports and wishes to impose on others because, according to his/her sentiment, they ought to act in accordance with them. Timasheff states that his type of introspection is analogous to Freud's psychoanalytic method of investigating the unconscious.

Mass observation is expressed in statistical data. In referring to this methodological procedure Timasheff is obviously advocating the use of quantitative information as found, for example, in the Uniform Crime Reports and the National Crime Survey. He explains that statistical study has "yielded the result that regularities were observable in the distribution of individual acts related to law, and that those regularities were quite different from those which arise when large numbers of human actions are observed in conditions similar to those prevailing in games of chance" (1941: 243).

Finally, Timasheff also suggests triangulating other methodologies. For example, he recommends that data obtained from ethnology, historical jurisprudence, comparative jurisprudence, and child psychology be used to test the validity of the results obtained through introspection and mass observation. At bottom, the goal of methodological techniques in the sociology of law is to investigate: (1) the "immediate juridical experience" given in the acts of legislators, authorities, electors, contracting parties, and of persons taking part in the juridical life of corporate bodies, and (2) the "juridical mentality," which includes the primitive revenge mentality, the retributive emotion, and the relative force of norms of conduct.

## VI. The Significance of Timasheff's
## Work for the Sociology of Law Today

The conceptual and methodological prescriptions that Timasheff explicated in *An Introduction to the Sociology of Law* will doubtless inspire a new generation of law and society scholars. Many of the proposals that he made in the book continue to await elaboration, modification, and verification. For example, Timasheff, in *Introduction*, attempted to formulate a "pure" theory of power (imperative coordination) that is independent of ethics and that would improve on the notion that "the essence of law must be searched for in the manner of imposing patterns of behavior" (p. 142). He proposed that the likelihood that commands will create imperative coordination depends on a power structure's "potential," or the relation between the force of the active center and the latent force of resistance from the periphery. To date, sociologists have not attempted to empirically quantify the potential values of different power structures.

It must not be assumed that in revisiting Timasheff's *Introduction* innovative directions in theory and research will automatically open up to the sociology of law. To be sure, given that throughout his work Timasheff rejected the use of a single conceptual model and relied instead on multiple frames of reference (behaviorism and interpretivism, systems-functionalism and conflict theory, individual observation and introspection) makes it so that his legal sociology risks placing current scholarship on multiple paths, but with little direction to guide it. Indeed, it is quite likely that this potpourri of theoretical perspectives and methodological modalities that tend to resist convergence was responsible for impeding Timasheff's attempt to successfully formulate a systematic theory—a logically coherent conceptual scheme—of law.

However that may be, his basic working hypothesis in *Introduction*—that the double nature of law consists of ethical and imperative coordination—and its subtle but noteworthy corollary—that people obey the law because of ethical conviction *and* fear of punishment—remain to be earnestly studied in tandem. Legal sociologists have yet to focus their investigations on the conceptual and empirical point at which ethical forces and power systems intersect.

Finally, it must be understood by contemporary scholars that Timasheff did not regard his 1939 statement as the final word on the matter. Indeed, he (1957: 432) expected to include two addenda in an updated edition of *An Introduction to the Sociology of Law*— addenda that would have continued to address the dialectic between the living law and the positive law.[7] First, he wished to place greater emphasis on the law as a "learned behavior tendency" (a concept, incidentally, that echoes Petrazycki's notion of "impulsions"). This elaboration requires understanding the legal order as the sum total of reactive tendencies of human beings. The reactive tendencies are intuitively acquired from the group conviction and, through repetition as well as through the application of the reward-and-punishment scheme, a learned behavior becomes ingrained in numerous group members (Timasheff, 1944: 78). In time the learned behavior produces a norm of conduct, an ideal pattern, that becomes law as it is fixed in a sufficient number of individuals and with sufficient intensity. This inductive understanding of the legal order in accordance with the general principles of learned behavior underscores "the law which is in force within the group," the living law.

Second, Timasheff intended to consider more fully the law as created by "verbal formulas"—the positive law—and as it determines reactive tendencies of behavior. This consideration is explained by a structure that is sequentially the "inverse" of the aforementioned one. It involves a deductive procedure in which "the intuitive recognition of values is directly expressed in verbal formulas and these are introduced into the system of ideal patterns in order to create new reactive tendencies" (Timasheff, 1944: 79).

These two extensions to his sociolegal theory (which Timasheff proposed in an article five years after *Introduction* was published) address recurrent questions that continue to plague contemporary sociology of law: Why do people obey the law? How are legal norms internalized? What is the relationship between ideal and actual behavior? Today, legal sociologists would do well to consult Timasheff in grappling with these and other fundamental problems which he pointed out all those years ago.

## Notes

1. Gurvitch's (1942) list of European and American founders of the sociology of law has not found consensus among legal sociologists.
2. The positive law/ living law distinction has a long tradition and is articulated in various forms: see, for example, Weber's (1978) formal rational law/substantive irrational law; Pound's (1910) law in books/law in action; Llewellyn's (1930) paper rules/real rules; Sumner's (1940) positive law/customary law; Petrazycki's (1955) positive law/ intuitive law; Gurvitch's (1942) organized law/intuitive spontaneous law; Kennedy's (1976) rules/standards.
3. This section is based, in part, on ideas—now extended and modified—that were previously articulated in my "Toward a General Theoretical-Methodological Framework for the Sociology of Law: Another Look at the Eastern European Pioneers" (1998).
4. This antiformalism is similar to Weber's (1978) substantive irrational type of lawfinding, Twining's (1973) "Grand Style" of adjudication, and Llewellyn's (1960) "situation sense."
5. Given that Timasheff sometimes downplayed the intensity of the law's coercive force, I prefer to use the term "control" in describing the law's internal (psychic) and external (social) regulating or coordinating influences. Kelsen (1945: 28-29) wrongly criticizes Timasheff for arguing against coercion as an essential element in law. Timasheff, to be sure, was well aware of the law's consensual *and* coercive elements. It would therefore be a mistake to place him in either the power-coercion or the pluralist-consensus camp. Johnson (1979), in contradistinction to Sheskin (1978), argues persuasively that the coercion and consensus images of law are both evident in Timasheff's legal sociology. As Timasheff himself states: "law *may* be used as an instrument of oppression, but also as an instrument of common welfare" (p. 378).

6.     Even though Sorokin, while in Russia, had taken a moderate behaviorist approach in *A System of Sociology*, he later reproached Timasheff for too much behaviorism in *An Introduction to the Sociology of Law.*
7.     If the dialectical tension is not properly attenuated it can lead to legal disequilibrium and legal disintegration; if adequately reconciled it produces legal and cultural change.

# References

Austin, John. 1961. "Lectures on Jurisprudence." Pp. 400-419 in *Society, Law, and Morality*, edited by F.A. Olafson. Englewood Cliffs, NJ: Prentice-Hall.

Bierstedt, Robert. 1970. "Nicholas S. Timasheff, 1886-1970." *The American Sociologist* 5(3): 290-291.

Ehrlich, Eugen. 1936. *Fundamental Principles of the Sociology of Law*. Cambridge, MA: Harvard University Press.

Górecki, Jan. 1975. *Sociology and Jurisprudence of Leon Petrazycki*. Urbana, IL: University of Illinois Press.

Gurvitch, Georges. 1942. *Sociology of Law*. New York: Philosophical Library and Alliance Book Corporation.

Hunt, Alan. 1979. "The Sociology of Law of Gurvitch and Timasheff: A Critique of Theories of Normative Integration." Pp. 169-204 in *Research in Law and Sociology*, Vol. 2, edited by S. Spitzer. Greenwich, CT: JAI Press.

_____. 1993. *Explorations in Law and Society: Toward a Constitutive Theory of Law*. New York: Routledge.

Johnson, Alan. 1979. "The Recognition of Differential Power in the Sociology of Law." *Mid-American Review of Sociology* 4: 57-70.

Kelsen, Hans. 1945. *General Theory of Law and State*. New York: Russell & Russell.

Kennedy, Duncan. 1976. "Form and Substance in Private Law Adjudication." *Harvard Law Review* 89(8): 1685-1778.

Llewellyn, Karl N. 1930. "A Realistic Jurisprudence—The Next Step." *Columbia Law Review* 30: 431-465.

_____. 1931. "Some Realism about Realism—Responding to Dean Pound." *Harvard Law Review* 44(8): 1222-1264.

_____. 1960. *The Common Law Tradition: Deciding Appeals*. Boston, MA: Little, Brown.

Mead, George Herbert. 1918. "The Psychology of Punitive Justice." *American Journal of Sociology* 23: 577-602.

Olivecrona, Karl. 1948. "Is a Sociological Explanation of Law Possible?" *Theoria* 14: 167-207.

Petrazycki, Leon. 1955. *Law and Morality*. Cambridge, MA: Harvard University Press.

Pound, Roscoe. 1910. "Law in Books and Law in Action." *American Law Review* 44: 12-36.

Scheuer, Joseph F. 1965. "Nicholas S. Timasheff and the Sociology of Recurrence." *Thought* (Autumn): 432-448.

Sheskin, Arlene. 1978. "A Critical Review and Assessment of the Sociology of Law." *Mid-American Review of Sociology* 3: 109-124.

Sumner, William Graham. 1940. *Folkways: A Study of the Sociological Importance of Usages, Manners, Customs, Mores, and Morals*. Boston, MA: Ginn and Company.

Timasheff, Nicholas S. 1922 [1964]. "Law as a Social Psychological Phenomenon." *Philosophy Today* 8 (Fall): 197-212.

_____. 1937a. "The Retributive Structure of Punishment." *The Journal of Criminal Law Criminology* 28: 396-405.

_____. 1937b. "What is 'Sociology of Law'?" *American Journal of Sociology* 43(2): 225-235.

_____. 1938a. "The Power Phenomenon." *American Sociological Review* 3(4): 499-509.

_____. 1938b. "Law as a Social Phenomenon." Pp. 868-873 in *Readings in Jurisprudence*, edited by Jerome Hall. Indianapolis, IN: Bobbs-Merrill.

_____. 1939a. "The Crisis in the Marxian Theory of Law." *New York University Law Quarterly Review* 16(4): 519-531.

_____. 1939b. "The Sociological Place of Law." *American Journal of Sociology* 44(2): 206-221.

_____. 1940. "Law in Pareto's Sociology." *American Journal of Sociology* 46(2): 139-149.

_____. 1941. "Fundamental Problems of the Sociology of Law." *American Catholic Sociological Review* 11(2): 233-248.

_____. 1942. "Gurvitch's Philosophy of Social Law." *Thought* 17: 709-722.

_____. 1942. *Religion in Soviet Russia, 1917-1942*. New York: Sheed and Ward.

_____. 1943. *One Hundred Years of Probation*. New York: Fordham University Press.

_____. 1944. "The Social Reality of Ideal Patterns." *Journal of Legal and Political Sociology* 3(1-2): 66-82.

_____. 1945. "On Methods in the Social Sciences." *American Catholic Sociological Review* 6(3): 169-176.

_____. 1946. "The Sociologist's Contribution to the Law." *Virginia Law Review* 32: 818-834.

_____. 1946. *The Great Retreat: The Growth and Decline of Communism in Russia*. New York: E.P. Dutton.

_____. 1947. "Petrazycki's Philosophy of Law." Pp. 736-750 in *Interpretations of Modern Legal Philosophies: Essays in Honor of Roscoe Pound*, edited by Paul Sayre. New York: Oxford University Press.

_____. 1948. "Observation in the Social Sciences." *American Catholic Sociological Review* 9(4): 259-271.

_____. 1949. *Probation in Light of Criminal Statistics*. New York: Fordham University Press.

_____. 1952. "The Basic Concepts of Sociology." *American Journal of Sociology* 58(2): 176-186.

_____. 1955. "Introduction." Pp. xvii-xl in *Law and Morality* by Leon Petrazcki. Cambridge, MA: Harvard University Press.

_____. 1955. *Sociological Theory: Its Nature and Growth*. New York: Doubleday; 2nd edition, Random House, 1957; 3rd edition, Random House, 1966.

_____. 1957. "Growth and Scope of Sociology of Law." Pp. 424-449 in *Modern Sociological Theory: In Continuity and Change*, edited by Howard Becker and Alvin Boskoff. New York: The Dryden Press.

Treviño, A. Javier. 1998. "Toward a General Theoretical-Methodological Framework for the Sociology of Law: Another Look at the Eastern-European Pioneers." Pp. 155-202 in *Sociology of Crime, Law, and Deviance*, Vol. 1, edited by Jeffrey Ulmer. Greenwich, CT: JAI Press.

Twining, William. 1973. *Karl Llewellyn and the Realist Movement*. Birkenhead, UK: Willmer Brothers.

Weber, Max. 1978. *Economy and Society*, Vols. I-II, edited by Guenther Roth and Claus Wittich. Berkeley, CA: University of California Press.

# Part IV

## Juristic Entities in the Study of Law and Society

# 9

# On Marshall B. Clinard and Peter C. Yeager, *Corporate Crime*

*Marshall B. Clinard*

"It has always seemed strange to me," said Doc. "The things we admire in men, kindness and generosity, openness, honesty, understanding and feeling are the concomitants of failure in our system. And those traits we detest, sharpness, greed, acquisitiveness, meanness, egotism and self-interest are the traits of success. And while men admire the quality of the first they love the produce of the second."—John Steinbeck, *Cannery Row*

*Corporate Crime*, published in 1980, is the first and still the only comprehensive study of corporate law violations by our largest corporations in the Fortune 500. The book laid the groundwork for the analyses of important aspects of corporate behavior and definitions to study corporate crime and found ways of locating corporate violations from various sources and even drew up measures of the seriousness of crimes. Much of this book still applies today to the corporate world and its illegal behavior.

This new introduction discusses the development of a criminological interest in corporate crime, explains the nature of corporate crime, and discusses a number of issues involved in its study and concludes with a comparative view of corporate crime twenty-five years after the publication of *Corporate Crime*.

Since the founding of the country and the chartering of corporations, serious unethical and law violations have characterized many large corporations. These have been the subject of journalists and other writers and even of an important sociologist, E.A. Ross, who, nearly 100 years ago directed attention to unscrupulous business operators whom he termed "criminaloids" (Ross, 1905). The first attempt to do a research study of corporate crime was made in 1949 by Edwin H. Sutherland in his *White Collar Crime* (Sutherland, 1949).

Things started to happen beginning in the 1960s due largely to consumer groups and others who strongly emphasized the need for more corporate social responsibility. This concern resulted in the creation of the National Highway Traffic Administration in 1966, which made it possible for the government to intervene in auto safety problems that the industry had ignored but resulted in needless deaths and tens of thousands of injuries. The Occupational Safety and Health Administration came into being in 1970 to regulate the safety of the workplace and to protect the workplace from harmful chemicals and other substances. Also, in 1970, the Environmental Protection Agency was created to control air, water, and chemical pollutants. After studies revealed a tremendous number of injuries to consumers from the use of unsafe corporate products, the Consumer Product Safety Commission came into existence in 1972 to ban the sale of unsafe and defective products. In 1977, in order to prevent widespread bribery of foreign officials by American corporations, the Foreign Corrupt Practices Act was passed. Already in existence was the Sherman Antitrust Act of 1890. The Food and Drug Administration was created in 1906 to protect consumers from impure foods and dangerous drugs and cosmetics.

Crime can be divided into three main types: conventional or ordinary; occupational; or organizational. *Conventional* includes crimes of violence, such as assault, rape, and murder, but mainly consists of property crimes such as theft, burglary, and robbery. Most of these are committed by persons of the lower and blue-collar classes. In *occupational* crime we find entirely different illegal behavior. Such crimes are committed by persons of the middle and upper social classes. Occupational crime involves the violation of law in the course of activity in a legitimate occupation. It is often referred to as "white collar crime" because the crimes are committed by individual businesspersons, politicians, government employees, doctors, pharmacists, lawyers, and labor union officials. Occupational crime also includes blue-collar workers in connection with their occupations, such as those by plumbers and auto mechanics. Finally, there is *organizational* crime, which is committed by large entities that use illegal methods to obtain a goal. Organizational crime is committed by large corporations, an industry, labor unions, and even a church hierarchy. Organizational crime, such as corporate lawbreaking, is carried out within a complex system, of boards of directors, presidents, chief executive officers (CEOs), middle managers, and supervisors.

*Corporate Crime* demonstrates that corporate lawbreaking covers a very wide range of misbehavior, much of it serious: among these violations are accounting malpractices, including false statements of corporate assets and profits; occupational safety and health hazards; unfair labor practices; the manufacture and sale of hazardous products and misleading packaging of products; abuses of competition that restrain trade such as antitrust and agreements among corporations to allocate markets; false and misleading advertising; environmental violations of air and water pollution, and illegal dumping of hazardous materials; illegal domestic political contributions and bribery of foreign officials for corporate benefits.

Since *Corporate Crime* was published, conventional crime has continued to attract far more interest, in part because of the complexity of corporations and the types of law violations. Another reason is that corporate illegal violations are not reported in central sources like the Uniform Crime Reports. To do research on corporate offenses there is a need for acquaintance with not only criminal law violations but those of administrative and civil laws as well. Finally, there is difficulty in securing necessary research funds, which are far larger than those needed for the study of conventional or occupational crime. These issues are discussed later in *Corporate Crime*.

Recognition of corporate crime is increasing, but corporate law violations are, on the whole, except for very large ones such as the WorldCom and Enron cases in the early 2000s, not highly publicized and rarely come to the attention of the public through the press and TV. Seldom are they ever on the front page or headline TV news, and studies have shown that nearly all the publicity of corporate law violations is in the *business section* of a newspaper, while a few occasionally are carried on the inside pages of a newspaper. Consequently, except for the few very large cases that come to their attention, the perception is that corporate law violations are generally not anywhere as serious or as numerous as conventional crimes, which gets nearly all the publicity. Actually, much corporate crime has a far wider effect on society than conventional or occupational offences. One who had studied illegal corporate offenses (Mokhiber, 1988) has put this succinctly in, "Why is it that despite the high number of victims, when people think of crime, they think of burglary before they think of monopoly (if they think of antitrust violations at all), of assault before they think of harmful pharmaceuticals, of street crime before they think of corporate crime?" (Mokhiber, 1998, p. 14)

## Seriousness of Corporate Violations

As has been pointed out, the consequences of corporate violations can be more severe than conventional or occupational offences. If corporations band together and eliminate the competitive price for their product, money is stolen from consumers. When corporations issue false and misleading statements of their assets and income, this can lead to defrauding of thousands of shareholders, investors, and those on a pension. By their very size, corporate income tax violations defraud the government of large sums of revenue.

When corporations produce and distribute unsafe products such as pharmaceutical drugs, foods, or even autos, this can result in injury or the death of thousands of consumers. Likewise, unsafe working conditions can result in serious injuries, or possibly death to the workers. A 2001 Public Broadcasting System TV series on the chemical industry revealed that hundreds of workers have been killed. It reported, "the Chemical Companies through their silence and inertia, subjected at least two generations of workers to excess levels of a potent carcinogen, vinyl chloride, that targets the liver, brain, lungs and blood forming organs." Thousands of citizens are injured by corporate pollution of air, water, and illegal disposal of hazardous products, such as dumping toxic chemicals on the land and into rivers.

According to the *Corporate Crime Reporter* the FBI reported that in 1998 that about 19,000 Americans were murdered. But the same year, 56,000 Americans died from work related diseases alone, such as corporation-caused asbestosis and black lung, but went unreported, as usual, in the FBI reports. Far more than these deaths, however, were those that result from corporate pollution and the manufacture of hazardous consumer products. As Thom Hartmann has reported in *Unequal Protection: The Rise of Corporate Dominance and the Theft of Human Rights*, "Today if you or I were to knowingly and willfully repair or build a car for somebody that killed them, we would go to prison for manslaughter or even murder. But if a corporation knowingly and willingly were to repair or build a car that killed a human, they now have a legal exemption. They would face only civil penalties and fines under the National Traffic and Safety Act" (Hartmann, 2002, p. 186). Unfortunately, it has taken the law to force social responsibility on corporations in numerous areas.

## Cost of Corporate Crime

The cost of corporate crime far exceeds the total for all the thefts, burglaries, arsons, and robberies put together. In 2003, the FBI estimated the cost for burglary and robbery alone at $3.8 billion. Even though this amount is very great, estimates for corporate crime have varied from several hundred billion dollars to one accounting professor's study in 1995 that added costs of price fixing, pollution, unsafe vehicles, workplace injuries, and accidents to an almost unbelievable total of three trillion dollars for the public cost of corporations' violations (Estes, 1996). Probably much more meaningful is to look at corporate costs in terms of individual cases. For example, a judge in 2004 put the punitive damage award for the notorious Exxon Valdez Alaska oil spill of 11 million gallons of oil in 1989 at $4.5 billion. WorldCom's bankruptcy of $103.4 billion in 2002 and Enron's in 2001 of $63.8 billion are the largest corporate bankruptcies in U.S. history. Both were followed by many criminal prosecutions. Lost alone in Enron's were $800 million employee pension investments and billions for other investors. Some idea of the cost of corporate crime can be gauged by the size of the fines levied on a sample of thirty-five of the Fortune 500 industrial and manufacturing companies between 1990 and 2004:

| Size of Fine and Settlement | Number of Corporate Violations |
|---|---|
| $200,000 to $1 million | 3 |
| $1 to $5 million | 18 |
| $5 to $10 million | 10 |
| $10 to $50 million | 9 |
| $50 to $100 million | 4 |
| $100 to $500 million | 9 |
| $500 million to $1 billion | 7 |
| Over $1 billion | 4 |

## The Law and Corporate Crime

Even though the title of the book is *Corporate Crime*, most corporate violators were not handled by the criminal law, although a large number might have been. A small number of corporate violators were handled under criminal law, but most were dealt with under administrative and civil law. Under administrative law, the corporation may be punished by such actions as consent agreements not to violate again, official warnings, the recall or destruction of a product, or by a monetary penalty. Under the civil law, a corporation can receive a fine even in the millions of dollars, a court injunction to refrain from further violations, and similar court ordered penalties.

In legal terms, then, corporate crimes are, as Sutherland stated in *White Collar Crime*, administratively segregated from conventional or ordinary crime. This differential treatment is a product in part of the power of corporations to influence legislation so that violations do not have the stigma of the criminal law. Another factor is that a corporation or corporate officials hardly fit the stereotype of the "criminal." A greater reason is the necessity for alternative sanctions, such as administrative and civil penalties, because of the legal difficulties in a criminal case and the total length of a criminal prosecution of a corporation or its officials. The corporation can employ a large number of highly competent legal talent, far greater than the government staff can have. Consequently a criminal trial may tie up much government legal personnel needed for other corporate cases.

To try all violations as a *criminal* law offense creates a difficulty because of the large number of serious corporate violations that must be dealt with. Among the serious corporate violations are the size of monetary losses to consumers, investors, or the government, the extent of physical damage to consumers and workers, the length of the violations, and the repetition of violations.

In *Corporate Crime*, 28 percent were considered serious (see page 118 for a definition of the seriousness of corporate violations), 34 percent moderately serious, and 38 percent minor. Two-thirds of the financial violations were serious, 20 percent of the manufacturing, 72 percent of trade violations, 40 percent of labor, but only 5 percent of environmental.

In the *Corporate Crime* study it was found that the seriousness of corporate violations is not necessarily related to the type of legal sanction employed. For example, a large number of the more serious law violations were handled under administrative law. Of the serious violations, two-thirds were dealt with by administrative law, less than one fourth by civil sanctions, and about 10 percent by a criminal sanction.

As will be pointed out later, events in the early 2000s, such as huge corporate bankruptcies involving fraudulent activities, often perpetrated by their corporate executives, resulted in Congress enacting the Sarbanes-Oxley Bill in 2002. The provisions of the bill greatly increased the possibility of using criminal sanctions more widely against corporations and their executives.

## Definition of "Corporate Crime"

Because of the reasons that have been outlined, the definition of a "crime" used in *Corporate Crime* is any act punishable by the state. This is essentially similar to the definition employed by Sutherland in *White Collar Crime*, in which he wrote: "The essential characteristic of crime is behavior that is prohibited by the State, as an injury to the State and against which the State may react, at least as a last resort by punishment. The two abstract criteria generally regarded by legal scholars as necessary elements in a definition of crime are legal description of an act as socially harmful and legal provision of a penalty for the act" (Sutherland, p. 31). The offenses that are discussed in *Corporate Crime* have the general criteria of criminal behavior, namely, legal definition of social injuries and legal provision of penal sanctions, but the use also of administrative and judicial procedures are different for these violations than for other violations of criminal law.

Many would disagree with this broad definition of "crime," which goes beyond that of a "crime" under criminal law. In legal terms, only those corporate offenses prosecuted under the criminal law can be termed "criminal." Moreover, if a corporation is fined a million dollars under administrative or civil law, it does not receive the "stigma" represented by prosecution under the criminal law. As far as a corporation goes, however, a civil or criminal fine are the same, except only one thing is missing: there is not the stigma, as may come with a criminal fine that may or may not mean anything to the corporation or to others.

Some argue that this wide definition means the appellation of "crime" is given to minor corporate offenses. The criminal law, however, includes minor offences or "misdemeanors," and these acts may be punishable by a fine or even imprisonment, though less in severity. As has been pointed out, it would be impossible to prosecute most serious offenses under the criminal law, consequently this would mean that no action would be taken in many cases.

## A Comparison of the Two Fundamental Studies, 1949 and 1980

As has been pointed out, only two extensive studies of corporate crime have been made, Sutherland's *White Collar Crime* (he claimed it took twenty-five years to develop and do the research) and *Corporate Crime*, a larger and more detailed study, which also examined the extent and nature of illegal activities and the relation of corporate structure and the economic setting in which violations occurred. It concentrated on 477 of the nation's 500 largest publicly owned industrial and manufacturing corporations (as listed in the Fortune 500). The annual sales for the corporations studied ranged from $300 million to $45 billion, with an average sales volume of $1.7 billion. Data covered all enforcement actions that could be found including those initiated and imposed by twenty-five federal agencies during 1975 and 1976. The study was supported by a grant of $300,000 from the National Institute of Law Enforcement and Criminal Justice of the U.S. Department of Justice. More detailed analysis is contained in *Illegal Corporate Behavior*, which was the research report submitted to the U.S. Department of Justice, and was printed in 1979 by the U.S. Government Printing Office.

*Corporate Crime* was basically similar in approach to that used by Sutherland: both studied the largest corporations and attempted to cover a wide range of types of violations and enforcement actions. Both define corporate "crime" as violations of administrative and civil as well as criminal law. They both excluded public utility, transportation, communication, and banking corporations on the grounds that these are mainly subject to regulation by commissions.

The differences between the two studies are extensive, in fact so extensive that only a few superficial comparisons of their findings are possible. For example, Sutherland made no study of the characteristics of corporations as related to violations other than the main type of industry; even this was done rather unsystematically. *Corporate Crime* made use of extensive economic and business data gathered on each corporation's structural and financial characteristics, including trend data, all of which was linked to the extent of violations.

Among other important differences between these two studies (termed here the first and the second) were the following:

1. *Sample*. The sample of the first study was seventy of the 200 largest nonfinancial institutions (mainly publicly but some pri-

vately owned); the second study studied only publicly owned corporations and included 477 of the 500 largest industrial and manufacturing establishments from the Fortune 500.

2. *Time Span*. The analysis in Sutherland's study covered the *life careers* of the seventy corporations whose average life was forty-five years; in the case of some corporations, the period covered was from 1890-1944 and in the case of five, actually prior to 1890. Sutherland's method of using cases over a wide variation of time periods makes his findings difficult to interpret. The second study was limited to cases during a two-year time period, 1975 and 1976.

3. *Scope*. Sutherland's study was restricted to decisions taken against a corporation by an administrative, civil, or criminal action. The later study covered all known *initiated* and *enforcement actions* against a corporation, whether administrative or court.

4. *Coverage*. When Sutherland was conducting his study, the only laws regulating corporations were primarily restraint of trade, illegal rebates, and certain illegal financial manipulations. Most of the government regulatory agencies of corporations were created after *White Collar Crime* was published in 1949. The second study covered some twenty-five federal agencies. Obviously this increased greatly the number of potential decisions even though the time span was limited to only two years. Sutherland included cases involving decisions in infringement of patents, trademarks, and copyright cases that do not constitute an actual federal offence since they are dealt with by private suits, while the second study used only federal cases.

5. *Data Sources*. Both studies recognized the difficulty in locating cases of corporate law violations. Sutherland gathered his from the *Federal Reporter*, the published decisions of the Federal Trade Commission, the Securities and Exchange Commission, the National Labor Relations Board, the Food and Drug Administration (but only for 1924-1927), and the Interstate Commerce Commission. The *New York Times* was the only newspaper used by Sutherland in his search for corporate violations.

   *Corporate Crime* used far more sources in the search for cases. Data sources consisted of all pertinent Law Service Reports, including the *Federal Reporter* and twelve different types of specialized reports such as those of the FDA, the National Labor Relations Board, the EPA, violation reports by corporations to the SEC (10K), violation and enforcement data from twenty-five federal agencies, and a computer search of all articles involving corporate law breaking appearing in the *New York Times*, the *Wall Street Journal*, and over fifty leading trade newspapers.

6. *Data Analyses*. The statistical analyses presented in *White Collar Crime* were simplistic; only simple counts of decisions were taken and averages were presented. In *Corporate Crime* data were ana-

lyzed in terms of averages and percentages but also complex statistical measures of degree of association of variables.

Although Sutherland did not make a sophisticated study, he made the pioneer theoretical interpretations of the subject. Many of these observations were undoubtedly derived from the analysis of much case material that he collected. Case materials were also extensive in *Corporate Crime* but not used to the extent that Sutherland did.

## Has Corporate Crime Increased?

It is impossible to state definitely whether corporate crime is greater in the 2000s than in the 1970s. Since then no studies comparable to *Corporate Crime* have been made. Consequently, it is impossible to test, for example, two important conclusions reached by the *Corporate Crime* study. The first was the discovery that about 40 percent of the corporations were not charged with law violations by twenty-five federal agencies during a two-year period. The second was that violations were concentrated in certain corporations. For example, only thirty-eight of 300 corporations were cited for one half of all the violations.

The impression one gets from reports in the media and a series of reports such as are contained in the *Multinational Monitor, Corporate Crime Reporter*, and numerous special reports such as "100 Corporate Criminals" is that corporate lawbreaking is greater than it was and also much more damaging. A number of factors indicate the likelihood of increased corporate lawbreaking in American society of which one element is the general greed, and a decline in ethical principles that now characterizes much of our society. In recent years, there have been serious violations of law, not only in industrial corporations, but in large accounting firms, banks, investment houses, large insurance companies, and other major financial organizations. For example, the major tobacco companies reached an agreement with the states in the 1990s amounting to $260 billion for deceiving the public as to the danger of tobacco smoking and encouraging the young to smoke. In 2004 the federal government charged them with racketeering and sought $280 billion, a record civil charge for deceiving the public for decades about the danger of encouraging the young to smoke. In early 2005, a federal appeals court ruled that the government could not force tobacco companies to turn over profits under the Civil Racketeering Act. The U.S. Department of Justice appealed the decision and instituted a suit under a different legal basis. As another example of corporate greed, the American International Group (AIG), among the world's largest insurance brokers, mainly for large corporations, in a 2004 SEC settlement agreed to pay $126 million and accept an independent monitor (*New York Times*, Nov. 25, 2004). They were charged with selling a structured insurance product that allowed companies to hide poorly performing assets and to inflate their earnings. It was also under investigation for other offenses and the founder and long term CEO was forced out by the board. AIG later uncovered at least $1 billion more in accounting problems to improve its financial condition. The previous month it had acknowledged that its accounting for a number of transactions was improper, and the aggregate effect on its net worth would have to be lowered by $1.7 billion or about 2 percent (*New York Times*, April 26, 2005). Shortly thereafter, on May 4, the *New York Times* reported that, "The Federal Bureau of Investigation has begun a nationwide review of insurance practices to determine whether the accounting irregularities uncovered at American International Group represent a pervasive problem in the industry."

Another factor has been the greatly increased size of corporations due largely to mergers and, as *Corporate Crime* revealed, the largest corporations committed a highly disproportionate number of violations. For example, the 43 percent of the sample of corporations that had more than $1 billion in annual sales amount for almost 75 percent of the violations and 72 percent of the serious violations. If, however, a comparison was made per unit size of firm (the number of offenses per $100 million in sales), it was found that large corporations were no more likely to break the law than the smaller ones were.

In the 2000s, one gets the definite impression that the concentration of violations and sanctions in large corporations continues to be the case. Moreover, at the time *Corporate Crime* was written, the offenses generally did not exhibit as high a degree as sophistication and cleverness that have characterized many of the corporate offenses in the early 2000s. This situation will be demonstrated later in the discussion of Corporate Accounting Frauds. All this possibly indicates that a much larger amount of corporate crime goes undetected.

In recent years there has been a decline in the adequate enforcement of many regulations affecting many corporations. For example,

Senator Jeffords, ranking member of the Senate Enforcement and Public Works Committee, stated in 2004 that, "I expect the Bush administration to consider the assault on regulations designed to protect health and the environment. I expect the Bush administration to continue undermining enforcement activities." He added, "The relaxed Bush approach [to enforcement of government regulations] will produce more illness, disease, and preventable deaths than simply putting the federal government's full resources into achieving compliance with the Clean Air Act" (*New York Times*, Sept. 13, 2004). While the Bush administration greatly increased the SEC budget to fight financial crimes affecting investors, it was not tough on other business areas. "When it comes to areas such as environmental protection and occupational and drug safety, corporations often have had their way according to critics" (Johnson, 2004, p. 204).

The *Corporate Crime* study revealed that a relatively small number of the large corporations violated repeatedly. There are indications that this may be more widespread, and if so would increase the number of violations. For example, thirty-eight corporations had ten or more sanctions imposed on them, or about twenty each. This recidivism among many corporations continues into the 2000s. General Electric, for example, as was pointed out in *Corporate Crime*, has been repeatedly charged with law violations in wide ranging areas. Even the Justice Department pointed out years ago General Electric's potentiality for frequent and persistent involvement in antitrust suits. *Multinational Monitor* ("Decades of Misdeeds and Wrong Doing," July/August, 2001) has compiled a list of forty-two major law violations of General Electric between 1990 and 2001. These included twenty-three environmental, air, or water pollution violations (five repeated acts of contamination of the Hudson River), a fine of $30 million for defrauding the government on defense contracts, several violations of plant safety, a $70 million fine for money laundering, a fraud related to the illegal sale of fighter jets to Israel, $13.5 million to the whistleblower, $3.25 million to consumers after deceptive light bulb advertising, and a $147 million fine to reimburse unfair debt collection practices.

Halliburton, the nation's largest corporation offering energy and other services worldwide, particularly in oil, has had a long history of troubles with the government. It was charged by the SEC with secretly changing its accounting practices so it would show that profits in 1998 and 1999 were substantially higher than they should have been. The fraudulent accounting charge dealt with the way Halliburton booked cost overruns. In 1995, it received a $1.2 billion fine and a $2.6 million civil penalty for sending oil-drilling equipment to Libya and Iraq that could be used to detonate nuclear weapons. Vice President Dick Cheney ran Halliburton from 1995 to 2000. In 2000 it was fined $2 million for overcharging maintenance and repairs at Fort Ord, CA. In 2004, Halliburton was fined $7.5 million, and an action was brought against two former officials by the SEC. In 2004, it was under SEC investigation involving possible illegal bribery payments in a joint venture in Nigeria in violation of the Foreign Corrupt Practices Act.

In 2004, during the Iraq war, Halliburton was again under investigation for substantial overcharging for gasoline, food, and equipment for the army and gasoline for the Iraq civilian population. All this was a reminder of the gross involvement of corporations in profiteering during World War II. As of the end of 2004, Halliburton had received over $10 billion in army contracts. There were many allegations of financial misdeeds by the corporation including overcharges that led to criminal, congressional, and Pentagon investigations of Halliburton's work in Iraq. As of early 2005, the investigations of Halliburton revealed:

1. A review by the defense agency concluded that Halliburton overcharged for fuel of $61 million.
2. An investigation found that Halliburton could not account for scores of items in Iraq worth millions.
3. A Pentagon audit found Halliburton charged the army for meals it never served to the troops. Halliburton repaid $36 million and set aside $140 million for a possible settlement.
4. A criminal investigation was made of whether kickbacks were given in Halliburton's use of a Kuwaiti subcontractor, without competitive bidding, that provided gasoline for Iraq's civilian market; the offense involved $6.3 million.

### Oil Industry: One of the Worst

Twenty-five years ago the oil industry was found to have 10 times its expected share of corporate violations. It was charged with one out of every ten cases of serious, or moderately serious, violations. It had a third of the serious and moderately serious environmental violations. Twenty-two of the twenty-eight oil-refining corporations violated the law at least once; twenty had one or more serious or moderately serious violations.

Turning to the 1990s and 2000s, we find similar large-scale oil industry violations. To select a few, Chevron, in 1992, pled guilty to sixty-five Clean Water Act violations, and was given $8 million in criminal and civil fines. Chevron also admitted to distributing wastewater prior to its being sampled so as to understate the actual amount of oil grease discharge that it had reported to the EPA. It also received another fine in 1992 of $6.5 million for damaging the environment. In 1991, Marathon Oil pled guilty to criminal violations of the Clean Water Act: it discharged pollutants from its refinery and was fined $900,000. Mobil, in 2004, was fined $5.5 million for oil spills on the Navajo Reservation in Utah. In 1994, Unalocal Corporation was given a criminal fine of $1.5 million for illegally discharging 8.5 million gallons of petroleum thinner over a fifty-year period, whereupon it could pass into state waters.

In 1990, Exxon was criminally fined $121 million in state claims over the Exxon Alaskan Valdez oil spill of 11 million gallons of crude oil spilled from the ship, the *Valdez*, which fouled 700 miles of Alaskan shoreline, killing birds and fish and diminishing the living standards of thousands of Alaskan Americans. There had been other corporate violations by Exxon. For example, in 1991 Exxon was given a criminal fine of $200,000 for spilling 567,000 gallons of home heating oil in a narrow waterway between New York and New Jersey. Another environmental violation resulted in a $125,000 fine.

A major problem in the oil industry was the well-publicized case in 2004 against the Royal Dutch/Shell Group, which operates in the United States and other countries and is the world's largest publicly owned oil corporation. Investigations by American and British security regulators found a very serious violation in Royal's reporting for years of crude oil reserves of 25 percent more than the company actually had. Shell thus misled investors for years about its financial health. A memorandum of the head of Shell exploration to the chairman in 2003 stated, "I am becoming sick and tired about lying about the extent of our reserves issues, and the downward revisions that have to be done because of far too aggressive, optimistic bookings" (*Guardian Weekly*, April 22, 2004). Shell later admitted it had substantially overstated its oil revenues; in 2002 it had been overstated by 41 percent. The corporation was fined $150 million and accepted the SEC finding that it had violated U.S. laws in its reporting, record keeping, and internal controls, and was also ordered to pay the SEC

$120 million. In 2004 the chairman resigned. The U.S. Department of Justice in 2005 was conducting a criminal inquiry into Shell's statement of its oil and gas reserves.

## The Pharmaceuticals: The Worst

*Corporate Crime* reported that pharmaceutical corporations committed one out of ten of all violations and one out of eight serious and moderately serious violations. All seventeen pharmaceutical corporations committed at least one serious or moderately serious violation. Two had twenty-one or more violations. Despite being by far the most prosperous of all U.S. industries since the 1980s (only in 2003 did it fall to third), making huge profits (Angell, 2004, p. 3), it is hard to explain their persistent violation of law. In 2002 the profits of the ten largest drug companies in the Fortune 500 ($35.9 billion) were more than the profits for *all* the other 490 businesses combined ($33.7 billion) (Angell, 2004, p. 11). These excessive profits are in part because drug prices are not controlled in the United States as in the case of most Western European countries, but also in many of the third world, like India.

The pharmaceuticals twenty-five years later still present a sordid history of noncompliance with the law as well as various unethical practices. In his 1984 book *Corporate Crime in the Pharmaceutical Industry*, Braithwaite pointed out that among pharmaceutical corporations, there is "a difference between the need for commitment to integrity and quality at operating levels of the organization, and the need for top management to suspend that commitment for decisions of major financial impact" (Braithwaite, 1984, p. 149).

Marcia Angell, an M.D. and the former editor-in-chief of the *New England Journal of Medicine*, which is among the most powerful positions in American medicine, strongly condemned the pharmaceuticals in her 2004 book, *The Truth About the Drug Companies: How They Deceive Us and What to do About It*. Her conclusions are that drug companies are corrupt, engage in deceptive research, greatly overcharge for drugs, produce inferior products, borrow their best research ideas from government-funded scientists, and constantly buy the affections of physicians with free trips and gifts. She points out that large pharmaceuticals "...would like us to believe that prices of their top selling drugs have to be high to cover their costs, including the costs of all drugs that never make it to the market.... The truth is that there is no particular reason to think that R &

D (research and development) costs, no matter what they are, have anything to do with drug pricing" (Angell, 2004, pp. 50, 51).

Big drug manufacturers have for some time encountered serious charges that some publish only favorable results of their drug tests and suppress the unfavorable results. A member of the AMA's Board of Trustees said, "We are concerned that this pattern of publication distorts the medical literature, affecting the validity and findings of systematic reviews, the decision of funding agencies, and ultimately the practice of medicine" (*New York Times*, June 16, 2004). One of the largest, GlaxoSmithKline, for example, made a settlement in 2004 of $2.5 million for suppressing adverse clinical evidence. They had been accused of hiding the negative test results of tests on its antidepressant drug of Seroxat on children and teenagers. Feeling that pharmaceutical companies often do not reveal the results of clinical tests that suggest that drugs that do not work or may even be harmful, the *New York Times* editorial of September 11, 2004 stated: "A useful lever for reform was provided by the 12 leading medical journals that announced they would soon refuse to publish their results of any clinical trial that had not been registered at the outset in a public database. Registration would make it harder for companies to bury bad results.... The best solution would be a federal law requiring that all significant clinical trials be registered in a public database and that results be made available. The American Medical Association favors a centralized registry covering drugs, biological agents and medical devices."

Some drug corporations have promoted so-called "off label uses" that are not described on the label, an illegal procedure. Several corporations have been involved with paying physicians or drug programs to prescribe or endorse their drugs. For example, MerckMedco Managed Care, one of the largest drug plan managers, was paid more than $3 billion in rebates in the late 1990s to promote sales of certain drugs. Many cases now involve Medicaid drug frauds. In 2003 seven states including New York, California, and Texas brought suits against GlaxoSmithKline and Pharmacia, two large pharmaceuticals who used unethical means to let consumer drug plans select the company's drugs over competing drugs. The suit claimed that this practice had cost the consumers and federal and state governments hundreds of millions of dollars over the previous years.

Ortho Pharmaceutical, a subsidiary of the large corporation Johnson & Johnson, was fined $8 million in 1995 for obstructing justice by persuading employees to destroy documents relating to a federal investigation of the company's RetinA public relations campaign. The company had an extensive public relations campaign that generated publicity for RetinA's use in the treatment of sun-wrinkled or photo-aged skin. The drug had been approved previously for the treatment of acne, and the FDA had never approved it for sun-wrinkled and photo-aged skin. The company later admitted directing employees to destroy the documents relating to the publicity. In 1999, F. HoffmanLaRoche Ltd, a giant Swiss pharmaceutical, operating also in the United States, was given a criminal fine of $500 million for antitrust violations involving the conspiracy of various pharmaceuticals in several countries to fix vitamin prices. In 2003 Schering-Plough was fined by the FDA for failing to manufacture its products safely.

In 1995 Warner-Lambert pled guilty and was given a criminal fine of $10 million for failing to notify the FDA about stability problems with a widely used drug for the treatment of epilepsy. In 1997, the corporation paid a $3 million fine for falsifying reports on the level of pollutants that its Puerto Rican plant was releasing into a river. In 1995, the corporation was given a criminal fine of $10 million by the FDA and in 2004 it was fined $430 million dollars.

Pfizer, the worlds largest pharmaceutical company, in 1999 received a criminal fine of $ 420 million for antitrust violations involving a conspiracy to set illegal prices, market shares, and the allocation of certain areas for the sale of drugs. In 2004, Pfizer was fined $5.5 million for marketing the drug Neurontin for inappropriate use.

In 2004 Bristol-Myers Squib, one of the largest pharmaceuticals, agreed to pay $150 million to settle the SEC accusation that the company inflated its sales and earnings in a series of accounting frauds, one of the largest penalties ever imposed by a federal agency in an accounting case. It came only days after Bristol-Myers agreed to pay $300 million in a class action suit over similar claims. According to the SEC, Bristol-Myers used several earnings management techniques to distort the corporation's true performance from early 2000 to the end of 2001. In fact, Bristol-Myers inflated its revenues by more than $1 billion going back, at least, to 1991. This was done through an aggressive accounting tactic known as "channel stuffing." In this, the company pressured its wholesalers to buy substantial amounts of pharmaceuticals above normal demand, thus generating revenue to meet reports of ambitious sales and earnings projections. The corporation used another accounting technique, called "cookie jar" reserves, using previous earnings to inflate its income by a total of $223 million in 2001. This series of illegal accounting practices enabled it to meet earnings goals and keep pace for investment purposes with rivals' income by claiming to report a professed double-digit growth.

Abbott Laboratories makes various pharmaceutical products and is the world's largest producer of intravenous solutions. In *Corporate Crime* it was noted that "investigations had revealed a history of problems with Abbott Laboratories' intravenous solutions including label mixups and contamination; an inspection of the firm showed that it did not provide sufficient control to insure detection of defective bottles" (p. 266). Twenty-five years later, Abbott continued to be in trouble with additional law violations. Abbott, in 1999, paid a fine of $100 million to the FDA to settle a long running investigation into the company's manufacturing plant in Lake Co., Illinois. Abbott also agreed to remove 125 products from the market and stop making them. In 2003, Abbott paid $622 million to settle an investigation into sales practices for liquids to feed the seriously ill. Abbott used marketing tactics in which the company gave tubes and pumps to deliver liquid food directly into patients' digestive tracts in exchange for large orders of the liquids. Some of the hospitals and nursing homes that received the equipment were suspected of billing Medicaid and Medicare for the free tubes and pumps. In 2001, TAP Pharmaceutical products, a joint venture of Abbott and Takeka Chemical Industries, pled guilty to conspiracy and paid $875 million, then the record for health fraud fines, to settle the accusations related to its marketing of the cancer drug Lupron. TAP was accused of giving Lupron to medical programs knowing that Medicare and Medicaid would be billed for the cost of drugs.

For the second time in less than six months, the U.S. Food and Drug Administration accused Abbott Laboratories in 2004 of false and misleading marketing of an AIDS drug (*New Mexican*, Nov. 11, 2004). The FDA ordered Abbott to immediately stop circulating print and advertisements for its drug Kaletra, the nation's most popular protease inhibitor for people with HIV, accusing the company of inflating the drug's benefits. Some ads, which have run in several publications targeting the HIV community and on restroom posters, show a multiyear sequence of pictures of a healthy-looking man and ask, "Where do you see yourself in five years?" One caption indicates that HIV is "still undetectable." "These promotional pieces overstate the effectiveness of Kaletra, and omit the indication and material information about the risks associated with Kaletra in the treatment of HIV infection," the FDA wrote in a letter. "Therefore, the promotional materials misbrand the drug [under federal rules]."

In the 2000s there have been many cases of Medicaid fraud committed by the largest pharmaceuticals. In 2004 ScheringPlough who, with sales of $8.3 billion, is one of the largest drug makers, agreed to pay $350 million in fines and plead guilty to criminal charges that it cheated the federal Medicaid program. Federal law requires drug makers to offer the lowest prices to Medicaid but Schering-Plough sold its products to private health care providers at a lower cost than to Medicaid. They used subterfuges such as "kickback fees" to the company purchasing disguised as "data fees" for information it was already getting. In another case, they offered a company open payments that were essentially free loans.

In the largest medical fraud ever, Bayer, the very large pharmaceutical, agreed in 2003 to a fine of $257 million and pled guilty to criminal charges for selling a widely used drug to Kaiser Permanente, one of the largest health care organizations, at lower prices than to Medicaid in violation of federal law. To cover up fraud charges, bottles of the drug were sold to Kaiser, relabeled with Kaiser's name and given a different identification number. In 1996, Bayer also labeled a blood pressure medicine with a Kaiser drug code so that it could give Kaiser a deeper discount. In 2003, GlaxoSmithKline agreed to pay $86.7 million to settle civil charges that it had overcharged the Medicaid program for two widely used drugs. The deal also involved relabeling medicine for Kaiser.

### Corporate Foreign and Domestic Bribery

When *Corporate Crime* was published twenty-five years ago there was considerable publicity given to the U.S. corporations bribing foreign officials in the third world by devices such as sending their children to college in the United States in order for the corporation to get the foreign contracts. A law, the Foreign Corrupt Practices Act of 1977, was passed to curb such bribery.

Since then, there still have been some cases of foreign bribery by American corporations. For example, General Electric in 1992 pled guilty to defrauding the federal government of $26.5 million in the sale of military equipment to Israel, and paid $69 million in fines of which $9.5 million was a criminal fine. The corporation pled guilty to diverting millions of dollars to a former Israeli Air Force general to secure favorable treatment in an F16 warplane contract. In 1993, Teledyne Inc. pled guilty to making false statements to the U.S. government relating to the payment of millions of dollars in commissions to a Taiwan consultant to obtain military contracts from the Taiwan government. The corporation was fined $1.5 million.

To get around the law, however the *New York Times* (Feb. 16, 2003) reported that a new practice called "offsets" had now become widely used by corporations to get around the law. They are equivalent to what might be done to bribe foreign officials but now the third world government itself is bribed. For the third world country to buy a corporation's products, the corporation agrees to various forms of aid to the country including direct investments in the country such as transferring subassembly jobs to the country or the construction of some needed plant. Boeing, Lockheed Martin, and Northrup Grumman did just that in the United Arab Emirates, spending millions on creating jobs, even financing a medical center linked to the Mayo Clinic and helping with oil spill cleanups. As of 2004, offsets are not illegal, but sooner or later this corporate practice will have to be outlawed because it is simply a "bribe" under another name that has been developed to undermine the 1977 law.

Domestic commercial or business bribery by corporations is to gain an advantage over other corporations. It is considered illegal by several federal agencies as well as some states. It takes various forms such as kickbacks, outright monetary payments, and a variety of other forms. Domestic bribery to influence purchases may take less direct forms. They include expensive dinners, theater tickets, and expensive gifts, particularly at Christmas. "For example, a former senior vice president and sales agent for Boeing said his company often arranged fishing and yachting expeditions for its customers. On one occasion, they hired John Wayne's yacht, the *Wild Goose* to 'entertain' customers. He added, 'I don't think we have done any more than the average American Business'" (Clinard, 1990, p. 1345). Years ago Reisman wrote that, "Illegal business bribery is so common that it has become almost as part of the American way of life" (Reisman, 1979).

Several large corporations have been involved in the domestic illegal bribery cases, including General Electric. For example, General Electric, along with two former top executives, were convicted in 1981 of paying a $1.25 million to a Puerto Rican operations manager of Puerto Rico's Water Resources Authority to obtain a $9.3 million power plant construction.

Boeing, in 2003 was involved in a somewhat subtle bribery scheme involving a top government official, a number 2 weapons buyer for the Air Force who was able to choose among bids of airplane manufacturers. In a case of what is termed "revolving door," the relationship was so cozy that it was as if she, the government official, were a "Boeing agent." Darleen Druyun passed along to Boeing, for example, proprietary data furnished by Airbus to the Air Force in connection with a $20 billion contract. Her goal, in favoring Boeing, was to secure first jobs for her daughter and future son-in-law, and later a position for herself. She steered billions of dollars in Air Force contracts to Boeing, and, in addition, sometimes overpaid the corporation by favoring them in a competitive bidding. She later admitted in one case selecting Boeing over four competing aircraft corporations, and later stated that from an objective analysis, the contract would not have been given to Boeing (*New York Times*, Oct. 2, 2004). After the case broke, she was fired by Boeing, along with the chief financial officer, Michael Sears. She received a nine-month prison sentence, and 150 hours of community service. The Boeing CEO and the former Boeing CFO later resigned and pleaded guilty to illegally negotiating a $250,000 executive position at Boeing while Druyen was reviewing whether Boeing should get a $33 billion contract to provide new refueling tankers to the Air Force.

At the time this case was going on, Boeing had already been barred from some $1 billion in Air Force business. The Air Force had discovered that Boeing had stolen over 25,000 proprietary documents belonging to Lockheed, which was also bidding for the contract. All this led to the *New York Times* top business story headline of Oct. 8, 2004, "A Growing Military Contracts Scandal: More Air Force Deals with Boeing are Questionable."

## Role of Accounting in Corporate Law Violations

A corporation's accurate accounting procedures are crucial to not only a true public corporate market picture but at another level, a true picture for the individual investor and stockholder. Corporate statements of assets, liabilities, cash flow, income, and the financial state of acquisitions must be accurate. But the picture can be manipulated by false accounting practices, and this is unfortunately often done. Corporate accountants, moreover, in this process are responding to the demand of corporate executives.

In this connection, *Corporate Crime* contains much information about illegal accounting practices twenty-five years ago and discusses some of the numerous cases of that day, including Lockheed, Allied Chemical, and Ashland Oil. Illegal accounting practices have continued since that time with increasing momentum. For example, in 2003, executives in Dynergy, Inc., a large producer of natural gas and electricity, reported in their accounting a $300 million loan as "cash flow" which gave a false picture of the corporate financial situation, for which they were fined.

As another example, the accounting fraud that went on in Computer Associates International, the world's fourth largest computer software company, was finally revealed in 2004. Seven executives including the CEO were indicted for securities fraud and obstruction of justice. The corporation later admitted that it had improperly booked more than $2 billion in revenue. The corporation general counsel even coached executives in misleading the investigators. Desperate to meet Walt Street's forecasting of quarterly corporate income, Computer Associates backdated billions of dollars by false accounting in business contracts. "The defendants," said Mr. Comey, the head of the U.S. Justice Department's corporate fraud task force, "are accused of perpetrating a massive accounting fraud that cost investors hundreds of millions of dollars when it collapsed. Then they allegedly tried to cover up their crimes by lying" (*New York Times*, Sept. 23, 2004). The company agreed to pay $225 million in restitution to shareholders and improve its accounting and ethics practices under the oversight of an independent monitor; in return, prosecutors dismissed security fraud and obstruction charges against the corporation in eighteen months, as long as the monitor finds that the company is abiding by the agreement.

Investors and stockholders have largely only one protection against false accounting practices, and that is the outside auditor who inspects and certifies the accuracy of the accounts and can call attention to false and misleading financial records. Unfortunately, large accounting firms such as Arthur Anderson, Arthur Young, and PricewaterhouseCoopers have not always carried out this responsibility. In the case of Arthur Young in the seventies, it did not exercise this responsibility in the Lockheed scandal (*Corporate Crime*, p. 196). A review committee reported to the SEC, "in spite of the detection of some unusual methods of payments, the outside auditors never terminated their relation to Lockheed.

When we move to the Enron case in the 2000s, Arthur Anderson did not exercise responsibility in its outside auditing. Anderson was required to look for deviations from accepted accounting procedures. The audit was supposed to include inquiries of management and corporate legal counsel about methods that might be illegal. Over the period from the third quarter of 2000 to the third quarter of 2001, Enron reported pretax profits of $1.5 billion. Had Arthur Anderson exercised its corporate responsibility, the profit would actually have been $425 million. The illegal activities were done by transferring bad corporate investments to what was termed "Raptors," which were "outside" units actually created inside the corporation as "partnerships" run by Enron's financial officer. It was a hall of mirrors. There was no purpose in this financial dealing except to hide the real situation. A committee of experts later created by the Enron board of directors reported, "the creation of 'Raptors' was perceived by many within Enron as a triumph of accounting ingenuity by a group of accountants." The committee reported that the "Raptors" was "little more than a highly complex accounting construct that was destined to collapse."

There are several reasons why large accounting firms sometimes do not carry out their auditing responsibilities. One reason is that a large accounting firm operates in a very competitive and lucrative business. For example, Enron paid Arthur Anderson in 2000 $25 million for auditing and $20 million for consulting. The "consulting relationship" often results in an interlocking relationship between a company doing the auditing and, in addition, consulting for the corporation, which adds up to a possible lack of integrity. As Charles Bowsher, a former U.S. comptroller general stated, "How independent can you be if you are also doing this kind of work for the management?" (*New York Times*, Feb. 8, 2003)

By being consultants, an accounting company can aid a corporation like Enron, in disguising their true financial condition. Anderson helped Enron, for example, to create its "Raptor off the books" partnerships in which Enron was able to drop assets off their books by creating "buyers" that Enron had actually created. Such sales could increase reports of earnings and cash flow, while the company's financial exposure to the partnership could, under accounting rules, remain hidden. In the first quarter of 2001, Enron restructured the Raptors and contributed a $1.2 billion of contingent common shares to Raptors in exchange for a $1.2 billion note. Anderson then booked the amount wrongly as a note receivable (an asset) instead of a charge against equity (like a debt).

According to a story in the *New York Times* (Feb. 8, 2003), the large incredible loans and bonuses given to top Tyco executives were approved by PricewaterhouseCoopers. The article asked, "At what point does an auditor's dual role become a problem either because an executive's role is compromised by an auditor's 'bribe' or because the auditor is compromised by a desire to keep both the individual executive and the management happy?" WorldCom, in the early 2000s, also used "the aggressive accounting" like Tyco did. For example, it established large reserves after the acquisition of another company to account for certain anticipated costs. By accounting, these reserves could actually be "reversed" into income.

In 2002, Arthur Anderson was indicted for obstructing justice, particularly by widespread destruction of documents relating to Enron. The indictment stated "tons of paper related to Enron's audit were promptly shredded as part of the orchestrated document destruction...a systematic effort was undertaken and carried out to purge the computer harddrive and email system of Enron related files." A jury found Anderson guilty and, within a few months, Arthur Anderson, one of the world's largest accounting firms, closed its doors. Anderson had been in serious trouble before. For example, in 2001 it paid a $7 million fine for helping Waste Management overstate its income from 1992-1996 in order to boost its value by more than $1 billion.

## Top Corporate Executives

Even though a corporation may be defined legally as a "person," by itself it cannot violate the law any more than a ship can technically go aground by itself. A ship requires someone at the helm in the same way a corporation requires at its helm a corporate executive officer (CEO), chairman of the board, and other top executives; it is their actions that drive a corporation "on the reef." Often the nature of the general corporate culture may help facilitate illegal decisions at the top as in the case of illegal behavior of the famed Enron case in the early 2000s. Many examples exist of the various subterfuges used by corporation executives. In 2002 the former chief executive of the Sunbeam corporation, one of the Fortune 500, agreed to pay a $500,000 fine and accept being banned from ever becoming an officer of a public company. According to the SEC, he engineered a large accounting fraud that increased the profits of Sunbeam. To falsely inflate profits, they used "buy and hold" sales in which barbeque grills would not be paid for or delivered until spring. This pumped up 1997 profits at the expense of 1998. In addition, he used the technique of "cookie jar reserves" that were created from sales, not acquisitions, and were used to create "profits" in later years, and also various other techniques to overstate sales and deceive the investor.

One thing has definitely changed in the corporate world in twenty-five years, and that is the enormous pay now generally given to corporate executives. The gap between corporate executives' salaries and hourly pay for plant workers was 43 times as great in 1980 as measured by *Business Week*; by 2000, it was about 400 times as great, cited in the *New Mexican*, April 20, 2003. Not only do CEOs still get their large salaries, but substantial bonuses are often added, long-term stock options as well as perks, which technically should be considered remunerative if the executive had to pay for them. A good example of the way monetary remuneration of top executives works is in the case of the 2000 payments to the CEO of General Dynamics, a major defense corporation. Nicholas Chabraja's $1 million salary was augmented by a $2.3 million bonus and $400,000 in non-cash benefits (including $200,000 worth of personal travel on the corporate jet). Nearly $4 million worth of General Dynamics stock was put into Chabaraja's long-term compensation account and the $7.6 million profit he realized by exercising options on 135,000 shares of stock. All together, he received a $15.2 million package in a year in which General Dynamics stock price and earnings per share declined.

The average compensation in 2004 for 200 CEOs of large corporations was approximately $10 million; the median was approximately $8.4 million. Some total compensations of CEOs were approximately: Abbott Laboratories $10.5 million, Alcoa $10.9 million, Clorox $7.8 million, GE $8.8 million, Honeywell International $16.4 million, Occidental Petroleum $38.6 million, Pfizer $21 million, Schering-Plough $12.9 million, Tyco International $21.3 million, Wyeth $10.6 million (*New York Times*, April 3, 2005). The chairman of Enron, Kenneth Lay's total compensation in 2001 was $104 million, and his CEO received $8.5 million.

In contrast, the highest top executive *combined* salary and other compensation in 1978 was $2 million paid to the board chairman and CEO of Norton Simon (*Corporate Crime*, p. 278). Salaries for CEOs in the 1970s were generally from $200,000 to $500,000. Even allowing for the differences in dollar value, twenty-five years later the salaries and compensation were comparatively enormous.

Several explanations can be offered for the large salaries in 2004. Some would say it is to reward their performance in the corporation, but several studies have found little connection between executive pay and corporate performance; in fact, in many cases, there is an inverse correlation—as profits decline, the executive pay often goes up. For example, *USA Today* (Aug. 12, 2003) in a sample of eleven large corporations whose stock declined between 28 and 59 percent, the CEOs received very substantial additional compensation; in fact, the CEO in the corporation that declined 59 percent received options worth $56.6 million. The defenses of CEOs in criminal trials (such as Ebbers of WorldCom and Lay of Enron) involve a tenuous contradiction. They claim they have been hardworking, closely involved in the corporation, hands-on CEOs, and largely this justifies their very substantial financial compensation. In their trials, they maintain they were simply "caretakers" for large issues who knew little of the details of the operation of the corporation and of, for example, accounting frauds.

Another explanation is that since the pay is high in other corporations, they must be paid high salaries to keep them content or keep them from leaving. Others say that since a corporation's earnings may be in the billions, CEOs should have a piece of the act, which, anyway, even if high, would be a comparatively infinitesimal amount.

An article in the *New York Times* (Dec. 18, 2002) offers still another explanation, namely that a corporation compensation committee made up of executives and others from other corporations often have too friendly ties with the CEOs and other top executives of the corporation to fairly evaluate their performance. "More than 200 large corporations including some of the nation's best known and most widely admired companies have had compensation committees with members who have close ties to the company or its chief executives" (ibid.).

In the 2000s, the list of corporate executives indicted, on trial or convicted, was large. Considering that corporate executives' compensation is extremely large, one can wonder why they risk their salaries to get even larger compensation. Some might argue that they were doing this not for personal advancement, but to increase or protect the corporation's bottom line. Perhaps both reasons are involved. As an example, the CEO, the former comptroller, and the director of accounting of WorldCom were indicted in 2002 on charges that they illegally conspired to hide billions of losses of the company (*New York Times*, Aug. 29, 2002). Specifically, they were charged with falsifying the corporation's losses and records, providing misleading information to the accounting auditors, and illegally monopolizing company information in conjunction with buying and selling securities and falsifying reports to the SEC. According to a later report of the corporation, the CEO was actively involved in securing a personal corporate "loan" of $400 million that was never disclosed to the stockholders. This loan was used for such things as the construction of a $1.8 million new house, $3 million for gifts and loans to family members and friends, and other personal services. The loan was recorded on the books as a help for the CEO to meet margin calls on personal loans secured by his own WorldCom holdings.

## The Prosecution of Corporate Executives

Back twenty-five years ago, few corporate executives were prosecuted under criminal law: Only 1.5 percent of all actions involved a corporate official convicted of not carrying out his corporate legal responsibility. Of the ninety-six executives convicted, 91 percent were convicted of federal antitrust violations. The major difficulty in prosecuting top corporate executives at that time and today is their claim that they did not know of illegal behavior going on in the corporation, did not want to know, or even may have told someone not to tell them. The delegation of authority within a corporation has made it often difficult to involve, for example, top corporate executives in accounting frauds, as was also pointed out in *Corporate Crime*.

Today the relationship of the CEO to a corporate offence is sometimes termed the "ostrich defense." Ebbers, the WorldCom CEO, and Lay, the Enron chairman, claimed that they knew nothing about illegal financial manipulations such as accounting fraud manipulations in their corporations. Ebbers testified that, "I do not know anything about finance and accounting," and also testified that he knew nothing about the accounting frauds (*New York Times*, March 4, 2005). At the trial of Ebbers, the WorldCom CEO, the defense claimed he was incapable of understanding complex accounting and incapable of devising a complex accounting fraud. His chief financial officer, Scott Sullivan, on the other hand, maintained that Ebbers was familiar with complex accounting issues. He testified that, "Bernie had a grasp of financial information that surpassed the level of a Chief Operating Officer" (*New York Times*, Feb. 8, 2005). Moreover he said that, "Ebbers was a very 'hands on' executive." The U.S. district attorney concluded, "It insults your intelligence that Ebbers could have built this company up from nothing in a 10 year period and still be clueless about its financial performance" (*New York Times*, March 4, 2005). The government finally showed that Ebbers effectively ordered the chief financial officer to reclassify in accounting procedures rising corporate expenses in order to meet the company's revenue growth targets. Ebbers was desperate to reverse the long slide in the corporation's share price, which also affected his own very large fortune in WorldCom stock. Enron's CEO, Lay, was also indicted for making false statements about Enron's financial prospects and has claimed ignorance of the accounting manipulations that brought him down. The trial is scheduled to begin January 6, 2006.

This situation, as well as many other problems in prosecuting corporations and their executives, has been greatly changed with the enactment of the Sarbanes-Oxley bill in 2002, also known as the Public Company Accounting Reform and Investor Protection Act of 2002, in which top executives were made criminally responsible for many of the actions taken in the corporation. The bill responded to the high profile scandals involving Enron, WorldCom, Arthur Anderson, Global Crossing, Tyco, and others, and had a significant impact on executives, accountants, shareholders, and government regulators. The bill significantly affected the regulation of accountants. It imposed new responsibilities and put liabilities on CEOs, CFOs, and boards of directors. It toughened criminal penalties in terms of both fines and prison sentences for corporate fraud, destruction of documents, and impeding investigations. Some of the more important provisions of the bill are (details derived from the Internet: McGuire Wood LLD, Press Room, Sarbanes-Oxley Act, 81—2002):

1. It significantly raises criminal penalties: the maximum penalty was raised to twenty-five years; there are new crimes with potential twenty-year sentences for destroying, altering, or fabricating records in federal investigations for any scheme or attempt to defraud shareholders. Fines and penalties were also increased for issuing false statements or failing to certify financial reports, to $5 million and a twenty-year sentence of imprisonment. The act requires preservation of documents relating to an audit (including emails) for five years and creates a ten-year penalty for destroying such documents. Charges for mail and wire fraud were raised to twenty years. In addition, the act prevents officers and directors guilty of securities fraud from discharging liability for securities fraud in a bankruptcy.
2. It requires each principal executive officer and principal finance officer to certify with respect to each periodic report containing financial statements.
3. It provides for certain illegal actions of the CEO or chief financial officer that they shall forfeit pertinent bonuses and profits.
4. It requires the chief financial officers of the corporation to be bound by a code of ethics and that any change or waiver to the code of ethics be reported to the SEC.
5. It created a Public Accounting Oversight Board to oversee the auditing of public companies.
6. It prohibits public accounting firms from performing specific services for their audit clients, including internal audit services and financial information systems design and implementation.

Enron started as a pipeline business and became an energy-trading powerhouse. Enron was the seventh largest U.S. company in sales in 2002, and filed for bankruptcy in 2002 in the amount of $63.8 billion, the second largest in corporate history. Following bankruptcy, a series of federal indictments were filed against top executives charging them with using aggressive accounting methods relating to Raptors, off the book "partnerships" to hide debt and inflate profits and assets. In 2004, the chairman, Kenneth Lay of Enron, was indicted for conspiring to deceive investors and employees about the company's financial difficulties, making misleading statements, wire fraud, bank fraud, and securities fraud. In a civil action, the SEC also sought $90 million in fines and penalties, accusing Lay of disposing of his stock at prices that did not reflect Enron's true, but much lower value. Also, it sought to bar him permanently from serving as an officer and director of a publicly held corporation. His trial is scheduled for 2006. The Enron former chief financial officer who was at the heart of the scandal, Andrew Fastow, was indicted in

2003. He was charged with ninety-eight counts, including fraud, money laundering, and insider trading. He later pled guilty to two counts of conspiracy and agreed to cooperate with federal prosecutors. Under his plea bargain, he would serve ten years in prison and return $29 million to the government. The former finance executive and aide to Fastow, Michael Kopper, pled guilty to fraud and money laundering charges in August 2002. He was cooperating with the government and awaiting sentencing in 2004. The former treasurer, Ben Glisan, Jr., pled guilty to conspiracy in September 2003. He was given a five-year prison sentence. Lee Fastow, former Enron assistant treasurer and wife of Andrew Fastow, pled guilty in May 2004 to tax evasion and was given a one-year sentence. Paula Ricker, former investor relations executive, pled guilty to insider trading in May 2004.

WorldCom collapsed in 2002 with the largest bankruptcy in corporate history with $103.4 billion. Its CEO, Bernard Ebbers, was convicted in 2005 of frauds amounting to $11 billion and sentenced to twenty-five years in prison. The judge said, "Ebbers' statements deprived investors of their money. They might have made different decisions had they known the truth." Ebbers started with a small long distance phone service and built it into the giant second largest telecommunications corporation. This was done largely by acquisitions, the financing of which was based on the increased value of the corporation's stock and the corporation's profits. In 1995 it changed its name to WorldCom. In 2002, it filed for bankruptcy. The CEO, Bernard Ebbers, was indicted in 2002 for falsifying the corporation's losses, providing misleading information to the company's auditors, and falsifying reports to the SEC. The conviction of Ebbers in March 2005 was top national news. He was found guilty of fraud, conspiracy, and seven counts of filing false reports to the SEC. Each count carried a sentence of five to ten years. The *Wall Street Journal* editorial comment on Ebbers' conviction was, "As this last chapter in WorldCom's story comes to a close, it's worth remembering what Mr. Ebbers wrought. WorldCom workers and shareholders lost billions of dollars. But the damage to our market system was—and is—even greater" (*Wall Street Journal*, March 16, 2005).

Several other top corporate executives of large corporations received lengthy sentences in 2005, including the CEO of Adelphia Communications, the sixth largest cable company, who received a sentence of fifteen years, and the chief financial officer, his son, of twenty years. They were convicted of looting hundreds of millions of dollars from the company and concealing its true debt load from investors.

### Criminal Sanctions for Corporations and Executives?

Crime control is not the only function of the criminal sanction. As Schlegel has pointed out, nor is deterrence the only principle upon which corporate punishments may be used. There is a "just deserts" explanation as well that regards the institution of punishment as representing society's moral condemnation of both the crime and the perpetrator. He feels that a reexamination is needed of the generally unsystematic corporate sentencing practices to include the element of just deserts. The amount of punishment must fairly reflect the seriousness of the offense. From his perspective, seriousness is determined on the basis of the harm caused or risked by the act, and the culpability of the offender (Schlegel, 1990).

An entirely different view from that of the use solely of punitive measures has been developed by John Braithwaite of Australian National University in several writings (Braithwaite, 1989, 2002). As opposed to the punitive approach to corporate crime he feels that there should be wider use of "restorative justice," and feels that this approach will be more successful in the long run. Braithwaite believes in corporate self-regulation and "conversational regulation" with government officials. Peter Yeager has written a comprehensive analysis of Braithwaite's views (Yeager, 2004) and states that Braithwaite believes that "persuasion of corporate managers and executives is likely to be more effective than an aggressive punishment oriented approach to compliance" (p. 898). Braithwaite argues "that restorative justice approaches fare better with corporate lawbreaking than do adversarial ones" (ibid.).

Yeager is somewhat critical of Braithwaite's restorative justice for corporate crime, even though it may be very effective for some conventional and occupational crime. Yeager has written, "Indeed, regulatory failure has been the most marked feature of the current crisis in corporate behavior. It reaches deep inside firms, into their financial and accounting controls, and spreads throughout the inner layers of compliant external review by their accountants, lawyers and bankers. Bedeviled by the sheer magnitude of companies' financial creativity, as well as by networks of professional and personal relations that generate conflicts of interest and/or lean toward the benefit of the doubt for client firms, both self-regulation (e.g., the New York Stock Exchange) and government regulation (the federal Securities and Exchange Commission) have reacted slowly and haltingly, leaving vigorous enforcement to a few states' attorneys general. This impressive pattern of fraud and regulatory failure reflects key features of the nation's (and world's) system of finance capital: its ever increasing centralization and its abstruseness. Importantly, these features together present formidable obstacles to restorative justice" (Yeager, 2004, pp. 908, 909).

Looking back twenty-five years ago, few corporate executives were then prosecuted or convicted and hardly ever given prison sentences. If they were sentenced to prison, it often involved only days or months, and very rarely a year or two. For example, the large price fixing conspiracy in the folding carton industry (a very large industry) in 1976 involved the indictment of twenty-three carton manufacturing concerns and fifty of their executives. It was a sordid antitrust conspiracy involving using code names in meetings that were held generally far from an office, exchanging mail on plain stationery, using only public telephones, and falsifying accounts of the meetings. As a result, sixteen executives were "imprisoned": eleven for less than one week, one for ten days, and one for fifteen. In addition, however, nearly all were fined and some given community service. Another example, in 1985, E.F. Hutton, a large investment company, pled guilty to 2000 felonies, admitting that it had engaged in a very large "check kiting" scheme with which it was able to deceive others of its true assets. The firm paid $2 million in fines. No one went to prison.

The collapse of WorldCom was followed by a landmark action in 2005. A suit was brought against the directors of WorldCom, whose bankruptcy was the largest in history and the largest accounting fraud scandal. The New York State Common Retirement Fund sued, stating, "WorldCom Board of Directors was utterly derelict in fulfilling the most basic function of the Board" (*Wall Street Journal*, Jan. 6, 2005). In March 2005, eleven out of twelve former directors agreed to a final settlement of $20 million to be paid out of their own pockets. The insurance companies that provided liability coverage to the directors and officers also paid $35 million as part of the settlement. The directors' personal payment was from the start a requirement of any deal. The payments account for 20 percent of an aggregate of a director's net worth, not counting his primary residences and retirement account.

An investment banker, Gary Lutin of Lutin and Company, felt that the accounting improprieties of WorldCom were of the type that could have been detected by any alert director familiar with the basics of the corporate budget. He said, "Management would not have been able to hide billions of dollars if even one member of the Board had done his job in reviewing the expenditures he had approved. The Board should certainly be responsible and share the pain that their lack of responsibility imposed on WorldCom shareholders" (*New York Times*, Jan. 6, 2005).

Over the years, there has hardly been any such action against directors or former directors. Michael Klamer, Stanford law professor, who has studied the personal liability of directors, found only four cases from 1968 to 2003 in which directors contributed their own money to settle a stockholder's lawsuit (*New York Times*, Jan. 6, 2005). A former SEC chief accountant concluded, "in the past Directors' personal wealth has not been at risk when they failed in their obligations to investors who elected them. Now if they don't get the job done you may very well pay" (*Wall Street Journal*, Jan. 6, 2005).

## An Examination of Causal Factors in Corporate Crime

Corporate unethical practices and law violations can be attributed to *internal* structure or to *external* factors such as an unfair or difficult position in the market. In large corporations, the complexity of the corporation itself and the structural relationships make it often difficult, in cases of illegal behavior, to disentangle economic factors, delegated authority, managerial discretion, the ultimate responsibility of the CEO and top management, and the role of corporate culture or corporate ethical history and practice. Moreover, the line between ethics and law violations is often not always clear. Many practices formerly "unethical" become "crimes."

It appears possible, however, to examine the causes of corporate crime in terms of three elements viewed singly or in some combination. One is the decline in corporate earning, profits, etc., the second is the role of unethical corporate cultures, and the other is the role of top management in unethical and illegal behavior.

### Economic Factors

Many might explain corporate violations of government regulations and laws as a consequence of the decline of their profits, the market value of the corporation's assets, or some other basic poor economic situation. This is a very complex situation to view. For example, one might be able to say that corporate violations in general are influenced by a poor economic situation but for certain industries this may not be true. For example, the oil and pharmaceutical industries show great profits but these industries have a long history of serious violations of law. In *Corporate Crime* a sophisticated study was made of corporate profitability, efficiency as defined by a corporation's total sales divided by its assets and liquidity defined as the firm's working capital. The relation of economic structure by the size of the corporation was fully examined.

The major conclusions were:

> Taken together, the results suggest that compared to nonviolating corporations, the violating firms are on average larger, less financially successful, experience relatively poorer growth rates and are more diversified. However, the relationships were only of moderate strength at best. When combined in statistical models to maximize our ability to predict the extent of firms' illegal behavior, the corporate characteristics examined proved not to be strong predictors. Indeed, knowledge of a firm's growth, diversification, and market power added virtually no predictive power when combined with size and financial measures, which were themselves not strong predictors of corporate involvement in illegal activity. Thus information on firm financial performance and structural characteristics is, by itself, insufficient for explaining corporate crime. (*Corporate Crime*, 1980, p. 132. Also see Clinard et al., *Illegal Corporate Behavior*, pp. 150-179. Later studies of some of these factors in relation to antitrust include Simpson, 1986, 1987).

A more satisfactory explanation is that economic pressures and other factors operate in a corporate environment that is conducive to unethical and illegal practices. On the other hand one may find extensive corporate violations where no financial pressures or structural characteristics are evident (ibid.).

*Corporate Culture*

Turning to the role of corporate culture, large corporations generally have a history of considerable length, including their founders, leading top management figures, economic changes, and standards of ethical conduct. Those corporations with high ethical standards may strongly influence the behavior of employees including middle and top management. Corporations, such as General Electric, Abbot Laboratories, and Halliburton, as been pointed out, have had an extensive history of illegal practices. Other corporations have a reputation of ethical standards and behavior such as Proctor and Gamble, Hewlett-Packard, and Borg Warner. Of course, there may be some

corporations with little history of either ethical or unethical practices, such as many technological corporations that came into existence in the late '90s and early 2000s.

In a study of the views of sixty-four retired Fortune 500 middle
management executives, many of whom over their careers worked
for several large corporations found that two thirds believe that corporations generally have an ethical or unethical culture. Among the
factors likely to produce an ethical or unethical culture are the importance of the basic principles of the corporation's founder or later
top management figure, and the idea that a corporation in a small
city rather than a big urban area promoted an ethical climate. In
corporations whose top management emphasized ethical and law-
abiding behavior, they felt there were six factors present. They were:
a history of top management's continuity in compliance; appointment of top management from within a corporation; top
management's explicit instructions for compliance with government
regulations; penalties for employees violating regulations; procedures for middle management to discuss problems with regulations
with top executives; middle management's respect for top
management's wishes to comply with ethical practices. Such description formerly and to a considerable extent today fits the large
Hewlett-Packard corporation, which has a history of ethical behavior (Rivlin and Markoff, 2005).

## Corporate Executives

Turning to the role of top corporate executives, the structure of
any large corporation has many components: the board of directors,
board chairmen, presidents, CEOs, other top management, middle
management, supervisory personnel, and workers. Within the corporate structure, each group has its own role and function related to
others; middle management is especially important because it is the
intermediary responsible for carrying out top management's objectives, and is often responsible for success in manufacturing, marketing, and in directing the supervisory staff.

Although theoretically the board of directors and stockholders
run corporations, in practice this is usually not the case (except in
corporations with large family holdings or where large financial institutions are involved, and therefore have much influence). It is the
CEO, president, or chairman of the board whose role, status, and
power enable them to participate in decisions and set policy about

running the corporations and also about the ethical direction that relates to workers, consumers, competitors, and the government.

> In many ways the ethical and legal problems of a corporation result from the modern corporate structure.... The typical corporation is a multiunit enterprise administered by a group of salaried managers; the board of directors exercises little direct power other than to hire and fire top management and, in general, it follows management recommendations. Corporate managers have great autonomy, therefore, over decisions regarding production, investment, pricing, and marketing." (*Corporate Crime*, p. 273)

Fortune 500 middle management executives felt that the chairman of the board or CEO often set the corporate ethical tone that influences the ethical behavior of other management positions (Clinard, *Corporate Ethics and Crime*, 1983, p. 71). As one middle management executive put it, "Ethics comes and goes in a corporation under top management. I worked under four corporation presidents and each differed. The first was honest, the next was a 'wheelerdealer,' the third was somewhat better and the last one was bad. According to their ethical views, varying ethical pressure was put on middle management all the way down" (Clinard, 1983, p. 133).

Many of the illegal actions taken by top corporate executives appear to be explained by their great power and their presumed virtual invulnerability. They believe their actions are difficult to discover because they have a staff of highly competent attorneys to help protect them, the difficulty of proving their responsibility for illegal actions, and the possibility of using complex accounting methods to prevent the discovery of any illegal behavior.

No corporate case has ever quite illustrated the power accruing to a CEO from corporate illegal activities than what happened to Tyco International. In 2001, Tyco was a global conglomerate with 250,000 employees and $40 billion in sales with profits of $4 billion. CEO Dennis Kozlowski was indicted in 2002 for systematically creating a culture of greed and looting the corporation of $600 million. For example, he secretly authorized the forgiveness of tens of millions of dollar loans to dozens of lesser executives to keep their loyalty. He also, without board approval, gave bonuses to fifty-one employees of $56 million and $39 million more to pay the taxes on bonuses.

A possible element is the personality or character of top management executives, which may influence the structure and direction of a corporation's ethical standards. There are several different types.

Some "financially oriented" executives, for example, are interested primarily in securing financial prestige and quick profits for the corporation, as well as increased compensation for themselves. These top executives are likely to engage to a greater extent in unethical practices than are more "technical and professional types" who have been trained for specialized areas such as engineering....

A similar definition, although different in terminology, has been made between "fiduciary" top managers and "entrepreneurial" managers. Fiduciary managers have an ethical commitment of service to beneficiaries; they do not make self-serving decisions, and they try promote the interests of the organization as a corporate entity. On the other hand, the entrepreneurial manager governs the corporate body on behalf of the owners, and his behavior is directed exclusively towards the corporation's profit maximization.... Still another distinction can be drawn between the ethics of top management persons who tend to be mobile, moving from one corporation to another and being recruited into a corporation from the outside. These executives are more likely to be aggressive, interested in their own rapid corporate achievements and consequently publicity in financial journals; they have limited concern for the corporation's long term reputation.... In contrast to these are executives who have come up from the ranks as supervisors or middle managers in production; they are likely to have had a long-term indoctrination into the corporate history, product quality, and pride in the corporation. They tend to occupy top management positions for lengthy periods of time, and they are less likely to tarnish the corporate name by permitting the corporation to engage in unethical or illegal behavior. (Ibid., pp. 136-137)

Shifting to another side of the issue, the personal behavior of some CEOs in adding unusually very expensive perks in addition to what they already they receive is somewhat hard to explain. The fact that their financial rewards are so great and that they have many perks already at their disposal may make them lose their sense of reality and get a sense of entitlement to even greater perks. They may see other CEOs of their status much more richly rewarded more than they are and they want to, in a sense, compete, even if illegally, to demonstrate their own status and power.

Something of this nature appears to have occurred in the behavior of the Tyco's Dennis Kozlowski. A later Tyco corporation report itemized millions in personal expenditures that the CEO made with corporation funds. They included his $16.8 million apartment on Fifth Avenue, New York City, along with $4 million in renovations and a $7 million apartment on Park Avenue for his former wife. According to the report, he also had the company secretly pay for items like an $80,000 American Express bill, a $72,000 fee to a yacht maker, a $17,000 traveling toilet box, a $15,000 dog umbrella stand, a $6,300 sewing basket, a $6,000 shower curtain, $5,900 for two sets of sheets, a $2,900 set of coat hangers, a $2,200 gilt metal wastebasket, a $1,650 notebook, and a $445 pincushion. A video was made of a $2 million week long Roman-themed party for

Kozlowski's wife held in Sardinia. Tyco corporation paid half the bill. As a former federal prosecutor later observed, "The worst penalty [would be] that Kozlowski has to give back some of the money, and that is a far better outcome than a guilty criminal verdict" (*New York Times*, July 16, 2004).

The criminal prosecution of Kozlowski and his finance officer were retried in 2005 after a mistrial was declared in their 2004 trial. Kozlowski and his financial office, Mark N. Schwartz were indicted for thirty-one criminal counts for stealing $170 million from Tyco by hiding details of their pay packages, and $430 million by selling Tyco stocks after artificially pumping up their price. They were convicted in July 2005 and both face up to twenty-five years in prison.

To most people, the corporate executives like those from Enron, WorldCom, and others were solely responsible for the massive greed and utter disregard for the thousands of employees and stockholders who had invested in the corporations. The primary causal role of corporate executives, however, has been challenged by a reviewer of a book dealing with Enron's failures. He feels aptly that the illegal behavior that occurred in Enron, WorldCom, Tyco, and Global Crossing runs much deeper. "Personal liability, however, grazes the surface of 'Enronization.' The phenomenon should force us to reckon with the larger issue: that an economy so singularly driven by finance and speculative trading may generate overwhelming pressures systematically to cook the books in order to sustain artificial values on the stock market. That is, 'Enronization' should cause us to re-examine the corporation as a public institution, one that ought to be subject to more, not less, regulation. Conventional wisdom to the contrary, shareholders are by no means the only constituency that counts. The economic reach and power of companies like Enron affect everyone—employees, suppliers, customers, whole communities and regions. 'Enronization' suggests that beyond the matter of determining personal responsibility lies the trickier terrain of policing institutional behavior. Otherwise, we can be certain that more Enrons are headed our way." (Steve Fraser, Review of *Conspiracy of Fools: A True Story*, by Kurt Echenwald, *New York Times Book Review*, March 27, 2005, p. 17)

\* \* \*

I appreciate the helpful suggestions of Peter Cleary Yeager. Fran Weldon prepared the manuscript for the printer and Michael Paley did the copyediting. My wife, Arlen Westbrook Clinard, gave much support in preparing the new introduction, for example, by laborious editing and other work such as computer drafts. A. Javier Treviño, editor of Transaction's Law and Society Series, was always encouraging.

## Note

The statistical research findings in *Corporate Crime* are derived from a detailed final report submitted to the U.S. Department of Justice that supported the corporate crime research (*Illegal Corporate Behavior*, Clinard et al., U.S. Government Printing Office, 1979).

## References

Angell, Marcia. *The Truth About Drug Companies: How They Deceive Us* (New York: Random House, 2004).

Bakan, Joel. *The Corporation The Pathological Pursuit of Power* (New York: Free Press, 2004).

Braithwaite, John. *Corporate Crime in the Pharmaceutical Industry* (London: Routledge and Kegan Paul, 1984).

Braithwaite, John. *Punish or Perish* (Albany: State University of New York Press, 1984).

Braithwaite, John. *Restorative Justice and Responsive Regulation* (New York: Oxford University Press, 2002).

Clinard, Marshall B., P. C. Yeager, J. M. Brissette, D. Petrashek, and E. Harries. *Illegal Corporate Behavior* (Washington, D.C.: U.S. Government Printing Office, 1979).

Clinard, Marshall B. *Corporate Ethics and Crime: The Role of Middle Management* (Beverly Hills: Sage Publications, 1983).

Clinard, Marshall B. *Corporate Corruption: The Abuse of Power* (New York: Praeger, 1990).

Estes, Ralph W. *Tyranny of the Bottom Line: Why Corporations Make Good People Do Bad Things* (San Francisco: BerretKoehler, 1996).

Fraser, Steve, Review of *Conspiracy of Fools: A True Story*, by Kurt Eichenwald, *New York Times Book Review*, March 23, 2005, p. 17.

Hartman, Thom. *Unequal Protection: The Rise of Corporate Dominance and the Theft of Huan Rights* (Rodale Inc., 2002).

Johnson, Carrie. "Open Season on Corporate Crime," *Washington Post* (Reprinted in the *New Mexican*, October 24, 2004).

Mokhiber, Russell. *Corporate Crime and Violence: Big Business and the Abuse of Trust* (San Francisco: Sierra Club Books, 1988).

Nader, Ralph. *The Good Fight: Declare Your Independence and Close the Democracy Gap* (New York: Regan Books, 2004).

Rivlin, Gary and Markhoff, John, "Tossing out a Chief Executive," *New York Times*, February 14, 2005.

Ross, E. A. *Sin and Society* (Boston: Houghton Mifflin, 1907).

Reisman, Michael W. *Folded Lies: Bribery Crusades and Reforms* (New York: Free Press, 1979).

Schlegel, Kip. *Just Deserts for Corporate Criminals* (Boston: Northeastern University, 1990).

Simpson, Sally, "The Decomposition of Antitrust: Testing a Multilevel, Longitudinal Model of Profit Squeeze," 51, December 1986, *American Sociological Review* 859-875.

"Cycles of Illegality: Antitrust Violations in Corporate America," *Social Forces* 65, June 1987, 943-963.

Sutherland, Edwin H. *White Collar Crime* (New York: The Dryden Press, 1949).

Yeager, Peter Cleary. *The Limits of the Law: The Public Regulation of Private Pollution* (New York: Cambridge University Press, 1991).

"Law Versus Justice: From Avdersaryism to Communitarism," *Law and Social Inquiry* 29, Fall 2004, 891-915.

Extensive use was made particularly of case material from: *New York Times, Wall Street Journal, New Mexican, Corporate Crime Reporter, 100 Corporate Criminals of the Decade* (Russell Mokhiber). Case and similar other materials are documented only in a few cases to increase the flow of the manuscript.

# 10

## On Hans Kelsen, *General Theory of Law and State*

*A. Javier Treviño*

Widely regarded as the most important legal theorist of the twentieth century, Hans Kelsen is best known for his formulation of the "pure theory of law"—within which the study of international law was his special field of work. The present volume, *General Theory of Law and State*, first published in 1945, allowed Kelsen to adjust his pure theory of law to American circumstances after World War II. It also afforded him the opportunity to present to English-speaking readers his latest ideas on the supremacy of international law. The volume, at over 400 pages in length, is divided into two parts: the first devoted to law, the second to the state. Together these two related topics constitute the most systematic and comprehensive exposition of Kelsen's jurisprudence up to that time.

### Life

Hans Kelsen was born to a German-speaking Jewish family on October 11, 1881 in Prague, in the Austrian part of the Austro-Hungarian Empire. His father was a mill owner, a circumstance that placed Kelsen's family in the middle class, thus providing him, as the eldest son, with a top-quality education. In 1883, when he was three years old, Kelsen's family moved to Vienna, where he attended the *Akademisches Gymnasium*. Later, as a student at the University of Vienna, Kelsen was initially interested in studying philosophy—a discipline with which he had a lifelong fascination—but given the practical considerations of making a living, he reluctantly decided to study law.

Despite Kelsen's initial lack of enthusiasm for the law, his interest in the subject grew increasingly during the course of his studies at the university. So much so that after obtaining his doctorate in law in 1906, Kelsen wrote his *Habilitation*, a higher doctorate, on the nature of legal norms. The *Habilitation* qualified him for an academic career, and in 1911 Kelsen began teaching state law and philosophy of law at the University of Vienna.

During World War I Kelsen served as legal adviser to the minister of war. In 1918 he became associate professor of law at the University of Vienna, and the following year he was made full professor of state and administrative law. After the war an independent German-speaking Austrian republic was created and Karl Renner, who was at the time chancellor of state of the provisional Austrian government, entrusted Kelsen with the task of helping to draft the new Austrian Constitution. An expert on constitutional law, Kelsen formulated the sixth main part of the Constitution, which gave primary consideration to the establishment of a Supreme Constitutional Court with specialized juridical functions. In 1921 Kelsen was appointed a member of the Constitutional Court, where, for many years, he exercised a strong influence over its many rulings. But it was his rulings on the issue of "marriage dispensation," in which he overturned the lower court's treatment of dispensations as invalid, that led to Kelsen's dismissal from the Court in 1930. Political opposition to his judicial support of marriage dispensation was so strong in Catholic Austria that Kelsen decided to permanently leave the country. His departure from Austria, which was motivated by politics, set in motion a series of similarly prompted relocations across Europe for several years to come.

From Vienna, Kelsen moved to Cologne, where he taught international law at the university. However, on April 13, 1933, just months after the Nazis took power, Kelsen was removed from his post. In the autumn of that year he left for Geneva with his wife and daughters to start a new academic career at the *Institut Universitaire des Hautes Etudes International*. Focusing chiefly on international law, Kelsen taught courses at the *Institut* (he was fluent in French) and wrote on such issues as the centralization of international law and the revision of the Covenant of the League of Nations. But with rising fascism and anti-Semitism in Geneva, and fearful that the secret police would implicate him in some way for possessing it, Kelsen wrapped his revolver in a banana peel, threw it into the Rhine, and with his family fled to Prague.

At the University of Prague, where he again taught international law, Kelsen not only encountered vehement anti-Semitic sentiments among his students, he was also overtly harassed and threatened. During his inaugural lecture at the university, fascists demanded that everyone who was not Jewish or a communist leave the lecture hall. The students who remained were beaten up. Kelsen had to continue teaching under police protection, but was eventually forced to resign from the university. He escaped from Prague after plans of a plot to assassinate him were discovered.

In 1940, at the age of sixty and with a poor knowledge of English, Kelsen immigrated to the United States and accepted a position as a research associate at Harvard. During his time there Kelsen delivered the prestigious Oliver Wendell Holmes Lectures at Harvard Law School. Five years later, with support from Roscoe Pound, the long-time dean of Harvard Law, Kelsen was given a permanent appointment in the Department of Political Science at the University of California, Berkeley. That same year he was made legal adviser to the United Nations War Crimes Commission in Washington, D.C. His task was to prepare the legal and technical aspects of the Nuremberg trials. Kelsen's years at Berkeley were immensely productive, having published several significant books and articles on such issues as the law of the United Nations, the U.N. Security Council, world peace, and state and international law. Even after his retirement in 1952, Kelsen remained highly active and productive as a scholar. Hans Kelsen died in Berkeley on April 20, 1973 at the age of ninety-two.

## The Work

During his almost seven-decade career, Kelsen produced nearly 400 academic publications, written in German, English, and French, and translated into as many as two- dozen languages. His major books include *Law and Peace in International Relations* (1942), a collection of his Oliver Wendell Holmes Lectures; *The Law of the United Nations* (1950), on the organization, sanctions, and functions of the United Nations; and *Principles of International Law* (1952), a systematic study of the distinguishing features and workings of international law.

The present volume, *General Theory of Law and State*, is not only a compendium of Kelsen's life-work up to that time, it is also an extension of his theories "to embrace the problems and institutions of English and American law as well as those of the Civil Law countries" (p. xxxv). Indeed, references to Continental European law are minimal compared with examples, scattered throughout the text, taken from the U.S. Constitution and several American court cases. That Kelsen, in *General Theory of Law and State*, considers the particular problems and institutions of English and American law is more than a concession to American readers; it signifies that his legal theory is truly general in that it accounts for the Common Law as well as the Civil Law. A systematic theoretical treatise on jurisprudence, *General Theory of Law and State* is a substantial reformulation of Kelsen's ideas articulated in several of his previous books, in particular *Allegmeine Staatslehre* (1925), which in turn was a considerably expanded version of his *Hauptprobleme der Staatsrechtslehere* (2d ed. 1923), and also in *Théorie générale du droit international public* (1932) as well as *Reine Rechtslehre* (1934). The book's Appendix, which consists of Kelsen's well-known study of Natural Law Doctrine and Legal Positivism, is an English translation of *Die Philosophischen Grundlagen der Naturrechtslehre und des Rechtspositivismus*, originally published in 1928. All of the sundry problems of jurisprudence that Kelsen addresses in *General Theory of Law and State*—the ought of law, legal hierarchy, the basic norm, the unity of state and international law—are premised on his unique legal science, which is set forth in full in this volume, a legal science he called the "pure theory of law."

The basic elements of Kelsen's pure theory of law are two. The first concerns Kelsen's endeavor to locate his jurisprudence in the nebulous and often contradictory intellectual space that lies somewhere between the idealism of morality and the banality of physical facts. The second is Kelsen's conviction that a legal order is a hierarchical system of norms, the validity of which relies on a hypothetical basic norm.

## The Purification of Legal Science

Kelsen's principle goal was to "purify" legal science by excluding, on the one hand, all subjective influences stemming from morals and ideology, and, on the other hand, all empirical connections made by the study of natural phenomena. Kelsen's goal was to create a unitary and objective jurisprudence for every field of law— private, criminal, administrative, constitutional, and international—

with a unique subject matter—positive, or real law—and method—rational cognition.

To begin with, in contradistinction to natural law doctrine, Kelsen's pure science of law is a theory of positive law wholly unconcerned with political or ideological issues given that these are based on extralegal premises. Preoccupied with morality, natural law posits that if there is a certain delict—an act committed against the intentions of the legal order—then there *must* be a certain sanction administered by the legal community against the delict. The reality, however, is quite different. Law, *qua* law, is simply and straightforwardly concerned only with the fact that if there is a delict, there *ought* to be a sanction. Viewed this way, the legal connection between delict and sanction is quite independent of any moral or political considerations.

Because Kelsen does not believe that absolute values should enter into a discussion of positive law, justice is for him an irrational, emotional ideal that has no place in the logic of legal science. All attempts to answer the question, What is justice?, either end in empty platitudes such as "Do good and avoid evil," or else are regarded from varying subjective and relative interpretations. Kelsen therefore sees justice neither in reference to some transcendental knowledge nor as a matter of some special form of juridical reasoning, but as an ideology borne by the conflict of interests. Kelsen's positivist jurisprudence soundly dismisses as untenable the ancient natural law doctrine that regards law either as a product of supernatural will—as in the bestowal of God-given inalienable rights—or of mere cognitive reasoning.

By the same token, Kelsen steers clear of the vulgar reductionism that characterizes the inductive sciences devoid of "philosophical" (read: deductive and theoretical) methods. For the standpoint of the pure theory of law, jurisprudence cannot be anything but a normative, not a descriptive, science: "The legal character of a phenomenon [such as a legal right] is not perceptible by the senses" (p. 79). This purely juristic consideration of valid norms puts Kelsen's theory of law in direct opposition to the sociological movement in law that sought to systematically observe and describe patterns of actual social behavior in relation to the phenomenon of law, and that had held sway since the beginning of the twentieth century. For example, both Roscoe Pound's sociological jurisprudence and Karl N. Llewellyn's legal realism were influenced by pragmatism, employed the inductive method, and perhaps most significant for Kelsen, very deliberately considered the "is" of sociolegal reality: the actual events of law (Llewellyn's "real rules") and the actual behavior of individuals.

Kelsen's normative jurisprudence also stands in opposition to the sociology of law advocated by Eugene Ehrlich and Nicholas S. Timasheff, given that theirs was very much of a nomographic science concerned with legal situations and their causal connections. As Kelsen explains, "The principle according to which natural [and social] science describes its object is causality; the principle according to which the [pure] science of law describes its object is normativity" (p. 46).

But Kelsen goes beyond the nomographic method of Ehrlich and Timasheff and also critiques Max Weber's ideographically informed *verstehen* approach, which considers the individual's social action as it is oriented (*orientiert*) to a legal order. Kelsen has no use for such an interpretivist approach that takes account of the individual's agency. "Human behavior pertains to the domain of the sociology of law," writes Kelsen, "not because it is 'oriented' to the legal order, but because it is determined by a legal norm as condition or consequence. Only because it is determined by the legal order...does human behavior constitute a legal phenomenon" (p. 178). Thus, the pure theory of law dismisses the metaphysical considerations of natural law doctrine, the factual pragmatism of legal sociology concerned with actual events, and Weber's idealist approach to understanding meaningful human behavior; instead it favors a jurisprudence that sees positive law as an order in the realm of the "ought."

*The Ought of Law*

As early as 1920, with the publication of his *Das Problem der Souveränität und die Theorie des Völkerrechts*, Kelsen had based his pure theory of law on the firm separation of "is" and "ought" (*Sein* and *Sollen*). For Kelsen, law, in the juridical sense, can only be a set of impersonal "oughts"—a combination of norms that state the court's duty relative to a delict. Whether the courts, *as a matter of fact*, react to the delict is of relevance only to the *Sein*-sciences (psychology, sociology, and so on), concerned as they are with "is" phenomena (of a physical, psychological, or sociological nature) related by causality. It is not, however, relevant to jurisprudence. Thus, for Kelsen, Oliver Wendell Holmes' famous declaration that law refers only to "the prophecies of what the courts will do in fact," is simply wrong. The jurist cannot predict what will happen if there is a delict—for example, whether the appropriate sanction will be applied—he can only say what *ought* to happen. Because observable facts cannot lead to a juridical conclusion, the jurist is more concerned with the *meaning* of the facts, and this meaning is made possible by the normative nature of law.

While the legal meaning of a factual act cannot be perceived by the physical senses—in other words, the judge can only cognitively *interpret* the act as, for example, arson—it is nonetheless the case that legal norms give juridical acts an "objective" meaning. Such an objective meaning is possible because all legal norms exist in the realm of the *Sollen*, a realm independent of any one individual's consciousness. In separating the "is" from the "ought," facts from meaning, Kelsen rejects the traditional jurisprudence that attributed the law's validity to its efficacy.

## Validity and Efficacy

Kelsen acknowledges that the meaning of a legal norm is ultimately premised on the notion of power, in that the state, or more accurately the "organs," or officials, of the state have the authority to apply coercive sanctions for violations of law. As a coercive order of the state, law must have some degree of efficacy—that is to say, it must be generally obeyed. While questions having to do with whether or not the legal norms are actually enforced or obeyed may be of crucial importance to legal sociology, they are, however, impertinent with regard to jurisprudence. The *existence* of a legal order depends not on its efficacy, says Kelsen, but on its validity—on the notion that the legal norms *ought* to be applied and obeyed.

For Kelsen, then, efficacy and validity are two completely distinct qualities. Whereas a legal norm's efficiency exists in the domain of *Sein*, of facts, its validity pertains wholly to the sphere of the *Sollen*, of the "ought." Thus, a legal norm can be valid, can possess a binding force, regardless of its being efficacious, actually applied and obeyed. What is more, "a legal norm is always valid, it cannot be nul, but it can be annulled" (p. 159), as in the case of the Eighteenth Amendment to the U.S. Constitution—a law that was annulled (repealed) because it was ineffective. But if the validity of a legal norm is not juridically linked to its efficacy (or, for that matter to Weber's notions of charismatic or traditional authority, given

238 Classic Writings in Law and Society

that these are metajuridical, or psychological and sociological, influences), what then gives it its legitimacy? The answer for Kelsen lies in the hierarchical structure and dynamic processes of the legal order.

## The Dynamic Hierarchy of the Legal System

According to Kelsen's pure theory of law, the legal order is best understood as a system of positive norms with a hierarchical structure. It is first of all a *system*, and not a mere aggregate, in that the plurality of legal norms that constitute it function in interrelation with regard to the progressive delegation of law creation. Its dynamic operations make it a closed or "unified" system because the interconnected norms are self-creating through the method of logical deductibility. The recursive law creating processes of progressive delegation and logical deductibility are not only intrasystemic, they are also, *ipso facto*, hierarchical.

The system of progressively delegated powers to create and apply laws runs in the direction from the top of the hierarchy downward. This means that each individual norm in the legal system is valid because it is based on a higher-echelon norm, which itself is based on a still higher one, all the way to the highest, most fundamental norm at the top of the hierarchy. Although the various norms are differentially positioned, there is unity among them in that all belong together in the same legal system. Kelsen refers to his explanation of this procedure of legal authorization as the "pyramid of law" (*Stufenbau des Rechts*) theory. The scheme of a pyramid of law consists of the individual norms (judicial and executive decisions, private contracts), which are juridically connected to general norms (court decisions, statutes, precedents), established by the courts, legislation, or custom, which are, in turn, determined by the constitution (it being the highest delegating norm given that it provides the procedure for the creation of all norms), which is itself based on the highest, the most supreme norm in the whole legal system whose validity we do not question—what Kelsen calls the "basic norm."

### *The Basic Norm*

The basic norm (*Grundnorm*) is not a positive norm; it is not a statement of fact. Nor, for that matter, is it dependent on philosophical, moral, or political considerations. It is a purely formal last presupposition, a superior postulate, that cannot be derived from any other higher norm. As the ultimate "source" of law, the basic norm gives fundamental validity to the plurality of norms of the legal system. What is more, the basic norm gives validity to the highest positive legal norm—the constitution—because it endows it with law-creating power. At the level of the national legal system, the basic norm is simply the impersonal fiat, "Make the norms of the country." But, in relation to international law, the basic norms of the different national legal orders are actually positive norms because they are themselves subordinate to the basic norm of the international legal order—articulated as, "The States ought to behave as they have customarily behaved"—on which is based the rule *pacta sunt servanda*, the legal foundation of all international treaties. It is the legal systems of state and international law, and the relations between the two, that most concern Kelsen, and to which he devotes approximately two-thirds of *General Theory of Law and State*.

## The Theory of State and International Law

Kelsen's first attempt in dealing with the nature and functions of international law was in his essay *Das Problem der Souveränität und die Theorie des Völkerrechts* written during World War I and published in 1920. The fact that he placed the subject of international law and its relations with state law at the center of his theoretical considerations sets Kelsen apart from other legal theorists, such as H.L.A. Hart and Ronald Dworkin, who either disregard international law or else accord it very limited treatment. Indeed, from early in his career Kelsen tenaciously advanced the then controversial notion that international law was law in its own right, a topic that he exhaustively analyzed in his jurisprudence.

Kelsen's general theory of state and law has as one of its basic contentions that there exists no difference in the nature and subject matter of state and international law. This position was in direct opposition to the two schools of jurisprudential thought prevalent at the time. The first, following Hegel, subsumed international law to state law and thus treated international law as merely a branch of state law. The other school, represented by the "pluralistic" theory, put forth the idea that state law and international law are two distinct, mutually independent legal orders separated according to their respective jurisdictions: state law is only concerned with relationships between the state and its subjects (public law) and with dealings between citizens themselves (private law), while international law only considers relations among states. In response to both the Hegelian and pluralistic approaches Kelsen proposed a "monistic" theory that made international law the only "objective" legal system, which encompasses and determines all state legal systems. Indeed, for Kelsen, international law incorporates into its sphere all human activities—a now commonplace conception in that international law is today primarily identified with protecting human rights.

## The Problem of Sovereignty

Kelsen's treatment of international law and state law as forming a unitary system compelled him to earnestly grapple with the problem of state sovereignty. If we identify a state with "that order of human behavior that we call the legal order" (p. 188), then the state's sovereignty, absolute liberty, must be based on the fact that its basic norm is not derived from, and subjected to, another legal order. If, on the other hand, we consider international law to be a valid legal order, then it is the case that international law, as a higher-order normative system, determines the national legal order's three spheres of validity: the territorial (its geographical space), the temporal (the period of its existence), and, indirectly through the medium of the national legal order, the personal (the persons residing within its territory). There are two points to be made here. The first is that, whether or not a state consents to them, the norms that regulate its territorial, temporal, and personal spheres of validity are "essentially and necessarily norms of international law" (p. 350); the second point is that, as such, the international and state legal orders constitute one inseparable whole.

If a state, as a member of a community of nations, is obliged to respect international law, it therefore cannot be sovereign. Moreover, the idea of the equality of states is credible only if states are not presupposed to be sovereign, that is, only if they are all subservient to a higher authority. As Kelsen explains, "The States are 'equal' before international law since they are equally subjected to international law and international law is equally applicable to the States" (p. 253). Accordingly, state legal orders are organs of international law, particularly since they are compelled to follow the international rule, *pacta sunt servanda*, which obligates states to behave in conformity with the treaties they have concluded. In so arguing, Kelsen not only challenged the traditional conception of international law as merely law between the states, he also inveighed against the idea of the supremacy of the nation-state. The upshot is that sovereignty, being paramount and exclusive, can only be attributed to the highest legal order, which is international law. It is the primacy and universality of international law that forms the basis of Kelsen's jurisprudence of the relations between state and international law.

## The Coercive Force of Law

Kelsen's *General Theory of Law and State* relies on understanding law as a normative order that can be hypothetically expressed as follows: When there is a legal norm, there ought to be compliance with it; and if there is noncompliance with the legal norm, there ought to be a sanction. For Kelsen, then, a legal duty (as opposed to one that is moral or religious in character) is defined by the socially organized sanction it entails: "It is because the legal norm attaches a certain sanction to a certain behavior that the opposite behavior becomes a legal duty" (p. 62). Accordingly, law is a "coercive order" (*Zwangsordnung*).

Any use of coercion in the international community can be characterized as either a *delict*, that is, a state's violation of international law (as when it invades the territory of another state without a specific reason), or a *sanction*, a reaction of the international legal community against the delict. Kelsen defines a sanction very specifically as the exercise or threat of physical force. As a coercive order international law has two types of sanction available to it: reprisals and war.

In Kelsen's view, war can only be an appropriate sanction of international law—a legitimate coercive act carried out by a state whose right has been violated by another state—when it is "just," that is, when it is an act of redressing a breach of international law. The ancient doctrine of the just war, or *bellum justum*—which forms the basis of important international covenants and treaties such as the Treaty of Versailles (1919) and the Kellogg-Briand Pact (1928)— had been expunged from the field of modern international law until the end of World War I, when it was revived, in simplified form, by certain legal philosophers such as Leo Strisower, Kelsen's former professor and one-time colleague at the University of Vienna. Apart from the case of *bellum justum*, which restricts the discretionary power of states to wage war, an unjust war is an illegitimate use of force and thus a delict. According to Kelsen, rejecting the theory of the just war was tantamount to denying the legal nature of international law.

## A Decentralized Legal Order

The two sanctions available under international law, reprisals (where national or private property is confiscated and other legal rights are infringed) and war (where human beings are killed, maimed, or imprisoned), are exacted, not by the international community per se, but by individual states in the form of self-help. This means that, compared to state legal orders, which provide for the application of sanctions by central juridical organs (i.e., the courts, the police), international law, at the time that Kelsen was writing, possessed no permanent and highly organized structure—neither a court nor an executive power—in which the enforcement of sanctions was concentrated. Accordingly, Kelsen viewed international law as relatively "primitive" or "decentralized" and thus had to develop, along the lines of the more advanced national legal systems, a centralized judicial body to authorize war as a sanctioning act. While international law is too decentralized to, organizationally, be considered a state, it can nonetheless be regarded as "true" law, although admittedly law *in statu nascendi*.

## A Universal System of Law

The movement toward a more centralized international law was first proposed by Kelsen in *Das Problem der Souveränität und die Theorie des Völkerrechts*, where he advocates a universal legal system premised on the ancient theological notion of *civitas maxima*. Reintroduced into eighteenth-century Enlightenment metaphysics by German philosopher Christian Wolff, the *civitas maxima*, or world community of humanity, would, according to Kelsen, find its organizational unity in international law. Although he does not use the expression *civitas maxima* in *General Theory of Law and State*, Kelsen nonetheless invokes the idea of a universal system of law, the legal unification of the world, with specialized juridical organs whose function is to ascertain the initial breach of international norms and execute sanctions against offending states. In centralizing and universalizing the international legal system, Kelsen inveighs against the idea of state sovereignty and argues instead for the submission to impersonal international norms.

## Kelsen's Theory of International Law in Light of Current Events

It is doubtless the case that in *General Theory of Law and State* Kelsen anticipated, if at times with only a shadowy understanding, the directions that international law has taken during the past half-century or so. For example, Kelsen's idea of a universal legal community is wholly consistent with the processes of globalization currently underway. These processes, however, are considered by many as no more than an affirmation of the Western world's hegemonic proclivities. From such a political perspective any international enforcement of sanctions carried out by a supranational authority—such as the so-called "Coalition of the Willing," made up of several countries led by the United States and Great Britain in the 2003 Iraq War—is bound, therefore, to be seen not as a legitimate action of legal sanction, but merely as an act of imperial aggression. To be sure, Kelsen was well aware that a practical distinction between war as a delict and war as a sanction was difficult, and in some cases even impossible, to make. Moreover, from Kelsen's method of rational cognition—his neo-Kantian epistemological assumption of the objective validity of law—the Iraq War may be regarded as an unjust war given that the U.N. Security Council never approved the military action, as U.N. Secretary-General Kofi Annan alleged in 2004.

In a slim but highly prescient volume, *Peace through Law*, which Kelsen published in 1944, the year before the appearance of *General Theory of Law and State*, he argues that the only way to guarantee a stable, universal peace among states is by compulsory adjudication of international disputes through the formation for a permanent and independent juridical organ—a world court—with the authority to resolve international conflicts and prosecute individuals for war crimes and crimes against humanity. It may be said that the turning point in the transition to a more centralized international legal order began the year *General Theory of Law and State* was published, in 1945, with the founding of the United Nations. Kelsen's proposal for an international court of justice, however, took much longer to be realized, but in 2002 the International Criminal Court (ICC), based in The Hague, Netherlands was finally established. While the ICC has the power to exercise its jurisdiction over persons for the most serious crimes of international concern—mass murder,

244 Classic Writings in Law and Society

genocide, and war crimes—it is not without controversy. Claming that the ICC may initiate politically motivated prosecutions against U.S. nationals, the United States, as of this writing, has not ratified the Court's treaty.

Two ad hoc International Criminal Tribunals, one for the former Yugoslavia (ICTY), established in 1993, and one for Rwanda (ICTR), established in 1994, have been set up within the framework of the United Nations for the purpose of bringing to justice individuals allegedly responsible for serious violations of international humanitarian law. On such individual is Slobodan Milosevic, the former Yugoslav president, who orchestrated a brutal campaign of ethnic cleansing during the collapse of the Yugoslav federation. As of this writing, Milosevic is being tried on war crimes charges by the ICTY. In 1998 the ICTR delivered the first-ever judgment on the crime of genocide by an international court when Rwanda's former prime minister, Jean Kambanda, plead guilty to six charges of genocide. With these and other prosecutions, both International Criminal Tribunals demonstrate a movement in the maturation of international law that Kelsen would have wholeheartedly approved: the direct adjudication of international law not only of "juristic persons," namely states, but also, and especially, of "real persons," that is, individuals who perform illegal acts in the exercise of their official function as state organs.

In the Preface to *General Theory of Law and State*, which he wrote in April 1944, when Europe was still under the jackboot of fascism, Kelsen contends that the most favorable situation for the reception of his general theory of law and state—a pure theory of law free from all political ideologies—is during "a period of social equilibrium" (p. xxxix). Whether such a period will actually be realized anytime soon, in an age of great sociopolitical instability, is a matter of pure speculation, and perhaps even a matter of the political ideology Kelsen wished to avoid. However that may be, we would do well to earnestly consider the juridical principles put forth by the most important legal theorist of the twentieth century, in endeavoring to achieve a genuine and enduring peace in the world of the twenty-first century.

# Part V

## Critical Perspectives on Law, Crime, and Society

# 11

# On Richard Quinney, *The Social Reality of Crime*

*A. Javier Treviño*

## I

Three decades after it was first published, Richard Quinney's *The Social Reality of Crime* remains an eloquent and important statement on crime, law, and justice. At the time of its appearance in 1970, the theory of the social reality of crime—as a critical reinterpretation of criminology—not only liberated the field from being mainly a recitation of the practices of the police, courts, and corrections, it also, and more importantly, represented a marked departure from the traditional analysis of crime that viewed criminal behavior as pathological in nature. Additionally, Quinney renounced the conventional conceptualization of law as an abstract, autonomous body of rules and instead reintroduced into sociology Roscoe Pound's notion of the law in action—that is to say, the law as a dynamic force that is continually being created and interpreted. Quinney's theory not only served to advance criminological and legal thought, it also inspired scores of students of crime, law, and society who had become disenchanted with the customary analyses, to reorient their perceptions of criminal justice.

Upon its publication, *The Social Reality of Crime* received wide acclaim and gave an entire generation of researchers the courage and legitimacy to seriously question definitions of crime and labels of criminality. The book's popularity quickly turned Quinney into a criminologist with an international reputation. Excerpts from the book's first chapter, which is devoted to the theory of the social reality of crime, are now routinely reprinted in anthologies on criminology and deviant behavior. The theory itself is discussed in most criminology textbooks.

There is no doubt that Richard Quinney has helped shape the course of criminology over the last thirty years. He (along with William J. Chambliss and Austin T. Turk) has contributed greatly to the further development of the conflict approach, placing it at the forefront of criminological theory. Quinney is not only the most prolific of the criminological conflict theorists—having produced over sixty-five articles and some fifteen books including, *Critique of Legal Order: Crime Control in Capitalist Society* (1974), *Providence: The Reconstruction of Social and Moral Order* (1980), *Marxism and Law* (1982), and *Criminology as Peacemaking* (1991)—he is also the most controversial. The controversy stems in part from his having shifted his paradigmatic orientation several times during his long and distinguished career.

Quinney's mark on the field is most apparent in the number of times he is referenced in criminology textbooks. He is, to be sure, the most widely cited of today's criminologists, ranking third in total number of references, exceeded only by the late Edwin H. Sutherland and the late Donald R. Cressey, ranked first and second respectively. Quinney's significance to criminology is perhaps best demonstrated in a 1982 article written by R.E. Hilbert and C.W. Wright for the journal *Deviant Behavior*, comparing Quinney's explanation of the inevitability of crime with that of the great French sociologist, Émile Durkheim.

In 1984, the American Society of Criminology (ASC) awarded Quinney the prestigious Edwin H. Sutherland Award for his contributions to criminological theory. In 1995, he was made a fellow of the ASC and, in 1998, was given the Major Achievement Award by the ASC's Critical Criminology Division. He is the only criminologist who has published two autobiographies, *Journey to a Far Place: Autobiographical Reflections* (1991) and *For the Time Being: Ethnography of Everyday Life* (1998).

## II

Quinney first became interested in the American legal system while a graduate student at the University of Wisconsin, Madison (from 1957 to 1962) preparing for his doctoral examination in criminology. At that time, he made three observations about law that would guide his thinking for the next several years: (1) that sociologists had not paid appropriate attention to the formulation of law in their studies of crime, (2) that law-breaking is related in some way to law-making, and (3) that law is not a system based on consensus, but tends to represent the interests of the powerful in society.

Shortly after receiving his Ph.D. and co-authoring *Criminal Behavior Systems: A Typology* (1967) with Marshall B. Clinard, Quinney began to politicize his analysis of crime. He cited such actions as refusing to pay income taxes used for military expenditures and picketing military bases, as evidence that the offenders were pursuing values different from the values of those groups that were formulating and administering law. The result was criminal behavior. Theories attempting to explain this criminal behavior, Quinney concluded, must include a knowledge of the political process.

With the publication of *Crime and Justice in Society* (1969), Quinney turned in earnest to the coercion or conflict-power model of society previously popularized by Ralf Dahrendorf and others. In this volume, Quinney considers the legal scholar Roscoe Pound's theory of interests, which, according to Quinney, provides one of the few starting points for the study of law as a social phenomenon. With the objective of proposing his own sociological theory of law, Quinney revises Pound's theory of interests so that it fits into a power of politics framework.

Quinney begins by rejecting the consensus, or integrative conception of society, that had led Pound to see law as reflecting the needs of a well-ordered society and, as regulating and adjusting people's conflicting claims and desires. In contrast, Quinney's vision of society is characterized by diversity, conflict, coercion, and change. Quinney further regards law not as independent of particular interests, but as a result of having been *created* by those interests. What is more, contrary to Pound who saw law as operating for the good of society as a whole, Quinney sees law as representing the interests of particular segments of society that have the power to translate their interests into public policy. Finally, while Pound's theory of interests is teleological in that he believed that society would create only that law which it needs, Quinney does not regard society's needs as inherent in the interests involved in formulating particular laws.

Based on the aforementioned suppositions, Quinney's sociological theory of interests maintains that: (1) law, as a form of public policy, is the creation and interpretation of specialized rules by authorized agents in a politically organized society; (2) a politically organized society is structured into different segments, each with its own interests; (3) the interest structure of a politically organized society is characterized by the unequal distribution of power and by conflict between the different segments; (4) within the interest structure of a politically organized society, law is formulated and administered by the segments of society with the power to incorporate their interests into the creation and interpretation of public policy. It follows, then, that by formulating law, some segments are able to control others to their own advantage.

In *The Problem of Crime* (1970), Quinney extended the idea that law is the creation and interpretation of specialized rules in a politically organized society, by formulating a new concept of crime—one that was more attuned to his evolving conception of science. In this work, Quinney contends that crime has meaning only when the concept of crime has first been constructed. Accordingly, his understanding of crime was now not only informed by the conflict-power approach, but also drew heavily from the philosophical tradition of idealism.

Idealism is based on a subjectivist position that sees knowledge as derived from sense experience. Thus, no facts exist independent of our knowledge of them. Reality, in other words, is a state of mind. Idealism is also based on a nominalistic position that posits that there is no reason to believe in the objective existence of anything. Quinney concludes, therefore, that there is no definite way of arriving at conclusions about the social world. Social reality, he maintains, is possible only to the extent that people mentally construct that social reality. For Quinney, the idealist approach promised to be fruitful (much more fruitful, in fact, than the positivistic mode of inquiry which he had relied on in *Crime and Justice in Society* but now rejected) in developing concepts that would be of maximum utility in a sociological analysis of the problem of crime.

Viewing crime as labeled conduct, Quinney focuses on the process of criminal defining, the behavior of the criminally defined, and the social reaction to crime. He then considers these three phenomena within the context of the "politicality of crime"—by which he means, first, that the actions of many criminally defined persons are actually political behaviors and, second, that the actions taken in the labeling of behavior as criminal are political actions.

It seemed only natural that, at this point in time when radical changes were taking place in American society, Quinney should become alert to the increased use of the criminal label in suppressing criminal behavior as well as to the increased politicality of the actions of the criminally defined. For Quinney, acts of conscience—such as the demonstrations outside the Democratic National Convention that took place in Chicago in 1968, and the so-called "Spock case" in which several men (including the famous pediatrician, Benjamin Spock), who opposed the military draft, were put on trial for returning their draft cards to the government—illustrated the politicality of crime.

### III

The ontological, methodological, and substantive positions that Quinney presents in *Crime and Justice in Society* and in *The Problem of Crime*—namely, the consideration of the conflict-power model of society, the sociological theory of interests, differentially segmented society, politically organized society, nominalism, and the process of criminal defining—are extended and synthesized in *The Social Reality of Crime*. Simply stated, through the formulation of an integrated theory—the theory of the social reality of crime—Quinney endeavors to explain the politicality of the social construction of crime.

The theory consists of six propositions derived from earlier work in criminology and sociology—most notably, the labeling perspective, George Vold's group conflict theory, social constructionism, and Edwin Sutherland's theory of differential association. Sutherland (who a half-century after his death in 1950 continues to be the model of what it is to be a criminologist) served as Quinney's main guide in developing the theory of the social reality of crime. Indeed, Sutherland's influence on the theory's structure (its systematic and integrative formulation and its articulation into propositions) and content (its focus on the concept of criminal definitions, the learning of behavior patterns, and differential social organization) is unmistakable. And just as Sutherland had previously taken the conventional criminological knowledge of the time—the late 1930s—and reformulated it into the theory of differential association, so also does Quinney attempt to reorient the study of crime into a theory that reflects the happenings of the time, the late 1960s.

The theory of the social reality of crime begins with the premise that criminality is not determined by the nature of the behavior itself; rather, crime is a category of human behavior that is created and imposed by authorized political agents (viz., the police, judges, and corrections authorities), through the formulation of criminal definitions. Crime is a judgment made by some persons about the behavior and characteristics of others. What is more, crime is an artificial construct created by the powerful segments of society to benefit their particular interests. In this sense, the formulation of all criminal law is a political matter.

Quinney states that those segments in society that have the power to translate their interests into public policy shape the enforcement and administration of criminal law. He further notes that the probability of powerful segments formulating criminal definitions becomes greater with an increase in the conflict of interests between segments of a society. The substantive and procedural laws that emerge from this conflict reflect the interests of the powerful in protecting themselves from the competing interests of the powerless. Conduct that is perceived to threaten or conflict with the interests of the dominant groups is designated as criminal. The dominant groups see to it that their particular definitions of criminality become enacted as law, ensconced in public policy, and protected by the operation of the criminal justice system.

When the behavior of members of subordinate groups clash with the law, they are less able to resist apprehension, prosecution, conviction, and incarceration for criminal charges. Because society's power segments formulate criminal definitions that reflect their own set of values, members of those segments of society whose behavior patterns are not represented in the development, application, and construction of these criminal definitions engage in actions that have relative probabilities of being labeled as criminal. Structural sources such as age, sex, social class, ethnicity, and race (as well as ecological areas and general cultural themes), influence who runs the greatest risk of officially being defined as delinquent or criminal. Youth, women, the economically disadvantaged, and minorities—that is to say, those with interests that are likely to conflict with the interests represented in law—will tend to be differentially processed thorough the criminal justice system.

The more the powerful are concerned about crime, the greater the likelihood that both criminal definitions and criminal behavior itself will increase. Furthermore, because of their reliance on power relations, criminal definitions are constantly changing so that they reflect the politically organized society. Thus, a particular criminal law may be intended for a particular interest at a particular time and then amended, implemented, or abolished at another time for some other interest. "Law," as Quinney puts it, "has its element of fashion" (p. 85).

Quinney further argues that the images of crime and criminals created by the powerful segments are diffused throughout the society in their effort to control the actions of the less powerful segments. Indeed, the term "crime" refers to conceptions of reality held by the powerful that are disseminated through various means of communication, including the news media. A criminal mythology—that is to say, an "official reality" with a common definition of particularly threatening behavior meant to arouse fear and anxiety—is subsequently constructed and those in power get others to believe in their definition of the reality of crime. In other words, criminal conceptions (or stereotypes) are created and communicated as part of the political process of promoting a particular set of values and interests. The end result is that criminal conceptions held by people with a great deal of power are imposed on others in the name of the whole society. Once these stereotypes of crime and criminals become stable, persons labeled as criminal begin to conceive of themselves as such and eventually come to play their role accordingly. This self-fulfillment of others' criminal definitions, in turn, increases the probability of further criminal definition.

This entire process legitimizes the authority of those in positions of power and allows them to establish official policies, in the name of the common good, that really protect and perpetuate their own private interests. The criminal justice system thus works to secure the needs of the powerful. In sum, Quinney argues that crime is a process whereby conceptions of crime are constructed, criminal laws are established and administered, and behaviors are developed in relation to these criminal definitions. He refers to this constructivist process as the social reality of crime.

## IV

Shortly after its publication, heavy criticisms were leveled at *The Social Reality of Crime*. For example, Taylor, Walton, and Young in *The New Criminology* described Quinney's theoretical orientation as "a confused relativist position" that seemed to be more the product of his existential *angst* than the result of "clear-headed theoretical analysis." Robert K. Merton, in *Sociological Ambivalence*, branded Quinney a total subjectivist and referred to his approach as "sociological Berkeleyanism," in reference to the idealist philosopher, George Berkeley, who doubted that the existence of the physical, objective world could be proved. This charge of total subjectivism is untenable given that Quinney's focus is on the structural origins, increased likelihood, and amount of crime in society. Thus, not only is the underlying conception of his theory the *segmental organization of society*, he is particularly interested in examining the *structural sources* (age, sex, social class, ethnicity, and race) of the *behavior patterns* that have a relative *probability* of being defined as criminal. Moreover, Merton considered Quinney's contention that "we have no reason to believe in the objective existence of anything" (p. 4), an unjust and erroneous distortion of W. I. Thomas's theorem—which, in attempting to explain the construction of subjective reality, states that, when people define a social situation as real, its consequences become real. Here again Merton's critique is wide of the mark because Quinney does not once mention Thomas in his book.

Others have taken the theory of the social reality of crime to task on several grounds: for assuming that the interests of the power segments in society are always in opposition to those of the subordinate groups; for implying that legally prohibited acts are wrong only because they are prohibited, without considering that they could also be objectively harmful to individuals and society; for its inability to specify the conditions under which law would not be simply an instrument of powerful interests; for proposing a highly abstract conflict model that is too simplistic and ultimately not very helpful in illuminating either the nature of criminal justice or the shape and significance of crime in society. This last criticism, while perhaps overstated, does have some merit. To be sure, Quinney's basic assertions are so self-evident that it is difficult to disagree with them. Who would argue, for example, with his conclusion that we live in a segmented society and that different segments have different interests?

While, on the face of it, the theory of the social reality of crime appears to be based on sound sociological premises, six shortcomings are nonetheless discernible. To begin with, although Quinney is careful to define or detail most of the terms that he employs (e.g., process, conflict, power, social action, interests), he is less than clear on the meaning of one of his most important concepts, that of social "segments." Quinney gives at least four characteristics of segments: (1) that, as types of social groupings, segments may or may not share the same values, norms, and ideological orientations; (2) that segments may or may not be organized in defense of those commonalties; (3) that different segments have different behavior patterns and normative systems, each of which is learned in its own social and cultural setting; (4) that, depending on their position in the political power structure, the various social segments possess varying degrees of influence to shape public policy.

Interesting as these attributes may be, they, neither singly nor collectively, serve as systematic guides for an empirical analysis of social segments. And while Quinney states that the interests power segments pursue "are not distributed randomly in society but are related to one's position in society [following] Marx's theory of economic production and class conflict" (p. 38), at the time that he wrote this, Quinney had little awareness of political economy and did not necessarily identify social segments with social classes.

Second, Quinney's observation that crime is created by criminal law is not particularly new. This notion is reminiscent of St. Paul who, two thousand years earlier, had noted a similar link between sin and law when he stated: "I would not have come to know sin except through the Law" (Romans 7:7). Similarly, during the early 1930s Jerome Michael and Mortimer J. Adler in *Crime, Law, and Social Science* had contended that not only was criminal law the formal cause of crime, it also gave behavior its quality of criminality. Thus, while Quinney's law-crime correlation is not unique, what is novel is that he extends it to include two interrelated propositions: one sociological, that the greater the amount of crime in society leads to a greater number of people who are defined as criminal; the other social-psychological, that those who are defined as criminal develop criminal self-conceptions.

Third, the theory of the social reality of crime is formulated at a middle-range level of abstraction and, as such, it should be possible to test it directly with empirical data. Yet, despite its middle-range articulation, the theory overreaches as it attempts to account for *all* crime instead of merely some of it. Little wonder that the theory, at times, appears too superficial as it glosses over variations and exceptions.

Fourth, Quinney contends that his theory is systematically constructed, composed as it is of propositions that are internally interrelated. His practice, however, is to shift back and forth between divergent theoretical positions depending on the argument that he wants to make. On the one hand, in explaining the formulation and application of criminal law, he employs the conflict-power conception of interest structure. On the other hand, when addressing the behavior of those defined as criminal, he relies on differential association, labeling, and other variables outside of the conflict-power perspective.

Fifth, in explaining how the power segments manipulate the criminal laws (including the enactments of legislatures, court decisions, and administrative rulings) to their own advantage, Quinney relies on a modified (i.e., non-Marxist) "instrumentalist" approach. Accordingly, he sees criminal laws in very rudimentary terms: as instruments or "political weapons" of the powerful. Aside from being overly simplistic, the instrumentalist approach is a static interpretation of law that suggests a deterministic view of society. Moreover, the criminal laws are not always just an instrument for the promotion of the interests of the powerful; indeed, considering that the powerless are more likely to be victimized by crimes of violence, laws against assault, murder, and rape, for example, are more likely to protect and advantage them. Only later, in *Class, State, and Crime* (1977) and during the late-Marxist stage of his career, does Quinney consider a structuralist view of law.

Finally, *The Social Reality of Crime* is so well documented and thoroughly researched that it has prompted one commentator to regard it as one of the most exhaustive collections of references on crime that he had seen since Blackstone's *Commentaries*. Yet, despite—or, perhaps because of—Quinney's footnoted citations of hundreds of case studies used to support his arguments, some of their findings and illustrations give the book as a whole a slightly outdated feel. Such findings have been outrun by numerous events that have transpired since the initial publication of *The Social Realty of Crime*, events that have forever altered the general public's attitudes toward crime, law, and criminal justice. These include Watergate; the Iran-Contra Affair; the impeachment of President Bill Clinton; *Roe v. Wade*; *Furman v. Georgia*, and *McKlesky v. Kemp*; the execution of Gary Gilmore; the enactment of the Racketeer Influenced and Corrupt Organization Act (RICO), Megan's law, and the "three strikes" law; the abolition of vagrancy laws and the nonenforcement of laws prohibiting "solicitation" by homosexuals; the War on Drugs and the crack cocaine-powder cocaine sentencing differential; the Attica and New Mexico prison riots; the police beating of Rodney King; the popularity of anti-heroes like D.B. Cooper; the O.J. Simpson case; President George Bush's manipulation of Willie Horton as a symbol of the criminal; the Knapp Commission's uncovering of widespread police corruption; the congressional hearings on the tobacco industry; the formation of special interest groups like Mothers Against Drunk Driving (MADD), Handgun Control, Inc., and Partnership for a Drug-Free America; the Savings and Loan scandal; the Cointelpro surveillance operation; the ABSCAM sting operation; the illegal contribution of campaign money to political action committees (PACs); the convictions of televangelist Jim Baker, mob boss John Gotti, investment broker Ivan Boesky, junk-bond king Michael Milken, and "death doctor" Dr. Jack Kavorkian; the popularity of real-life crime shows like "COPS" and "America's Most Wanted"; the crimes of serial killers Ted Bundy, the Son of Sam, John Wayne Gacy, and Jeffrey Dahmer; the bombing of the World Trade Center and the Murrah Federal Building in Oklahoma City; the Unabomber; the attempted assassination of President Ronald Reagan; the school shootings in Jonesboro, Arkansas, Pearl, Mississippi, Springfield, Oregon, West Paducah, Kentucky, and Littleton, Colorado; and the hate-crime slayings of Matthew Sheppard and James Byrd, Jr.

Other legal and attitudinal changes that have taken place since the initial publication of *The Social Reality of Crime* are apparent from the fact that some actions used as examples in the book, like abortion and vagrancy, are no longer considered crimes. (Quinney anticipated other actions, such as the decriminalization of public drunkenness.) Moreover, while computer crimes were virtually unknown at the time, other events, such as "race riots," which were not uncommon then, now tend to occur with less frequency. But particular statistics, such as the number of executions and the number of inmates under sentence of death in state and federal prisons, have increased dramatically—with the numbers rising from two (in 1967) to 74 (in 1997) and from 435 (in 1967) to 3,335 (in 1997), respectively.

## V

Notwithstanding the many momentous events that, during the past three decades, have transformed American society and its criminal justice system, the theory of the social reality of crime remains as fresh and pertinent today as it was when Quinney first set out "to provide an understanding of crime that is relevant to our contemporary experiences" (p. 3). The theory of the social reality of crime has, at least thus far, had more of an impact on both criminological thought and deviant behavior studies than Quinney's later Marxist, prophetic, and peacemaking approaches. What is more, the theory has exerted an indelible and direct influence on the development of subsequent criminological theorizing. For example, Thomas Bernard's "unified conflict theory of crime" presented in *Theoretical Criminology* incorporates variables derived from the social reality of crime. Similarly, Jeffrey Reiman, in *The Rich Get Richer and the Poor Get Prison*, also draws on Quinney's notion of the construction of the social reality of crime in developing his own "Pyrrhic defeat theory." Even scholars like Taylor, Walton, and Young, who have been hostile to Quinney's nominalistic position concerning the formulation and administration of criminal law, proposed their "new criminology" in opposition to it. More generally, the theory of the social reality of crime has also made an impact on sociology. The German sociologist, Richard Münch, in the third volume of his *Sociological Theory*, for example, sees Quinney's social reality of crime theory as a conflict approach that has advanced knowledge of the symbolic processes of labeling.

Perhaps the most fitting description of the theory of the social reality of crime is that which Quinney offered of Sutherland's theory of differential association in his assessment of it in 1966. To paraphrase: Although there are shortcomings in the theory, one must keep in mind that it was formulated nearly a third of a century ago. In the end, the theory's truly remarkable feature is its basic logical consistency. This republication of *The Social Reality of Crime* will doubtless renew excitement for Quinney's conflict-social constructionist perspective that has been so significant to the development of theoretical work in the fields of criminology, social problems, and the sociology of law.

# 12

# On Evgeny B. Pashukanis, *The General Theory of Law and Marxism*

*Dragan Milovanovic*

## Introduction

Evgeny Bronislavovich Pashukanis (1891-1937) was at center stage in the development of Marxist law during the highly creative and challenging historical period of 1917-1937 in Russia. He was, perhaps, the most significant figure to develop a fresh, new Marxist perspective that was to have a dramatic impact in the sociology of law for many years. Although he was "withered" away by the Stalin purges in early 1937 and his writings were expunged from the law universities in the developing Stalinist state by Andrei Ia. Vyshinsky, Pashukanis, nevertheless, left a legacy which gained a new momentum in the late 1970s.

Apart from Pashukanis's activist political interventions in molding the legal landscape in post-revolutionary Russia, his so-called commodity-exchange theory of law spearheaded a perspective that traced the form of law, not to class interests, but to capital logic itself, a logic to which both rich and poor were enslaved. His later critics—to which he gradually deferred more and more—argued that he had omitted the nature of Soviet law during the "transitional period" of the dictatorship of the proletariat. But up until his death, Pashukanis continued to argue for the ideal of the withering away of the state, law and the juridic subject. He eventually arrived at a position contrary to Stalin, who was attempting to consolidate and strengthen the state apparatus under the name of the dictatorship of the proletariat. Needless to say, Pashukanis met his fate in January,

1937 when he was branded an enemy of the revolution. His works were subsequently taken off the shelves, and his ideas were subjected to a one-sided critique led by Vyshinsky. However, in 1954, he was "rehabilitated" by the Soviets and restored to an acceptable position in the historical development of Marxist law.

In Europe and North America, it was not until the late 1970s that a number of legal theorists rediscovered his work, subjected it to careful critical analysis, and realized that he offered an alternative to the traditional Marxist interpretations that saw law simply and purely as tied to class interests of domination. By the mid-1980s, the instrumental Marxist perspective which was in vogue in Marxist sociology, criminology, politics, and economics was to give way—due to a significant extent to Pashukanis's insights—to a more structural Marxist assessment of the relationship of law to economics and other social spheres.

## Biographical Sketch

Little is known about Pashukanis prior to the 1917 Revolution. We do know that he studied at the University of St. Petersburg before World War I and that he completed his legal training at the University of Munich. He subsequently returned to post-revolutionary Russia, became a Bolshevik, served as a judge in the Moscow area, and in the early 1920s he conducted legal advice for the People's Commissariat of Foreign Affairs. In 1924 he wrote what is probably his most influential piece, *The General Theory of Law and Marxism*, and in the second edition, 1926, stated that this work was not to be seen as a final product but aimed, rather, at "self-clarification" in hopes of adding "stimulus and material for further discussion." A third edition was printed in 1927.

Pashukanis's direct involvement in shaping the legal culture of post-revolutionary Russia, particularly from the 1920s through the mid-1930s, was extensive and had a significant impact. From 1924 to 1930, he assumed a number of important positions in the Soviet political and academic structure. These posts included membership in Piotr I. Stuchka's Section of Law and State and the Institute of Soviet Construction, as well as his tenure as head of the Subsection of the Institute of Soviet Construction on the General Theory of Law and State. Under the auspices of the Section of Law and State, Pashukanis, in 1925, co-edited *Revolution of the Law*, a collection of papers on Lenin's understanding of Marxism and law. That same year he joined the law faculty at Moscow State University and the Institute of Red Professors. Pashukanis was to become a prolific writer on various aspects of law and Marxism. As such, he was involved with various editorial responsibilities of scholarly journals, including his position as founding editor of *Revolution and Culture* which dealt with the cultural aspects of the October Revolution.

By 1930, Pashukanis's influence was pronounced in legal circles, and his commodity-exchange theory of law was dominant in the law curriculum. Within the Communist Academy, two wings of the commodity-exchange perspective were to emerge by the late 1920s: the more moderate wing, initiated by Stuchka, and the more radical wing, represented by Pashukanis. This tension between the two factions led to a great deal of discussion about the function of law in the transitional period. Stuchka was Pashukanis's main rival in this analysis, but outside of the Communist Academy, A.A. Piontkovsky—a member of the competing Institute of Soviet Law—was also a critic. From 1927 to the early 1930s, the exchange between Stuchka and Pashukanis was to persuade the latter that some of his early statements made in *The General Theory of Law and Marxism* should be qualified to include class dimensions in the overall analysis.

In June, 1930, the Sixteenth Party Congress saw some of the disagreements between Pashukanis and his critics come to a head. Already, in 1929 Stalin, as General Secretariat, had warned that the class struggle had reached a critical level and that the dictatorship of the proletariat needed consolidation and strengthening. Furthermore, this was the time of the first Five Year Plan, and forced collectivization and massive industrialization were occurring. The Sixteenth Congress, ipso facto, rejected the idea of the gradual withering away of state and law. At this Congress, Stalin was poignant: "We are for the withering away of the state, while at the same time we stand for strengthening the dictatorship of the proletariat which represents the most potent and mighty authority of all the state authorities that have existed down to this time" (cited in Beirne and Sharlet, 1990: 34). It was at this moment, according to Beirne and Sharlet, that the commodity-exchange theory of law was decisively undermined, preventing it from contributing to an understanding of the transitional dynamics of law toward the "higher" order. The tide of criticism was hereafter to relentlessly grow.

Pashukanis subsequently qualified his position especially in his 1932 article, "The Marxist Theory of Law and State," where he argued that "law cannot be understood unless we consider it as the basic form of the policy of the ruling class," and that the "particular role of the legal superstructure is enormous in the transitional period when its active and conscious influence upon production and other social relationships assumes exceptional significance" (Pashukanis, 1980 [1924]: 297). Meanwhile, the Seventeenth Party Congress (1934) called for greater legal formalism, a position directly opposed to Pashukanis's and others' (such as Nikolai Krylenko's) views of legal nihilism. In 1936, Pashukanis further recanted and said, "We also insisted that Soviet Law must enjoy the maximum mobility and flexibility during the period of full-scale socialist offensive" (Pashukanis, 1980: 358). We recall that in his 1926 and 1927 editions of *The General Theory of Law and Marxism* he had already begun his re-thinking. Nevertheless, his ideas were still too inconsistent with the developing dictatorship of the proletariat and the demands of the transitional period, so said Stalin through his spokesperson Vyshinsky, Procurator General of the Soviets. In January, 1937 Pashukanis was arrested and made to "disappear." Vyshinsky then assumed the role of further dismantling and vilifying Pashukanis's works and of rebuilding the Soviet legal system according to the ascending notion of Soviet law, the law of the transitional period.

## Writings: Marx and the Commodity-Exchange Theory of Law

From 1924 to 1936 Pashukanis produced a number of works on Marxism and law. It is remarkable that Pashukanis was so active in both theoretical work and practice. During this time, he was simultaneously refocusing the law school curriculum, actively contributing to building the new order, and refining his analysis of Marxism and law, particularly as it led to the eventual withering away of the state and law. His contributions in various scholarly debates during the post-1917 years were squarely centered on the meaning of law in the new Soviet society. But the key work by Pashukanis was his 1924 book-length manuscript, *The General Theory of Law and Marxism*.

This significant, comprehensive statement on Marixst law detailed his commodity-exchange perspective. While the theory was to undergo some modifications in the second and third printing of *The General Theory*, it nonetheless maintained its central focus on the development of the form of law that emerges in the capitalist mode of production.

The theory attempts to explain how the core of law can be traced to the exchange of commodities in the competitive (laissez-faire) market place. It draws inspiration from the first 100 pages of Karl Marx's *Capital,* where the notion of the fetishism of commodities is discussed. Note, Marx's position draws from Hegel. Pashukanis indicated that a homology existed between the development of the commodity and legal form and that this development occurred "behind people's backs," regardless of class standing. Capital logic, he contended, produces such abstractions as the juridic subject, the "reasonable man in law," and principles such as the "due process clause" and the "equivalence principle," both articulated in the Fourteenth Amendment to the United States Constitution. Capital logic was also to find its way into various slogans verbalized during revolutions around the world which were subsequently given "idealized expression" in the various "declarations of independence." Let us summarize Pashukanis's theory as developed in his initial publication of 1924. Following this, we will look at some of the critiques and the impact of this perspective.

## Theory: Commodity-Exchange Perspective

The legal form, Pashukanis argued, developed directly out of the exchange of commodities in a competitive capitalist market place and in a parallel fashion (homologous) to the commodity form. Let us briefly summarize.

A commodity is constituted by two aspects, its "use-value" and its "exchange-value." The use-value of a commodity can, in turn, be seen as incorporating two elements: an unequal amount of labor in its production, and the unequal amount of benefit that it brings. Use-value, thus, incorporates differences. Whenever we produce for direct use, we have products and not commodities. In competitive capitalism, however, objects produced and exchanged take on the form of commodities. When two commodity owners meet at the market place to exchange commodities the initial use-value undergoes a change to an "exchange-value."

Exchange-value reflects a ratio of exchange. One commodity is exchanged with another in a specific quantitative ratio. Two gallons of milk, for example, could be exchanged for one pound of butter. This is a mathematical relationship of equivalence (two gallons of milk are equal to one pound of butter). Inherent differences in the use-value are now replaced by a ratio of exchange. What began as a qualitative relationship (e.g., inherent differences in the use-value) is, through commodity exchange, translated into a quantitative relationship.

Further, money becomes the "universal equivalent": two dollars can purchase either two gallons of milk or one pound of butter. A masking has taken place. "The memory of use-value," Marx tells us, "as distinct from exchange-value, has become entirely extinguished in this incarnation of pure exchange-value" (1973: 239-40). What has disappeared from consciousness are the inherent differences, now replaced by their representative. Quality has been changed into quantity, substance into form, and money is now worshipped as the universal equivalent. This is the process of the fetishism of commodities. It is also known as the law of equivalence, or capital logic, and it occurs "behind people's backs."

But this process is also the basis of the development of the legal form, according to Pashukanis. The development of the abstraction, the juridic subject, the "reasonable man in law," and notions of formal equality have their origins in the process of the exchange of commodities. The commodity exchangers enter the market-place as inherently different from others (i.e., they have different interests, wants, needs, and desires). They are similar to the notion of use-value reflecting inherent differences. But two inherently different commodity exchangers enter an exchange situation in a definite relationship. At the exact moment of exchange three specific phenomenal forms appear. First, the two commodity owners enter a relationship of equality. Each recognizes the other as an equal in the very moment of exchange. Even as there are inherent differences between the two, at the moment of exchange there is equivalence. Second, at this moment there is also recognition of free will. Each of the parties sees the other as freely exchanging a commodity. Finally, each recognizes the other as a rightful owner of the commodity that is being exchanged.

The constant exchange of commodities in the market-place produces these three phenomenal forms: the notion of equality, free will, and the proprietorship interests. The idea of the bearer of rights develops out of this instance, and lawyers have provided "idealized expression" for these emergent forms. The juridic subject as the bearer of these abstract rights is now similar to the notion of "exchange-value." A person has been transformed into the reasonable man in law, equivalent to other juridic subjects. As Pashukanis has said, "the legal subject...assumes the significance of a mathematical point, a centre in which a certain sum of rights is concentrated" (p. 39). The equivalence principle, derived from capital logic, is thereafter elevated to the heavens as a sacred right and incorporated in many emerging constitutions that resulted from social transformations. In sum, just as the commodity was transformed from use-value to exchange-value, so too is the person. Differences have been brought under the relationship of equivalence. Pushed away from consciousness is not only the unique and idiosyncratic, but also the historical production of the commodity and the person.

Along with the abstract development of law and the juridic subject there appeared the need for formalistic contracts. For Pashukanis, "[i]n the logical system of legal concepts the contract is only one of the forms of transaction in general, i.e., one of the methods of concrete expression of the will with whose aid the subject acts upon the legal sphere around him" (p. 43). "Outside contract," he continues, "the very concepts of subject and will exist only as lifeless abstractions in the legal sense" (p. 43).

In the U.S. Constitution, the equivalence principle can be found in the Fourteenth Amendment's "equal protection clause" which argues that equally situated should be equally treated. The juridic subject becomes a universal equivalent. Law finds its own legitimation principle within the logic of equivalent exchange, and the "rule of law" is elevated to the heavens. Both rich and poor are brought within its purview and are formally equal before the law. By bringing diverse subjects under a similar measure, many critics in the 1980s following Pashukanis's logic, argued that the result was repressive formalism. This had already been anticipated much earlier in the work of Max Weber (Milovanovic, 1989).

Pashukanis's insights into the development of the legal form outlined in 1924 were subsequently questioned. He was to make some changes, but his essential position concerning the homology between the legal form and the commodity form remained intact to the end. Additionally, Pashukanis argued that commodity exchange must be altered if these fetishisms were to be transformed, and that only in the "higher forms" of communism would the need for the state, law, and the juridic subject disappear. During the transitional period, he wrote, "human relationships will for a time involuntarily be limited by the 'narrow horizons of bourgeois law'" (p. 7). Desirable, therefore, following Marx and Lenin, was the movement toward the higher forms. But it was this very question that was strongly debated during the "transitional period" of the dictatorship of the proletariat, especially during the creative and fertile years between 1917-1937. What was to become of Soviet law during this period?

## Law, Morality, Crime, and Punishment

Pashukanis's theory of commodity-exchange and the development of equivalent exchange (capital logic) find their expression in notions of morality, crime, and punishment. For Pashukanis, ideas on morality are derived from the constructed fetishisms of rationally calculating egoists and from the development of the abstract concept of social equality. As he tells it, "[i]f moral personality is nothing other than the subject of commodity production, then moral law must reveal itself as the rule of exchange between commodity owners" (p. 64). Notions of justice are, therefore, derivative from commodity-exchange.

Similarly, with the violation of law, equivalent exchange materializes itself in the form of equivalent punishment. It is only at a certain stage of economic development—where equivalent exchange dominates—that we also find punishments fully expressed and articulated in the form of equivalent exchange. Ancient law, Pashukanis goes on to say, knew only collective responsibility. Bourgeois-capitalist law, on the other hand, invents the notion of individual responsibility and liability and a "gradation of liability." The equivalence principle becomes dominant: "Deprivation of freedom—for a definite term previously indicated in the judgment of the court—is the specific form in which modern, that is, bourgeois capitalist criminal law, realizes the basis of equivalent retribution" (p. 81).

Pashukanis explains that there is a difference between retribution and social defense as responses to crime. The latter would go beyond the abstract equivalence principles of the former inasmuch as "[i]t would require...a clear description of *symptoms* characterizing a socially dangerous condition and the development of those *methods* which must necessarily be applied in each given case for social defence" (p. 85). In other words, for Pashukanis, the social defense approach must return to the notion of the law of differences, not equivalences in dealing with those who break the law. He concludes his general treatise on Marxism and law by stating that abstract notions of crime and punishment will only begin to disappear when the "general withering away of the legal superstructures begins" (p. 86). His tautological conclusion is that to the extent these categories are disappearing, "narrow horizons of bourgeois law are disappearing" (p. 86).

Historical examination indicates that Lenin's early statements that only "excesses" will exist in the higher form and that some type of social defense is the initial ideal response under the dictatorship of the proletariat, gradually gave way by the mid-1930s to Stalin's and Vyshinsky's return to retribution theory (Solomon, 1996). By this time, both men's writings had already generated much momentum for the return of legal formalism.

## Critiques and Revisions

Pashukanis, from mid-1920s to 1936, was to be attacked for his position in the development of law on a number of fronts. It should be mentioned that prior to 1919 there was no lively discussion or debate on Marxist law in Russia (Beirne, 1990: 48-49). With the revolution came the dismantling of the Tsarist form of law and courts (Solomon, 1996: 17-48). Certainly, a vacuum existed as to the question of what form law should take during the transitional period.

The key critical theorists who provided the basis for revisions by Pashukanis were Piotr I. Stuchka, Nikolai Krylenko, and Andrei Vyshinsky. Stuchka, a significant figure in the emerging Soviet society, criticized Pashukanis for his neglect of class in the development of law during the transitional period. Three years prior to Pashukanis's 1924 manuscript, Stuchka had published *The Revolutionary Role of Law and State* which provided much discussion on Marxist law. While Stuchka praised Pashukanis's work in the book's third edition, he nevertheless disagreed with the exclusion of class in Pashukanis's analysis of Marxist law. For Stuchka, the transitional period demanded a Soviet law which would aid in the eventual transformation into the classless society of communism. For Pashukanis, on the other hand, Soviet law was inherently a continuation of the previous bourgeois law.

It has been suggested by Sharlet, Maggs, and Beirne (1990: 55) that Stuchka provided the logic necessary to support a Soviet legal system not only for the transitional period but for some time thereafter. In fact, for these authors, Stuchka, albeit inadvertently, supplied the logic that would undermine the notion of the withering away of law. This logic was later to contribute to Stalin's and Vyshinsky's articulations of Soviet law. But Stuchka's position also suggested a simplification of the legal process. Regrettably, Stuchka died from natural causes in 1932, at a time when his voice could have contributed to further productive debates about the nature of Soviet law.

Whereas Stuchka's position on the law's development was focused on the primacy of superstructural practices, Pashukanis's position was focused on the workings of the "base" in the Marxian conceptualization of the base-superstructure metaphor. Pashukanis had written that,

> Comrade Stuchka...correctly identified the problem of law as a problem of a social relationship. But instead of beginning to search for the specific social objectivity of the relationship, he returned to the usual and formal definition... [L]aw figures not as a *specific* social relationship but, as with *all* relationships *in general, as a system of relations which corresponds to the interests of the ruling class and which protects it with organized force* (p. 22).

Pashukanis goes on to state that Stuchka's definition of law "was tuned to the needs of the practicing lawyer. It shows the empirical limit which history always places upon legal logic, but it does not reveal the deep roots of this logic itself. This definition reveals the class content included in legal forms, but it does not explain to us why this content adopts such a form" (p. 23).

The position Pashukanis took in 1924 was that understanding class relationships, alone, does not go to the deeper sources of the particular legal form that develops. However, it was just this position that was the focus of the attacks that cumulated in Pashukanis's purge in 1937. He did, however, later qualify his central argument in the commodity-exchange perspective. We find, for example, in his 1927 article, "The Marxist Theory of Law and the Construction of Socialism," a concession to Stuchka's criticism. He states emphatically:

> I readily agree that [my 1924]...essay in many respects needs further development and perhaps reworking. A whole series of problems could not be covered in the book and indeed, at that time simply did not come within the author's field of vision. Such for example, is the problem of the law of the transitional period, or Soviet law, fully posed by Stuchka, which is among his outstanding contributions to the theory of law (Pashukanis, 1980 [1927]: 194).

But Pushukanis immediately follows with, "I did not view the process of the withering away of law as a 'direct transition from bourgeois law to non-law'" (1980 [1927]: 194). And he dismisses

Stuchka's critique of "economism" against him. Here, Pashukanis reminds Stuchka that the "economic subjects" as exchangers of commodities and the social division of labor are "facts" and that they are not inherently connected with the wishes of the state. These "facts," for Pashukanis, "contain the basic and principal prerequisites for a legal relationship" (1980 [1927]: 194.). Pashukanis does, however, give credit to Stuchka for noting the importance of state power in the transition from one form of the mode of production to another. Concerning this, he tells us that Stuchka is "absolutely right."

In 1932 we see Pashukanis returning to this question in his article "The Marxist Theory of State and Law." Here, he notes the significance of the independent influences on law by superstructural practices: "we cannot deny the real existence of the legal superstructure, i.e. of relationships formulated and consolidated by the conscious will of the ruling class" (1980 [1932]: 296). It seems that at this point Pashukanis was developing a new, more integrated form of his commodity-exchange perspective, for he goes on to say,

> But to study law only as relationships of production and exchange means to confuse law with economics, to retard the understanding of the reciprocal action of the legal superstructure and its active role. At the same time as production relations are imposed on people regardless of their will, legal relationships are impossible without the participation of the conscious will of the ruling class (1980 [1932]: 296).

Here, Pashukanis anticipated many of the revisionist theories later developed by Louis Althusser and Nicos Poulantzas from the late 1960s to the late 1970s. The emerging notion—contrary to the dominant form of instrumental and class-oriented Marxism in the 1960s—was that a number of relatively autonomous spheres existed (viz., the economic, political, ideological, and juridical) and appeared historically in relatively stabilized articulations, producing the actual substance of law itself. At different historical junctures, one of these social spheres may, indeed, be the more dominant. Pashukanis seemed, already, to be acknowledging this with his comment in this same 1932 article when he stated, "A legal relationship is a *form* of production relations because the active influence of the class organization of the ruling class transforms the factual relationship into a legal one, gives it a new quality, and thus includes it in the construction of the legal superstructure" (1980 [1932]: 297). Pashukanis is indicating the interconnected nature of the various spheres of influence, where one may be the more dominant. For example, he states that "the revolutionary role of the legal superstructure is enormous in the transitional period when its active and conscious influence upon production and other social relationships assumes exceptional significance. Soviet law, like any law, will cease to exist if it is not applied" (1980 [1932]: 297).

But Pashukanis's various reconceptualizations fell short of keeping his attackers at bay. He still maintained that Soviet law was to be "seen exclusively as a legacy of class society imposed on the proletariat and which haunts it until the second phase of communism" (1980 [1932]: 299). Pashukanis continued with this thesis in a 1935 work (co-authored work with L. la. Gintsburg), *A Course on Soviet Economic Law*, where he once again notes the "class nature" of Soviet economic law. He even advocates, in a 1936 article entitled, "Sate and Law Under Socialism," that Soviet law must be given "maximum mobility and flexibility during the period of full-scale socialist offensive."

At this point, there is a certain irony at work. Vyshinsky, during this time, was suggesting a re-establishment of formal law for social stability and argued for blending socialist and revolutionary legality. Krylenko, on the other hand, as noted above, had been debating Vyshinsky and was advocating the idea of law as analogy and for the simplification of law. Stuchka, who died in 1932, contributed in many ways to this debate, providing much support for Vyshinsky's call for formalism in law. Stuchka, for example, believed that formalism and the adversary process were high cultural accomplishments that had to be maintained. Pashukanis's position shifted from his initial, strong argument for the exclusive analysis of relations of exchange in the development of law and for the withering away of the state and law to his revised position of the early and mid-1930's. This latter stance was one in which he advocated state intervention in the social formation with a recognition that the law's roots still resided in commodity exchange; this reconsideration added a rich dimension to the debate. Pashukanis was at odds with Vyshinsky and Stuchka, but had some sympathy for Krylenko's position. Nonetheless, Pashukanis—who in the mid-1930s seemed to be persuaded to accept some form of Soviet law during the transitional period to the higher forms—must have seen Krylenko's position as being out of touch with the emerging society.

Perhaps Pashukanis's downfall had to do with the fact that he was unable to provide convincing analysis of how law should look during the transitional period, in order for the higher form to develop from it. It seems that a dialectical position was required which advocated a form of Soviet law, during the transitional period, that had embedded within it sufficient tension for the gradual transition to the withering away of law itself. This would have also called for discernment in how to organize the productive and exchange spheres in such a way that the dialectical tension would aid in the transition to the higher form. Pashukanis was already suggesting something along these lines in the mid-1930s, indicating that he was, indeed, working on a more fully developed theory. This insight is indicated by his 1936 article in which he suggested a reciprocal effect between the base and superstructure and the desirability for guidance from the superstructure in the form of Soviet law.

Krylenko's effect on Pashukanis emerged out of the former's increasingly hostile debates with the rising Vyshinsky during the early 1930s (see Huskey, 1990: 174). As an old Bolshevik and as the Commissar of Justice until his arrest in January 1938, Krylenko's view of law was considered one of the more extreme, a perspective identified as legal nihilism. Whereas Krylenko advocated the simplification of law, Vyshinsky, ironically, advocated legal formalism as a way of providing stability in society. In retort to a proposed draft of the criminal law offered by Krylenko in 1935—with the thrust that judges should merely orient themselves to law, not be bound by it—Vyshinsky responded that it went against Stalin's earlier speech, which advocated stricter adherence to the law. During the next two years this public debate continued and Vyshinki was accused by Krylenko of re-inventing legal retribution, a bourgeois form of punishment for dealing with offenders (Huskey, 1990: 181; see also Stalin's return to retributive forms of law, Solomon, 1996: 227).

Vyshinsky, who was appointed as the Procurator General of the U.S.S.R. in 1935, continued his purging of rival theorists: Pashukanis, Stuchka (in abstentia), and Krylenko. No public trial took place for Pashukanis, nor were formal charges initially made. However, subsequent to his disappearance he was attacked by Vyshinsky: "The pseudo-scientific positions of Pashukanis and his group in the field of law have been completely shaped by the counterrevolutionary 'theories' of Trotskyism and the rightists (in particular by the anti-Leninist views of Bukharin)" (Vyshinsky [1937] cited in Sharlet and Beirne, 1990: 153). In 1937, Stuchka was cited as "a propagator of

harmful ideology and a deliberate wrecker in the field of jurispru-
dence" (Medvedev, cited in Sharlet, Maggs, and Beirne, 1990: 47).
Vyshinsky, in 1938, called Stuchka the advocate of "the
Bukharinist perversions of Marxism-Leninism" (cited in Sharlet,
Maggs, and Beirne, 1990: 47). As for Krylenko, the charge was,
"the uncritical repeating of the 'ideas' of Pashukanis" (cited in
Barry, 1990: 166).

Krylenko was arrested in early 1938—one year after Pashukanis's
arrest—and purged. According to one source, "he was accused of
ties with a right-wing anti-Soviet organization that was supposedly
headed by Bukharin, of having created a wreckers' organization in
agencies of the justice system and having carried out subversive
activities, and of having personally recruited 30 people" (Feofanov
cited in Barry, 1990: 166). At the end of a twenty-minute trial, on
July 29, 1938, Krylenko was sentenced to be shot.

So there ended a social experiment, an attempt at revolutionary
change from below. The rich debate concerning law during the transitional period was answered by the purges of 1937-1938. Stalin,
aided by Vyshinsky's rhetoric and revisionism of law, prevailed,
placing a lid on the possibilities that were embedded in the revolution of 1917. An experiment, started in 1917 with the fertile possibilities of liberating human potential, was delivered a death blow.

### Legacy: Historical Lessons Often Withered Away

What possible benefit can be gained in re-visiting Pashukanis, to
have yet a newer edition of his works published? Haven't the historical lessons already been learned? Are would-be revolutionaries
so well acquainted with the notion of the dialectics of struggle that
nothing can be gained by reviewing Pashukanis's work and the context for its development and subsequent dismissal? What value do
we place on the meticulous and clear-headed research and writings
of those such as Beirne and Sharlet, Hunt, and Solomon dealing
with those critical years in post-revolutionary Russia?

Pashukanis's work is significant on a number of levels. In the late
1970s and early 1980s a number of theorists teased out the various
implications of his early version of the commodity-exchange theory
of law. By the mid-1980s there was a decisive switch in Marxist
analyses in the social sciences away from instrumental Marxism and
toward structural Marxism that was, in many ways, informed, either
directly or indirectly, by Pashukanis's work.

The structural form of Marxism indicates the interplay of relatively autonomous spheres (the economic, political, ideological, and juridical) which can be studied in their historical manifestation in terms of relatively stable configurations. It is the active intervention by the juridic sphere in other social spheres, through such mechanisms as "interest balancing," that the subject of late capitalism is no longer perceived in a unitary manner; rather, there has been a historical transformation from status to contract, and increasingly back to status. One's rights and duties become increasingly connected with one's position, one's status in the social formation (i.e., free citizen, prisoner, juvenile, mentally ill, welfare recipient, unionized worker, soldier). Given this relative stability, phenomena must be seen as overdetermined. It may very well be that Pashukanis's initial (1924) statement of the commodity-exchange perspective was congruous with nineteenth-century laissez-faire forms of capitalism, but twentieth-century political economy with its tendencies toward "legitimation crises" (Habermas, 1975) brought with it greater intervention by the state, the superstructure. Subsequent revisions by Pashukanis of his 1924 statement—especially in response to the critiques of Stuchka—seemed to indicate that Pashukanis was indeed developing a more sophisticated model that would take into account capital logic, class interests, superstructural practices, and the reciprocal effects among these.

The full development of this reciprocity was not theorized until the mid-1980s. The contemporary era of critical social science research no longer privileges dogmatic forms of Marxism. Certainly there is the old guard protecting the sacred tablets of truth. But more contemporary works such as those of Laclau and Mouffe (1985) and Laclau (1990, 1996) question some of the concepts of Marxism interpreted by critical social scientists. The question of the category of "working class" itself has been central. Is there such a thing as a homogenous working class? Laclau (1990, 1996) questions whether it is still a useful concept because class in late capitalism does not reflect the variety of factions in existence. Similarly, Butler (1990) has examined the question of gender and has indicated its inherent instability. Recent research is beginning to examine the question of the intersections of class, gender, and race (see Schwartz and Milovanovic, 1996).

Doubtless, the old guard attempts, at all costs, to hold on to this sacred concept of class. But contemporary research has indicated a much more dynamic form of political economy which necessitates new ways of thinking about law. In fact, the very "dislocations" and "structural undecidabilities" (Laclau, 1990: 61; 1996: 88, 97, 100-102) in existence in postmodern society are opportunities for the development of new, more humanistic articulations (Lash and Urry, 1994). Consequently, Pashukanis's work is still central in this creative time of reevaluation, refinement, deletion, and the development of law.

Connected to this are some of the inexcusable and deplorable contemporary forms of "praxis" that are not rooted in historical lessons. We only have to examine the Cuban experience and post-revolutionary Nicaragua under the Sandinstas to see both the good and bad in activism. Pashukanis's work shows us the complex forces that exist at the time of revolutions. During revolutions, creative possibilities, good and bad, emerge. However, those activists who are not sensitive to historical examinations of these vacuums can easily fall into Stalinist forms of expression, or even become—as Marx himself had warned with his (and Gramsci's) notion of hegemony—their own gravediggers. And over-zealous, would-be reformers, unguided by some notion of fairness and understandings of historical specificities outside of their own ends-justify-the-means rhetoric can quickly engage in negative forms such as political correctness, reversal of hierarchies, schmarxism (dogmatic marxism), moral hate (Groves, 1991), "hate politics" (Cornell, 1991), and exorcism (Milovanovic, 1991).

Pashukanis's work has also sensitized us to the notion of "repressive formalism." This idea, which demands scrutiny of abstract principles that on the face seem fair, indicates that new notions of fairness need to be researched, developed, and instituted. Marx's offering of the notion, "from each according to his ability, to each according to his needs" is still relevant today. Here, rather than "formal equality" rooted in capital logic, new operative principles must be developed that recognize the uniqueness of the humanbeing. See, for example, Laclau and Mouffe's privileging of the "logic of difference" rather than the "logic of equivalence" (1985: 130, 154-155, 176, 182; Laclau, 1996: 43, 53-56; see also Cornell, 1991, 1998).

Beirne and Sharlet (1990: 40) have also offered some keen observations concerning revolutionary change. First, they note that even if a dictatorship of the proletariat is necessary, Marx and Lenin had argued that it should be restricted in duration and extent. Second, societal elements, structures, and institutions developed within the transitional phase, "must dialectically contain the capacity for self-transformation." Chaos theory's conceptualization of "dissipative structures" is an especially appropriate concept here (see Milovanovic, 1997; see also Unger's "transformative agenda" which looks very much like far-from-equilibrium conditions replete with emerging dissipative structures advocated by chaos theorists, 1987). And third, the form of social relationships themselves must be transformed; this process is informed by historical analysis. This has everything to do with the mode of production and political economy. Pashukanis had already informed us that "a society which is compelled to preserve equivalent exchange between labour expenditure and compensation in a form even remotely resembling the exchange of commodity values, *will be compelled* also to preserve the form of law" (p. 9). From my own analysis above, I would add, as a fourth point, being aware and sensitive to the dialectics of struggle as a necessary component to an emancipatory form of transpraxis. Pashukanis's work certainly provides much context for understanding these central concerns in social struggles.

## Conclusion

This republication of Pashukanis's work on law at the turn of the millennium is timely. It beckons us to be sensitive to historical struggles and their outcomes. It provides us with an understanding of how social transformations can take unintended directions with the emergence of Stalin-like figures. But it also indicates the creative potential that can provide the basis of a new, more humane order. The more recent Russian revolution of 1989-1990 still awaits the visionary who will come forth in a time of turmoil to pronounce a thesis equivalent to that of Pashukanis's.

## References

Barry, Donald. 1990. "Nilolai Vasil'evich Krylenko: A Reevaluation." In Piers Beirne (ed.) *Revolution in Law: Contributions to the Development of Soviet Legal Theory, 1917-1938*. London: M.E. Sharpe, Inc.
Beirne, Piers. 1979. "Empiricism and the Critique of Marxism on Law and Crime," *Social Problems* 26: 373-85.
_____ (ed.). 1990. *Revolution in Law: Contributions to the Development of Soviet Legal Theory, 1917-1938*. London: M. E. Sharpe, Inc.
_____. 1980. "Editor's Introduction." In Piers Beirne (ed.) *Revolution in Law: Contributions to the Development of Soviet Legal Theory, 1917-1938*. London: M.E. Sharpe, Inc.

Beirne, Piers and Alan Hunt. 1990. "Law and the Constitution of Soviet Society: The Case of Comrade Lenin." In Piers Beirne (ed.). *Revolution in Law: Contributions to the Development of Soviet Legal Theory, 1917-1938*. London: M.E. Sharpe, Inc.

Beirne, Piers and Richard Quinney (eds.). 1982. *Marxism and Law*. New York: John Wiley.

Beirne, Piers and Robert Sharlet (eds.). 1980. *Pashukanis: Selected Writings on Marxism and Law*. New York: Academic Press.

_____. 1990. "Toward a General Theory of Law and Marxism: E.B. Pashukanis." In Piers Beirne (ed.). *Revolution in Law: Contributions to the Development of Soviet Legal Theory, 1917-1938*. London: M.E. Sharpe, Inc.

Butler, Judith. 1990. *Gender Trouble: Feminism and the Subversion of Identity*. New York: Routledge.

Cornell, Drucilla. 1991. *Beyond Accommodation: Ethical Feminism, Deconstruction and the Law*. New York: Routledge.

_____. 1998. *At the Heart of Freedom: Feminism, Sex and Equality*. Princeton, New Jersey: Princeton University Press.

Groves, Byrone. 1991. "Us and Them: Reflections of the Dialectics of Moral Hate." In Brian MacLean and Dragan Milovanovic (eds.). *New Directions in Critical Criminology*. Vancouver, Canada: Collective Press.

Habermas, Jurgen. 1975. *Legitimation Crises*. Boston: Beacon Press.

Hazard, John (ed.). 1951. *Soviet Legal Philosophy*. Cambridge, MA: Harvard University Press.

Huskey, Eugene. 1990. "Vyshinsky, Krylenko, and Soviet Penal Politics." In Piers Beirne (ed.) *Revolution in Law: Contributions to the Development of Soviet Legal Theory, 1917-1938*. London: M.E. Sharpe, Inc.

Laclau, Ernesto and Chantal Mouffe. 1985. *Hegemony and Socialist Strategy*. London: Verso.

Laclau, Ernesto. 1990. *New Reflections on the Revolution of Our Time*. London: Verso.

_____. *Emancipations*. 1996. London: Verso.

Lash, Scott and John Urry. 1994. *Economies of Signs and Space*. London: Sage.

Marx, Karl. 1973. *Grundrisse*. New York: Random House.

Milovanovic, Dragan. 1981. "The Commodity-Exchange Theory of Law: In Search of a Perspective," *Crime and Social Justice* 16: 41-49.

_____. 1987. "The Political Economy of 'Liberty' and 'Property' Interests," *Legal Studies Forum* 11: 267-293.

_____. 1989. *Weberian and Marxian Analysis of Law: Structure and Function of Law in a Capitalist Mode of Production*. Aldershot, England: Gower Publishers.

_____. 1991. "Schmarxism, Exorcism and Transpraxis," *The Critical Criminologist* 3(4): 11-12.

_____. 1997. *Chaos, Criminology, and Social Justice: The New Orderly (Dis)Order*. Westport, CT: Praeger.

Pashukanis, Evgeny B. 1980 [1927]. "The Marxist Theory of Law and the Construction of Socialism." In Piers Beirne and Robert Sharlet (eds.). *Pashukanis: Selected Writings on Marxism and Law*. New York: Academic Press.

_____. 1980 [1932]. "The Marxist Theory of State and Law." In Piers Beirne and Robert Sharlet (eds.). *Pashukanis: Selected Writings on Marxism and Law*. New York: Academic Press.

Schwartz, Martin and Dragan Milovanovic (eds.). 1996. *Race, Gender and Class in Criminology: Intersections*. New York: Garland Publishing.

Sharlet, Robert, Peter Maggs and Piers Beirne. 1990. "P.I. Stuchka and Soviet Law." In Piers Beirne (ed.). *Revolution in Law: Contributions to the Development of Soviet Legal Theory, 1917-1938*. London: M.E. Sharpe, Inc.

Sharlet, Robert and Piers Beirne. 1990. "In Search of Vyshinsky: The Paradox of Law and Terror." In Piers Beirne (ed.). *Revolution in Law: Contributions to the Development of Soviet Legal Theory, 1917-1938.* London: M.E. Sharpe, Inc.

Solomon, Peter. 1996. *Soviet Criminal Justice under Stalin.* Cambridge: Cambridge University Press.

Unger, Roberto. 1987. *False Necessity.* New York: Cambridge University Press.

# 13

## On Richard Quinney, *Critique of Legal Order*

*Randall G. Sheldon*

After more than three decades, the works of Richard Quinney continue to be influential. During the past few years I have assigned graduate students in a seminar on "law and social control" to read excerpts from three of Quinney's books: *Crime and Justice in Society* (1969), *The Social Reality of Crime* (1970) and *Critique of Legal Order: Crime Control In Capitalist Society* (1974). Most of these students know little of Quinney's works, except perhaps what they have read in other books (usually undergraduate criminology or criminal justice textbooks). Without exception the students have consistently marveled at the contemporary relevance of most of what Quinney wrote so many years ago. The same can be said of several generations of criminologists, for Quinney ranks among the giants of twentieth-century criminology, as indicated by the many awards he has received (especially the prestigious Edwin Sutherland Award from the American Society of Criminology), plus the fact that he has been cited more than any other American criminologist, save for Sutherland and Donald Cressey (largely because of their classic text, *Criminology*).

What is most interesting about Quinney is the evolution of his thinking and writing over the years. In a recent interview appearing in *Contemporary Justice Review* Quinney notes that "one lifetime isn't enough for all that we need to experience.... I guess I see so many possibilities of experiencing the world, that you experience it one way and that opens up another way and then, rather than continue on that one experience, you want to see the world in another way. That's one reason why I think I've gone from one theory to another, at least in early times." This helps explain Quinney's seemingly dramatic shifts in perspectives over the course of his career, especially during the 1970s and early 1980s. His earlier writings reflected a classic "liberal" perspective, as one of the foremost representatives of the popular "labeling" approach in the late 1960s and early 1970s (as evidenced in *Crime and Justice in Society, The Problem of Crime* and especially in *The Social Reality of Crime*). *Critique of Legal Order*, however, represented a rather significant shift toward a Marxist view of crime and the legal order. This perspective was expanded upon with the publication of *Class, State and Crime* in 1977, which Quinney revised in 1980 for a second edition. But just when we were getting used to his Marxist orientation toward crime and justice, Quinney wrote something totally different in *Providence: The Reconstruction of Social and Moral Order* (1980). In this book his aim was to connect the material life (exemplified in the works of Marx) with the spiritual life; more specifically, he wrote about the possible fusion between material existence and sacred essence; about Marx's critical analysis of material existence and the prophetic theology of culture. Here Quinney's writings took him back to one of his original interests in graduate school, the sociology of religion. With his *Social Existence: Metaphysics, Marxism and the Social Sciences* (1982) it was obvious that Quinney was heading in a completely different direction, as he began to take a more existentialist and spiritual path.

Quinney wasn't entirely leaving the world of criminology, however, as he co-edited (with Hal Pepinsky) *Criminology as Peacemaking* in 1991, along with a third edition of *The Problem of Crime* in 1991 (but with a significant subtitle added: *A Peace and Social Justice Perspective*) and a third edition of his classic *Criminal Behavior Systems* in 1994. Most recently he has completed a co-edited book (with Kevin Anderson), *Erich Fromm and Critical Criminology*, bringing forth a series of articles that link Fromm's work with the problem of crime and justice, including two new translations of Fromm's early articles on crime and justice, previously unpublished in English.

During the past twenty years or so Quinney has, through several different writings (including two auto-biographical books, *Journey to a Far Place* and *For the Time Being*), demonstrated his existentialist views and his Buddhist orientation toward life, along with his skills as a photographer. Today he remains an inspiration to many generations of criminologists, as is clearly demonstrated by the large attendance whenever he is on a panel at a conference (especially the American Society of Criminology).

Placing *Critique of Legal Order* in the context of Quinney's lifetime of work is not an easy task. It seems best to begin by reiterating that this book represented a significant break from Quinney's previous work. It may seem appropriate to suggest that Quinney was offering a new "paradigm" for criminology, in the sense used by Thomas Kuhn (1970). Here he clearly provided a new way of looking at the phenomenon of crime control. The emphasis of this work is on the *control* of crime, and the manner in which it is done in a *capitalist* society. He was practically alone among American criminologists in connecting the Vietnam War with what was occurring in America. In the preface Quinney writes that: "The legal system at home and the military apparatus abroad are two sides of the same phenomenon; both perpetuate American capitalism, the American Way of Life." This is a serious charge, and one that has been amply documented in the works of such well-known critics as Noam Chomsky, Howard Zinn, and Michael Parenti (to name just three) who have written about the various forms of repression abroad, supported by American tax dollars, which served "American interests"—meaning in reality, the interests of the ruling class.

Quinney's overall critique of capitalism and criminology's role in crime control is still relevant and provides some guidelines for the future. One of the leading points Quinney makes is that crime control in modern capitalist societies is not so much aimed at reducing crime and suffering as it is at preserving the established order and controlling the "dangerous classes," the "rabble" or the "surplus population" (Shelden and Brown, 2000; Shelden, 1999a, 1999b; Shelden, 2001).

It becomes obvious in the first chapter of this book that Quinney is extending his analysis of the criminal justice system, begun years earlier in *Crime and Justice in Society* with his "sociological theory of criminal law," in which he proposes, via four propositions, an "interest group" theory of law. In *Crime and Justice in Society*, he was clearly departing from conventional practice by suggesting that powerful interests shape the law, rather than the interests of all (known as the "consensus" view). This theory was expanded upon in *The Social Reality of Crime*, where he offered six propositions, among which included the proposition that criminal definitions describe behaviors that conflict with powerful interests. The theory was based on the social constructionist mode of thought, which suggests that rather than being some objective truth, reality is socially created. Thus, "crime" and the "criminal justice system," are *social products*.

In *Critique of Legal Order*, however, Quinney engages in a critique of all previous modes of criminological thought, including his own. In the first chapter he outlines and critiques three of the ways we normally think about reality: the positivist, the social constructionist and the phenomenological. He then proceeds to outline a critical mode of thinking, one which involves the "demystification, the removal of the myths—the false consciousness—created by the official reality." He completes this first chapter by outlining six propositions for a "critical philosophy of the legal order." In these propositions he clearly departs from his previous work by advancing a version of what has come to be called *instrumental Marxism*, arguing that the state serves the interest of the ruling class and that criminal law is "an instrument of the state and ruling class to maintain and perpetuate the existing social and economic order" (p. 16). In his sixth proposition he offers a form of socialism as a solution to the crime problem. It can be said that in this light the volume represents more than a mere critique of the legal order; it represents a "call to arms," so to speak, for citizens (and criminologists) to help bring about the replacement of American capitalism with a new society, based upon socialist principles. Quinney was treading on ground rarely covered then (and now) by mainstream criminology.

*Critique of Legal Order* was perhaps a reflection of someone who had become disenchanted with American capitalism. As a humanist, Quinney was deeply and genuinely disturbed by what he saw around him. In the preface, Quinney suggests that capitalism is in deep trouble and thus "will increasingly rely on repressive, authoritarian measures to secure its own survival" (p. vi). Writing at the time of Watergate, COINTELPRO, the Vietnam War, and other key sociopolitical events, it is understandable that he would predict that worse things would transpire. However, it seems obvious that Quinney, like Marx, underestimated the resiliency of capitalism and the power of the ruling class. It could even be argued that he underestimated the predictive power of his own analysis of the role of ideology and the ways in which, as Noam Chomsky has suggested, "necessary illusions" are produced, thereby "manufacturing consent" (Chomsky, 1989; Herman and Chomsky, 1988). In other words, it could be argued that Quinney did not go quite far enough in his own analysis. A more careful reading of Marxist literature reveals the importance of ideological rule ("hegemony"), that ruling classes in "democratic" societies cannot become too authoritarian.

The balance of the book consists of a critical analysis of not just the legal order per se, but of how such an order fits into society as a whole. He begins, in Chapter 2, with an analysis of the relationship between "knowledge and order" and levels one of his most serious charges, calling his fellow criminologists "ancillary agents of power" who provide "the kinds of information that governing elites use to manipulate and control those who threaten the system" and who "inform the managers of social order" (p. 27).

Quinney noted that conventional knowledge tends to support the established social order. He further noted that the "official reality of the state and the interests of social scientists are the same" (p. 17). Moreover, it is the "search for order" (the so-called "Hobbesian problem of order") that has dominated intellectual thought since the seventeenth century. The solution to this "problem" came to be the establishment of a set of norms that limit legitimate action. There are, of course, serious threats to this "order." What is most interesting here is Quinney's observation that, as de Tocqueville noted long ago (and more recently Noam Chomsky) that the biggest threat to the prevailing order is *democracy*, not its traditional notions, but true democracy which would involve extending democratic principles to the economy and to everyday life (Chomsky, 1996).

For Quinney the ultimate source of social order is the "legitimacy" of the system, noted by Max Weber. Weber was famous for developing his ideal types of "authority," noting that in modern, bureaucratic societies "legitimate" authority (based on *positions* supported by *law*) is the most prevalent. This legitimacy lies not in the people, but rather in the state. Law, from this view, is one of the ultimate and most rational forms of authority. The legal system is not to be questioned because it is legitimate. Therefore it is to be obeyed. The demand for "law and order" was of paramount importance when Quinney wrote this, as it certainly is today. We constantly hear the phrase that this is a nation under the "rule of law," not the rule of men. Quinney's observation a quarter of a century ago, however, rings just as true today: while it is technically true that there is due process, that is, a system of basic rights theoretically accorded to all, such an ideal "is negated by the fact that the entire legal system is played according to rules formulated and enforced by a legal estab-lishment that is part of the capitalist ruling class" (p. 21). In other words, we have "rights" but only within narrowly defined param-eters (for a similar view see Chomsky, 1989, 1994 and Herman and Chomsky, 1988).

Quinney has consistently argued throughout his career for a need to visualize possibilities other than the taken-for-granted existing social order. That requires a *critical* perspective. This was made clear when he noted that the present legal order "is being presented to us (by the legalists in a capitalist society) as the only rational means for the achievement of social order. Other possibilities for social exist-ence are excluded" (p. 22).

Finally, Quinney, in Chapter 2, becomes a critic of established criminology. In a statement that is almost identical to a thesis of-fered by Chomsky in his famous essay "On the Responsibilities of Intellectuals" (1987), Quinney argues that criminologists "provide the kinds of information that governing elites use to manipulate and control those who threaten the system. As 'experts,' criminologists inform the managers of social order." Rather than being an explicit conspiracy, the relationship "is much more natural and subtle" be-cause criminologists rarely question their own assumptions. "By pursuing a narrow scientific model, supported by an ideology of social order, the criminologist finds his interests tied to those of the state. Both parties have an interest in preserving existing arrange-ments" (pp. 27-28). In many of his published works and public speeches, Chomsky has criticized intellectuals for providing "scien-tific" rationalizations of the existing social order, with all of its injus-tices. Such intellectuals have been gradually socialized through es-tablished schools of higher education so that by the time they re-ceive their degrees they have become fully indoctrinated and begin to receive handsome rewards for serving the interests of the power-ful.

Quinney provides a superb example of how criminologists serve the existing order and those in power—by the mere fact that they unquestioningly rely on a state definition of "crime." The control and prediction of "crime" is the goal of the criminologist, since he or she follows the scientific tradition of positivism. Quinney quotes one of the most famous textbooks, that of Sutherland and Cressey, in which they note that "theoretical knowledge is increased most significantly in the efforts at social control" (p. 29). Indeed, Quinney states "crime control is good business for the criminologist." He notes that many criminologists have specialized in the field of corrections, since the prison provides a steady supply of data for which to test various criminological theories. Quinney notes that if we eliminated prisons we would remove "one of the crucial sites for criminological research" (p. 30). This continues to be true today as crime control has become a huge industry, which has even captured the attention of Wall Street. Indeed, several noted brokerage houses (e.g., Smith-Barney, Merril Lynch) have on several occasions issued "buy orders" to invest in various crime-control businesses, such as Corrections Corporation of America. Likewise many criminologists "follow the money" dripping from the almost unlimited coffers of the federal government (Shelden, 1999).

The remainder of Chapter 2 consists of a sampling of what Quinney calls "Scholarship in the Service of Social Control." Here he begins a lengthy analysis of various research projects funded by government agencies through universities all over the country. Especially prominent is the money coming from the (now defunct) Law Enforcement Assistance Administration (LEAA). One could easily update his list to include the most recent research projects, the bulk of which, says Quinney, are "intended to make the existing [criminal justice] system more rational or more respectable" (p. 30).

Quinney notes sarcastically that a good deal of funding goes toward the development of criminal justice programs in colleges and universities. He was one of the first criminologists to critically examine this new phenomenon. Most of these programs were, in effect, little more than "police training" programs, begun partly as a result of President Johnson's Crime Commission reports (the various "Task Forces" that appeared in the late 1960s) which strongly urged that we "professionalize" and "humanize" the police and the rest of the criminal justice system. Quinney sums up what this really meant in practice, by quoting a report by Lee Webb in an obscure publication, *The University-Military-Police Complex* (published by the North American Congress on Latin America). Webb stated that "professionalization of the police means exactly what it does in the Army: a fascination with technique and modern equipment, a depolitization of the department, and a readiness to carry out any orders from above" (p. 34). By the early 1970s LEAA was in full gear. The Department of Justice was funding a variety of research projects in an attempt, said Quinney, to secure the allegiance of scholars. As

the "crime control industry" was beginning Quinney wrote propheti-
cally that: "The study of crime, from an approved perspective, becomes a worthwhile subject for the young scientist" (p. 35).

It is appropriate to quote two other scholars who have made their
mark in fields other than criminology, but whose writings nonetheless relate strongly to the field. First, Howard Zinn once criticized
mainstream historians. In his book *The Politics of History* (1990),
Zinn begins a chapter appropriately titled "Knowledge as a Form of
Power" (which reads much like Chapter 2 of *Critique of Legal Order* and has a similar title), with comments about how the usual
publications of historians have produced "the largest number of in-
consequential studies in the history of civilization." Zinn further remarks that "historians occasionally emerge from library stacks to
sign petitions or deliver a speech, then return to produce even more
of inconsequence." He suggests that historians "read the titles of
doctoral dissertations published in the past twenty years, and the
pages of leading scholarly journals for the same period, alongside
the lists of war dead, the figures on per capita income in Latin
America, the autobiography of Malcolm X." In short, Zinn states
that historians "publish while others perish" (1990: 5).

It is interesting to note that Zinn first published the above remarks
in 1970, meaning he was actually writing them in the late 1960s.
About the same time, another leading social critic, Noam Chomsky,
wrote a piece in the *New York Review of Books* (Feb. 23, 1967),
entitled "The Responsibility of Intellectuals." At the time Chomsky
was best known for his work in linguistics. He crossed the line into
politics with this famous article and stated that: "It is the responsibility of intellectuals to speak the truth and to expose the lies." His
reasoning was simple. Intellectuals are in a unique position in that
they have the time and access to a wide variety of information and
freedom of expression. They do not have to rely solely on "official"
publications. Chomsky further noted that, "For a privileged minority, Western democracy provides the leisure, the facilities, and the
training to seek the truth lying behind the veil of distortion and mis-
representation, ideology, and class interest through which the events
of current history are presented to us" (1987:60).

It should be noted that both Chomsky and Zinn remain two of the
most outspoken critics of American foreign and domestic policies.
In their writings and public speeches both continue to follow these
responsibilities. It is clear that what they wrote four decades ago

seems just as relevant today—perhaps more so. Clearly, Quinney's writings have played the same role over the years.

How does one assess the importance of *Critique of Legal Order* nearly thirty years later? In making a few general observations about some of Quinney's assertions in that book, the evidence seems quite overwhelming. Since that time numerous studies have extensively documented the following charges that he made:

(1)   That there is in fact a "ruling class" and they indeed *rule* the country (Domhoff, 1998; Rothman, 1999);

(2)   That members of this class play a major role in defining not only what is designated as "criminal" but also in defining the dominant crime control policies, both on the national and local level; what Quinney never explored is the impact of local or regional ruling class members on crime control policies within states and municipalities (some examples include: Chambliss and Zatz, 1993; Reiman, 1998; Greenberg and Humphries, 1993; Barnett, 1993; Humphries and Greenberg, 1993; for an example of elite influence on the "war on drugs" see Baum, 1997 and Webb, 1998); No one, except Baum and Webb, actually identified specific offenders to the extent that Quinney did. Ironically, both Baum and Webb are journalists, rather than criminologists;

(3)   That the brunt of enforcement efforts is felt very disproportionately by minorities in particular and the "dangerous" classes in general, who obviously pose a threat to the established order and that this is especially evidenced by the "war on drugs" and the "war on gangs" (Klein, 1995; Shelden, Tracy and Brown, 2001; Baum, 1997 and Currie, 1995 and 1998);

(4)   That the bulk of criminological research continues to follow the proverbial money trail and is concerned primarily with assisting the state in controlling conventional crime which is committed by members of the underclass and minorities; much of this research still focuses on improving the criminal justice system, making it more "efficient" and making better use of available technology to identify "potential criminals;" if anything, this tendency is even greater than what Quinney described in his book (consider the latest advertisements for funded projects by the National Institute of Justice or Office of Juvenile Justice and Delinquency Prevention and casually review articles appearing in mainstream journals);

(5)   That this research is further adding to what we have called the "crime control industry" or "criminal justice industrial complex;" it is important to note that Quinney was one of the first to point this out when he talked about "crime control bureaucracies" in *Critique of Legal Order* and then had a chapter devoted to the "criminal justice industrial complex" in *Class, State and Crime*; little did he realize how expansive this system would become within the next 25 years (more than

$150 billion spent yearly on the formal criminal justice system alone; see Chambliss, 1999);

(6)    That it is rare for criminologists to focus much attention to crimes committed by corporations and especially the state; a few isolated studies have documented such crimes and they are extensive, but other than Quinney, Reiman and a handful of other criminologists (notable examples include, Coleman, 1994, Friedrichs, 1996 and Simon and Hagan, 1999), there has been little consistent effort to link such crimes to the very nature of capitalism itself (some of the best work on crimes of the state is found in the works of non-criminologists, such as Chomsky and Michael Parenti);

(7)    That the media contribute greatly to the standard images of crime was a major part of *The Social Reality of Crime* and Quinney continued this line of thinking in *Critique of Legal Order*; a good deal of work has been done since that time, documenting the critical role of the media (a set of giant corporations in itself) in perpetuating certain images of "crime" and "criminals" (see Surette, 1998 and Anderson, 1995), an image of street crimes, drug crimes and gang-related crime committed almost exclusively by African-Americans and Hispanics (crimes by the rich are buried in the back pages of the *Wall Street Journal*, if they are reported at all); some excellent work on "moral panics" and crime have appeared in recent years (see McCorkle and Miethe, 1998; Goode and Ben-Yehuda, 1994).

These seven statements are just a few of the key portions of *Critique of Legal Order* that are still relevant today, and well supported by research. What is especially relevant here is Quinney's critique of not only crime control policies but especially the crime control bureaucracies like the Department of Justice and its various branches (e.g., the FBI). This is where Quinney broke fresh ground, for few criminologists dared to seriously question the concept of crime control in the context of state bureaucracies and the vested interest they have in perpetuating themselves and preserving the capitalist system. While most criminologists were (and still are) busy conducting "empirical studies" of the police, prosecution, the prison subculture, and treatment modalities, Quinney was the only one at that time looking at the entire structure of crime control and the overall role of the state, of which the criminal justice system is merely one part, and how the "state" supports the ruling class and the capitalist order. Quinney, along with a few other radical criminologists, has consistently tried to make connections between the very nature of capitalism (e.g., the inherent inequality, the class structure, alienation, the creation of a "surplus population") and crime.

In the final chapter of *Critique of Legal Order*, entitled "Toward a Socialist Society," Quinney offers some rather vague sketches of what is to be done and how a socialist society should look. For those who wanted (and still desire) a blueprint of the "ideal society" Quinney fell short. But a "blueprint" is not what is needed, for such a model may end up as a confining straight-jacket that does not allow for alternative visions. What Quinney offers is merely a vision, with the lament that "we have much to do." His last paragraph is one of caution, as he argues that we make changes in society through constant struggle suggesting that, "Our theory and practice are formed in the struggle to make a socialist society."

One of the major weakness of Quinney's argument appears in Chapter 3 where he extends his instrumentalist perspective and tries to demonstrate that the ruling class has some sort of direct control over crime policies by noting the class backgrounds of members of various commissions (e.g., President's Commission, Riot Commission). His definition of the "ruling class" would have benefited from a closer look at the work of William Domhoff, whom he cites in this chapter. Quinney says that this class consists of those who "own the means of production" and "those who benefit in some way from the present capitalist economic system" (p. 55). To include those who benefit "in some way" lacks precision and opens the door to criticism. Subsequent pages in this chapter consist of a listing of dozens of names of those sitting on these various commissions, which many readers will doubtless find boring and repetitive.

Quinney's analysis of the "state" took the *instrumentalist* Marxist perspective. Marx once stated that, the *state* was originally a system set up to support ruling class interests and was, in effect, an inevitable outgrowth of a division of labor based upon class exploitation. In fact, the "state" was only necessary when class divisions arose. This instrumentalist perspective has received a number of important criticisms, which can be applied to *Critique of Legal Order* (Lynch and Groves, 1989: 23-24). First, there is a tendency to exaggerate the cohesiveness of the ruling class and the ability of this class to always act in a unified manner (sounding too much like a "conspiracy" theory). Second, this approach is overly deterministic, emphasizing the economic variable above all else. Third, there is an assumption that *every* law serves the interests of the ruling class only, and that the state never serves (and cannot by definition serve) the interests of ordinary people. Finally, such a simplistic view ignores the various conflicts and contradictions within the ruling class itself (Chambliss and Zatz, 1993).

*Critique of Legal Order* was frequently subjected to scathing criticism, much of which was overdone. To many in the mainstream of criminology, Quinney had gone "off the deep end" or was out there in "fantasy land" and his writings were too "bombastic and polemical" (Gibbons and Garabedian, 1974). It is also interesting that Quinney was not only criticized by mainstream criminology, but by many on the Left (see Platt and Takagi, 1982; see Wildeman, 1984, for an excellent response to these criticisms). As already noted, Quinney was sensitive to the criticisms, especially those concerning his instrumentalist perspective. With the publication of *Class, State and Crime*, Quinney addressed some of his critics and wrote from a more structuralist perspective. Despite these criticisms, what Quinney wrote in *Critique of Legal Order* more than a quarter century ago is still relevant today. It should be re-read by criminologists and the doors and windows he opened should be re-opened, this time with new visions, new methodologies and hopefully greater wisdom. As Quinney says in the final passage of this volume, this is indeed a "critical life." As we begin a new millennium, life remains critical indeed.

# References

Anderson, D. C. *Crime and the Politics of Hysteria.* New York: Times Books, 1995.

Barnett, H. "The Enforcement of Anti-Monopoly Legislation." Pp. 641-648 in D. Greenberg (ed.), *Crime and Capitalism* (2nd ed.). Philadelphia: Temple University Press, 1993.

Baum, D. *Smoke and Mirrors: The War on Drugs and the Politics of Failure.* Boston: Little Brown/Back Bay Books, 1997.

Chambliss, W. J. *Power, Politics, and Crime.* Boulder, CO: Westview, 1999.

Chambliss, W. J. and M. S. Zatz (eds.) *Making Law: The State, the Law, and Structural Contradictions.* Bloomington, IN: Indiana University Press, 1993.

Chomsky, N. *The Chomsky Reader.* New York: Pantheon Books, 1987.

———. *Necessary Illusions: Thought Control in Democratic Societies.* Boston: South End Press, 1989.

———. *Class Warfare.* Monroe, ME: Common Courage Press, 1994.

———. *Year 501: The Conquest Continues.* Boston: South End Press, 1993.

Coleman, J. W. *The Criminal Elite* (3rd ed.). New York: St. Martin's Press, 1994.

Currie, E. *Crime and Punishment in America.* New York: Metropolitan Books, 1998.

———. *Reckoning: Drugs, the Cities, and the American Future.* New York: Hill and Wang, 1993.

Domhoff, W. *Who Rules America? Power and Politics in the Year 2000.* Mountain View, CA: Mayfield, 1998. (originally published by Prentice-Hall in 1967).

Folbre, N. and the Center for Popular Economics. *The New Field Guide to the U.S. Economy.* New York: The New Press, 1995.

Friedrichs, D.O. *Trusted Criminals: White Collar Crime in Contemporary Society.* Belmont, CA: Wadsworth, 1996.

Gibbons, D. C. and P. Garabedian. "Conservative, Liberal and Radical Criminology: Some Trends and Observations." Pp. 51-65 in C. Reasons (ed.), *The Criminologist: Crime and Criminology.* Pacific Palisades, CA: Goodyear, 1974.

Goode, E. and N. Ben-Yehuda. *Moral Panics: The Social Construction of Deviance.* Cambridge, MA: Blackwell, 1994.

Greenberg, D. and D. Humphries. "The Co-optation of Sentencing Reform." Pp. 621-640 in D. Greenberg (ed.), *Crime and Capitalism* (2nd ed.). Philadelphia: Temple University Press, 1993.

Hanh, T. N. *Peace is Every Step.* New York: Bantam Books, 1991.

Herman, E. and N. Chomsky. *Manufacturing Consent: The Political Economy of the Mass Media.* New York: Pantheon, 1988.

Humphries, D. and D. Greenberg. "The Dialectics of Crime Control." Pp. 463-508 in D. Greenberg (ed.), *Crime and Capitalism* (2nd ed.). Philadelphia: Temple University Press, 1993.

Klein, M. *The American Street Gang.* New York: Oxford University Press, 1995.

Kuhn, T. *The Structure of Scientific Revolutions* (2nd ed.). Chicago: University of Chicago Press, 1970.

McCorkle, R. and T. Miethe. "The Political and Organizational Response to Gangs: An Examination of a `Moral Panic' in Nevada." *Justice Quarterly* 15:41-64, 1998.

Messner, S. and R. Rosenbaum. *Crime and the American Dream* (2nd ed.). Belmont, CA: Wadsworth, 1997.

Miliband, R. *The State in Capitalist Society.* New York: Basic Books, 1969.

Parenti, M. *Power and the Powerless.* New York: St. Martin's Press, 1978.

———. *Land of Idols: Political Mythology in America.* New York: St. Martin's Press, 1994.

———. *Against Empire.* San Francisco: City Lights Press, 1995.

Platt, A. M. *The Politics of Riot Commissions, 1917-1970.* New York: Collier Books, 1971.

Platt, T. and P. Takagi. "Meeting the challenge of the 1980s." *Crime and Social Justice* (Summer, 1982).

Quinney, R. *The Social Reality of Crime.* Boston: Little, Brown. 1970.

———. *Criminal Justice in America: A Critical Understanding.* Boston: Little, Brown, 1974.

———. *Class, State and Crime.* (2nd ed.) New York: Longman, 1980.

———. and J. Wildeman. *The Problem of Crime: A Peace and Social Justice Perspective* (3rd ed.). Mountain View, CA: Mayfield, 1991 (originally published by Quinney in 1970 as *The Problem of Crime*, New York: Dodd Mead).

Reiman, J. H. *The Rich Get Richer and the Poor Get Prison* (5th ed.). Chicago: Allyn and Bacon, 1998.

Rothman, R. A. *Inequality and Stratification: Race, Class and Gender* (3rd ed.). Englewood Cliffs, NJ: Prentice-Hall, 1999.

Shelden, R. G. "The Prison Industrial Complex." *The Progressive Populist* 5, 11 (Nov. 1) 1, 12-12 1999a.

———. "The Prison Industrial Complex and the New American Apartheid." *The Critical Criminologist* 10, 1 (Fall) 1, 7-9, 1999b.

———. *Controlling the Dangerous Classes: A Critical Introduction to the History of Criminal Justice.* Boston: Allyn and Bacon, 2001.

Shelden, R. G. and W. B. Brown. "The Crime Control Industry and the Management of the Surplus Population." *Critical Criminology* 9 (Autumn), 39-62, 2000.

Shelden, R.G., S. K. Tracy and W. B. Brown. *Youth Gangs in American Society* (2nd ed.). Belmont, CA: Wadsworth, 2001.

Simon, D. R. and F. E. Hagan. *White Collar Deviance*. Boston: Allyn and Bacon, 1999.

Surette, R. *Media, Crime and Criminal Justice* (2nd ed.) Belmont, CA: Wadsworth, 1998.

Webb, G. *Dark Alliance: Crack, the CIA and the Contras*. New York: Seven Stories Press, 1998.

Wildeman, J. "Richard Quinney vs. the New Orthodoxy: Some Recent Developments in Radical Criminology." Paper presented at the annual meeting of the American Society of Criminology, November, 1984.

Zinn, H. *The Politics of History* (2nd ed.). Urbana, IL: University of Illinois Press, 1990.

# Contributors

**Piers Beirne** is professor of criminology at the University of Southern Maine. He is the author of several books including *Marxism and Law* (with Richard Quinney), *Criminology* (with James Messerschmidt), *Comparative Criminology*, and *Inventing Criminology*. He has served as editor of the journal *Theoretical Criminology*.

**Marshall B. Clinard**, emeritus professor of sociology, University of Wisconsin-Madison, is widely known for his publications in the fields of criminology and deviant behavior, including four books on corporate crime.

**Tim Griffin** has advanced degrees in philosophy and law, and has taught philosophy and legal theory courses at a number of universities. He is a priest in the Episcopal Church.

**Alan Hunt** is professor in the Departments of Sociology and of Law at Carleton University in Ottawa, having previously taught in England. He is the author of *Governing Morals: A Social History of Moral Regulation*, *Governance of the Consuming Passions: A History of Sumptuary Regulation*, *Foucault and Law* (with Gary Wickham), *Explorations in Law and Society*, *Reading Dworkin Critically*, *Marx and Engels on Law* (with Maureen Cain), and *The Sociological Movement in Law*.

**Dario Melossi** is professor of criminology at the University of Bologna, Italy. He is the coauthor (with Massimo Pavarini) of *The Prison and the Factory: Origins of the Penitentiary System*, author of *The State of Social Control: A Sociological Study of Concepts of State and Social Control in the Making of Democracy*, and editor of *The Sociology of Punishment*.

**Dragan Milovanovic** is professor of criminal justice at Northeastern Illinois University. He has written several books and numerous articles on critical criminology and law. He has served as editor of the *International Journal for the Semiotics of Law*.

**Dante J. Scala** teaches politics at Saint Anselm College in Manchester, New Hampshire. His research interests include the development of the concept of corporate personality and the role of taxation in American political development.

**Randall G. Shelden** is professor in the Department of Criminal Justice, University of Nevada, Las Vegas. He is the author of *Controlling the Dangerous Classes: A Critical Introduction to the History of Criminal Justice, Criminal Justice in America: A Sociological Approach*, and coauthor of *Girls, Delinquency and Juvenile Justice* and *Youth Gangs in American Society*.

**A. Javier Treviño** teaches sociology at Wheaton College in Massachusetts. He is the author of *The Sociology of Law: Classical and Contemporary Perspectives* and coeditor (with Susan Guarino-Ghezzi) of *Understanding Crime: A Multidisciplinary Approach*. He serves as editor of Transaction Publisher's Law & Society Series.

**Klaus A. Ziegert** is head of the Department of Jurisprudence, University of Sydney, and director of the Center for Asian and Pacific Law, Sydney, Australia.

# Index

Marxism, 31, 41, 43, 48, 50, 56(n24),
57(n24), 57(n33), 99, 133, 134, 135,
259, 260-262, 266, 273, 280, 283
instrumentalist, 256, 260, 269, 272,
282, 289
structuralist, 256, 260, 272-273, 290
*Marxism and Law* (Beirne and Quinney),
248
"Marxist Theory of Law and State, The"
(Pashukanis), 261-262, 269
"Marxist Theory of Law and the Con-
struction of Socialism, The"
(Pashukanis), 268
*McKlesky v. Kemp*, 256
Mead, George Herbert, 180
mechanical jurisprudence (*see* jurispru-
dence, analytical)
"Mechanical Jurisprudence" (Pound), 90
Megan's law, 256
Melossi, Dario, xxi, xxii, 42, 43, 56(n15),
57(n24), 57(n27), 58(n35)
Menger, Anton, 124(n1)
MerckMedco Managed Care, 206
Merton, Robert K., 254
Michael, Jerome, 255
Milken, Michael, 257
Mills, C. Wright, 99
Milosevic, Slobodan, 244
Milovanovic, Dragan, xxi, xxiv
modernism, xi, xix
modernity, x, xii, xviii, xxi, xxv(n4), 47,
58(n34), 88, 90
Molotov-Ribbentrop pact, 40, 55(n7)
Montesquieu, Charles de Secondat, x
Moore, Wilbert E., 134, 137
"Moral Philosophy and the Moral Life,
The" (James), 85
Mothers Against Drunk Driving
(MADD), 257
Mouffe, Chantal, 273, 274
multiculturalism, xx, 99
*Multinational Monitor*, 200, 202
Munch, Richard, 258
Myrdal, Gunnar, 109-110, 126(n24)

National Highway Traffic Administra-
tion, 192
National Labor Relations Board, 199
National Traffic Safety Act, 195
"Nature of Morals and Rights, The"
(Durkheim), x

"Need of a Sociological Jurisprudence,
The" (Pound), 91
Negri, Antonio, 57(n28), 57(n31)
Nelken, David, 126(n22), 127(n35),
128(n42), 128(n46), 128(n57),
128(n58), 128(n60), 129(n70)
Nelson, Leonard, 32
Neumann, Franz, 37-38, 55(n7), 55(n8),
56(n10), 56(n11), 56(n17)
*New England Journal of Medicine*, 205
*New Criminology, The* (Taylor, Walton,
and Young), 57(n24), 253
Noriega, Manuel, 172
normative facts, 148-149, 153, 168
norms, 113, 116, 121, 122, 168, 173-
174, 238
norms of decision, 113, 120
Northrup Grumman (corp.), 210

Oakeshott, Michael, 18, 19(n14),
20(n58), 20(n59), 20(n60)
obligation (*see* duty)
Occidental Petroleum (corp.), 215
Occupational Safety and Health Admin-
istration, 192
"On the Responsibilities of Intellectuals"
(Chomsky), 284
*One Hundred Years of Probation*
(Timasheff), 165
Ortho Pharmaceutical (corp.), 206
"ought," 113, 171, 173, 174, 178-179,
234, 236-237
*Outlines of Lectures on Jurisprudence*
(Pound), 82

*pacta sunt servanda,* xiv, 239, 240
Paley, Michael, 228
Parenti, Michael, 281, 288
Pareto, Vilfredo, 58(n35), 175, 179
Parsons, Talcott, xii, xx, 3, 88, 132
Partnership for a Drug-Free America, 257
Pashukanis, Evgeny B., xi, xiv, xv, xix,
xx, xxi, xxiv, 57(n30), 160(n10),
259-277
*Path of Law, The* (Holmes), 65, 78
Pavlov, Ivan, 164, 175, 179, 182
*Peace through Law* (Kelsen), 243
Peirce, Charles Sanders, 66, 71-72
*Penal Philosophy* (Tarde), xvi, xxii, 21-
29
Pepinsky, Hal, 280

women, 49-50
WorldCom, 193, 195, 214, 216-218, 220,
    222-223, 228
Worms, René, 29(n2)
Wright, C.W., 248
Wright, Chauncey, 66
Wundt, Wilhelm, 125(n12), 179
Wurzel, Keal Georg, 124(n1), 125(n7),
    125(n12), 126(n17)
Wyeth (corp.), 215

Yeager, Peter C., xi, xvi, xx, xxiii,
    xxv(n7), 191-230

Yntema, Hessel E., 170
Young, Jock, 54(n24), 253, 258

Zander, Hartwig, 35, 38, 41, 47, 55(n1),
    56(n14), 56(n15), 56(n24), 57(n29)
*Zeitschrift für Sozialforschung* (journal),
    33
Ziegert, Klaus A., xxi, xxiii, 126(n21),
    127(n40), 128(n45), 128(n60),
    128(n61), 129(n74), 129(n79)
Zinn, Howard, 281, 286